Gibbons v. Ogden,
Law, and Society
in the Early Republic

Gibbons v. Ogden, Law, and Society in the Early Republic

THOMAS H. COX

OHIO UNIVERSITY PRESS

Athens

Ohio University Press, Athens, Ohio 45701
www.ohioswallow.com

Printed in the United States of America
Ohio University Press books are printed on acid-free paper ⊗ ™

16 15 14 13 12 11 10 09   5 4 3 2 1

Library of Congress Cataloging-in-Publication Data

Cox, Thomas H.
  Gibbons v. Ogden, law, and society in the early republic / Thomas H. Cox.
    p. cm.
  Includes bibliographical references and index.
  ISBN 978-0-8214-1845-1 (cloth : alk. paper) — ISBN 978-0-8214-1846-8 (pbk. : alk. paper)
  1. Gibbons, Thomas, 1757–1826—Trials, litigation, etc. 2. Ogden, Aaron, 1756–1839—Trials,
litigation, etc. 3. Fulton, Robert, 1765–1815—Trials, litigation, etc. 4. Interstate commerce—
Law and legislation—United States—History—19th century. 5. Inland navigation—Law and
legislation—United States—History—19th century. 6. Steamboats—Law and legislation—
Hudson River (N.Y. and N.J.)—History—19th century. I. Title.
  KF228.G528C69 2009
  343.730815—dc22
                                    2009012770

CONTENTS

ILLUSTRATIONS

PREFACE

"THE GALLING SHACKLES with which a few lordly monopolists have, for some years past, contrived to fetter our navigation and intercourse with our sister state, have been at length broken by the Ithuriel spear, whose-all-powerful touch makes every unrighteous decision to crumble into dust," exclaimed an article in the *Elizabethtown Gazette* of Elizabethtown, New Jersey, on March 15, 1824. Borrowing imagery from John Milton's *Paradise Lost,* the article compared the appellate power of the U.S. Supreme Court to a holy weapon that, in the hands of the angel Ithuriel, had uncovered Satan's deceptions with a single touch. In spring 1824, the justices of the High Court had used their powers of discernment to strike down a New York steamboat monopoly law as a violation of interstate commerce in the landmark case of *Gibbons v. Ogden.* Created by Chancellor Robert R. Livingston in 1798 and used to defend a steamboat empire built by his partner, Robert Fulton, the monopoly had dominated local steam travel along the Hudson River and across New York Harbor for over twenty years. Long beset by stifled competition and exorbitant fares, citizens of both New York and New Jersey applauded the Gibbons decision. The *Gazette* article captured the popular sentiment, condemning the monopolists for "their appalling system of monopoly injunctions, penalties, and imprisonments against all who should dare, *without their purchased leave,* use the two most common elements of nature, in facilitating the intercourse between neighboring ports."[1]

The origins of *Gibbons v. Ogden,* popularly known as the great "steamboat monopoly case," lay in a dispute between rival Elizabethtown steamboat operators Aaron Ogden and Thomas Gibbons. In 1824, Chief Justice John Marshall upheld the congressional control of interstate trade by asserting that Gibbons's federal license trumped a state grant issued to Ogden by the Fulton-Livingston steamboat monopoly. Legal scholars have consistently ranked *Gibbons*—the first Supreme Court case to confirm Congress's power over interstate commerce— among other landmark Marshall Court cases such as *Marbury v. Madison* (1803) and *McCulloch v. Maryland* (1819), which promoted federal authority over states' rights.

In 1919, U.S. senator and constitutional scholar Albert J. Beveridge stated in his foundational *Life of John Marshall* that *Gibbons v. Ogden* "has done more to knit the American people into an indivisible Nation than any other one force in our history, excepting only war." Pathbreaking works such as Charles Warren's

Supreme Court in United States History (1922), and Charles Haines's *Role of the Supreme Court in American Government and Politics, 1789–1835* (1944) likewise depicted *Gibbons* as a bold statement of nationalist principles in an era dominated by states' rights. Even Maurice Baxter's *Steamboat Monopoly* (1972), the only full-length treatment of the case, discussed primarily the constitutional and political rather than the economic and social dimensions of *Gibbons v. Ogden*. As Baxter acknowledged, "Though I have undertaken the first lengthy study of the case, there is naturally much more that could be said if one were to be 'exhaustive.'"[2]

This book examines *Gibbons v. Ogden* as a legal conflict in which three different groups—steamboat entrepreneurs, local elites (including state officials), and federal judges—sought to control the development of steam power in the young nation. In the late 1700s and early 1800s, working-class inventors with dreams of continental steamboat empires sought alliances with landholders eager to develop steam power on the local level through state-granted monopolies. Yet in 1824, steamboat entrepreneur Thomas Gibbons and Supreme Court justices John Marshall and William Johnson, already disliked by many among the American gentry, adopted a nationalistic view of commerce that resulted in a popular Supreme Court decision with long-term implications not only for the regulation of interstate commerce but also for wide-ranging social issues such as the sale of alcohol or the desegregation of busing across state lines.

Scholars have long sought to link the shifting alliances of business elites to the larger economic and social transformations of the United States in the early 1800s. In 1991, Charles Sellers's influential work, *The Market Revolution,* posited that encroaching commercialism, with its emphasis on economic individualization, displaced a traditional agrarian world of subsistence farmers in Jacksonian America. Daniel Fellers and Daniel Walker Howe, however, have persuasively argued that Americans across class lines rushed to embrace the economic opportunities created by the transportation and communications revolutions. Perhaps nothing symbolized the economic growth of the young nation more than the spectacle of steam power, a scientific marvel that promised economic progress through technological innovation with minimal social upheaval. Unlike British factories, which invoked images of oppression and drudgery, steamboats appeared to early Americans as floating symbols of progress that would bring raw goods to market and refinement to the backcountry. Controversy over the pros and cons of steam travel paralleled similar debates over internal improvements, federal patents, and incorporation laws. In each of these controversies, Americans from a variety of backgrounds enthusiastically supported economic and technological development. They primarily disagreed as to whether state or federal governments could most effectively promote such progress.[3]

Throughout the late 1700s, working-class inventors such as John Fitch and James Rumsey were inspired by the success of the American Revolution and the promise of a stronger central government under the U.S. Constitution. These entrepreneurs sought federal patents and political support from national political figures, including George Washington and Benjamin Franklin, to protect their inventions. Fitch and Rumsey believed that such patronage would help them cultivate reputations as heroic inventors whose steamboats would in turn encourage trade and thus strengthen the bonds of political union. Weak patent laws and the scarcity of capital, however, forced subsequent steamboat entrepreneurs such as Nicholas Roosevelt and Robert Fulton to ally with landed elites who, for the moment, remained the principal power brokers in American society. Businesspeople pursued steam power to gain wealth and social status. Country squires such as John Stevens of New Jersey and Chancellor Robert R. Livingston of New York, on the other hand, dabbled in such technology to maintain reputations as paternalists who would bring scientific progress to their less fortunate neighbors. In 1798, Livingston secured a New York legislative monopoly over steam travel in local waters, and he partnered with Fulton to produce the first practical steamboat in 1807.

Over the next decade, Fulton and Livingston defended their monopoly from rivals through price wars, steamboat races, advertising, and public testimonials. When these methods failed, the partners hired famed attorney Thomas Addis Emmet to defend their monopoly interests in state and federal court. Emmet privately dismissed the monopoly as unconstitutional but publicly defended the measure as a legitimate expression of New York's right to regulate commerce and encourage science within its borders. Landholding members of the New York legislature and court system sympathetic to Livingston's interests consistently agreed. In 1811, Chancellor James Kent of the New York Court for the Correction of Errors ruled in *Livingston v. Van Ingen* that as a vested right, the steamboat monopoly should be protected from the majoritarian impulses of the time. Livingston and Fulton widely circulated Emmet's legal arguments and Kent's decision in newspaper articles and pamphlets to ensure that their rights were protected in both the courtroom and the court of public opinion. And for a brief time, the Fulton-Livingston steamboat empire flourished. Other elites, including Stevens, John R. Livingston, and former New Jersey governor Aaron Ogden, quickly cast their lots with the monopoly.

Ironically, the steamboat monopoly eventually fell not because of any advancing democratic tide against the perfidy of vested interests, but because of the efforts of three wealthy landholders who, as economic visionaries and social mavericks, had little to lose by adopting a nationalistic view toward steamboat development. In 1816, Thomas Gibbons, a disgraced planter turned New Jersey steamboat promoter, joined forces with an obscure sloop captain named Cornelius Vanderbilt to destroy Aaron Ogden's steamboat business between New York and New Jersey through cutthroat competition. Ogden immediately sued his opponent in the Court of Chancery of New York for violating the monopoly that state had awarded him. Gibbons's attorney, Daniel Webster, argued that his client held a federal license authorized under an act passed by Congress in 1793 to promote domestic trade by giving ship captains the right to conduct business in any American port. When Gibbons appealed the case to the U.S. Supreme Court, Chief Justice John Marshall viewed the matter with apprehension. Marshall was a Virginia Federalist who had recently handed down nationalistic but unpopular decisions in *McCulloch v. Maryland* (1819) and *Cohens v. Virginia* (1821). The chief justice thus sought to craft a moderate decision that would skirt both the states rights approach adopted by James Kent, chancellor of the New York Court of Chancery, in previous steamboat monopoly cases and the strongly nationalistic views of William Johnson, an associate justice of the U.S. Supreme Court.

In March 1824, Marshall handed down one of the most significant decisions in American judicial history. The true strength of the Gibbons decision lay in its delivery and timing. By invoking broad appeals to nationalism and free trade, Marshall successfully depicted the federal government as the champion of economic opportunity and social progress. He also steered away from the difficult issue of state commercial regulation by handing down a decision designed to appeal to different groups of Americans at the same moment in time.

By that same token, *Gibbons v. Ogden* became popular with successive generations of Americans who used the case as a precedent to argue that the state and federal governments had important roles to play in the regulation of commerce, not merely for the sake of economic efficiency but also for the well-being of society. For instance, opponents of alcohol and immigration in the 1830s and 1840s used *Gibbons* to argue that states retained a sphere free from federal control in which their own police powers could be used to regulate the social good. Following the Civil War, *Gibbons* alternatively served as a precedent to limit or expand federal commerce authority. Beginning with New Deal cases in the 1930s, attorneys cited *Gibbons v. Ogden* to justify sweeping federal regulation of economic and social matters, and in the post–World War II period, reformers used *Gibbons* in cases involving labor standards and civil rights. Then, at the close of the twentieth century, the Supreme Court cited *Gibbons* to limit congressional commerce power over gun control in *United States v. Lopez* (1995) and over women's rights in *United States v. Morrison* (2000); yet just a few years later, the court cited the same decision to uphold the federal regulation of marijuana in *Gonzales v. Raich* (2005). *Gibbons v. Ogden* thus helped solidify federal powers over commerce regulation, and its very broadness allowed different generations of Americans substantial latitude in determining in what form, and on what governmental level, such power would be expressed.

This book begins with a discussion of previous scholarly work on *Gibbons v. Ogden* as well as the current legal significance of the case. Chapter 1 traces attempts by rival steamboat inventors John Fitch and James Rumsey to develop steam power and secure patent rights for their inventions in the post-Revolutionary United States. The origins of the partnership between Fulton and Livingston and their creation of the New York steamboat monopoly form the basis of chapter 2. Chapter 3 examines the rise of the first serious competition to the Fulton-Livingston syndicate from John Stevens, Chancellor Livingston's brother-in-law and former partner. Chapter 4 explores Fulton and Livingston's attempts to establish steamboat monopolies on the Mississippi, Ohio, and Hudson rivers. Chapter 5 discusses how Fulton and Livingston fended off challenges from competitors such as Henry Miller Shreve and created partnerships with rivals, including Aaron Ogden.

Centering on the relationship between Ogden and Thomas Gibbons, chapter 6 examines their personal and professional rivalries to control the lucrative steamboat business between New York and New Jersey—rivalries that spanned twenty years. Chapter 7 discusses attempts by Thomas Gibbons to defeat Ogden and the stockholders of the North River Steam Boat Company (often referred to by contemporaries as the "North River Company") in federal court. Highlighting the events of late February 1824, chapter 8 details the arguments used by Gibbons and Ogden before the Marshall Court. Chapter 9 investigates Chief Justice Marshall's decision and the public reaction to that decision. Chapter 10 discusses the successful attempts by John R. Livingston, one of the original supporters of the monopoly, to defeat the North River Company in both the New York Court of

Chancery and the New York Court for the Correction of Errors. A brief conclusion summarizes *Gibbons v. Ogden*'s role as a legal precedent in subsequent Supreme Court cases dealing with interstate commerce.

The *Gibbons v. Ogden* case was significant on a number of levels. First, it provided a window into the alliances that inventors and landholders struck to promote their financial interests and social status in the tumultuous years of the early American steamboat industry. Second, it revealed the ways these individuals used the state and federal court systems to advance their economic interests in a twenty-year process in which litigants, lawyers, judges, and juries came to see federalism and free trade as more beneficial to the development of steam power than state-granted monopolies. And third, as a sweeping decision that relied on nationalism and a broad definition of commerce, *Gibbons v. Ogden* became an important precedent, an "Ithuriel spear" with which the Supreme Court would rule on a variety of issues involving trade over the next two centuries.

ACKNOWLEDGMENTS

It is with pleasure that I acknowledge the following individuals for their contributions to this book. I am particularly grateful to my doctoral dissertation adviser, Richard E. Ellis, whose sound advice and patience guided this project to completion. Michael H. Frisch, Tamara Plakins Thornton, and Donald M. Roper helped me to place *Gibbons v. Ogden* within the greater context of American social, cultural, and legal history. Doron Ben-Atar, Michael Les Benedict, Patricia Cline Cohen, Edward Countryman, Richard Demarjian, Songho Ha, Richard Hull, Victoria Jackson, Charles McCurdy, Harry Scheiber, Sandra Van Burkleo, and Edward C. Walterscheid also lent their insight to this book.

The staff of Ohio University Press has been a pure joy to work with. Tremendous thanks go to Gillian Berchowitz for her support in bringing this project to fruition. My external reviewers, Daniel W. Hamilton and Richard Hamm, provided a number of excellent comments that have greatly enhanced the quality of my work. Rick Huard, my editor at Ohio University Press, likewise labored for long hours to make the manuscript detailed, nuanced, and accessible to a popular audience. My thanks also go to Richard Comfort for creating the index for this book. I am particularly indebted to Paul Finkelman, whose scholarly advice and encouragement proved invaluable in the completion of this book.

Jim Folts, director of the New York State Archives, and Jean Schoenthaler, of Drew University Library, helped me to mine the rich collections of their institutions. My colleagues at the State University of New York at Buffalo, University of Nebraska at Kearney, and Sam Houston State University were very supportive of my work. Kersten Biehn, Terry Bilhartz, Ty Cashion, Caroline Crimm, Brian Domitrovic, Ken Hendrickson, Nick Pappas, and Robert Shadle commented on several chapters of this book. Jeffrey Littlejohn helped secure the illustrations that adorn the following pages. Herbert A. Johnson provided advice on several early chapters of my work. And Gregory Witkowski offered a Europeanist perspective on every chapter. I am particularly indebted to Jim Olson for proofreading this manuscript and adding his wit and wisdom to its contents. H. Robert Baker offered guidance and a sympathetic ear as well as feedback on the entire manuscript. A special note of thanks goes to Jeremy Schneider for critiquing every line of this book, often several times over.

I was fortunate to receive funding from several sources for this project. Two Larry J. Hackman Research Residency Awards from the New York State Archives

Partnership Trust and a Gilder Lehrman Dissertation Fellowship from the Gilder Lehrman Institute of American History helped me to access the rich historical resources of New York State. Stipends to attend the 2002 Supreme Court Historical Society Summer Seminar on Federalism, the 2003 Law and Society Graduate Student Workshop, the 2007 Institute for Constitutional Studies Summer Seminar, and the 2007 Fulton-Livingston Steamboat Bicentennial Symposium at Bard College afforded me opportunities to discuss my research with fellow scholars: my special thanks go to Maeva Marcus for her extraordinary efforts to sustain such sorely needed scholarly gatherings. A Clements-DeGolyer Research Grant from the Clements Center for Southwest Studies at Southern Methodist University allowed me to research the development of steam travel in the southern United States. I also received generous support from the State University of New York at Buffalo in the form of a College of Arts and Sciences Dissertation Writing Fellowship and a Graduate Student Association Mark Diamond Research Grant. The State University of New York at Buffalo History Department also provided generous funding through a Milton Plesur Dissertation Fellowship and two Thomas B. Lockwood Dissertation Fellowships. A generous Faculty Enhancement Grant from Sam Houston State University and a Library Research Grant from Princeton University allowed me to conduct vital, last-minute research on *Gibbons v. Ogden* and to gather additional material for a forthcoming biography of Thomas Gibbons. Finally, a yearlong position at the Birmingham Civil Rights Institute in Birmingham, Alabama, first inspired me to pursue a career in American constitutional and legal history.

Throughout my career, I have been sustained by a wonderful group of friends and colleagues. J. David Fraley, David Furber and Diana Dimitrova, Songho Ha, Edward S. LaMonte, Patricia Mazon, Kenneth Moore, Erik Seeman, Samuel Shepherd, and Michael Vorenberg have provided excellent advice over the years. After spending so much time with the Livingston, Fulton, Ogden, and Gibbons clans, I have learned to appreciate the importance of family. My own has been very supportive of my passion for history. William and Johanna Horton, Beth Hilleke, the Reverend Dr. Marion C. and Theodora Stapf Cox, the Reverend Jasper and Georgia Cox, Dr. Jonathan and Darcy Cox, Walter and Esther Meyer, Thomas and Kay Meyer, Judy Cox, and Matt Cox have supported my career in many ways. I dedicate this book to my father, the Reverend Dr. L. Hughes Cox, professor of philosophy, Centenary College of Louisiana.

Gibbons v. Ogden,
Law, and Society
in the Early Republic

CHAPTER 1

Steam Power and Patent Law
Development in the Eighteenth Century

Perseverance against Great Odds

O N MONDAY, AUGUST 20, 1787, a crowd gathered at the Front Street wharves on the banks of the Delaware River in Philadelphia. Curious, the people had come to watch John Fitch and Henry Voight launch their experimental steamboat, aptly named *Perseverance*. The inventors were an interesting pair. Fitch radiated detached impatience, whereas the jovial Voight conversed with the speculators in the crowd. A "crank-and-paddle" engine, which consisted of six sets of steam-powered oars, propelled the narrow craft. Hoping to attract investors, Fitch offered free rides aboard *Perseverance* to influential observers. Several leading politicians, including Oliver Ellsworth (who would later serve as the second chief justice of the U.S. Supreme Court), Samuel Johnson, Rufus King, and Edmund Randolph, accepted rides in the strange-looking craft, which churned several hundred yards upstream before returning to the dock. Johnson later sent a congratulatory certificate to Fitch; however, neither he nor any of the other spectators offered financial support.[1] While Fitch and Voight promoted their invention, Johnson, Ellsworth, and their colleagues at the Philadelphia Convention meeting three blocks away sought support for their own creation, the U.S. Constitution. On August 18, two days before Fitch and Voight's

John Fitch. "Portrait of John Fitch," in James T. Lloyd, *Lloyd's Steamboat Directory and Disasters on Western Rivers* (Cincinnati, OH: James T. Lloyd, 1906), 18

demonstration, James Madison had spearheaded the debate over a constitutional clause for the "promotion of useful arts," which the convention approved on September 12, 1787.[2]

Attempts by Fitch and his colleagues to create steamboat businesses in an era of economic uncertainty and rapid political change were the subject of a vital chapter in the history of American transportation. Fitch hoped that the fledgling federal government would provide European-style legal protection for his inventions. In the sixteenth and seventeenth centuries, industrial development had unleashed advancements in iron forging, building construction, and steam power. Modernization had also created powerful nation-states that granted patents and other exclusive monopolies to increase royal authority. European inventors often secured aristocratic patrons who helped them obtain royal patents in return for a share of the profits. Yet in America, despite the abundance of land and waterways that made it a natural arena for the development of steam power, European patent systems were unrealistic because of the sheer size and sparse population of the frontier.

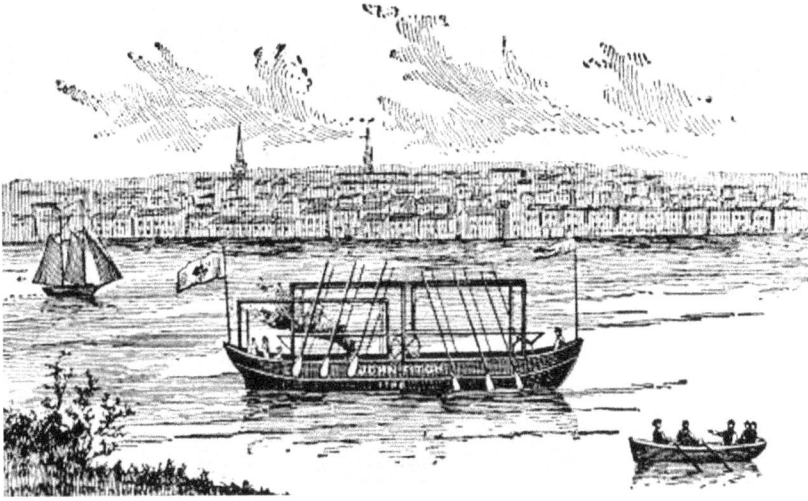

John Fitch's steamboat at Philadelphia. "John Fitch's Steamboat at Philadelphia," in
E. Benjamin Andrews, *History of the United States from the Earliest Discovery of America to the Present Time* (New York: Charles Scribner's Sons, 1894), 2:290

Early inventors such as Fitch and Voight had to find new methods to legally defend their inventions. Rather than discovering a single solution for their problems, these entrepreneurs learned to rely on a combination of state-granted monopolies and personal reputations to discourage competitors. In particular, Fitch learned than in an increasingly democratizing American society, cultivating a reputation as a heroic scientist who was laboring for the public good would help him secure the customers, patrons, and public support that strong patent laws would have provided in European circles. In this regard, Fitch did more than pioneer steam technology. He developed legal precedents and business techniques that future steamboat inventors would adopt with increasing regularity.

The Industrial Revolution

The framers of the U.S. Constitution were not the first political leaders to consider the merits of regulating scientific inventions.[3] Since the late Middle

3

Ages, European governments had recognized the value of encouraging technological achievements by promising inventors certain exclusive rights over their discoveries. In the 1400s, the English government took the lead in promoting scientific development through royally granted monopolies. Under that system, monarchs issued monopolies to political allies to raise money or to protect local industries from foreign competition. In 1449, to protect English products from cheaper Italian imports, Henry VI awarded the first British patent to John of Utynam, for stained-glass manufacturing. And throughout the fifteenth and sixteenth centuries, the English monarchy granted patents to ironworkers, stonemasons, shipwrights, and other artisans. These franchises took several legal forms: charters to private corporations, letters patent with directives to the public, and closed letters that provided private instructions to key individuals. Just as titles of nobility gave landowners the right to govern peasants who lived on their lands, patents gave promising inventors exclusive rights to reap the profits of their inventions. In time, these monopolies became an accepted part of English common law.[4]

As part of her efforts to create a modern nation-state, Elizabeth I granted monopolies to promote English mining, iron working, and shipbuilding. In 1557, she granted the Stationers Company a powerful monopoly over all printed material in England. Elizabeth also used patents to attract Dutch, French, and German artisans to England with the promise that they could receive monopoly rights as original inventors, even if they imported only the work of others.[5] In 1623, Parliament drew from medieval guild laws to pass the Statute of Monopolies, limiting the number of exclusive franchises the monarchy could grant. Just as master craftsmen could bind apprentices to two seven-year terms and thus control their labor, inventors could now gain the profits from their inventions for a maximum of fourteen years. The statute also stipulated that when a monopoly expired, its details would be made available to the public.[6] Parliament subsequently passed the Statute of Anne in 1710, which distinguished copyrights from patents and gave authors control over their written work for limited periods. Because of two landmark legal cases, *Millar v. Taylor* (1769) and *Donaldson v. Beckett* (1774), Parliament declared authors had a common-law right to their intellectual property for twenty-eight years, but grants to inventors were based on royal prerogatives. These precedents formed the basis for English patent law until the mid-nineteenth century, and they were part of the English legal tradition that settlers brought with them to North America.[7]

Social Consequences of Technological Change

By the mid-1700s, the creation of English patent law had achieved its desired result—the industrial development of Great Britain. Canals, clocks, foundries, mechanical looms, toll bridges, gristmills, sawmills, whiskey stills, windmills, and rudimentary steam engines dotted the English landscape. The rise of machines redefined labor and forced industries that could not afford new technology to increase the productivity of their human workforces. As a result, industrialization had a cumulative effect on increasing the rate of production in the workplace. These trends soon became apparent not just in Britain but also in much of western Europe.[8]

Of all the technological developments in the late eighteenth century, steam power had perhaps the most diverse range of industrial uses. British inventor Thomas Newcomen perfected the first steam engine capable of industrial use in 1712. Matthew Boulton and James Watt became partners in 1775 and created an engine based on a high-pressured steam boiler and piston, as opposed to earlier models that relied on condensation to operate. Boulton and Watt patented their invention and opened the first steam engine factory. Following a successful steamboat trial in Lyons, French inventor Claude-François-Dorothée, marquis de Jouffroy d'Abbans, obtained a French patent over steam travel in 1783.[9] Industrialists used the rudimentary engines to pump water out of coal mines and to run power looms. The development of "vessels powered by fire and steam" visibly had far-reaching social effects and created new communication and trade networks. The evolution of steam engines on both sides of the Atlantic captured the public's imagination, and the engines became a symbol of increased industrialization.[10]

Development of Steam Technology in North America

Effective patent policies helped Britain emerge as the leading producer of steam technology in the world. Given their shared history and culture, when Americans sought to establish their own industrial and legal systems, they did so with British precedents in mind. Chronic labor shortages, the need for fast and reliable transportation, and the opportunity to settle the frontier made the idea of steam power popular in eighteenth-century North America.[11] Steamboat inventors made frequent trips to Europe, seeking capital and advice for their experiments. Conversely, English, Scottish, and Irish mechanics well versed in steam power emigrated to work in the foundries and shipyards of Philadelphia, Boston, and New York City.[12]

One such émigré was Christopher Colles, an Irish native and former protégé of Richard Poacoke, a well-known Anglican bishop and anthropologist. Colles perfected his mathematical and engineering skills by constructing a canal across the Shannon River before departing for America with his family in August 1771. Skilled at attracting European patrons, Colles was disheartened when a lecture at the American Philosophical Society on the benefits of steam power met with roaring applause but little financial support. He therefore sent pamphlets to leading Philadelphia citizens and colonial legislatures to propose a canal system in return for governmental land grants, the one form of wealth readily available in the colonies. In 1774, the Philadelphia City Council agreed to fund a plan by Colles to supply the city with water using a steam engine. Unfortunately, a lack of funds with which to purchase much-needed equipment and the services of skilled artisans led to the eventual failure of the project.[13]

One individual who learned much from Colles's pioneering endeavors was John Fitch. The son of hardscrabble Connecticut farmers, Fitch used his affinity for mathematics to escape rural life. After brief careers as a mechanic, a craftsman, and a land speculator, he became interested in steam travel. Fitch later wrote in his memoirs that a chance encounter in April 1785 with a wealthy man in a horse-drawn carriage inspired him, in a dramatic moment of insight, to design a steam-powered carriage: "I soon thought that there might be a force procured by Steam and set to and made a draft. And in about one weeks time gave over the Idea of Carriages but thought it might answer for a Boat or better yet for a first rate man of war."[14] More probably, Fitch got many of his ideas from William Henry, a Pennsylvania gunsmith and inventor who perfected plans for a functional steamboat but who, like Colles, failed to secure financial support to create a working engine.[15]

While Fitch struggled with his designs, rival inventor James Rumsey cultivated support for his own fledgling steamboat business. A Maryland native, Rumsey worked as an innkeeper and amateur engineer. He possessed a keen mind but, unlike the impulsive Fitch, tempered his creativity through methodical experimentation. In 1780, Rumsey built a working model of a steam-powered boat that pushed its way along riverbeds by a series of poles.[16] Drawing from European precedents, Rumsey courted the friendship and patronage of wealthy Americans—

including George Washington, Thomas Jefferson, James Madison, and John Marshall—who frequented his inn.[17]

The Race for Public and Private Patronage

In 1783, Rumsey borrowed from Colles's techniques to ask the Continental Congress for a grant of western land that he could use or sell to finance his research in steam travel. To his chagrin, he learned that Philadelphia inventor James McMechen had already petitioned Congress for a land grant to finance a pole-powered steamboat, which bore a strong resemblance to the vessel in Rumsey's own blueprints. Congress appointed a subcommittee to examine the competing claims, and on July 11, 1783, it produced a report that lauded McMechen's goals but postponed giving him support until he developed a working steamboat. In 1784, McMechen publicly renounced his claims as inventor of the pole boat in exchange for a partnership with Rumsey. The two men jointly appealed for additional funds. Since Rumsey carried the written support of George Washington and Thomas Jefferson, Congress took his petition seriously.[18]

Hugh Williamson, who chaired the congressional subcommittee appointed to resolve the steamboat controversy, wrote to Washington and Jefferson for confirmation of Rumsey's reliability. Washington voiced his support, whereas Jefferson nonchalantly admitted to having seen a demonstration of Rumsey's boat.[19] On May 11, 1785, Rumsey and McMechen received a congressional promise of twenty thousand acres of land west of the Ohio River—if they could produce a steamboat that ran fifty miles a day for six consecutive days without repairs.[20] Riding a wave of success, Rumsey successfully lobbied the Virginia, Maryland, and Pennsylvania state legislatures for monopolies on steam travel. Nonetheless, he faced considerable opposition in Virginia and won a steamboat monopoly in the Old Dominion only with Washington's timely support.[21]

Desperate to make up for lost time, Fitch attempted to imitate Rumsey's methods in securing wealthy patrons and federal protection for his steamboat experiments. In 1785, he presented his steamboat plans to the American Philosophical Society. Fitch also petitioned various state legislatures for monopoly privileges, and on August 30, he asked Congress for his own western land to support steamboat experiments.[22] Congress, having already pledged support to Rumsey, returned Fitch's documents to him the following day. In his autobiography, an infuriated

7

Fitch blasted the "Ignorant Boys of Congress" for their lack of foresight.[23] The disgruntled inventor then wandered through Pennsylvania, Maryland, and Virginia seeking help from anyone who would listen to him, including Benjamin Franklin and George Washington. The retired general politely heard what Fitch had to say but explained that he had already given his support to Rumsey. Consumed with anger, Fitch lashed out against Rumsey, his patrons, and the world in general.[24]

Franklin considered Fitch's plans unworkable and reportedly offered him a meager $4 for his blueprints. Franklin himself entered the steamboat controversy in September 1785, delivering a paper titled "Mechanical Inventions" to the American Philosophical Society. Borrowing heavily from a work published in 1769 by Italian inventor Daniel Bernoulli, he rejected paddle wheels as an inefficient means of propulsion. He instead promoted plans for a steam-powered boat that propelled a jet of water through the stern to move the vessel forward. Franklin's engine bore similarities to pressure-powered water pumps, which the inventor had installed on Philadelphia fire engines. Following the lead of America's foremost scientist, many inventors rushed to develop their own jet engines.[25]

Feeling exploited by Franklin and the wealthy members of the philosophical society, Fitch appealed to working-class Americans as a fellow mechanic in need of assistance. He also established a partnership with Henry Voight, a Dutch-born silversmith and owner of a wire-making mill who suggested pursuing a paddle-powered steamboat. In addition, Fitch received the support of a number of Philadelphia mechanics, including Christopher Colles, and he used their influence to create a steamboat company in April 1786, selling shares at a modest $20 each. The company raised $300 in less than a month—mostly from fellow inventors and small business owners in Philadelphia. But despite his promising start, Fitch repeatedly argued with his investors and began to lose financial support. New Jersey attorney Richard Stockton, who served as president of Fitch's corporation, tried to calm the volatile inventor and pacify his backers. Fitch also faced legal pressure from several competitors. Inspired by Franklin's water-jet plan, Pennsylvania inventors Arthur Donaldson and Levi Hollingsworth collaborated to build a marketable steamboat. To circumvent Donaldson, Hollingsworth, and Rumsey, Fitch applied for steamboat monopoly grants in Delaware, Pennsylvania, New Jersey, and New York. Such a patchwork of overlapping legal claims led to an intense debate in the Pennsylvania state legislature, dubbed the case of *Fitch v. Donaldson.*[26]

In his petition to the Pennsylvania General Assembly, Fitch asserted he was the true inventor of the steamboat. He portrayed himself as a reasonable man who had offered his rival a partnership. Donaldson countered that he had invented the idea of a water-jet steam engine, adding that he had, in fact, created an engine based on steam-powered wheels or turbines. Fitch argued he should receive a broad patent for his invention because it offered correspondingly wide benefits to society. He contended that legislatures should create coherent patent laws designed not to enrich a few inventors but to reward inventors whose work enriched the lives of all citizens.[27]

In particular, Fitch insisted upon a patent that excluded similar grants for others during his fourteen-year patent term. A legal arrangement of that type would give him control over future inventions that conflicted with his projects. Donaldson argued there were no precedents for such a patent under English law.[28] Invoking republican rhetoric, Fitch retorted that the English were "neither wiser nor more virtuous than the inhabitants of Pennsylvania." While waiting for the legislature to end its deliberations, he received word from his friend Caleb S. Riggs, a New York attorney, that he had triumphed over other contenders, including inventor John Stevens, and received a steamboat monopoly in New York. Riggs reported, "It is now become a Law of this State that you should have the exclusive rights of building all boats to be propelled by the force of steam agreeable to the prayer of your petition and that for the term of time you worked for."[29] Two weeks later, on March 28, 1787, the Pennsylvania legislature granted Fitch similar rights to operate steamboats within state borders.[30]

With his legal base secure, Fitch petitioned Virginia congressman James Madison to support a national monopoly on steam travel, and he again implored the Continental Congress for land grants to support his endeavors. But Fitch's latest plea for aid failed when a group of congressmen led by Andrew Ellicot demanded the inventor produce a functional steam-powered vessel before they would consider the matter of support. Undeterred, Fitch announced to the Philadelphia press in December 1787 that his steamboat was completed and ready for public demonstrations.[31]

Promoting "Scientific and Useful Arts" at the Constitutional Convention

The Philadelphia Convention represented a defining, though inconclusive, moment in the development of U.S. patent law. During the colonial period,

9

the English monarchy technically retained the right to grant patents in the North American colonies, though popularly elected colonial legislatures frequently assumed such powers. Massachusetts issued the first colonial patent in 1646, awarding it to Joseph Jenkes for a mill that manufactured wheat scythes. By the mid-1700s, a variety of patent systems existed throughout the colonies, all of which operated alongside British patent law. South Carolina, however, was the only colony to pass legislation that specifically recognized the rights of inventors to their work for a limited number of years. Following the Revolutionary War, many inventors appealed to the confederation government for patents. Lacking the specific power to recognize patent claims, the Continental Congress referred such matters back to the states. Although Madison and other Constitution framers cited patent reform as a pressing political need, the subject was barely addressed at the Philadelphia Convention. In August 1787, after delegates had forged compromises on representation and slavery, they turned to the issue of promoting inventions.[32]

The delegates at the Constitutional Convention also faced outside pressure to develop an effective patent policy. Tench Coxe, a Philadelphia merchant and former Loyalist turned ardent Federalist, supported a strong federal patent system as a precondition for industrial development. On August 9, 1787, he claimed in a well-received speech that governmental support for inventions would "with great convenience enable an enlightened society, established for the purpose, to offer liberal rewards in land for a number of objects of this nature."[33] Convention delegates took Coxe's suggestions to heart. On August 18, James Madison and Charles Cotesworth Pinckney proposed that Congress control the power "to secure to literary authors their copyrights for a limited time" and to "encourage by premiums and provisions, the advancement of useful knowledge and discoveries." By linking the patent process to the social good, Madison and Pinckney borrowed from British precedents. Both men first considered a council of state similar to the British model that encouraged inventions, but they rejected the notion as too "European." Madison and Pinckney instead suggested a system of patents and other entitlements to promote agriculture, trade, and manufacturing. Perhaps eager to dispose of the issue without opposition, the delegates referred the matter to the convention's Committee of Detail.[34] After two weeks of debate, on September 12, 1787, the committee presented a statement that became Article I, Section 8, Clause 8, of the U.S. Constitution: "Congress shall have the Power . . . To promote the Progress of Science and useful Arts, by securing for limited Times to Authors and Inventors the exclusive Right to their respective

Writings and Discoveries." Records of the convention contain little information on the debates over the measure.[35]

The lack of discussion about the patent clause at the Constitutional Convention carried through to the ratification debates. Although Massachusetts, New Hampshire, and North Carolina called for provisions against monopolies in general, the intellectual property clause failed to generate controversy.[36] The delegates possibly agreed that the federal government, following English legal traditions, should maintain the right to grant patents. As Madison noted in *Federalist* no. 43, "The copyright of authors has been solemnly adjudged, in Great Britain, to be a right of common law. The right to useful inventions seems with equal reason to belong to the inventors." States could not defend patent rights, and most had granted such authority to Congress.[37]

Attempts to Develop Steamboat Companies

Having secured governmental protection for their inventions, Fitch and Rumsey realized that funding for their inventions would have to come from ordinary Americans as much as wealthy benefactors. Public demonstrations were therefore necessary to attract public attention and potential investors. Rumsey kept McMechen at a distance and enlisted his brother-in-law, Joseph Barnes, to help adapt a Newcomen engine and create a water-jet-powered steamboat. The inventor carried out a successful steamboat demonstration on December 3, 1787, on the Potomac River near Shepherdstown. Before a throng of enthusiastic spectators, Rumsey invited several young women aboard, and with his assistant Charles Morrow at the helm, he steamed half a mile upstream, reversed course, and passed the town before docking to a cheering crowd. Another successful steamboat experiment followed eight days later.[38] To promote his project, Rumsey also published a pamphlet entitled *A Short Treatise on the Application of Steam*.[39] Primarily a sales brochure, the treatise contained a chronology of Rumsey's steamboat experiments, a technical description of his vessel, and affidavits testifying to its success. Fitch countered with a publication entitled *The Original Steam-Boat Supported; or, a reply to Mr. James Rumsey's Pamphlet*, which asserted his claim as the inventor of the steamboat and accused Rumsey of stealing his ideas.[40] Joseph Barnes responded in turn with *Remarks on Mr. John Fitch's Reply to Mr. James Rumsey's Pamphlet*, which attested to the originality of Rumsey's jet-powered boat.[41]

Rumsey moved from Shepherdstown to Philadelphia in March 1788 to publicly defend his interests. With support from his cousin William Rumsey, as well as Washington and Franklin, he presented his steamboat plans before the American Philosophical Society. At Franklin's urging, wealthy Philadelphia residents formed the Rumseian Society to counter Fulton's steamboat company.[42] Rumsey also sought to appear benevolent in the eyes of the public by offering Fitch a reconciliation and suggesting a merger of their corporations. Insulted by the offer of a mere one-eighth of the profits, Fitch turned down the proposal. Rumsey then traveled to England to buy a Boulton and Watt engine and hire engineers. Worried that Fitch might try to follow suit, Franklin and his associates John and Benjamin Vaughn wrote to British investors discrediting Rumsey's rival.[43]

In Paris, Rumsey stayed with the American ambassador, Thomas Jefferson.[44] Then, in the summer of 1788, he traveled to Great Britain to meet with Matthew Boulton and James Watt, who were so pleased by Rumsey's plans that they offered him a partnership. Specifically, they sought permission to use Rumsey's plans for a spiral boiler. Both had experimented with the concept of passing water through spiral tubes enclosed within the engine's firebox. Rumsey inverted Boulton and Watt's idea, sending heat through tubes enclosed in water. Boulton and Watt were suitably impressed, and they promised to withdraw their own patent rights so that Rumsey could place a legal claim to his work.[45]

Boulton and Watt's initial positive impression of Rumsey broke down shortly after their first meeting. In the United States, Rumsey was a gentleman of standing, with considerable support from leading citizens. But in Great Britain, his public reputation meant nothing. Boulton and Watt expected him to cut his ties to the Rumseian Society and form a partnership with them. Rumsey shot back with a threat to take his newly acquired engine to Ireland, where British patent laws did not apply. He reminded Boulton that British patents were not legal in the United States and insisted that his steam engine ideas were superior to those of any competitors. The situation deteriorated, and Rumsey ultimately refused any offer of partnership.[46] While in London, he continued to experiment with steam power and kept abreast of his ongoing conflict with Fitch in the United States. He confided to Charles Morrow, "I am astonished at Fitch's perseverance and rascality. I wish you had got him taken with a writ, however on the whole I think his Exertion will operate against him."[47] By 1791, Rumsey had secured three British patents for spiral boilers and, with the backing of several patrons, built a ship named the *Columbian Maid.* He had worked hard to cultivate a popular reputation in Great Britain as a successful inventor, yet at the same time, Rumsey had incurred great debt as his steamboat experiments dragged on. To help stave off financial collapse, he accepted the humiliating position of secretary and agent for his own creditors.[48]

Fitch faced similar financial problems in Philadelphia, and in 1787 and 1789, stockholders reorganized his firm and reduced his voting power. Fitch also suffered technical setbacks. In the summer of 1788, during a test run on the Delaware River, *Perseverance*'s engine failed: passing boatmen taunted Fitch and Voight as the hapless inventors waited for the tide to carry their vessel back to shore.[49] Fitch's situation temporarily improved, however, with the assistance of stockholder William Thornton. Thornton was a man of exceptional intelligence. Born in the Virgin Islands, he was trained as a physician in Scotland, but he also excelled as a painter, composer, engineer, and architect. In 1786, he emigrated to Philadelphia, where he designed the headquarters for the Library Company of Philadelphia. He would also plan several buildings in the future national capital of Washington, DC. Thornton bought out several members of Fitch's company and worked with the beleaguered inventor on his steamboat. On April 16, 1790, Fitch, Voight, and Thornton arranged a trial run on the Delaware River and pushed *Perseverance* to a speed of eight miles an hour. Although they declined to provide financial support, the governor and the Council of Pennsylvania capitalized on Fitch's newfound popularity and presented him and his partners with a silk flag to commemorate their achievement.[50]

The Struggle to Establish a Federal Patent System

While Rumsey struggled to obtain British recognition for his inventions, Fitch and other steamboat promoters demanded comprehensive legal protection for their work in America. The intense debate about the issuance of state monopolies and federal patents reflected the political turmoil of the 1780s and the need for legal reform. In their quest for governmental recognition, engineers such as Fitch and Rumsey wielded considerable influence in the development of American patent policy. Under pressure from inventors, manufacturers, and President Washington, Congress enacted a patent act on April 10, 1790. The act gave the Department of State the authority to issue patents, and it required a panel consisting of the secretary of state, the secretary of the treasury, and the attorney general

13

to determine "useful" and "important" requests. Upon approval, an inventor paid a fee, registered the invention, and received a federal patent.[51]

The Patent Act of 1790 appeared simple, but in practice, it proved unworkable. Many inventors complained that federal patents were expensive, hard to obtain, impossible to enforce, and limited in scope. Secretary of State Thomas Jefferson condemned the very concept of patents as antidemocratic. In truth, he and his colleagues lacked the time to review applications. On February 4, 1791, Jefferson lobbied Congress to revise existing U.S. patent law. Three days later, he submitted a bill that made the application process more costly and time-consuming. Specifically, the bill required an applicant to petition the secretary of state for a warrant that testified to the usefulness of the invention. After paying a fee directly to the treasury, the inventor then had to register with every U.S. federal district court and publish notices of the invention three times in a major paper in each of those districts to warn away other competitors.[52]

While Jefferson drafted the bill, the Patent Board reviewed requests from John Fitch, James Rumsey, Henry Read, and John Stevens. To avoid confrontations, the board canceled a hearing with the inventors and urged them to wait for the passage of the new patent bill, which was before Congress at the time.[53] Fitch protested the bill, stating he "had no idea that he must go all the way from Kentucky to Cape Cod, and quite the Distance of Province of Main[e] to publish his inventions, and to pay out large fees wherever he goes for the same."[54] For once on the same side as Fitch, Joseph Barnes published a polemic that condemned Jefferson's bill for favoring European technological discoveries over American inventive genius.[55] Despite Barnes's strong words, the ever-wary Fitch suspected Jefferson and Rumsey of collusion to keep him from developing a steamboat franchise.[56]

Jefferson resubmitted his bill to Congress early in March 1792. The measure now required an applicant to register with the secretary of state, pay a fee, and provide a short description and model of the invention. The inventor, however, still had to file and register the patent in every judicial district in the United States. The new bill also allowed an offender to claim ignorance of the law or irrelevancy of the patent in question as valid defenses. It specified that patents were the private, intellectual property of their owners and that the public would not be allowed to view related documents until the originals expired. In addition, the bill asserted that federal patents trumped any state licenses granted before the ratification of the U.S. Constitution. Furthermore, applicants had to be American citizens.[57]

When Congress reconvened in January 1793, it appointed a committee, chaired by Hugh Williamson, to consider Jefferson's bill. The following month, the bill passed both houses of Congress to become the Patent Act of 1793. In 1800, Congress revised the act to allow resident aliens to apply and to set heavy fines for those who infringed on patent rights.[58] However, like its predecessor, the revised act allowed applicants to secure patents for inventions regardless of how similar their discoveries might be. Fitch, Rumsey, Read, and Stevens quickly secured federal patents for their steamboats under the new federal guidelines. However, realizing the worthlessness of such documents, the inventors quickly turned to the states to protect their work.[59]

Rumsey did not live to see his federal patent approved. He died in 1792 of an aneurysm while attempting to rekindle public interest in his steamboat experiments through an address to the British Society of Arts in London. Fitch traveled to France at the invitation of Aaron Vail, one of his stockholders and the U.S. consul in L'Orient. But in addition to a lack of diplomatic skills, Fitch suffered from horrendous timing. He arrived at the height of the French Revolution, and with the nation in turmoil, he was unable to find financial backers for his experiments. He then traveled to Britain, only to find that no British investor would support him given the rumors spread by Franklin and Rumsey. With no funds left, Fitch worked his way back to America as a common sailor.[60] Facing economic ruin and emotional collapse, he wandered throughout the United States for several years before settling in Bardstown, Kentucky. Without success, he continued to experiment with steamboats. As Fitch had spent much of his life attempting to attract investors and patrons, he now felt the need to publicly justify his life. He thus wrote a lengthy autobiography that alternated between detailed descriptions of his steamboat experiments and embittered diatribes about his inability to profit from such work. Almost as if composing his own epitaph, a despondent Fitch at one point wrote, "The day will come when some great powerful man will get fame and riches from my invention, but nobody will believe that poor John Fitch can do anything worthy of attention."[61]

In 1798, Fitch committed suicide, combining a lethal dose of opium pills with wine. In many ways, his failure reflected the inability of the young nation to develop a coherent patent system. Although the United States proved eager to develop new forms of technology, it espoused, for the moment, a republican culture that stressed communal responsibility and civic virtue over commercial acquisition and individualism. In the 1790s, Thomas Jefferson attempted to create a federal patent system based on republican principles, by which issues regarding

15

scientific achievement would be better settled between gentlemen and the success of an invention was guaranteed by that invention's superiority. More appropriately, he left states as the logical spheres in which to defend intellectual property rights. Because the patent clause of the U.S. Constitution provided only vague guidelines for the protection of intellectual property, American inventors defended their interests at the regional level through state-granted monopolies.

It is important to note that inventors such as Fitch and Rumsey only reluctantly forged alliances with state leaders to protect their inventions. Both men initially petitioned both national political figures and Congress for support in much the same way that a medieval courtier might have pursued a European monarch for letters patent. They learned to their misfortune that Washington, Franklin, and Jefferson possessed neither the authority nor the mindset of an Elizabethan ruler. The federal patents Fitch and Rumsey secured were essentially worthless in the unregulated economy of the 1790s. So in addition to forming steamboat companies and securing state monopolies, Fitch and his contemporaries turned to newspapers, brochures, presentations at scientific societies, and direct demonstrations to cultivate investors and customers. Even if they remained unaware of the effects of their larger actions, Fitch and Rumsey helped popularize steam travel and monopolies. John Fitch's autobiography served as a cautionary reminder to future steamboat entrepreneurs that scientific brilliance alone was not enough to ensure success in the early United States. Future inventors would have to create personas as not merely clever inventors but also savvy businessmen and leading citizens concerned with the public good. Nevertheless, as the United States began to look westward with the advent of the Jeffersonian age, steamboats still appeared to be lucrative investments in which to risk one's efforts and reputation. By the 1790s, other steamboat enthusiasts, including Robert R. Livingston, John Stevens, and Nicholas Roosevelt, had begun to study Fitch's methods in the hopes of succeeding where he had failed.[62]

CHAPTER 2

Origins of the
Fulton-Livingston Monopoly

"A New State of Things Is Rising Up"

"THE PRESENT MOMENT will long be remembered as an auspicious era in the history of our state. A new state of things is rising up," declared the *New York Columbian* on January 26, 1820. Expounding on the greatness of the Empire State, the article boasted, "She is capable of unfolding her immense resources, in every noble improvement but connected with civil policy, but that she is also capable of uniting her moral strength, and displaying, under the banner of truth, her genius, her virtue, and her power."[1]

Such an optimistic appraisal conveyed the aspirations shared by many early nineteenth-century New Yorkers. Six years of British occupation during the American Revolution had drained New York's population, flooded its roads with refugees, and depressed its economy. By the 1790s, however, the region bustled with new economic life. The tight fiscal policies of Treasure Secretary Alexander Hamilton encouraged domestic manufacturing. The forcible removal of Native Americans from their ancestral homes in central and western New York opened up land to speculators who resold it to white settlers. And recognition of American independence granted New Yorkers access to French, Spanish, and eventually British markets. In addition, European conflicts created a demand for American foodstuffs and flooded New York City with cheap immigrant labor. The city soon became a clearinghouse for upstate produce, New England textiles, Virginia tobacco, and Deep South cotton destined for export overseas.[2] Increased commercialization also brought a new generation of merchants and attorneys who championed the goals of delayed gratification and capital acquisition. Professionally trained stockbrokers aggressively haggled over commodities at the Tontine Coffee House at the intersection of Wall and Water streets. Lawyers began to specialize in banking, incorporation, insurance, and patent law. From the 1790s to the 1820s, the New York state legislature actively promoted the development of canals, turnpikes, and post roads; the dredging of rivers; and the creation of new inventions such as steamboats.[3]

No individual epitomized the changes in New York society more than Governor DeWitt Clinton. As a young attorney, Clinton learned the art of political survival while serving as personal secretary to his uncle, George Clinton, the only colonial governor to retain his office throughout the American Revolution. His imposing physique and penchant for quoting Greek and Roman classics while opposing ratification of the U.S. Constitution in 1788 gained him the lifelong nickname "Magnus Apollo." He became a popular Republican mayor of New York City, a U.S. senator, and New York lieutenant governor. Yet his opposition to Thomas Jefferson's embargo policies, his lukewarm stance to the War of 1812, and his failed run for the U.S. presidency in 1812 left Clinton out of power. The resourceful politician created a new public identity as a commissioner and champion of the Erie Canal, a massive engineering project designed to connect the Hudson River to the Great Lakes. Clinton became New York governor in 1817, and for the next eight years, he commissioned legions of mostly immigrant laborers to complete a seven-hundred-mile "ditch" from the Hudson River to Buffalo. The canal carved a wide swath through the New York backcountry and through the popular imagination of New Yorkers, seeming to herald a new era of scientific, economic, and social progress.[4]

To be certain, the commercialization of the Empire State was neither seamless nor inevitable. "Putting out systems," in which nonspecialized workers focused on a single task in the completion of a final product, existed in tension with artisan shops until the eve of the Civil War. Mechanics, backcountry farmers, and landed tenants effectively used republican rhetoric and informal methods of resistance to defend traditional ways of life well into the 1840s. Yet as ordinary Americans turned to wage labor to subsidize family businesses and cash crops to preserve family homesteads, the market became ever more intertwined with

Chancellor Robert R. Livingston.
John Vanderlyn, *Chancellor Robert R. Livingston*, 1804, New-York Historical Society

their lives. Even many provincial landowners, the traditional power brokers in agrarian society, looked to the market for income to offset the falling values of their ancestral lands, the traditional source of their prestige. As a result, a considerable number of country squires agreed with the author of the *New York Columbian* article that the classical republican values of "truth," "genius," and "virtue" could be supported, not destroyed, by the "power" of economic growth. After all, landholders still held the levers of political power throughout the state governments and could control economic development through patronage, permits, and legislation. If they had to encounter economic and social change, why not do so on their own terms? One such individual, cautiously optimistic about the future, was Chancellor Robert R. Livingston.[5]

Robert R. Livingston: Industrious Agrarian

The patriarch of one of New York's oldest, largest, and wealthiest families, Livingston was described by biographer George Dangerfield as "something of an enigma, a slaveholding aristocrat in an era of rapidly democratizing politics."[6] The Livingston dynasty began with Robert R. Livingston's grandfather, also named Robert Livingston, a Scottish-born, Dutch-educated merchant who immigrated to North America in 1673. Fluent in English and Dutch, the elder Livingston thrived as a political leader, merchant, and landholder in Albany, New York. He pursued an aristocratic lifestyle, demanded deference from his tenants, and bequeathed to his descendants an impressive fortune and a regal family name to uphold. Born in 1746 in New York City, Robert R. Livingston quickly learned from his father, a colonial assemblyman and judge, how to function in a world of hierarchy and patronage. The young heir continued to build social networks while studying law, political philosophy, mathematics, science, and the classics at King's College. However, Livingston's promising political career as a New York City recorder and colonial assemblyman ground to a halt with the outbreak of the war with Britain in 1775.[7]

Livingston and the Revolutionary Experience

Although loyal to the Patriot cause, Livingston remained, at best, a cautious revolutionary. Like many landholders, he sought to free America from Britain—but not necessarily to liberate his tenants from their quitrent fees. Livingston left the Second Continental Congress early to attend to family business and thus missed the opportunity to sign the Declaration of Independence. In 1777, he collaborated with John Jay and Gouverneur Morris to draft a moderate state constitution, complete with property requirements for voting and a strong executive branch. Not surprisingly, Livingston became the first state chancellor under the newly formed state constitution. He relished the moniker, for although titles of nobility were frowned upon in post-Revolutionary America, the title "chancellor" bespoke a person of social importance under any system of government. Livingston became a Federalist, defended the U.S. Constitution as a delegate to New York's ratification convention, and read the first presidential oath of office to George Washington in New York City in 1789. Yet as a country squire and powerful state official, he warmed to Thomas Jefferson's vision of a nation based on agrarian virtues and states' rights. The chancellor also felt slighted by the Washington administration for not being offered a position on the U.S. Supreme Court.[8] In 1791, he became a Jeffersonian Republican and intermingled his agrarian sensibilities with a fascination for new industrial and scientific opportunities.[9] Through participation in the Society for Promoting Agriculture, Arts, and Manufacturing as well as local internal improvement projects, Livingston confirmed his self-image as an "eighteenth-century amateur scientist . . . who believed that the physical universe might at any moment yield any one of its innumerable, its extraordinary secrets to some fortuitous experiment or sudden flash of insight."[10] Like many in the founding generation, he remained fascinated by the new and the exotic. Over time, he became particularly interested in developing steam travel as a way to supplement his wealth and leave a lasting legacy to the citizens of New York.[11]

An Uneasy Partnership

Livingston's interest in steam power grew from conversations in 1797 with his brother-in-law, John Stevens of Hoboken, New Jersey.[12] By all accounts, Stevens and Livingston enjoyed cordial relations and frequently corresponded on family news, European politics, and advances in steam technology.[13] Although both men were landholders, Stevens had overinvested in western land speculations in the 1780s. He thus pursued steam power to stave off the loss in social status that insolvency would certainly bring.[14] Stevens first realized the potential for steam power in the summer of 1787 while witnessing one of John Fitch's paddleboat demonstrations on the Delaware River. The New Jerseyite pestered Fitch and Rumsey for technical advice, immediately built his own steamboat, and lobbied the New York state legislature for monopoly rights. Stevens admitted to Livingston that his steamboat rested upon the work of others, but he argued that investors often "discovered some happy mode of adapting and applying this power which has long since been made use of for various purposes." He also invoked social progress to complain that needless delay would "deprive the public for a considerable time of the benefit of it [his steamboat], provided it turns out to be good for anything," adding that "if it does not I shall injure no one but myself."[15] Nevertheless, a state legislative committee dismissed Steven's steamboat as an obvious copy of Rumsey's.[16] The flimsy federal patent Stevens received two years later did little to secure his reputation as inventor of the steamboat.

In 1797, Stevens struck up a partnership with Nicholas Roosevelt, a brilliant but unpredictable engineer. The son of a New York shopkeeper, Roosevelt showed an early aptitude for mechanics. After the Revolutionary War, he borrowed money from friends and built a metal foundry and shop in Second River (later

Belleville), New Jersey, naming it the Soho Works after Matthew Boulton and James Watt's famous Birmingham foundry. Roosevelt aggressively recruited talented engineers, such as German-born mechanic Charles Stoudinger and James Smallman, a former employee of Boulton and Watt. He also secured lucrative contracts to build a steam engine for the Philadelphia waterworks and a rolling mill to provide copper for federal warships. When the U.S. Navy failed to construct the promised ships, however, Roosevelt sank into insolvency.[17]

Stevens and Roosevelt realized the commercial possibilities of steam travel, but they lacked the funds to pursue their business plans. Consequently, the partners turned to Robert R. Livingston for help. The chancellor realized that he held the advantage, and in February 1797, he offered harsh terms to Stevens and Roosevelt: Livingston and Stevens would each receive 44 percent of the corporate profits, whereas Roosevelt would garner a mere 12 percent of the franchise and no profits from future steamboat lines. Stevens and Roosevelt grumbled but agreed to the arrangement.[18] The chancellor provided not only financial assistance but also mechanical advice, based on his eclectic readings. Stevens and Roosevelt humored their patron, hid their impatience, and struggled to maintain some control over the project.[19] After repeated disagreements, the partners launched their experimental vessel, the *Polacco,* on the Hudson River in spring 1797.[20] When the steamboat failed after the first attempt, Livingston remarked that he was "more mortified than surprised at the failure of the engine." He demanded that Stevens and Roosevelt stand by "the terms of our agreement to make up my loss at least by repaying what I have advanced with interest and making what you please of the engine if you think it is good for anything."[21] Roosevelt retorted, "Moderation and justice ought to govern us in this endeavor, this is your as well as our interest for the security of the patent which I look upon as valuable."[22]

Dismayed at such setbacks, Livingston took steps to ensure his own control over steam travel in New York. In 1798, he campaigned for a repeal of John Fitch's still valid 1787 steamboat monopoly law, on the assumption that Fitch was either dead or unwilling to invoke his claims. Two months later, Livingston received the state monopoly previously awarded to Fitch, with the proviso that he construct a boat within a year that weighed at least twenty tons and traveled no less than four miles per hour against the current. He was also to operate a steamboat line between New York City and Albany. The new monopoly law made no mention of Livingston's partners.[23] In October 1798, Stevens and Roosevelt successfully ferried the *Polacco* across New York Harbor.[24] Aware that the slow-moving vessel

could not meet the standards of his new monopoly, Livingston secretly petitioned James Watt for a British-made steam engine. "The small number of work-
men that understand the business" in America made steamboat construction "a
slow and expensive operation," complained the chancellor. Watt, however, failed
to respond with either sympathy or a steam engine.[25]

Frustrated with his partners, Livingston once again returned to the world
of politics. In 1800, his younger brother, Congressman Edward Livingston, rallied
support for Thomas Jefferson in that year's controversial presidential election.
To reward the Livingston family and neutralize a possible opponent, Jefferson appointed Chancellor Livingston as minister to France in order to determine if
Napoleon controlled Louisiana and, if so, to negotiate access to the port of New
Orleans.[26] While in France, Livingston met Robert Fulton, a gifted young engineer and shameless self-promoter. Interested in a variety of projects that ranged
from canals to floating mines, or "torpedoes," Fulton understood much of the
current literature on steamboats. After months of negotiations, the two men
began a partnership that, in time, would become one of the most successful col-
laborations in American business history.[27]

The Varied Career of Robert Fulton

Early nineteenth-century America teemed with opportunistic young
men, each claiming to possess a fabulous invention or unique investment opportunity. In this world of "projectors" and "stock jobbers," Robert Fulton emerged
as an unequivocal success story. He was born in 1756 to a Scotch-Irish farming
family in Little Britain Township, Pennsylvania. As a child, Fulton absorbed an
informal education from a local library supported by the inventor William Henry,
whose plans for steam engines had inspired a young John Fitch a decade earlier.
After his father died in debt, Fulton made his way in Philadelphia as a silversmith
and amateur artist. The young tradesman eagerly partook of the city's vibrant
scientific culture, including Fitch's steamboat demonstrations. In 1787, Fulton departed for London to study under the famous American painter Benjamin West,
a favorite in the court of King George III.[28] West introduced Fulton to the literary
and scientific elite of London. Painting portraits granted Fulton access to the world
of the British gentry. But he also pursued exotic projects such as building marble-
cutting saws, iron bridges, aqueducts, canals, and steamboats. Such projects

23

Robert Fulton. George
Parker, *Robert Fulton*, 1840,
Stapleton Collection,
Bridgeman Art Gallery,
c. 1830–68

attracted the interest of wealthy patrons such as William Courteney, the Earl of
Devon, and Robert Mahon, the Earl of Stanhope, Fulton frequently dazzled public gatherings with displays of knowledge on a variety of topics.[29]

To avoid acquiring the reputation of a mere projector, Fulton drew from
Adam Smith's *Wealth of Nations* and from colleagues such as Robert Owen and
John Dalton at the Literary and Philosophical Society of Manchester to construct
an intellectual framework for his endeavors.[30] He quickly assumed the role of an
inventor who borrowed from the work of others in society to create useful products, which he would then "return" to the public. As such, Fulton frequently employed proselytizing rhetoric to attract supporters.[31] In 1796, he published *A
Treatise on the Improvement of Canal Navigation,* in which he argued that "canals
must be considered like the looms of the draper or hosier; or those improved machines, which reducing the labor, yet multiply the produce; and consequently
render the necessaries, and conveniences, of life more abundant." Investments in
such projects, he declared, "have been the progressive steps of civilization; and
to which there appears to be no boundary!"[32]

Although Fulton dazzled British elites with his knowledge and charm, he failed to understand them as a class. He frequently entered "gentlemen's agreements" with potential investors. Such alliances were not formalized in writing, and Fulton merely discarded partners as better opportunities emerged. As an outsider, he failed to grasp that these agreements carried substantial weight in the culture of honor shared by the British gentry, and he soon developed a reputation as a "man on the make," which hurt his business opportunities. Unable to attract new patrons, Fulton hurriedly left for France in June 1797.[33]

He arrived on the Continent in the later stages of the French Revolution. He hoped to convince French authorities that canal investments would help modernize their largely agrarian nation.[34] In Paris, Fulton became fast friends and probably lovers with American poet Joel Barlow and his wife, Ruth. The Barlows tutored Fulton in Parisian art, science, and culture; invested in several of his projects; and introduced him to French elites.[35] In November 1797, the French directorate rejected Fulton's request for a patent on a canal boat. In retaliation, Fulton authored pamphlets titled *Thoughts on Free Trade, To the Friends of Mankind on the Advantages of Free Trade,* and *The Republican Creed,* in which he argued, for example, "Industry will give abundance to a virtuous world and call mankind to unbounded feats of harmony and friendship. The liberty of the seas will be the happiness of the earth."[36]

Negotiations, Delays, and Further Experiments

Abandoning his plans to promote canals in Paris, Fulton spent the next three years unsuccessfully attempting to develop a practical submarine. Then, in late 1801, the Barlows introduced him to Chancellor Robert R. Livingston. Through the following spring, the young inventor courted Livingston with conversations on ship propulsion, construction, expenses, and potential profits. In June, Fulton boldly proposed an equal partnership to construct a steamboat based on his expertise and Livingston's capital.[37] After several months of deliberation, the chancellor signed a formal agreement with Fulton on October 10, 1802. The contract stipulated that the two men would form a company and take out a federal patent for a steamboat to ply the Hudson River between New York City and Albany, carry at least sixty passengers, and travel no slower than eight miles per hour. Livingston would provide funds, and Fulton would oversee construction of a

25

prototype boat. If the vessel failed to operate within two years, Fulton would repay Livingston half the investment plus interest.[38] Each investor could sell off up to 40 percent of his business shares, but purchasers would gain no voice in company policy. If either Fulton or Livingston died, an heir with twenty shares would be considered an active partner, but the surviving partner would maintain control over his half of the business. To avoid the problems he had encountered with Stevens and Roosevelt, Livingston retained the right to withdraw from the agreement after an initial investment of £500.[39]

After finalizing his agreement with Fulton, Livingston wrote his brother-in-law Thomas Tillotson, New York's secretary of state and a member of the powerful Council of Appointment, to secure new monopoly rights for both himself and Fulton. The chancellor claimed that all of his old partners had given up on steamboats, but he insisted that he had found a new associate in Fulton. Livingston reported, "We are now actively making experiments on a large scale upon the Seine. Should we succeed it would be mortifying to have any other compete for my advantage."[40] Tillotson replied that he had placed the petition into the hands of "friends" in the legislature who would see to its passage.[41] Livingston chose a fortuitous moment to renew his monopoly. George Clinton, who was, for the moment, a Livingston family ally, had just been elected to his seventh term as governor of New York. Many of the Republicans who dominated the New York Assembly owed political favors to the Livingston family. Passage of the steamboat monopoly bill was assured. Even Livingston's role as a negotiator with Napoleon's government to procure New Orleans proved useful. On April 11, 1803, the French leader offered to sell the entire Louisiana Territory for $15 million. Livingston urged President Jefferson to overcome constitutional qualms and accept a treaty that effectively doubled the size of the United States.[42]

With Livingston engaged on several fronts, Fulton sent frantic letters to Matthew Boulton in a futile attempt to secure a steam engine. In desperation, he then combined the discoveries of predecessors such as the marquis de Jouffroy d'Abbans, Lord Stanhope, Rumsey, and Fitch with his own calculations to produce a prototype steamboat in spring 1803.[43] Fulton bragged to the director of the French Conservancy of Arts that he had designed a vessel "to put it in practice upon the long rivers of America where there are not roads suitable for haulage."[44] When the experimental craft broke in two and sank, Fulton risked his health to refloat the ship. On August 9, he pushed the repaired and reconstructed boat to three miles an hour while towing two other boats before a Parisian crowd.[45]

Plans and Experiments

Fulton enjoyed widespread popularity across Paris for his successful experiments with steam travel. However, he squandered the goodwill by embarking on a two-year quest to interest the French and British governments in his torpedo experiments. Distrusted by both sides, he failed to find any financial backers for his experiments in naval warfare. In desperation, he sought new business opportunities in the United States and traveled to Washington, DC, to offer his torpedo schemes to the U.S. Navy. While staying with the Barlows, Fulton attended a dinner on January 14, 1807, to honor the famed explorer Meriwether Lewis, who had recently returned from his transcontinental expedition. At the banquet, Joel Barlow entertained the crowd with a poem that suggested renaming the Columbia River in honor of Lewis. "Let our Occident stream bear the young hero's name, / Who taught him his path to the sea," recited Barlow.[46] Not to be outdone, Robert Fulton led a toast to "the American Eagle—when she expands her wings from the Atlantic to the Pacific Ocean, may she quench her thirst in both."[47] Like many young Americans, Lewis, Barlow, and Fulton viewed the frontier in Jeffersonian terms—as a place to create a uniquely American culture. They hoped that the West, if opened to settlement, would spawn a technologically advanced yet virtuous society of people who lived in harmony with their natural surroundings.[48] Fulton conceived of himself as an agent of destiny, whose experiments in steam power would create a better society and secure his personal fame and fortune.[49]

To that end, Fulton wrote to Livingston and stressed the need to determine whether the Hudson or the Mississippi would provide the most profits for their steamboat plans. Fulton hoped to pursue a steamboat line on the Mississippi and arranged with Secretary of War Henry Dearborn to measure the speed of the river's current. The inventor hinted, "I hope this work will promote the interest of the country."[50] Livingston, however, remained skeptical of the value of any western ventures. As an attorney, the chancellor knew quite well that territorial governments could not adequately defend monopoly and patent rights. A steamboat line on the Hudson River would be more lucrative and easier to control. Furthermore, every steamboat that navigated up the Hudson past Clermont, the Livingston family estate, would testify to Livingston's public reputation as a patron of the arts.[51]

Fulton and Livingston quarreled over the issue throughout fall 1806. In the short run, the chancellor won out, as Fulton journeyed to New York in March

1807 to begin work on a steamboat to operate on the Hudson River.[52] The chastised inventor hired shipbuilders, blacksmiths, and carpenters to begin construction of a steamboat at Charles Brownne's shipyard in lower Manhattan. While Fulton poured more than $20,000 of capital into the endeavor, Livingston petitioned the New York state legislature to extend their monopoly privileges for another two years.[53] After a failed attempt, in July, to sink a mothballed navy brig in New York Harbor with his torpedoes, Fulton made final modifications to his steamboat.[54] At one o'clock in the afternoon on August 17, 1807, a crowd gathered at the New York Battery to witness the trial run of the functionally named *North River Steam Boat*. Livingston family members and their wealthy friends waited patiently aboard the vessel. Fulton attempted to bring the ship up to steam, but a minor problem with the boiler caused the engine to shut down. As both the passengers and the crowd on the shore became impatient, he effected repairs and restarted the engine. Then, as the vessel churned to life against the current, the spectators began to cheer.[55]

Not all were taken by the spectacle. Sloop owners complained that the vessel polluted the Hudson River with its vile smoke, and farmers dismissed the noisy craft as the work of Satan. All who witnessed the steamboat on its 120-mile trip up the river heard Fulton and his passengers singing popular ballads and Scottish laments deep into the night. The voyagers arrived at Clermont precisely twenty-four hours later, where Chancellor Livingston warmly welcomed Fulton into polite society by announcing the engagement of the inventor to his niece, Harriet Livingston. Fulton and his passengers then traveled to Albany the next day in a record eight hours before returning in triumph to New York City. The potential of steam power had now been proven to the residents of the Hudson River valley.[56]

Livingston and Fulton had done more than merely triumph over technical problems and jeering critics to create the first practical steamboat. They had also overcome their own differences to create an extremely successful business partnership. Livingston wanted a small-scale steamboat empire on the Hudson River, which would provide him with a lucrative income and showcase his talents as a gentleman scientist. Fulton, by contrast, wanted to create an expansive steamboat network on the Mississippi River, which would facilitate the westward development of the United States and make him a living legend on both sides of the Appalachian Mountains.

Such contrasting goals made the prospects of an effective partnership difficult at best. Nonetheless, both men rose to the occasion. Livingston provided

Map of the state of New York, 1831. William Williams, "The Tourist's Map of the State of New York—Compiled from the Latest Authorities in the Surveyor General's Office" (Utica, NY: William Williams, 1831)

much of the capital, which allowed Fulton to complete the *North River Steam Boat*. The chancellor also learned to let Fulton alone when it came to planning and construction. And for his part, Fulton mustered enough patience to put aside his ambition to tame the Mississippi with steam power and maintain a long-term partnership.

Together they succeeded where others had failed. Nonetheless, their work rested on the creativity and scientific knowledge of many who had come before. It was only a matter of time before challengers emerged to contest their claims of control over steam travel in New York State. This development would test their partnership to the core.

29

Corporate Negotiations

*Private Gain and the Public Good
in the Early Steamboat Industry*

SHORTLY AFTER HIS triumphant return to New York City on August 20, 1807, Robert Fulton reported to Joel Barlow, "The power of propelling boats by steam is now fully proved." The jubilant inventor also confided, "Although the prospect of personal emolument has been some inducement to me, yet I feel infinitely more pleasure in reflecting on the immense advantages that my country will draw from the invention."[1]

Fulton's attempt to balance the conflicting goals of personal gain and public service reflected dilemmas faced by many steamboat promoters. The Louisiana Purchase, secured in the first decade of the nineteenth century, opened western lands to a burgeoning population and created a demand for new forms of transportation. However, there were no quick and easy navigational charts to success in the early American steamboat industry. Capital often remained bound up in land and agricultural products.[2] States provided support for internal improvements but often on an ad hoc basis.[3]

Given such economic instability and the competitive and uncertain market, Fulton and Livingston used a variety of techniques to protect their steamboat interests. Their use of printed testimonials, pamphlets, and public demonstrations to attract public support drew directly from techniques pioneered by Fitch and Rumsey a decade earlier. The partners also frequently brandished their state monopoly to intimidate opponents from running steamboats in New York. But lawsuits were time-consuming and expensive, and early state and federal courts often relied upon persuasion rather than coercion to enforce their decrees. Under these circumstances, the steamboat monopoly was primarily a symbol of honor, a stamp of state approval on a flourishing business. Fulton and Livingston often used the monopoly as part of their sales pitch, to convince the public that they enjoyed the favor of local government and their competitors did not. In the short run, the two men proved quite adept at using threats of lawsuits with promises of profits to co-opt rivals such as John Stevens and Nicholas Roosevelt into their growing steamboat empire. Yet by constantly threatening their opponents with legal action, Fulton and Livingston also invited the first public examination of their legal claims. In particular, John Stevens began a systematic investigation of the New York monopoly grant. Although financial pressure ultimately forced him to give in to Livingston's demands for a partnership, Stevens pioneered many of the legal arguments that would be used against the steamboat monopoly in *Gibbons v. Ogden*.[4]

Attempts to Secure a Steamboat Monopoly on the Hudson River

In fall 1807, Fulton and Livingston took steps to form a steamboat company to ply the Hudson River. Fulton listed steamboat schedules and fares in local papers and registered the *North River Steam Boat* with New York authorities. He also published testimonials from passengers that boasted of the safety and comfort of the trip. Over the next year, *North River Steam Boat* passenger numbers increased, on average, from twelve to ninety customers per trip. Fulton estimated that at $7 per passenger, the vessel would produce $700 in profit per week. By any standard, Fulton and Livingston's gamble had emerged as a full-blown success. Still dreaming of a western steamboat empire, Fulton spent his spare time calculating profits for projected steamboat lines on the Missouri and Mississippi rivers.[5]

Despite Fulton's accomplishments, however, many leading New Yorkers doubted that he could sustain a profitable company. Peter Augustus Jay inspected the *North River Steam Boat* two weeks after its initial excursion. Fulton boasted to

Jay that his vessel could reach Albany in thirty-two hours and travel five miles an hour in still water. Jay reported to his father, former U.S. chief justice and New York governor John Jay, "The greatest objections to the invention arise I think from the expense of the boat and the little room it contains." The elder Jay confirmed, "Perhaps the steamboat may yet be so improved as to be useful and less expensive—in the present state I doubt its proving advantageous to the owners."[6]

While on a visit to the Barlows in Washington, DC, Fulton raised the possibility of obtaining a federal patent. Livingston had second thoughts about obtaining such a document, for a federal patent might undermine their state grant because it would essentially acknowledge the superiority of federal law over state law. He argued that it would be more practical to consider their monopoly a public service to meet the transportation needs of New Yorkers, rather than a unique invention. In any event, he said, weak federal patents were no substitute for solid state and territorial monopoly grants.[7] Fulton countered that a federal patent law would place their monopoly rights on a national footing. He also wrote the U.S. Patent Office for an opinion that would make manifest the benefits of a federal patent. Unfortunately for Fulton, William Thornton had just been appointed superintendent of the Patent Office. Thornton was still bitter over the setbacks that he and John Fitch had faced in their attempts to manage a steamboat company in the 1790s. Although he still harbored hopes for a successful steamboat franchise, Thornton recognized the need to accommodate Fulton in the short run. He thus concurred with Fulton that states could not grant exclusive navigation rights over major rivers. Nonetheless, lingering doubts over the originality of his work and Livingston's reassurances that the monopoly faced no immediate danger prompted Fulton to abandon his quest for a federal patent. This decision would later prove a costly mistake.[8]

Growing Rivalries in the Steamboat Industry

While in Washington, Fulton petitioned President Jefferson and the Navy Department to fund further torpedo experiments. When he returned to New York City in December to refit the *North River Steam Boat* for the spring thaw, he found a host of rivals eager to capitalize on his successes. A Canadian company established a steamboat service to run on Lake Champlain, and closer to home, John Winants and James Smallman, former Livingston employees, formed their own steamboat company.[9] To make matters worse, in a heated letter, William Thornton demanded an equal partnership with Fulton and Livingston; if that demand was not met, he would secure a patent on John Fitch's steamboat designs. The Patent Office chief also brandished a Spanish monopoly for steam travel on the Mississippi River, which he claimed was still valid under federal law. When Fulton failed to respond, Thornton created his own steamboat company. The endeavor quickly went bankrupt, and its failure prompted Thornton to begin amassing evidence and witnesses in anticipation of the day when he could take revenge on Fulton.[10]

While Thornton was pressuring Fulton, John Stevens again pushed Chancellor Livingston for access to the Hudson River. Stevens threatened to register his vessel under a federal coasting license and oppose the monopoly in federal court. "What is to be done in such a case?" Stevens asked Livingston. "Will an action brought against the owner of this vessel in the Federal Court of New Jersey avail any thing? Will this court conceive itself bound to pay any respect to an act of the legislature of the State of New York passed in direct contravention of the spirit and letter of the Constitution of the United States?" And even if a federal court were to uphold the monopoly, he continued, "will a Jury in the State of New Jersey be much inclined to give very heavy damages for the infringement of a law granting a monopoly so injurious of the public?"[11] Stevens sought to place the dispute before the public by promising to abandon the matter if his vessel failed to surpass the speed of the *North River Steam Boat* in a fair and open race.[12] He was thus the first to suggest that the steamboat monopoly could not survive indefinitely without the support of both the U.S. Constitution and popular opinion.

Livingston, in return, asked if inventors should be defrauded "merely because another person has at a later day found another mode of doing the same thing?" The chancellor reasoned, "Surely the late comer would have no right to complain if his invention is not taken from him but merely prohibited, where it is not wanted or where prior engagements interfere with it."[13] Certainly, he argued, the U.S. Constitution did not preclude state-based monopolies created for the public good.[14]

Having fleshed out his arguments, Livingston offered Stevens a one-fifth partnership for $9,000, provided that he confined his steamboat service to either New York City and New Brunswick, New Jersey, or Trenton, New Jersey, and Philadelphia. Stevens would also have to publicly acknowledge Fulton as the true inventor

33

of the steamboat. Livingston placed additional pressure on Stevens with the false assertion that he and Fulton held a federal patent for their steamboat.[15] Stevens now faced two undesirable choices. He could swallow his pride and acknowledge Fulton as inventor of the steamboat. Or he could face the humiliation of bankruptcy by giving up the financial support provided by his brother-in-law. To play for time, Stevens implored his sister, the chancellor's wife, to seek an indirect reconciliation with Livingston; Mary Stevens Livingston obligingly plied her husband with flattery.[16] Yet as his sister undertook these efforts, privately Stevens fumed, "Monopolies are very justly held, in every free country, as odious. A monopoly gives an unlimited power to one man or set of men to lay heavy contributions on all the rest of the community." Regardless of the appearance of congeniality, Stevens and Livingston thus remained divided by their economic interests.[17]

New Steamboats on the Hudson River

On April 11, 1808, the *New York Commercial Advertiser* reported the launch of Stevens's new steamboat, the *Phoenix,* from the Hoboken shipyards. Five days later, the New York legislature passed a law that extended Fulton and Livingston's thirty-year monopoly by five years for every additional steamboat they put into service. The measure also allowed the men to seize unlicensed steamboats in New York waters, although it did not detail the process by which the partners could take such vessels.[18] The new monopoly law spelled disaster for Stevens. Although he was a wealthy man, his fortune lay in lands that he had heavily mortgaged to pay his land speculation debts and finance his steamboat experiments. For the moment, he survived on Manhattan Bank notes endorsed by Chancellor Livingston. On April 21, Stevens contritely wrote his brother-in-law to apologize for selling banknotes endorsed by Livingston at a discount. Yet he simultaneously asked the chancellor to endorse several new notes. Not even a flattering letter from Mary Stevens Livingston to her husband could soften the blow.[19]

Two weeks later, Livingston responded with a pointed lecture on financial responsibility. Stevens then mentioned that the chancellor still owed $3,186 for a bond Stevens had loaned him in 1796. He also asked Livingston not to destroy their friendship over such a trivial matter. Livingston replied that, though he regretted the loss of their friendship, he could not endorse any more notes without risking his own credit and "being stamped a bankrupt."[20]

As his relationship with Stevens deteriorated, Livingston's partnership with Fulton continued to bloom. In June 1808, Fulton informed artist Charles Wilson Peale, "My steamboat is now in complete operation and works much to my satisfaction making his voyages from or to New York or Albany." In addition, he noted that "the people of this state are much pleased and our success in passengers has been encouraging."[21]

In July 1808, Stevens offered his home in Perth Amboy, New Jersey, as collateral if Livingston would only endorse more notes to him.[22] When the beleaguered inventor threatened again to obtain a federal coasting license, Fulton bellowed, "What is an invention but an exact demonstration of such combinations and principles as will produce a new and desired effect which was not known before? What is the object of a patent but to secure such mutual property?" Fulton assured Livingston that he was the true inventor of the steamboat, that the *North River Steam Boat* was superior to the *Phoenix,* and that Stevens would never violate their monopoly.[23]

Having issued his threats, Stevens approached Richard Harison, a prestigious New Jersey attorney, with several legal questions. Could a state prevent a federal patentee from using his patent provided that doing so did not harm the public good? And did the U.S. Constitution protect free intercourse between states? Critical of Fulton and Livingston, Stevens claimed, "I have been engaged in similar pursuits, and have expended, I believe, more money than they have in the prosecution of them solely under a reliance on my patent from the United States."[24] Harison concurred that states could not infringe upon federal patent rights and that only Congress could regulate interstate trade.[25]

Expanding the North River Company

Fulton and Livingston sought to outmaneuver Stevens by granting the chancellor's brother, John R. Livingston, the rights to construct and run a steam ferry between Manhattan, Staten Island, and New Brunswick. The decision to partner with John Livingston was a controversial one. As a privateer during the American Revolution, Livingston had traded with both Patriots and Tories. For that reason, it was feared he might put his own interests ahead of those of the partnership. Fulton and Chancellor Livingston wisely limited their new partner to operations from New York City to New Jersey ports.[26] While the Livingstons closed ranks behind the steamboat monopoly, Stevens field-tested the *Phoenix.* The vessel averaged five and a half miles per hour, but it succumbed to an over-heated boiler and paddle wheels that rotated at different speeds. Undeterred, Stevens publicly sold stock at $75 a share for a company to run steamboats from New York City to New Brunswick, Trenton, and Philadelphia.[27]

In October, Chancellor Livingston reported to his brother-in-law that the Manhattan Bank was demanding security for several notes issued to Stevens. Livingston told him he had hoped that "your sense of what was due to your character would long before this have led you to perform the promises which you so repeatedly and solemnly made me." The chancellor urged Stevens to discharge his duties, which "every man of honor considers a sacred obligation."[28] While Livingston expatiated on the virtues of honor, a letter appeared in the New York–based *American Citizen,* titled "A Friend to Useful Invention and Justice." The author claimed to be a potential investor who wanted to pose several pointed questions to Stevens. Did Stevens have a federal patent that could prevent competition from other vessels? Did Fulton and Livingston not have a federal patent and a state monopoly? Had Stevens not rejected a partnership offer from Fulton and Livingston? Had Stevens inflated his passenger estimates and speed records? What security could Stevens provide for investors, since it would be impractical to bring multiple lawsuits to recover investments of only $75 each? Although the letter was written anonymously, draft notes found in Chancellor Livingston's handwriting leave little doubt as to the identity of its author. The letter damaged Stevens's reputation, and after selling only fifty-one shares of stock, he declared bankruptcy and doled out refunds to his investors.[29]

As Livingston manipulated Stevens from behind the scenes, Fulton made conciliatory gestures toward their rival. He argued that further competition would only hurt everyone. Stevens could join the New York syndicate if only he would acknowledge Fulton and Livingston's patent and monopoly rights. Defining the matter in terms of personal honor, Fulton claimed he made his offer from a desire to help Stevens and not because he considered the New Jerseyite a threat.[30] Curious as to why his rivals wanted recognition of their patent rights, Stevens wrote William Thornton for a copy of Fulton's federal steamboat patent.[31] In response, Thornton informed Stevens that Fulton possessed a patent for a simple steam-powered poleboat, not a paddle-driven steamboat.[32] On learning this, an infuriated Stevens drafted his own letter to the *American Citizen,* which dismissed Fulton's contributions to steam power. Reminding the public of his own experiments with steam power, he pushed for "open and unrestrained competition and the opportunity to offer the results of my genius and experiments to the public," free from character attacks or threats.[33]

More Attempts at Compromise

Aware that Stevens could expose their false patent claims to the public, Fulton and Livingston sought a rapprochement with their rival. Chancellor Livingston passed along a partnership offer through his wife, Mary Stevens Livingston: Stevens could have his choice of steamboat routes below the Hudson, provided he acknowledged Fulton and Livingston's legal rights. Even if he refused their terms, Stevens could still transfer passengers to Fulton's boats if he agreed to limit himself to one steamboat line. Livingston gave Stevens a week to respond.[34] Fulton also expressed regret to Stevens for their quarrels and offered to help him construct a new steamboat. The inventor hoped that after sober reflection, Stevens would "not accuse the chancellor or me of sinister writings, or illiberality towards you." Fulton reasoned that if Stevens's *Phoenix* proved faster, "there is no cause of complaint on our part, the race of science is a noble exertion of humane faculties, and he who fastest runs should win."[35] Such attempts at diplomacy belied Fulton's intense worry that Stevens could damage his reputation. Accordingly, Fulton submitted an avalanche of diagrams and affidavits to Secretary of State James Madison along with a request for a proper steamboat patent. Madison promptly forwarded Fulton's correspondence to William Thornton, who registered a patent for himself before issuing one to Fulton eleven days later. Despite Thornton's obvious duplicity, he would continue to press his claim as inventor of the steamboat for years to come.[36]

John Stevens was not the only one to realize the precariousness of Fulton's patent claims. Nicholas Roosevelt deduced that his own experiments in paddle wheel technology had formed the basis for much of Fulton's steamboat designs, and in spring 1809, Roosevelt contacted his father-in-law, Benjamin Henry Latrobe, with a plan to publicly declare that he, not Fulton, had invented the paddle wheel. Latrobe was a British-born, Prussian-educated military veteran who was literate in five languages; known as the "father of American architecture," he had laid plans for the U.S. Capitol building and, in fact, for much of Washington, DC. As a well-respected member of Washington society, Latrobe carried more weight than his frequently insolvent son-in-law. He discreetly mentioned Roosevelt's experiments with paddle wheels to Fulton and suggested a "nice connexion founded on mutual friendship and interest" to settle the matter.[37] Fulton met with Latrobe and insisted that he was not bound by any previous agreements made by the chancellor. Furthermore, he stressed that his patent claims stemmed not from paddle wheels per se but from "proportioning the boat to the power of the engine and the velocity with which the wheels of the boat turn, as to move with the medium of the velocity attainable by the power and the construction of the whole machine." Fulton lamented that he could not grant Roosevelt a portion of the New York state monopoly, but he hinted at the possibility of a partnership to develop steamboats on the Mississippi River.[38]

Having dealt with Roosevelt, Fulton and Livingston threatened to sue John Stevens for running the *Phoenix* between New Brunswick and New York City. Livingston also promised to reduce his fares to one-third Stevens's prices to bring his opponent to reason.[39] In retaliation, Stevens demanded that Fulton supply a copy of the federal patent he had supposedly violated. Fulton agreed but insisted that Stevens reveal his steamboat plans in return. When Stevens refused, Fulton stated that he had just as much right to protect his inventions, and he then ordered Thornton not to disclose his patent to Stevens under any circumstances. Thornton played for time by asking U.S. attorney general Caesar A. Rodney to clarify whether, under federal law, ordinary citizens could request patent copies.[40]

Although his patent rights and personal reputation remained vulnerable, Fulton proceeded with his plans to create a western steamboat company.[41] In spring 1809, he commissioned Nicholas Roosevelt to construct and pilot a steamboat from Pittsburgh, Pennsylvania, to New Orleans.[42] Equal parts scientific experiment, promotional tour, and investment opportunity, Fulton's proposed voyage would spearhead future steamboat lines throughout the Mississippi River valley. Roosevelt readily agreed and arranged to take his wife, Lydia Latrobe Roosevelt, with him on the trip. Benjamin Latrobe promised his daughter that the voyage "will give you a charming jaunt, and will effect a separate housekeeping, an object of first importance to your happiness." Domestic concerns aside, Latrobe hoped that Lydia would help keep her husband fiscally accountable.[43]

In June 1809, Nicholas and Lydia Roosevelt arrived in the booming frontier town of Pittsburgh, at the intersection of the Ohio, Allegheny, and Monongahela rivers. Accustomed to East Coast elegance, the couple puzzled over the muddy streets and clapboard houses they encountered. They mingled with local elites and commissioned a customized flatboat from a local boatyard. With a small crew, they departed for New Orleans in fall 1809. Roosevelt measured river currents and widths. He also left mounds of coal by the banks of the Ohio River in anticipation of future steamboat traffic. The Roosevelts arrived in New Orleans in December and then returned to New York City to deliver their report.[44] When spring arrived, they went back to Pittsburgh, sold company stock, and began construction of a four-hundred-ton steamboat named the *New Orleans*. Over the next six months, Roosevelt grappled with timber shortages, wage disputes, and constant summer floods. To make matters worse, he channeled corporate funds into a snuffbox factory and a distillery.[45] Against the advice of his father-in-law, he even bartered away his partnership agreement in return for a salaried position with Fulton and Livingston.[46]

More Problems in New York

Unaware of Roosevelt's malfeasance, Fulton and Livingston struggled to solidify their New York operations. In June 1809, they launched a second steamboat, the *Car of Neptune,* in New York Harbor to help offset profits lost to Stevens. More spacious and elegant than the *North River Steam Boat,* the *Car of Neptune* attracted increased business for the run between Albany and New York City.[47] The following month, Stevens received good news from Thornton: any American citizen could request copies of a registered patent. The Patent Office chief jubilantly promised Stevens a copy of Fulton's patents. Thornton had already secured an affidavit from David Voight that showed Fulton's steamboat plans clearly rested on John Fitch's designs. He promised Stevens that, as they could now beat Fulton in court, their rival would certainly see reason and negotiate.[48]

Armed with the knowledge that Fulton's patent claims were a sham, Stevens secretly negotiated with Livingston to secure a stagecoach service that would link their steamboat lines from Philadelphia to New York City. Fulton and Livingston tried once more to tempt Stevens with a partnership, this time merely for his private, written acknowledgment that Fulton had invented the steamboat. If he refused, they warned that the North River Company would license third parties to run steamboats against the *Phoenix* on the Delaware River and destroy Stevens without even risking their own capital.[49] In response, Stevens cleverly offered to allow groups of skilled, impartial mechanics to determine whether his or Fulton's steamboat plans were original. Such a move would threaten not merely Fulton's steamboat plans but also his public reputation. Further, if Fulton

39

and Livingston harmed his Delaware interests, Stevens said he would launch his own steamboat lines on the Hudson.[50] These tactics took Fulton by surprise. He denied any attempts to intimidate Stevens, saying that rival steamboat companies continued to pressure for licenses to run boats on the Delaware River and that he was merely reporting the news. However, such competition revealed the practicality of a shared partnership over economic warfare on every river in the nation.[51]

After a brief cooling-off period, Fulton and Stevens met to forge an alliance. Fulton and Livingston clung to their interests on the Hudson, Ohio, and Mississippi rivers, and Stevens received monopoly rights to the Delaware, Chesapeake, Santee, Savannah, and Connecticut rivers. All parties would share patents and plans. The bargain rested on Fulton's flimsy patent rights and was therefore more of a gentlemen's agreement, the success of which would depend on voluntary cooperation. The document also carried the implicit understanding that steam power had truly become a national issue—even if the partners still sought to defend it primarily at the state level.[52]

The initial goodwill shared by Fulton, Livingston, and Stevens did not survive the inking of their contract. At the last moment, Fulton inserted an addendum that based their agreement solely on the authority of his patent rights. Stevens flinched but signed the contract anyway.[53] When the chancellor demanded that his brother-in-law admit the superiority of Fulton's steamboat designs, Stevens coolly replied that he had already signed an agreement with Fulton.

Conflict among the partners subsided for the moment, primarily because recent British seizures of American vessels and sailors gave Fulton the hope that the U.S. government might be ready to support his torpedo project.[54] In spring 1810, he accepted $5,000 in federal funds to pursue torpedo experiments, but he failed to deliver a functional prototype. Humiliated before a congressional subcommittee, Fulton eagerly returned to his Hudson River and Mississippi River steamboat ventures in December 1810.

Eastern Dreams and Western Realities

Anxious to legally protect their Mississippi River interest, Fulton and Livingston petitioned state and territorial legislatures for exclusive monopoly rights. As historians from Frederick Jackson Turner to David Waldstreicher have noted, early Americans looked to the West as a symbol of national growth. Westerners were highly aware of their role in the national imagination and contested their peripheral status in American society. Many correctly predicted that population growth would soon make their region the most powerful section of the young republic, and they viewed the steamboat as a crucial ingredient for the economic development of the frontier.[55] Consequently, Fulton's success with the *North River Steam Boat* generated much enthusiasm among frontier residents. But westerners had little use for monopolies. They remembered all too well the deposit fees and trade disruptions of the Spanish colonial period. State monopolies —even those advanced by the inventor of the steamboat and the architect of the Louisiana Purchase—appeared to backcountry farmers as nothing more than elements of yet another plot by jealous easterners to hamper western destinies. Inhabitants of the Mississippi River valley would harbor hostility toward the steamboat monopolies until the Supreme Court put the matter to rest in 1824.[56]

Fulton and Livingston brushed aside such considerations to petition the Ohio and Kentucky state legislatures as well as the governors of Tennessee, Indiana, and the Orleans, Upper Louisiana, and Mississippi territories for exclusive monopoly rights. In their appeal to the Kentucky state legislature, they boasted that their steamboats could carry goods for one-third the time and cost of normal freight operations. On those grounds, they demanded a twenty-year monopoly with an additional five years for every boat added to their western fleet, up to thirty years.[57] The pair met with little success. The Indiana territorial legislature agreed to sanction a steamboat company, to be called the Ohio Steam Boat Navigation Company, but refused to grant a monopoly. Ohio representatives passed a monopoly bill, only to see their efforts defeated in the state senate. And Senator John M. Breckenridge crushed a monopoly petition on the floor of the Kentucky statehouse. The senator warned his constituents, "It would be dangerous and impolitic to invest a man or set of men with the sole power of cramping, controlling, or directing the most considerable part of the commerce of the country for so great a period." Stymied by defeat after defeat, Fulton and Livingston seized upon one last opportunity to secure a monopoly in the Orleans Territory at the mouth of the Mississippi.[58]

Politics and Personalities in the Crescent City

To influence Louisiana legislators, Fulton and Livingston tried to make their way through the complex legal and cultural avenues of New Orleans society. Descendants of French, Spanish, African, and Native American Creoles, known locally as the *ancienne population,* dominated the Crescent City, which was also home to East Coast lawyers, merchants, clerks, doctors, and planters such as Governor William Charles Cole Claiborne and Edward Livingston, the younger brother of Chancellor Livingston.[59]

In 1803, Thomas Jefferson had appointed Claiborne, a fellow Virginian and supporter during the "revolution of 1800," as governor of the Orleans Territory.[60] Trained as a lawyer, Claiborne struggled to establish a territorial government in the former French and Spanish colony. French inhabitants resented the American occupation of Louisiana, and they feared for the future of their legal and cultural traditions. Claiborne consequently emerged as a convenient whipping boy for New Orleans natives.[61] He stood in stark contrast to Edward Livingston, who benefited from a childhood spent among New York's manorial elite. Like his brother, Livingston had supported the U.S. Constitution as a Federalist in 1788 only to secure electoral votes for Thomas Jefferson as a Republican in 1800. While serving as a federal district attorney, Livingston faced an embezzlement scandal that ruined his political career. He fled to New Orleans in 1804. Unlike Claiborne, who clung to his Virginia ways, Livingston learned French, married a wealthy Haitian émigré named Louise Moreau de Lassy, and carved out a niche in the French Creole community of New Orleans.[62] In fall 1810, Robert R. Livingston enlisted Edward to secure Claiborne's support for a steamboat monopoly grant from the Orleans territorial legislature. Realizing an economic opportunity, Claiborne met with Chancellor Livingston in March 1810 in Washington, DC, while presenting a petition to Congress for Louisiana statehood. After a journey to New York and a ride on one of Fulton's steamboats, Claiborne agreed to lobby the Orleans legislature for monopoly rights.[63]

In 1810, the possibilities of the Fulton-Livingston partnership seemed endless. After five years of struggle, the two men had created a cost-effective steamboat, monopolized steam travel on the Hudson River, and stood poised to gain a similar franchise on the Mississippi River. Chancellor Livingston had successfully deployed his image as a stern patriarch with substantial money and influence to keep John Stevens in line. However, he had also resorted to attacking Stevens in the press (albeit anonymously), essentially making their private, family feud a public confrontation. Meanwhile, Robert Fulton had based his status as an inventor on legally worthless federal patents—and Stevens, Thornton, and Roosevelt were quick to exploit such a weakness. Although Fulton succeeded in buying off Roosevelt, he could not indefinitely postpone a showdown with either Stevens or

Thornton. Until that time, Fulton stayed on the offense by portraying himself as a single-minded businessman with no time to quibble. His decision to avoid conflict in the short run would come back to haunt him in future years. Furthermore, John Stevens's public rivalry with Fulton and Livingston had publicized their arguments for and against federal patents and state monopolies, arguments that would later be used in *Gibbons v. Ogden*.

CHAPTER 4

Defending the Monopoly

New Competitors

IN 1810, ROBERT FULTON and Robert R. Livingston began an aggressive campaign to expand their steamboat operations across the nation. Their petitions to western state and territorial legislatures combined Livingston's methods of courting local politicians for regional monopolies with Fulton's ambitions of bringing steamboats to the Mississippi River valley. Fulton hoped that a network of steamboats plying the Ohio and Mississippi rivers would secure his fortune and fame as the inventor of the steamboat. The more practical Livingston realized the need to protect the New York monopoly, which remained the partners' primary source of income and prestige. Fulton might dream about conquering the frontier with steam power, but the Empire State would remain the primary battlefield for steamboat development in the United States.

Throughout the 1810s, old rivals such as John Stevens joined new competitors such as James Van Ingen and Daniel French to launch steamboats on the Hudson River. These opponents effectively used well-staged steamboat launches and races in conjunction with wars of words in local newspapers calculated to siphon customers and profits away from Fulton and Livingston. The monopolists were unable to intimidate or buy off such a large number of opponents, and they were thus forced to follow through on their frequent threats to sue their competitors. With the aid of sympathetic state court judges such as Chancellor James Kent of the Court of Chancery of New York, the partners defeated their opponents in the short run. Yet by resorting to litigation, Fulton and Livingston revealed that their partnership could no longer survive the rigors of open competition. Constant litigation and aggressive advertising would keep the monopoly afloat for another fourteen years. But the turn to such tactics marked the beginning of the end for the Fulton-Livingston steamboat empire.

As Fulton and Livingston negotiated for monopoly rights on the Mississippi, a group of Albany businessmen led by James Van Ingen organized to challenge their New York interests. Van Ingen was a wealthy Albany lawyer, merchant, sailing sloop owner, and former clerk for the New York Assembly. Like Alexander Hamilton, he was a strong Federalist, related to the influential Schulyer family by marriage. But he was also part of a Dutch-descended community in Albany that chafed against the economic and cultural domination of downstate Anglo-American landholders such as the Livingston family. The thought of Livingston's steamboats controlling trade on the Hudson River was an unsettling prospect. In 1807, Van Ingen therefore formed a syndicate of like-minded Albany businessmen, informally known as the Albanians. He and his partners hired Elihu Bunker, a Nantucket shipwright and sailing sloop captain of Quaker descent, to construct two steamboats loosely patterned after the *North River Steam Boat*. Bunker, who had been forced into bankruptcy by competition from Fulton the previous year, was amply motivated to complete the project.[1]

In anticipation of legal action, Fulton and Livingston shrewdly consulted attorney Thomas Addis Emmet. An Irish native, Emmet had sacrificed a promising career as a Dublin attorney to participate in an abortive uprising against British rule in 1798. He served a lengthy jail term before migrating to New York. Emmet overcame nativist prejudice to become one of the most sought-after attorneys in the nation. In fact, he used public perceptions of his heritage to craft a colorful image as an Irish barrister who could charm juries and judges alike. His advice, however, was not music to Fulton and Livingston's ears. Emmet bluntly informed his new clients that a court decision to uphold their monopoly "would annihilate the most useful powers of Congress . . . open the door to constant collisions and quarrels between the federal and state governments, and eventually subvert the union itself."[2]

46

Thomas Addis Emmet.
William G. Jackman, *Thomas Addis Emmet,* c. 1800–1830, Library of Congress, Prints and Photographs Division, Washington, DC

Not surprisingly, Fulton and Livingston disregarded Emmet's advice. The partners had poured effort, capital, and their own prestige into the success of the project and had much to lose. They preferred to gamble on the appearance of a legal claim, which could still be a strong card to play in business negotiations. Such strategic bluffs might allow them to collect profits for years to come. Fulton remained acutely aware of his legal and social vulnerabilities. He boasted to his former patron, Lord Stanhope, of the success of his steamboats but confided that, "attempts are now making to evade my patent rights, and deprive me of my mental property." The inventor urged Stanhope to locate plans they had devised twenty years earlier to help bolster his claims as inventor of the steamboat.[3] In the meantime, Livingston pressed for a New York law that strengthened his ability to seize unlicensed steamboats and forbade the removal of any cases that arose from such incidents to federal court.[4]

In March, Fulton and Livingston received the good news that Governor William Claiborne had delivered their petition to the legislature of the Orleans Territory, the southernmost district carved out of the Louisiana Purchase. Claiborne assured the assembly, "I feel confident that the introduction of steamboats on the Mississippi and its waters would greatly conduce to the convenience and welfare of the Inhabitants of this Terr[itory]."[5] He likewise repeated to Chancellor Livingston, "I feel desirous that the exclusive privilege solicited may be granted by Law, since I am convinced that the introduction of steam boats on the Mississippi and its waters will conduce greatly to the convenience of the whole western country."[6] Three weeks later, the territorial legislature granted Fulton and Livingston exclusive rights to operate steamboats at the mouth of the Mississippi, provided their services remained at least 25 percent cheaper than any competitor's. Control over the Orleans Territory effectively gave the New Yorkers a stranglehold over all upper river traffic as well. When Louisiana achieved statehood on April 30, 1812, Fulton and Livingston's monopoly grant became state law. Four days later, Fulton and Livingston agreed to incorporate the Mississippi Steam Boat Company to oversee their western interests.[7]

Five months after the creation of the Louisiana monopoly, the *Pittsburgh Gazette* reported, "With pleasure we announce, that the Steam Boat lately built at this place by Mr. Roosevelt (from an Experiment made Tuesday last) answers the most sanguine expectations that were formed of her sailing." On October 20, the *New Orleans* steamed onto the Monongahela before a crowd of amazed onlookers. Eastern papers also reported on the construction, deployment, and voyage of the *New Orleans*.[8] The steamboat's journey down the Ohio and Mississippi rivers provided all the ingredients of a Washington Irving novel. Nicholas and Lydia Roosevelt departed with only a few sailors and servants onboard, for despite advertisements promoting the trip, no passengers had dared sign up. Throughout its voyage, the *New Orleans* provoked the same public curiosity and anxiety that the *North River Steam Boat* had incited four years earlier on the Hudson. For instance, Louisville, Kentucky, residents mistook the hiss of the ship's boiler for a comet striking the river. Frontier elites such as John James Audubon and Henry Miller Shreve accepted jaunts on the *New Orleans* and marveled at its speed.[9]

Roosevelt and his followers successfully navigated the Ohio rapids in time to encounter the aftershocks of an earthquake centered on the New Madrid fault line. It was one of the strongest earthquakes ever to hit the contiguous United States, and it must have shaken the crew of the *New Orleans*. Unaware of the nature of plate tectonics, the voyagers witnessed surreal spectacles such as currents that ran backward, islands that disappeared, deserted villages, and floods that destroyed all landmarks. As the *New Orleans* entered the Mississippi River, the current regained a semblance of normalcy. Crowds gathered to watch the arrival of the steamboat in St. Louis and in Baton Rouge. Claiborne optimistically wrote to Livingston, "The arrival of the steamboat at this port, is daily expected. We have heard of her progress down the river, & this whole society manifests a deep interest for her."[10]

47

On January 10, 1812, the *New Orleans* safely arrived in the city that shared its name. A crowd led by Governor Claiborne wildly cheered as the steamboat pulled into a wharf within view of the Place d'Armes. The *Louisiana Monitor* remarked that the vessel "is intended to make regular trips from New Orleans to Natchez and it is generally believed that success will answer to what is proposed by the Entrepreneurs Messrs. Livingston & Fulton of New York, who have attained a patent to this effect." The *Louisiana Gazette and Daily Advertiser* quipped less enthusiastically, "Had Mr. Fulton's torpedoes succeeded equal to his Steam boats, we might now laugh at the thunder of the British Navy."[11]

Upon the arrival of the *New Orleans,* Governor Claiborne assembled a committee of local citizens to certify the ship. Delegates confirmed that the *New Orleans* had been built on a western river, could maintain a speed of four miles an hour in calm water, and therefore fulfilled the conditions of the monopoly grant. Claiborne then assured the chancellor, "The practicability of propelling Boats by Steam against the Current of the Mississippi has been fully proven."[12] The *New Orleans* became a popular sight as Roosevelt ferried potential investors across the Mississippi River. On January 23, he commenced operating a steamboat line from the Crescent City to Natchez. Three months later, Fulton gloated to Barlow, "The Mississippi, as I before wrote you, is conquered; the steamboat which I have sent to trade between New Orleans and Natchez, carried 1,500 barrels, equal to 150 tons, from New Orleans to Natchez, against the current, 313 miles in seven days, working in that time 84 hours." He enthusiastically added, "These are conquests perhaps as valuable as those at Jena," drawing a comparison to Napoleon's decisive victory over the Prussians in 1806.[13]

The New York Monopoly before the Courts and the Public

Fulton and Livingston relished this victory yet still had to contend with the Albanian threat. Throughout spring 1811, Van Ingen and his associates awaited the completion of two steamboats, aptly named the *Hope* and the *Perseverance.* Both were obvious copies of the *North River Steam Boat,* for they differed only slightly in length and width. After successful trial runs in April, the Albany Company announced plans to run the *Hope* from New York City to Albany. Fulton and Livingston promptly launched a suit in U.S. circuit court. Normally distrustful of federal courts, the chancellor appeared willing to risk the matter partly because his cousin, Supreme Court justice Henry Brockholst Livingston, had agreed to preside over the case in his capacity as justice for that circuit.[14]

Like Chancellor Livingston, Brockholst Livingston grew up among the colonial New York elite. Although initially a Federalist, he became a supporter of Thomas Jefferson in 1790 and was rewarded with a Supreme Court appointment in 1806.[15] As a member of the "Manor" branch of the Livingston family, Brockholst maintained cordial, if not warm, relations with Chancellor Livingston. In fact, he had served as his cousin's personal attorney on several occasions.[16] But these family connections also created problems when *Livingston v. Van Ingen* came before Justice Livingston in 1811. Concerned with his public image, he hoped to avoid a decision that hinted of privilege. Furthermore, despite his Republican affiliations, he consistently backed the nationalist decisions handed down by the Marshall Court; thus, he may have been unwilling to rule in favor of a state monopoly that contested federal supremacy.[17]

Fulton and Livingston brought their suit at a fortuitous time, for at ten o'clock in the morning on June 22, 1811, the *Hope,* under the command of Captain Bunker, sailed from New York City for Albany with fifty passengers aboard. Newspaper accounts stated that several thousand people gathered to cheer the vessel. A Pandean band complete with flutes, pipers, and drums played "Washington's March" and other patriotic songs. As the *Hope* ventured up the Hudson, passengers composed and sang an impromptu ballad to mark the occasion. Several stanzas articulated the popular dislike for the steamboat monopoly:

> Our rivers and bays, by great nature's decree,
> Have been given in common, and must ever be free:
> To prove this axiom, needs not figures nor trope,
> But still will we prove it—and that by the HOPE.
> Our wishes and views are the public to serve;
> For which, be assur'd, we will strain every nerve;
> But no matter what boats with ours may cope—
> We're sure to have passengers always in HOPE.[18]

The author of an article in the *New York Columbian* agreed that attempts by the North River Company to seize the *Hope* through an injunction would probably fail. Although Fulton and Livingston's steamboat endeavors would, he said, "engrave their names on the tablet of history among the benefactors of mankind," the Albany Company boats would, it was hoped, be allowed to remain in business. If both companies shared the Hudson, they could clear enough profits for all concerned and create "a public accommodation without equal or similarity in the world."[19]

Despite such an auspicious send-off, the *Hope* broke down several miles up-river and returned to New York City on one paddle wheel. Passengers nevertheless signed a testimonial that complimented the luxuriousness of the *Hope* and the professionalism of its crew. Another favorable newspaper account downplayed the setback and quipped, "We note the above circumstances to show that it was an injunction from *Chance* and not Chancery which prevented her arrival at this port."[20]

After learning of the *Hope*'s launching, Fulton angrily announced to Barlow his intention to legally "crush 22 Pirates who have clubbed their purses and copied my boats and have actually started my own inventions in opposition to me." He fumed, "A more infamous and outrageous attack upon mental property has not disgraced America." Fulton asked his friend to secure from the U.S. Patent Office copies of an agreement to transfer half of his patent rights to Livingston. He also insisted that Barlow get Thornton to sign a deposition recognizing his achievements in steam navigation. Although Thornton provided the requested documents, he not surprisingly declined to formally acknowledge Fulton's role as inventor of the steamboat.[21]

The North River Company and the Albany Company did more than merely face each other in court. They also fought each other for public approval through price manipulation, superior accommodations, and boat races. In a race held on Saturday, July 27, at nine o'clock in the morning, the *Hope* and the *North River Steam Boat* departed Albany. As the boats neared a bend in the river called Paddock's Point, the crew of the *North River Steam Boat* tried to overtake the *Hope* but struck the larger vessel and forced it aground. The pilot of the *North River Steam Boat* offered to pay for the damages, and the two vessels returned to Albany.[22] Supporters of the Albany Company quickly claimed that Fulton and his associates had staged the accident to avoid losing the race. Defenders of the monopoly countered that the *Hope* had maneuvered to prevent the *North River Steam Boat* from passing. *Hope* pilots John T. Haviland and David Morris denied before Albany special judge Garrit Gilbert any attempt "to run the *Hope* in the way of the *North River* to prevent her passing the *Hope* at any time during the passage from Albany."[23]

The inconclusive outcome of the race left open the question of whose steamboats were faster and more efficient. Captain Andrew Bartholomew of the *North River Steam Boat* publicly challenged Captain Bunker to another race. To cultivate the image of a prudent public servant, Bunker responded, "The *Hope* was built for the accommodation of the public as well as the advantage of the proprietors. Her owners request public patronage no longer than they shall be found to merit." He concluded, "It does not consist with Capt. Bunker's sense of propriety (after his recent experience) to enter into a gambling arrangement for the trial of her speed against the North River Boat."[24]

While New Yorkers thronged to watch the two companies compete for business, Fulton and Livingston prepared their arguments for the U.S. circuit court. They hired a formidable legal team. Cadwallader D. Colden, the senior attorney, shared a friendship with Fulton that stretched back to their days as amateur engineers in London. The son of an influential colonial politician and a former federal district attorney, Colden was a prominent specialist in commercial law. Richard Harison wielded similar experience as a former law partner to Alexander Hamilton and as a U.S. district attorney who had drafted much of American maritime law. Chancery court lawyer Caleb Riggs had helped John Fitch secure the first New York steamboat monopoly twenty-four years earlier. Josiah Ogden Hoffman offered experience as a former Federalist leader in the New York State Assembly and as state attorney general. He was also Colden's son-in-law and a distant cousin of New Jersey governor Aaron Ogden, who would later play a pivotal role in the unfolding of the steamboat monopoly case.[25]

The Albanians retained an equally distinguished group of attorneys. Born into a wealthy New York Dutch family, Abraham Van Vechten had studied law with former Albany mayor and future New York chancellor John Lansing and served as Albany city recorder, a state senator and assemblyman, and state attorney general. He was a strong proponent of internal improvements and public education. Van Vechten was also the brother-in-law of James Van Ingen. Another member of the Albanians' legal team was Edmund Henry Pendleton. Although a Georgian by birth, Pendleton had migrated north and established a thriving law practice in New York. Also on the team was David A. Ogden (yet another cousin of Aaron Ogden), who was born in Morristown, New Jersey, graduated from Columbia College, and became a successful lawyer before both the New Jersey and New York bars. He held considerable legal experience both as a private attorney and as an associate justice for the New York Court of Common Pleas.

51

In addition, Jonathan Wells, Thomas Addis Emmet's partner, participated as a skilled commerce law attorney and an ardent Federalist who frequently wrote for anti-Republican newspapers. The youngest member of the defense team, Lucius Horatio Stockton, served as a U.S. district attorney.[26]

Arguments for the plaintiff commenced on July 26. Colden asserted that the Albany Company's construction and deployment of the *Hope* and *Perseverance* on the Hudson River violated his clients' patent and monopoly rights. As state courts would only bury the matter in endless litigation, he argued that Fulton and Livingston's only hope for justice lay in getting a federal injunction that would shut down the Albany Company's steamboat operations on the Hudson River.[27] For the defense, Van Vechten coolly but forcefully argued that a federal circuit court could neither hear a case advanced by citizens of the same state nor rule on an equity issue.[28] After a week of arguments, Justice Livingston rendered his decision. He noted the "importance and novelty of the case" and conceded that Fulton and Livingston were "eminently entitled to the favour of the public."[29] Livingston nevertheless stressed the need for caution before issuing an injunction without the benefit of trial. Since all the litigants involved with the case were New York citizens, the U.S. circuit court wielded no authority over the matter. To maintain public support, federal courts should not overstep their own jurisdiction. Certainly, Livingston said, the "great and wise men who composed the legislature that organized the judiciary" understood the necessity of judicial discretion. The Judiciary Act of 1789 was likewise "prepared by a committee consisting of a member from each state, most if not all professional men." Consequently, he stated, "it cannot be believed that, in a law drawn with so much care, and embracing such a variety of provisions, so important an omission was casual."[30]

Livingston concluded that a state court was the proper forum in which to settle such a common-law dispute. In any event, he said, "a court, constituted like this, is not to reason itself into jurisdiction from considerations of hardship," when the lines of federal jurisdiction were clear.[31] Several New York papers printed an article that approved Livingston's brief ruling, maintaining, "It was not thought proper to express any opinions, nor was any given or hinted at."[32] Dismayed at the decision, Fulton wrote Joseph Gales, reporter for the U.S. Senate and coeditor of the Washington-based *National Intelligencer.* The inventor enclosed an article on the defense of patent rights that he wished to have anonymously published. Gales, however, realized that the article attacked Van Ingen and his associates for not being "gentlemen and moral members of the community." When Gales threatened to expose the matter, Fulton backed down but ranted about the inefficiency of both patent laws and the federal court system.[33]

New Problems and Strategies

The U.S. circuit court's ruling temporarily opened the Hudson River to unfettered steam travel. Forced to compete in an open market, Fulton's steamboats rapidly lost profits. Captain Bartholomew was aware of the public discontent, and he warned his employers, "We have all of Albany against us."[34] He also counseled, "The people of this country cannot be drove into any measures whatever but if you start right they will be led by the nose to almost anything." Fulton and Livingston should not lose hope, he said, for "I have seen this time up people to come on board & view my boat and acknowledge my accommodations were far superior, and after all be persuaded to take passage in the *Hope,* crowded into a berth better fit to a Coffin than to sleep in."[35]

In September, a *New York Evening Post* article announced that Connecticut engineer Daniel French had patented a new steam engine at half the cost of Fulton's. Declaring that the North River Company had failed the public, French promised to sell stock for a steamboat line between Long Island and Norwich, Connecticut. "With respect to State Grants, it is now well known the Grant of this state to Messrs. Fulton and Livingston is totally illegal and altogether void," taunted French. Furthermore, he said, "neither Mr. Fulton nor colonel Stevens, does or will now pretend to claim to any particular privileges under the state law."[36] Two weeks later, Fulton responded in kind. "This correspondent must have much assurance to state that, in a public paper, as a fact, which has not been decided by the tribunals of the state," bellowed the inventor. Warning "innocent individuals, not to permit themselves to be deceived by designing men," Fulton predicted that "a few months more will decide the validity of the State law, after which adventurers will understand the subject better."[37]

While Fulton squabbled with French, John Stevens continued to run fifteen trips and fifteen hundred passengers per day between Hoboken and New York City.[38] The *New York Spectator* bragged of the *Phoenix*'s speed and accommodations. In response, a *New York Daily Post* article written by a "Car of Neptune passenger" dared "foreigners who say we have no talent for improvement to point to an equal mode of conveyance where there are so many enjoyments combined

53

into one machine, that wafts passengers as if by enchantment between Albany and New York City." The author concluded, "To our countrymen then and our arts let justice be liberally and honestly measured out."[39]

Like print wars, steamboat races represented opportunities to generate public support for steamboat entrepreneurs. In early November, Livingston's *Raritan* raced Van Ingen's *Hope* near New Brunswick. The captains of both vessels overstoked their boilers and enveloped the boats in a cloud of smoke. The *Hope* won the contest but lost a similar race to the *Juliana* four days later. An account by an individual writing under the pseudonym "Particeps Lineteris" bragged, "There must be a great superiority in the construction of the machinery on board the *Juliana*."[40] He added boastfully, "As the *Juliana* now not only reigns victorious over the waters of the Hudson, but may be said to have distanced the triumphant *Hope*, the lovers of sport will probably not very soon be gratified with any more Steam Boat Races."[41] Another article in the same paper defended the monopoly in terms of human progress: "When we look back to past ages, and view mankind wrapt in the night of ignorance, and but little above the Brute Creation, what a striking contrast presents itself between them and the present state of mankind!" The article concluded, "How it behooves us to encourage talents or ingenuity, wherever it is found, and lend the fostering hand to every exertion of improvement and genius in the arts and sciences."[42]

Setback in Chancery Court

While Fulton competed with his rivals on the waterways of New York and in the headlines of local papers, Chancellor Livingston followed the advice of his cousin Brockholst and prepared to sue the Albanians in the Court of Chancery of New York. Unlike federal district courts, which were bound by precedent and written laws, state chancery courts dealt with matters of equity, or "natural justice," grounded in traditional notions of fairness. Turning to a chancery court represented another calculated risk for Livingston. For although the court could not award him monetary damages for infringements to his monopoly rights, it could issue injunctions to bar competitors from operating steamboats on New York waters. Taking no chances, Livingston attempted to lure Van Vechten away from the Albany Company with a hefty retainer, but the attorney declined and cited his kinship to Van Ingen as a conflict of interest. Thomas Addis Emmet, though he believed the steamboat monopoly was unconstitutional, agreed to represent Fulton and Livingston. In September, Emmet and Colden filed a suit against the Albanians in chancery court.[43] The case soon appeared before Chancellor John Lansing Jr., a leading figure in New York politics. Following the American Revolution, Lansing had translated a fortune in confiscated Loyalist land and promissory notes into positions as a state assemblyman, a U.S. congressman, constitutional framer, and New York state chancellor.[44] Unbeknownst to Livingston, Lansing also had financial ties with Albany interests. In August 1810, he had contacted William Thornton in Washington, claiming to represent a group of Albany businessmen who wanted to create a steamboat line on the Hudson River. Critical of Fulton and Livingston's legal claims, Lansing had suggested an alliance based on Thornton's patent claims and the economic resources of the Albany syndicate. The Albanians had freely accepted Thornton's plans and advice but declined his offers of a partnership.[45]

Given his financial ties to the case, Lansing had an even greater reason than Brockholst Livingston to act with caution. He therefore ordered the Albany Company to provide a valid defense against an injunction by the next court session.[46] Chancellor Livingston wrote in frustration to his brother Edward, "We are head over heels in the law, what the issue will be I know not." Livingston further lamented, "We cannot expect justice from our enemies and our friends are fearful of granting it, lest it appear they love us."[47] Publicly, however, the chancellor continued to press his rights in court.

In November, Van Vechten and his associates argued that as the Fulton-Livingston monopoly regulated trade between New York and New Jersey, it violated the commerce clause of the U.S. Constitution. In any case, a court could not issue an injunction until it had ruled on the legality of the steamboat monopoly.[48] To ask a state judge to overturn the steamboat monopoly was one thing. But to expect him to do so by interpreting the U.S. Constitution was quite another matter, particularly in an era when judicial review, while established by the Supreme Court in *Marbury v. Madison* (1803), was still an embryonic legal concept among judges and attorneys. Lansing, however, rose to the occasion, and on November 18, 1811, he rendered a decision in the case of *Livingston v. Van Ingen*. He began with an acknowledgment of the "important and novel questions" inherent in the case. Although New York held the sovereign power to regulate commerce within its borders, it could not monopolize all steam travel on state waters. Steam merely combined natural elements such as fire, air, and water.[49]

55

As the Byzantine emperor Justinian had stated in the sixth century, "The source of the right to the common enjoyment of air and water [is] paramount to his authority, and bestowed, as a common boon, by the hand of nature, or, as we would express the same sentiment, by Nature's God." Medieval sources concurred that public access to waterways constituted a common-law right.[50] Lansing conceded that "the incalculable utility and convenience which the public experience from the invention, merit every consideration in favor of the inventors."[51] But if the New York legislature could regulate steam travel, might it not regulate rowboats or sailboats? Did the framers intend that "any portion of the citizens of an individual state, described by their age, their occupations, or estates, should have the exclusive right of using the navigable waters of each state?" Livingston thought not and struck down the New York monopoly as unconstitutional.[52]

Alarmed by this development, Fulton and Livingston immediately appealed to the New York Court for the Correction of Errors. Fulton also increased steamboat traffic on the Hudson to keep pressure on the Albany Company, and he traveled to Washington to lobby for an extension on his two federal patents. He accused Thornton of masterminding the competition against the North River Company and threatened to file a lawsuit if the Patent Office chief further interfered in his affairs.[53] Fulton also complained to Secretary of State James Monroe that Thornton "takes patents, exchanges barters and then disputes the rights of all who interfere with his pretensions."[54] In a letter to fellow inventor Oliver Evans, Fulton warned his colleague to "change the parts of your engine [design]" and "involve yourself in lawsuits to defend your [patent] claims." Following his own advice, he worked with Livingston throughout the winter of 1812 to refine their legal strategy.[55]

In the meantime, the public received Lansing's decree favorably. At a dinner hosted by the New York State Artillery Regiment, opponents of the monopoly raised a toast to "Commerce, the main spring to the whole: may it meet no impediment but the winds, no resistance but the waves."[56] A newspaper editorial noted the increase in steamboat traffic along the Hudson and boasted, "The excellence of the accommodations and the certainty and rapidity of the passage, on this great thoroughfare, are unquestionably without parallel and example in the habitable globe."[57] Furthermore, steamboat races continued to draw attention, as the captains of the North River Company and Albany Company touted their victories and explained away their defeats in the local press.[58]

As Fulton fumed over the repeated attacks on his profits and reputation, Livingston struck a more positive note. In a letter to Arthur Roorbach, the newly appointed captain of the steamboat *Paragon,* Livingston remarked, "The pirates are detested, and were the question taken at this moment from the vote of the citizens, and strangers in this city they would be put down by a majority of at least eight to one." Livingston also feigned impartiality on the subject of the monopoly: "Knowing our cause is to be both legal, and just, I feared only popular prejudice, but since there is none with us I think we have nothing to fear."[59] Livingston had good reason to be optimistic. Unlike other state courts, the New York Court for the Correction of Errors consisted of both state supreme court justices and senators, many of whom were landholders and conservatives. State supreme court chief justice James Kent was one such figure. Born in Putnam County, New York, in 1763, Kent became a successful attorney and leading Federalist in the 1780s. After working as a law professor at Columbia College and a state assembly member, he joined the New York Supreme Court in 1798, and became chief justice six years later. Kent brought his extensive learning and compulsion for order to bear on the cases set before him. He consistently displayed a preference for legal tradition over democratic impulses. Kent cultivated the reputation of a methodical judge who crafted authoritative opinions "to discuss a point as never to be teased with it again, and to anticipate an angry and vexatious appeal to a popular tribunal by disappointed counsel." Over time, Kent's image as a brilliant and thorough jurist allowed him to become one of the foremost legal authorities in the early Republic, frequently using English common-law precedents to construct a distinctive American jurisprudence.[60] Yet monopoly opponents would use Kent's reputation for meticulousness as a weapon against the justice in future cases.

In January 1812, Josiah Hoffman, Cadwallader D. Colden, and Caleb Riggs delivered several familiar arguments to the New York Court of Errors. They stressed that New York enjoyed the sovereign right to grant monopolies for canals, toll bridges, turnpikes, ferries, and public markets. English and colonial precedents proved that rivers could be regulated for the collective good, and the state legislature had repeatedly upheld the legality of the monopoly. The federal commerce clause did not prevent concurrent state regulation. Fulton and Livingston were possessors, not inventors, of new steam engine technology. "The appellants have endured all the ridicule and contempt cast upon them, as rash and chimerical projectors," Hoffman insisted. Yet now, "when they are just about to reap the fruits of their enterprise, the respondents seek to deprive them of the honor and profit of the establishment."[61] Having upheld the steamboat monopoly, Emmet and Colden argued that an injunction was the necessary remedy for

Chancellor James Kent. Daniel Huntington, *James Kent,* n.d., National Portrait Gallery, Washington, DC

their clients. To delay justice would allow the Albany Company to profit from its own crime. The legislature had encouraged Fulton and Livingston's experiments, and it was therefore "bound, in honor and good faith, to protect them against those who, without incurring any risk, now seek to deprive the appellants of the profits of a successful enterprise."[62]

Abraham Van Vechten, John Wells, and William Henry refuted these arguments by endorsing a strict dual federalism. If states were given concurrent power over foreign and interstate commerce, "it would introduce that infinite confusion and diversity which the Constitution intended to prevent."[63] They further argued that the steamboat monopoly was not a contract, for it could not compel Fulton and Livingston to keep their side of the bargain. By changing their status from inventors to possessors, Fulton and Livingston cunningly hoped to circumvent federal patent law. Van Vechten concluded, "The appellants claim this monopoly against all the world, and the respondents, though not patentees, have a right to call their claim into question."[64]

Emmet retorted that Fulton and Livingston should be rewarded, not punished, for introducing valuable steamboat technology from Europe. Great Britain used such monopolies to encourage invention, internal improvements, and commerce. In similar fashion, he asked, "Can this country expect to take its eagle flight, and to reach its high destinies, by the strength of its own genius alone, without the aid of foreign invention?" He further argued that even if the Albany Company possessed a federal patent, the New York grant would still be valid as a concurrent measure. Emmet asked rhetorically, "What, then, becomes of the doctrine that patent inventions may force themselves into our fields and habitations, and stride over the land as a blessing or a pestilence, while the states must bow in homage, or reverential horror, to the potent and pestilential patent."[65] "Has not the *steam-boat* cleared the *Hudson* of the bar of ignorance and prejudice, and conferred an equal benefit on the public?" he asked, concluding, "It would be an act of perfidy in the state not to perform the contract on their part. Such a breach of good faith would level genius, public honor and integrity in the dust."[66]

On March 12, 1812, the justices of the Court of Errors delivered *seriatim* opinions in favor of Fulton and Livingston. Justice Joseph Yates began by observing, "The importance of this decision must be evident to everyone that hears me; no question has, perhaps, ever presented itself to this court of greater magnitude, involving principles so highly interesting to the community."[67] He then defended the New York steamboat monopoly as a legitimate expression of state power, arguing that to overturn the measure would endanger all of New York's internal improvements.[68] Justice William Van Ness concurred with Yates, whereas Justice Ambrose Spencer declined to speak because he was related to some of the involved parties.[69]

Justice Smith Thompson's opinion provided the most expansive interpretation of the case. As a sovereign state, he observed, New York could certainly grant monopolies. The job of the state judiciary was to determine the constitutionality, not the effectiveness, of such laws. As both the state legislature and the Council of Revision had upheld the steamboat monopoly, the New York Court of Errors would be hard pressed to strike it down without good reason. Furthermore, he contended, Congress could not grant patents and regulate trade at the expense of states' rights. Although Chancellor Livingston's forfeiture law of 1808 was somewhat vague, it was still better to grant an injunction now rather than to risk additional lawsuits later. In conclusion, Thompson stated, "I entertain a clear and decided opinion in favor of the validity of the appellants' rights, as granted by the acts of the legislature, and that they are entitled to the remedy asked for to protect and secure them in the enjoyment of it."[70]

In a thorough opinion, Chief Justice Kent elaborated on points made by Yates and Thompson. The New York legislature had ruled five separate times on the matter—in the last instance, he observed, well after the current steamboat controversy had begun. The creators of the monopoly "had been deeply concerned in the study of the constitution of the *United States*" and "were masters of all the critical discussions which had attended the interesting progress of its adoption."[71] Consequently, "a decree prostrating all these laws would weaken, as I should apprehend, the authority and sanction of law in general, and . . . the public confidence."[72]

Having acknowledged the importance of the case, Kent asserted that every sovereign government, such as New York, could encourage internal improvements. The framers of the U.S. Constitution, as "men of the most powerful talents, and with the most animated zeal for the public welfare," understood the need to encourage scientific development at the local level. The founders had furthermore "bestowed intense thought" and "deeply studied the history and nature, the tendency and genius of the federal system of government" to create a limited central government. Excess powers, such as the right to grant monopolies, naturally fell to the states.[73]

Kent admitted that it was hard to distinguish between interstate and intrastate commerce. It would nevertheless be a "monstrous heresy," he said, to strike down a state law merely because it might conflict with a future federal statute.[74] Kent concluded, "It is impossible for any act to be committed, which attracts more universal notice, and if wrong and illegal, none which has a more fatal influence upon the general habits of respect and reverence for the legislative authority." The chancellor warned, "The boats cannot but run in the face of day, and in the presence, as it were of the whole people, whose laws are set at defiance, nor without seducing thousands, by the contagion of example, into an approbation and support of the trespass." In summation, Kent compared American jurisprudence to that of antiquity through the assertion that "we follow a purer and nobler system of morals, and one which teaches us that right is never to be violated." He cautioned, "This principle ought to be kept steadfast in every man's breast; and above all, it ought to find an asylum in the sanctuary of justice." The state senate reinforced Kent's decision by a unanimous thirty-to-zero vote to uphold the monopoly and grant the injunction.[75]

Fulton and Livingston received the decision with relief. Livingston reminded his partner, "Your law suit could have been carried on by no one but myself as has been so [since] its commitment. Nor could the necessary funds have been raised as we wanted them without my credit."[76] Fulton was too elated to disagree. As he wrote to Barlow, "I have beat my enemies in law, the court of Errors has laid their boats under an Injunction . . . I am now tranquil on this important point."[77] With his legal claims secure, Fulton refitted the elegant *Paragon* and commissioned two ships, the *Jersey* and the *Firefly*, to add to his North River fleet. But his troubles were not entirely over. In June 1812, Van Ingen petitioned the legislature for a law that would place the Albany Company in receivership until its stockholders could sue Fulton and Livingston in federal court. Chancellor Livingston journeyed to Albany and lobbied quietly behind the scenes to defeat the measure.[78]

To improve his public image, Fulton instructed Colden to buy the *Hope* and *Perseverance* from the Albany Company. He felt that "the advantages which the law and the just feelings of the public have put in our power" encouraged him to make such a gesture.[79] To sweeten the deal, he offered his rivals steamboat rights on Lake Champlain. In December 1812, the Albany Company officially sold both vessels to Fulton.[80] Then, in early 1813, Elihu Bunker, the former shipwright for the Albanians, decided to test the depths of Fulton's graciousness. Bunker publicly approached Fulton with an offer to jointly construct a deep-keeled steamboat for service from New Haven, Connecticut, to New York City. Trapped by his own recent overtures of peace, Fulton agreed to build the boat privately, but he heaped constant scorn on the project. Even Bunker's clever decision to name the experimental craft *Fulton* did little to mollify the inventor.[81]

With his financial, legal, and social status momentarily secure, Fulton threw a celebratory cruise aboard the *Paragon* for his friends and investors. In June, the elegant vessel steamed up the East River through the Buttermilk Channel and down to Staten Island before returning to Manhattan. Guests were treated to live music, a huge banquet, and an eighteen-gun salute from a battery on the shore. Fulton had good reason to celebrate. He and Livingston had deftly used a combination of threats, negotiations, print wars, lawsuits, and public displays to maintain public support for their steamboat monopoly and discredit their competitors. They had preserved their New York monopoly and looked forward to constructing a fleet of steamships on the Mississippi. They had been aided in no small part by James Kent. Kent's conservative disdain for competition, especially the cutthroat variety popular among a rising generation of steamboat promoters, figured prominently in his Van Ingen decision. In many ways, Kent's

61

dicta recalled the vision of a simpler America, grounded in republican virtue, that he felt was rapidly declining in an age of cynical materialism. This helps explain why Kent, a High Federalist to the end, could endorse a strong states' rights position in apology for monopoly that would become the primary line of defense used by the monopolists and their attorneys in future cases, such as *Gibbons v. Ogden*.[82]

Although successful for the moment, Fulton and Livingston still faced a steady stream of rivals on both the Hudson and the Mississippi. The New York monopoly still hinged on Livingston's political clout, Fulton's aggressive business tactics, and the personal reputation of both men. A troubling question now emerged and would eventually have to be addressed: could the monopoly survive the death of one, or both, partners?

CHAPTER 5

Interstate Competition

Beset on All Sides

THROUGHOUT 1812, the profits of the North River Company continued to soar, and Fulton tenaciously pursued his dream of a steamboat franchise on the Mississippi River. Two new adversaries, however, quickly emerged to contest the New York monopoly—former New Jersey governor Aaron Ogden and former planter and Savannah mayor Thomas Gibbons. Both men were members of Robert R. Livingston's generation, successful colonial elites who had weathered the American Revolution (albeit on different sides) and brought a lifetime of business and political experience to bear in pursuing their steamboat interests. Gibbons and Ogden would prove themselves experts at creating steamboat companies, engaging in price wars and aggressive advertising, and defending their interests in court. Although they were initially partners, personal and familial differences would drive them to rivalry. Their private quarrels would later become publicly intertwined with their reputations and economic interests. And eventually, both men would risk their entire fortunes to destroy one another in state and federal court. In doing so, they would put the complicated matter of interstate steamboat commerce before the U.S. Supreme Court.

Despite the victory Fulton achieved over the Albanians, his legal status remained precarious. In April 1812, he declared, "If the nation could respect the labours of mind and do justice to them as is done to the labours of every Vulgar pair of hands we might become as rich as some cotton planter or merchant."[1] But the trade embargoes of the Jefferson and Madison administrations and the economic disruptions caused by the War of 1812 had created new opportunities for domestic trade. Shipbuilders, captains, and sailors laid off by the decline of overseas business also provided a cheap source of labor for local steamboat companies. Putting aside his misgivings about the state of property law, Fulton aggressively expanded his business interests.[2] To accommodate public demand, he rebuilt the *Car of Neptune* and added the *Richmond* and *Washington* to his New York fleet. Fulton and his wife's brother-in-law, William Cutting, also secured a charter from the Common Council of New York to create a new corporation, the Fulton Steam Boat Company. The partners were required to have at least two steam ferries to provide service between lower Manhattan and Brooklyn. Fulton immediately launched the steam ferries *York, Jersey,* and *Nassau* to link New York City to New Jersey and Brooklyn and the oceangoing *Fulton* to carry passengers between New York City and New Haven, Connecticut. Fulton housed these boats at new dock facilities on the corner of Courtland and Washington streets in New York City.[3] His boats revolutionized travel throughout the Hudson Valley, New York Harbor, and Long Island Sound. In 1814, Fulton and Livingston earned $85,000, most of which went to the construction of more vessels.[4]

Fulton also solidified his Mississippi River interests. In June 1812, he sold off corporate stock originally promised to Edward Livingston, offering his associate a monopoly on the Red River in compensation.[5] Throughout 1812 and 1813, Fulton also made repeated attempts to contact Nicholas Roosevelt, his agent in Pittsburgh who was under orders to construct more steamboats for the Ohio and Mississippi rivers. Receiving no reply, Fulton wrote to Benjamin Henry Latrobe, accusing Roosevelt of embezzlement. The architect defended his son-in-law but secretly warned Roosevelt that Fulton and Livingston's "confidence has been entirely lost, and never can be restored."[6] Aware of Roosevelt's spending habits, Fulton appointed his wife's uncle and Chancellor Livingston's second cousin, John Livingston, as agent for the Ohio Steam Boat Navigation Company.[7] Livingston journeyed to Pittsburgh and seized the *New Orleans* and company offices from Roosevelt. Not content with Roosevelt's declaration of bankruptcy, Fulton offered his former partner's position to Latrobe as a final insult. To appear magnanimous and to keep Roosevelt silent, Fulton negotiated a settlement that involved offering Lydia Roosevelt and her children one-third of the profits made from the *New Orleans.* However, he warned Latrobe that if Nicholas Roosevelt "made difficulties he will compel a scrutiny which I fear will end in his dishonor and ruin."[8] Ambition eventually trumped family loyalty, as Latrobe accepted Fulton's offer in January 1815.

In the meantime, however, Latrobe had to sort out the jumble of paperwork left by Roosevelt. Latrobe arrived in Pittsburgh in late fall 1813 only to find himself beset with high labor costs and scarce construction supplies, problems that had plagued his predecessor. Finally, in May 1814, he launched the *Buffalo,* the latest addition to Fulton and Livingston's Mississippi fleet.[9] When Fulton complained of cost and time overruns, Latrobe accused his partner of "a diabolical malignity, and an upstart pride which disfigures even your hand writing."[10] The outraged inventor quickly fired Latrobe, who promptly became an ally of Fulton's archrival, U.S. Patent Office chief William Thornton.[11]

Seeking to explore new markets, Fulton commissioned attorney John Devereux Delacy to survey possible steamboat routes throughout the Southeast. The Irish-born Delacy possessed a friendly disposition—and an unsavory past as a failed land speculator.[12] He replicated the business tactics pioneered by Fitch, Rumsey, and Fulton by incorporating local steamboat companies throughout the southern states and raising capital by selling stock. In the meantime, Fulton and Livingston made plans to petition state legislatures for monopoly grants. Within a year, Delacy incorporated three new business entities—the Elizabeth, the Robert Fulton, and the Charleston steamboat companies—to ply the waters of Virginia, North Carolina, and South Carolina. In summer 1813, Fulton predicted that within a year, he would be free of debt with a line of steamboats that ran from "Lake Champlain to Charleston, South Carolina, distance 1,500 miles."[13]

Despite his successes, not all was well with Fulton. The first conflict, ironically, came from within his own household. For the previous six years, Robert and Harriet Fulton had endured a tepid marriage. A member of one of the most powerful families in New York, Harriet Livingston Fulton was a well-educated and insightful woman, keenly aware of her second-class status as a female in antebellum society. She had been raised in an atmosphere of power and influence but could not seek employment, own property, or even serve as legal guardian to her children. She also felt alienated by her husband's intimate relationship with the Barlows.[14] Fulton tried to fill the void in his marriage by promising his wife the profits from the *Jersey,* reasoning that since a ferry differed from a steamboat, it did not fall under his partnership agreement with Livingston. The chancellor,

65

however, noticed the discrepancy in profits and demanded compensation. Cleverly playing to masculine pride and anxiety, Harriet Fulton accused Livingston of committing a "horrible sin against a defenseless woman." Claiming that her husband had promised her the proceeds of the *Jersey* as financial support for their children, she asked, "Sir, have I not a prior right? In honor is it not mine?"[15] An outraged William Cutting also blamed Livingston and Fulton for dishonoring his sister-in-law. When Livingston failed to relent, Fulton sided with the chancellor but appeased his wife by taking out a will in December 1813 that left his family a sizable inheritance in case of his death. Fulton may have calmed the waters temporarily, but this failed to placate Cutting.[16]

Fulton was not the only one searching for loopholes. In 1810, John Stevens realized that his agreement with Fulton failed to mention several rivers in Virginia and North Carolina.[17] He consequently petitioned both states for monopoly grants; he failed in Virginia but gained supporters in North Carolina. In a terse letter, Fulton accused Stevens of enticing his workers, running steamboats on the Hudson without a license, stealing the credit for inventing the steamboat, and expressing a general ingratitude. "I came forward and granted you great privileges which I hope you would at least see the policy of acknowledging and maintaining," wrote a bitter Fulton. "But the anxious desire to be thought an inventor has kept you at open war with Livingston and Fulton, particularly with me, my interest and your own through me." He concluded, "Where justice fails the law must make up the deficiency."[18]

Delacy raced to Greensboro, North Carolina, to rally legislative opposition to Stevens's petition.[19] But in December 1812, the North Carolina state legislature, incensed by Fulton's grandiose claims, granted Stevens a monopoly over steam travel.[20] When further negotiations failed, Stevens dismissed Fulton for his "tissue of arrogance" and "disgusting egotism." He also shrewdly attacked Fulton for not sharing credit with Chancellor Livingston for his successful steamboat experiments.[21] In response, Fulton blamed their rivalry on Stevens's pursuit of profit. Rather than surrender to "pretenders" such as Stevens, Fulton threatened to reveal the secrets of his inventions to the public and "take my reward in the honor of having extended steam boats to every navigable water in the United States." Stevens could hope to avoid future lawsuits only by putting up a bond to ensure his good behavior and painting on the top beams of his engine frames, in large letters, the title "Livingston's and Fulton's Patent."[22]

Stevens secretly offered Chancellor Livingston half the profits from his North Carolina monopoly in exchange for permission to operate steamboats on the

Hudson River.[23] Fulton and Livingston countered with the offer of a license to run steamboats from New York City to New Jersey for two-thirds of the North Carolina grant.[24] The offer provoked the anger of Chancellor Livingston's younger brother and partner, John R. Livingston, who began to withhold his steamboat profits from Fulton. An enraged Fulton in turn threatened Livingston and Stevens with legal action.[25] To avert a confrontation, Stevens agreed to dismantle his steamboat, the *Juliana,* and ship it to Connecticut by land for future use as a steam ferry.[26] Behind the scenes, however, he secretly arranged for his son Robert to sail the vessel to New England. Learning of Stevens's plan, Fulton dispatched six steamboats to seize the *Juliana.* On August 3, Stevens and his crew led their pursuers on a spirited chase through Long Island Sound to safety in Connecticut waters.[27]

Fulton and Livingston also faced additional challenges from William Thornton. In 1813, Thornton testified before the House Judiciary Committee, criticizing the weakness of federal patent laws and asking for public funds to undertake steamboat experiments.[28] Thornton also petitioned the Virginia legislature to prevent Fulton and Livingston from obtaining a steamboat monopoly in the Old Dominion. Fulton complained to Latrobe that he would defeat such "pirates and pretenders" as Thornton. In particular, he confidently predicted that he could prove himself the inventor of steamboats through the twenty years of correspondence that he had saved.[29]

Fighting for Control

On February 25, 1813, Chancellor Livingston suffered a massive stroke and died at Clermont. The same day, Fulton received word that Joel Barlow had also passed away, in Poland. The double loss of two such close friends devastated him.[30] Although he and Livingston were often at odds, Livingston's experience had meshed well with his own energetic brilliance. In addition, Livingston had provided the financial and legal resources necessary to sustain their monopoly. As Livingston failed to dispose of his steamboat company shares through his will, his portion of the steamboat business passed to his wife, Mary Stevens Livingston, and his sons-in-law (not to mention cousins) Edward P. Livingston and Robert L. Livingston.[31]

Robert L. and Edward P. Livingston shared a similar heritage, but they were drastically different individuals. Scholarly and amicable, Robert served briefly as a New York state senator but relished the refined life of a country squire. He

67

became his father-in-law's business manager and assumed more of his daily affairs as the chancellor declined in health. In contrast, Edward P. Livingston was a hot-headed lawyer and state senator with definite political ambitions. Both men were eager for profits from the monopoly: Robert wished to shore up the Livingston family's declining land values, and Edward needed funds to fuel his political career. Consequently, they frequently quarreled with one another and with Robert Fulton over their rightful shares of Chancellor Livingston's steamboat stock.

Mary Livingston was in an unusual position in this conflict. As the executrix of the chancellor's estate and the owner of half of his steamboat stock, she wielded considerable influence over her sons-in-law. Furthermore, as the sister of John Stevens, she possessed a unique opportunity to mediate the differences between the Livingstons, Fulton, and Stevens. Yet like her niece Harriet, Mary Livingston, despite her wealth, did not enjoy full legal rights to own or dispose of property or manage a business under New York law. Furthermore, she had worked for much of her adult life to establish a reputation as the matriarch of one of the most influential families on the East Coast. She stood to gain nothing by publicly participating in the same types of sordid disputes that had poisoned relations between her husband and brother. She accordingly hired attorney William Wilson, a family friend, to discreetly settle her inheritance claims.[32]

These developments created new problems for Fulton. As the surviving partner, he now wielded a majority interest in the North River Company. However, Robert L. and Edward P. Livingston showed a constant lack of interest in defending, managing, or funding the corporation. At one point, Fulton exclaimed, "Neither of you have aided me in the least in my enterprise, hence I have to the extent of individual exertion done in all cases that which I thought our mutual interest."[33] In response, the Livingstons demanded that Fulton reduce corporate expenses and abandon plans to build new boats while somehow simultaneously selling company stock and increasing steamboat service.[34] The final insult came in fall 1813 when the Livingstons offered Fulton full control over the company if he would give up his partnership in return for a salaried position. In a scathing response, Fulton claimed that under his 1802 agreement with Chancellor Livingston, "my voice is equal to all other owners." In addition, he said that all steamboat operations beyond New York "are to be conducted by me as I think proper without consulting anyone."[35] When Robert L. Livingston broke off contact, Fulton demanded that they work together against competitors such as Stevens; otherwise, he warned, "we must confine ourselves to the North and East Rivers."[36]

To make matters worse, the Mississippi River Steam Boat Navigation Company literally and figuratively ground to a halt in summer 1814 when the *New Orleans* sank near Baton Rouge and the *Vesuvius* ran aground on the Tennessee shore. Fulton naively instructed John Livingston to contact the governors of Kentucky and Tennessee and ask them to provide militia troops to refloat the *Vesuvius*. The inventor predicted that such labor "would be honorable to a state giving such generous protection to a new and noble art" and that "those noble warriors who defend their country will take pride in protecting her arts."[37] The governors flatly denied his requests. Two months later, to the relief of Natchez merchants who eagerly awaited the resumption of trade, Livingston repaired the *Vesuvius* without military aid. In June 1814, Fulton and the Livingstons renegotiated the terms of the Mississippi Steam Boat Navigation Company. The following month, they also agreed to a new partnership on the Hudson River in which Fulton received two votes on all company decisions and half the profits from his New York steamboats; the Livingstons accepted one vote and a quarter of the profits each and, in return, promised to reimburse Fulton for the business expenses he had assumed on behalf of the original partnership with Chancellor Livingston.[38]

Interstate Rivalries

Sensing weakness, rivals of the North River Company made repeated efforts to break the New York monopoly. In May 1813, Fulton patented a steam-powered towboat that could warp its way up rapids by use of a steam-powered crank, or windlass, normally used to raise anchors. John Langdon Sullivan, a civil engineer, physician, and superintendent of the Middlesex Canal in Boston who had experimented with a similar invention, rushed to oppose him. As the son of former Massachusetts governor James Sullivan and nephew of Revolutionary War general John Sullivan, James Langdon Sullivan enjoyed considerable public support. He also received the public endorsement of William Thornton, who still had a score to settle with Fulton.[39]

In August, Benjamin Henry Latrobe suggested that Fulton allow a panel of three neutral inventors (including Eli Whitney, who invented the cotton gin) to settle the matter. Fulton, Delacy, and Sullivan met with the commissioners in Hartford and New Haven, Connecticut, in fall 1814. On December 28, Whitney informed Fulton, "The broad principle of towing belongs equally to yourself and Mr. Sullivan in common with the rest of mankind."[40] Since the arbiters had failed to determine the originality of the steam-powered windlass, Sullivan quickly secured a federal patent for the device.[41] In 1815, he also obtained from the Massachusetts legislature a twenty-eight-year monopoly over steam towboats on the Connecticut River. Armed with these documents, Sullivan began to ply his vessels on Long Island Sound in direct violation of the Fulton-Livingston monopoly. In frustration, Fulton appealed to Secretary of State James Monroe with accusations that Sullivan and Latrobe had stolen his inventions. He failed to reach a settlement with Sullivan, however, because he soon became preoccupied with yet another challenge to his monopoly. This time, the conflict would come from Aaron Ogden, the former governor of New Jersey.[42]

Aaron Ogden and Thomas Gibbons Enter the Steamboat Business

Fulton and the Livingstons could not have chosen a more formidable opponent than Aaron Ogden. Born into a wealthy Elizabethtown, New Jersey, family, Ogden attended Princeton and defied his father to join the Continental army, in which he attained the rank of colonel. After serving with distinction, he gained admission to the New Jersey bar in 1784. Early in his legal career, he worked with former comrade-in-arms Alexander Hamilton to resolve land disputes with the state of New York. In one sensational case, the two lawyers lost to Chancellor Robert R. Livingston.[43] Ogden used his legal career to cultivate a network of political allies throughout New York and New Jersey. Capitalizing on his impressive war record, he became a Federalist senator and governor of New Jersey during the War of 1812. Ogden lost in his bid for reelection the following year.[44] His political career in tatters, he returned to Elizabethtown and directed his attention to developing a ferry service he owned with Jonathan Dayton. Dayton was a Continental army veteran, a Second Continental Congress delegate, a constitutional framer, and a Federalist congressman whom Ogden had known for over thirty years. It therefore came as a shock when it was learned that Dayton secretly sold his share of the franchise in 1812 to a wealthy Georgian by the name of Thomas Gibbons, a man who would become a major player in steam travel.[45]

Gibbons's personality and experiences provided an interesting contrast to those of Ogden. The son of a wealthy Georgian rice planter, Gibbons trained for

Aaron Ogden. David Broderick Walcutt, *Portrait of New Jersey Governor Aaron Ogden,* 1856.

the law in Charleston, South Carolina. When the American Revolution broke out, his family strongly backed the American cause, but Thomas Gibbons became a Loyalist and spent the war defending the property rights of fellow Tories in British-occupied Savannah. The willingness of the Gibbons family to divide their loyalties during the war may have resulted from a pragmatic decision to ensure that no matter which side won the war, their wealth in plantations and slaves would remain intact. Gibbons's Loyalist status certainly did not preclude his marriage in 1779 to Ann Miles Heyward, whose father and uncle were leaders of the South Carolina Patriot movement. The couple had three children—Thomas Heyward, William, and Ann—and survived the war on the proceeds of Gibbons's law practice.[46]

In the postwar period, Gibbons fought to gain American citizenship and re-cover his family estates, which had been confiscated during the war. He regained his fortune and served several terms as mayor of Savannah. He and his family escaped sultry southern summers by purchasing a summer home in Elizabethtown. In New Jersey, Gibbons enjoyed the life of a gentleman. He rode about town in an elegant two-horse coach trimmed with silver, managed a popular tavern known as the Union Hotel, speculated in land, and invested in the Elizabethtown Bank.

Thomas Gibbons. Artist unknown, *Thomas Gibbons,* n.d., Drew University Library

These activities brought Gibbons into contact with Aaron Ogden. Initially, the two men enjoyed a cordial relationship. Ogden introduced Gibbons to local elites, and the two dined frequently at each other's homes. In June 1803, they jointly sued Walter Rutherford in state court over a land dispute. Gibbons sensed the economic potential of northern New Jersey. And knowing that his Loyalist past, his reputation as a duelist, and rumors that he had helped rig a congressional election in 1791 precluded a future in Georgia politics, Gibbons permanently moved his family north in 1811.[47]

Despite the difficulties posed by the New York monopoly, both Ogden and Gibbons were eager to convert their ferry business to steam power. In 1804, Ogden hired Daniel Dod, a Connecticut clock maker and inventor, to build a steam engine factory. Dod was a versatile individual who combined studies in literature and theology with an interest in mechanics. More important, he possessed several federal patents for steam boilers that might prove useful in a legal confrontation with Robert Fulton. To break into the New York steamboat trade, Ogden allowed Fulton and John R. Livingston to take on passengers and supplies at his dock on the run between New York and New Brunswick. When he felt his position was strong enough, he petitioned Fulton for a license to operate steamboats in New

York waters. Fulton agreed but demanded an exorbitant fee that he knew Ogden could not pay.[48]

To pressure Fulton, Ogden voiced his grievances to the New Jersey state legislature. In January 1811, the legislature decreed that whereas "the citizens of New-Jersey have a full and equal right to navigate and to have and use boats upon all the waters lying between the States of New-Jersey and New-York," steamboats registered in New York would be seized upon entering New Jersey waters. Unlike their New York colleagues, New Jersey legislators carefully worded the act so as not to interfere with federal authority. The New Jersey law would stand until the Empire State rescinded the Fulton-Livingston monopoly.[49]

After consulting with several lawyers, Ogden borrowed heavily to complete his vessel, the *Sea Horse,* whose twelve-horsepower engine cruised the New Jersey shore at nine miles per hour. Upon its completion, Ogden ordered Dod to test the New York monopoly with runs from Elizabethtown to New York City.[50] Gibbons followed Ogden's progress through conversations with Thomas Addis Emmet and Cadwallader D. Colden, whom he kept on retainer.[51] With the passage of Chancellor Livingston's stringent monopoly act in April 1811 and the outcome of *Livingston v. Van Ingen* ten months later, Ogden again pushed the New Jersey Assembly for tougher steamboat legislation. Since New York now permitted New Jersey boats to be arbitrarily seized, Ogden asked that "a law . . . be passed containing countervailing provisions." In February 1813, the legislature complied by passing a measure that reinforced their 1811 steamboat seizure law.[52]

Origins of the Ogden and Gibbons Feud

Ogden squared off against not merely the New York monopoly but also his own partner. Troubles between Ogden and Gibbons began when disagreements over their ferry business intersected with domestic disputes within the Gibbons household. Thomas Gibbons had given half of his stock in the Elizabethtown ferry service, including waterfront property and several sloops, in trust to his only daughter, Ann. Her husband, John M. Trumbull, was to serve as executor of Gibbons's will. It was not a discreet choice. Trumbull was the black sheep of one of Connecticut's leading families. His grandfather had served as governor of Connecticut and adviser to George Washington during the American Revolution. His uncle (also named John) was one of America's foremost painters in the late

73

1700s. And his brother Joseph had succeeded as a private attorney and president of the Hartford Bank. Yet John M. Trumbull was a pariah, having lived off family wealth for much of his life and failed in several business ventures. Rumors persisted throughout Elizabethtown that he had seduced Ann Gibbons and that their marriage was merely a sham to preserve the honor of the Gibbons family.[53]

The already strained relations between the Trumbulls and the Gibbonses ruptured in August 1814 when Trumbull pleaded with the Connecticut General Assembly for an act of insolvency. It was an act of public humiliation, but Trumbull was desperate to raise money to satisfy his creditors. Scrambling to find some future source of income, Trumbull insisted that Gibbons leave his daughter one-third of his estate in his will, and he urged Ann to sue her father if he refused their terms. Gibbons would not accede to the threat, and beyond that, he rewrote his lease agreement with Ogden to deprive the Trumbulls of income, an arrangement that made Ogden uneasy. George Johnson, a family friend, chastised Gibbons for failing to provide for his daughter: "It has been your daughter's misfortune, in choosing a husband, to make a bad selection, you are not justifiable in aggravating it by leaving her to starve." Johnson reminded Gibbons that he was accordingly "bound by sentiments of decency and propriety to make a provision for your child."[54] Gibbons retorted, "I don't know any clause, or paragraph, or section in the laws of honor that is applicable to this case. I thought it a matter of accounts and figures. I find there is a difference between a knowledge of figures and a knowledge of accounts."[55] He promised to make "mince pie" of Trumbull's claims. Johnson in turn defended Trumbull, noting, "I understand it very well, but as according to the old proverb there are none so blind as those who won't see, so possibly there may be none so stupid as those who won't understand."[56]

Through 1813, relations between Gibbons, Ogden, and the Trumbulls deteriorated even further. Seeking to distance himself from the situation, Ogden quietly contacted Daniel D. Coit, a successful lawyer in Elizabethtown, "to pursue such separate course to secure the benefit of my enterprize as circumstances seem to require."[57] When the Trumbulls offered to lower the lease rates, Ogden threatened to divide the ferry business to get a more favorable offer.[58] Disgusted with the entire affair, Gibbons demanded that Ogden buy him out of the business. He further insisted that Ogden allow the Trumbulls an equal partnership, whereas Ogden wanted a cash settlement. When Ogden failed to budge, Gibbons sent a petition to the New Jersey state legislature designed to publicly humiliate

Ogden by accusing him of cheating Ann Trumbull and her children out of their rightful share of the business.[59]

Attempts to Repeal the New York Steamboat Monopoly

In January 1815, Ogden, on the advice of William Thornton, asked the New York legislature to rescind the Fulton-Livingston monopoly. He also publicly circulated his petition as a broadside to rally popular support against the North River Company. Ogden personally argued his case before the state assembly, whereas Emmet and Colden appeared on behalf of the monopolists. Colonel Ogden reminded the delegates of his wartime service and stressed the expenses he had incurred to develop his steamboat business. He also asserted that a federal coasting license and patent formerly owned by John Fitch (sold to Ogden by William Thornton for $1) granted access to any port in the United States. Highlighting the need to provide for his family, Ogden asked the legislature to repeal the Fulton-Livingston monopoly.[60]

The New York Assembly referred Ogden's memorial to a subcommittee chaired by William A. Duer. As a Democratic-Republican, landholder, and cousin on his mother's side to the Livingston family, Duer should, in theory, have been among the strongest supporters of the monopoly. Yet he was also a longtime advocate of Aaron Burr, whom the Livingstons had helped defeat in the electoral crisis of 1800. Furthermore, Duer's constituents in Rhinebeck, New York, would benefit economically from increased steamboat traffic on the Hudson River. It was not surprising, then, that he denied a request by attorney Cadwallader D. Colden for a delay in the committee's hearings so that Fulton could be produced to testify on behalf of the monopoly.[61]

To stall for time, Thomas Addis Emmet delivered a six-hour speech that described his client as a tireless public servant who strove to better society. Emmet brilliantly depicted Fulton as the victim of a noble, albeit naive, heart. "You rely too implicitly on the strength of your rights, and the sanctity of the obligations on which they are founded," Emmet chastised an imaginary Fulton, subtly underscoring the fact that Duer had not afforded his client the opportunity to appear in person. "You expect too much from your well earned reputation, and the acknowledged utility to mankind of your life and labours." In an emotional conclusion, Emmet warned Fulton in absentia, "I have fearful forebodings, that you may hereafter find in public faith a broken staff for your support, and receive from public gratitude, a broken heart for your reward."[62] Despite Emmet's clever improvisation, Fulton sensed defeat and offered Ogden an equal partnership in the North River Company, which angered John R. Livingston. As with Stevens, Fulton insisted that Ogden acknowledge the legitimacy of his patents, monopoly, and reputation as inventor of the steamboat. When Ogden refused on the grounds that he sought to defend his state as well as his personal interests, Fulton lambasted his rival for attacking his public reputation and property rights.[63]

On March 8, the legislative committee reported that Fulton's steamboat was clearly based on Fitch's designs and recommended that the New York Assembly rescind the steamboat monopoly.[64] Fulton at last arrived in Albany to demonstrate his newfound humility in a last-minute plea before the legislature. He contrasted his altruistic attempts to bring steamboats to New York to Ogden's selfish efforts to turn a profit. Fulton provided depositions from Charles Stoudinger and Benjamin Henry Latrobe that attested to the originality of his steamboat designs. The inventor even produced a letter written to Lord Stanhope in 1793 that discussed the use of paddle wheels to power steamboats. Emmet reinforced these claims in a summation that again depicted Fulton as a noble but tragic figure constantly beset by smooth-talking interlopers determined to destroy his interests.[65]

After proposals to repeal the monopoly proved unpopular, the assembly sponsored a compromise bill that acknowledged the importance of public trials to defend property rights in "cases of conflicting and doubtful claims, more especially those in great public interests and [where] constitutional questions are involved."[66] The bill suggested leaving the steamboat monopoly intact, yet it stipulated that the 1811 seizure law should be repealed. The measure passed the House but lost in the Senate by a margin of fifty-one to forty-three. Once again, Fulton had staved off disaster through a combination of threats, brilliant legal maneuvering, and appeals to public sentiment. Worrying that he had overplayed his image as an altruistic inventor, Fulton speculated that New Yorkers would now want him to produce more boats out of gratitude. "I have fulfilled every part of my contract," he observed. "I cannot risque more of my fortune without a declaratory act on the laws in my favor and complete protection."[67]

Fulton's problems were far from over. On March 26, 1814, Mary Stevens Livingston passed away in Washington, DC. As she left no will, Fulton dismissed Robert L. and Edward P. Livingston's partnership claims and demanded immediate payment on their debts to the company. He continued to quarrel with the Livingstons over the Hudson River operations while watching his western steamboat interests disintegrate. The inventor also dismissed Delacy, whom he accused of embezzlement and land speculation. All the while, Fulton continued to lobby the navy in regard to plans for torpedoes and a steam-powered warship. Just as the War of 1812 raged across the United States and British troops burned Washington, DC, Fulton's business ventures began to crumble.[68]

Attempts to Repeal the New Jersey Steamboat Monopoly

Despite his defeat in Albany, Ogden continued to dominate the waters of New Jersey. He cunningly took passengers from Elizabethtown to Bedloe's Island, a peninsula off New York Harbor, where they transferred to a horse-powered "team boat" that proceeded to New York City. Similarly, John R. Livingston ran his steamboat to Staten Island, where passengers boarded sailboats bound for New Jersey. Angry at Ogden's circumvention of the New York monopoly, Livingston complained to Mahlon Dickerson, a New Jersey Supreme Court justice. Certainly Dickerson, a fellow Jeffersonian Republican, landholder, and advocate of industrialization, would lend a sympathetic ear. Yet when Livingston argued that he stood to lose a fortune to the New Jersey monopoly, Dickerson nonchalantly responded that such seizure laws were designed not to punish individuals but to contest New York State's navigation claims up to the New Jersey coastline.[69]

Fulton and the Livingstons bided their time and watched the upcoming statewide elections in New Jersey with interest. When the Jeffersonian Republicans won a huge victory at the polls, John R. Livingston petitioned the state legislature to repeal Ogden's monopoly.[70] Fulton also asked Emmet for any mutual correspondence, dating back to 1802, that might corroborate his steamboat claims.[71] In addition, he obtained sworn affidavits from Captains Bartholomew and Roorbach verifying the fact that their employer had invented the *North River Steam Boat*. Aware of the desperation of his situation, Fulton secretly sought a partnership with a New Jersey businessman he cryptically referred to as the "Gentleman of Monmouth"—possibly Trumbull.[72] Offering his breadth of knowledge and experience in the construction of steamboats, he asked that men such as Delacy and Roosevelt not be involved in any business dealings. Fulton resolutely stood by his legal claims and insisted that his patents gave him exclusive control

77

over all steamboats in American waters, even in New Jersey. He argued that the Republican legislators in New Brunswick certainly would not deprive their state of the advantages of steam power merely to satisfy the interests of a few wealthy citizens. "Surely not[.] [T]hey are disposed to encourage useful science come from whence it may," Fulton reasoned.[73]

Caught in a strange situation for monopolists, the Livingstons sought, through their petition, to distinguish between the New York and New Jersey grants. They relied heavily on the fact that New Jersey's economy was largely dependent on trade with the wealthier New York. In the long run, therefore, New Jersey would suffer financially more than New York would from a steamboat monopoly law. Furthermore, fellow Republicans now dominated the New Jersey legislature. The Livingstons thus adopted a series of brazen arguments in defense of the monopoly but opposed to the New Jersey measure. Although these arguments may have seemed contradictory from a logical point of view, they allowed the New York monopolists to invoke state pride and appeal to residents back home, make a prima facie legal case against New Jersey, and give the New Jersey legislature enough of an excuse to repeal their monopoly.

John R. Livingston reviewed the history of the monopoly to show that such legislation did not infringe upon the waters of New Jersey but merely protected inventors. The New Jersey monopoly, in contrast, merely hurt local investors with stock in New York steamboat companies and denied Jerseyites trade with their neighbors. To tamper with the New York monopoly would waste precious time and undercut Livingston's profits.[74] The Livingstons also argued that the New Jersey monopoly unfairly "appears to favor that of a particular act against a particular person or persons; and that, in consequence of its not being general, may be construed as unconstitutional."[75] The petitioners furthermore contended "that the laws of New-York never were intended to militate against the state of New-Jersey or its waters; that the machinery in Col. Ogden's Boats is not an improvement and has been used in other Boats," and "that the most respectable mechanics do determine that there is nothing in principle different from Mr. Fulton's." The New Jersey law should therefore be repealed, they stated. Like their New York counterparts, the New Jersey legislators convened a special committee to determine the validity of Ogden's monopoly.[76]

Ogden seized the chance to challenge the New Yorkers on his own home ground. From behind the scenes, he and Thornton assembled a group of Fulton's embittered associates, including Evans, Delacy, Latrobe, Roosevelt, Stevens, and even Fulton's own partner and in-law William Cutting. Each rival produced testimony to contest Fulton's legal claims and reputation. Aware of the growing threat, Fulton hurriedly assembled affidavits to buttress his achievements in steam travel. In doing so, Fulton learned of Thornton's scheme to secure a federal patent based on his steamboat design six years earlier. Fulton promptly wrote to Secretary of State James Monroe, accusing Thornton of using his position as Patent Office superintendent to receive plans for promising inventions and surreptitiously patent them for himself. Weary of Thornton's schemes, Monroe promptly forbade Patent Office employees from securing patents of their own.[77] Thornton struck back with a pamphlet titled *A Short Account of the Origin of Steamboats* that trivialized Fulton's claims as an inventor.[78] When Fulton threatened a lawsuit for slander, Thornton hired attorneys James Greenleaf and Fernando Fairfax to comb through courthouses and secure witnesses against his opponent.[79]

Confrontation in Trenton

Realizing that Fulton was distracted by his feud with Thornton, Ogden prepared his own legal confrontation. On January 12, 1815, he asked attorney Samuel L. Southard to present an "entertaining and interesting" case to the New Jersey legislature. Southard was a leading Jeffersonian in the New Jersey Assembly and would later serve as both treasury secretary and secretary of war to President John Quincy Adams. Hoping Southard's connections with fellow Republicans in the legislature would prove useful in the upcoming conflict, Ogden asked the young lawyer to name his fee.[80] He also secured the services of Joseph Hopkinson, one of the most notable lawyers in the nation. Hopkinson had successfully defended backcountry farmers charged with treason for defying federal whiskey taxes, helped Benjamin Rush win a famous libel suit, and saved U.S. Supreme Court justice Samuel Chase from impeachment charges in 1804. He would eventually argue famous cases such as *Trustees of Dartmouth College v. Woodward* (1819), *Sturges v. Crowninshield* (1819), and *McCulloch v. Maryland* (1819) before the U.S. Supreme Court before becoming a federal judge in his own right. Hopkinson was well known for using puns and a dry wit to win cases, skills that would serve him well in his confrontation with Fulton.[81]

The hearings into Ogden's monopoly began in Trenton on January 24, 1815. The affair was open to the public, and spectators crowded the lobby and gallery of the New Jersey statehouse. What had started as a debate over monopolies rapidly turned into a referendum on Fulton's reputation as an inventor and gentleman. As counsel for Roosevelt, Delacy insisted that Fulton had stolen the concept of paddle wheels from his client. Emmet responded with the affidavit Roosevelt had signed four years earlier that acknowledged Fulton's claims. Delacy then maintained that Roosevelt had signed the affidavit only under duress. While the legislative committee recessed for a week, Fulton journeyed to Trenton to testify.[82]

When the committee reconvened, Emmet argued that Ogden had no grounds to seek a monopoly, as his partner, Thomas Gibbons, had not agreed to the matter. On his own behalf, Ogden replied that he had not sought to create a personal monopoly but wanted only to end the New York grant by the sole means available. His offer to withdraw the New Jersey monopoly, if New York would do likewise, was met with cheers from spectators in the crowded galleries. Next, Ogden's attorneys produced examples of Fitch's writings to prove that his experiments had been successful. Using Fulton's own techniques against him, Joseph Hopkinson and Southard depicted Fitch as a brilliant but tragic figure whose repeated failures at the hands of interlopers such as Fulton had led to his suicide. Hopkinson and Southard also drew on the fact that the *Sea Horse* was faster and more cost effective than Fulton's boats.[83]

Ogden and his attorneys finished their case with an attack on Fulton's moral character as they summoned John Stevens to testify. Stevens insisted that as the first person to pursue steamboat experiments in New Jersey, he himself deserved monopoly rights if anyone did. In principle, however, monopolies were incompatible with a free society. Hopkinson and Southard also produced an affidavit signed by William Cutting stating that in 1805, Aaron Vail had confided in him that Fulton had borrowed Fitch's plans for several months, while in France. In addition, Ogden's attorneys castigated Fulton for the alleged theft of a rope-making machine from a British inventor.[84] Fulton responded personally to these attacks. The enraged inventor insisted that he had never claimed to invent a rope-making machine but had merely imported one from Great Britain to France. He also insisted that he had never copied Fitch's plans. As proof, he circulated the 1793 letter he had written to Lord Stanhope that mentioned his experiments with paddle wheels. Ogden, however, held the letter up to the light and revealed a watermark that identified the paper as an American product manufactured in 1796. Fulton tried to explain that he had merely copied the original, a claim his opponents met with sarcasm.[85]

Sensing weakness, Ogden and his counselors pressed home the attack. Hopkinson argued that New York had no right to claim open waters up to the New Jersey shoreline. Furthermore, he asked, if Fulton's federal patent claims were valid, what need did he have for a state monopoly? Fulton burst out that, regardless of how the legislature ruled, he would seize the *Sea Horse* and personally shoot Ogden if he ventured onto the Hudson. Hopkinson swiftly took advantage of the outburst. He magnanimously admitted that Fulton deserved some measure of credit but that it could not erase his selfish ambitions. Fulton was not a heroic scientist but an unscrupulous "capitalist" passing off the inventions of others as his own: he was not even above using false names and perjury to advance his interests. Caught off guard, Emmet fell back on his earlier strategy of depicting Fulton as a modern Christopher Columbus whose scientific explorations had opened a new continent of steam travel for ordinary Americans. Such hyperbole was unconvincing.[86]

Ogden and his followers realized that any victory they might achieve would be far from complete. After all, Ogden's patent claims and state grant were as dubious as those held by Fulton. Furthermore, the state legislature remained dominated by Republicans who were friendly with the Livingston clan and bore no love for the former Federalist governor. Aware of Ogden's vulnerability, Fulton criticized his opponent for cobbling together legal claims from diverse documents. "Suppose you were to collect a basket of old ballads and bad verse without ideas, but rhyming and containing the twenty-four letters of the alphabet," he retorted.[87] "Could you not, from those parts used by Pope, prove that he did not conceive or invent the *Dunciad,* or 'Essay on Man and Criticism?'"[88] Fulton also threatened to launch suits of $5,000 each against Thornton and Cutting for slander.[89]

In early February 1814, the New Jersey Assembly and Council, voting along party lines, rescinded the steamboat monopoly by votes of 21 to 18 and 7 to 6, respectively.[90] Even as Fulton continued to threaten lawsuits, John R. Livingston negotiated with Ogden behind the scenes. In May, they reached an agreement. Ogden received the right to run a steam ferry from New York City to Elizabethtown for ten years. In return, the colonel agreed to pay $600 annually and share his wharf in New York City with the North River Company. In an attempt to mollify Livingston, Ogden also agreed "that he [would] not, either directly or indirectly during the continuance of this agreement, be concerned in any steam boat or steam boats, to run to or from any other place or places than to and from Elizabeth Town Point."[91]

The encounter at Trenton shook Fulton's resolve. On the journey home, he stopped at the Jersey City shipyard to inspect his newly constructed steam frigate *Fulton*. To save time, Fulton, Emmet, Colden, and their colleague William Sampson attempted to cross the frozen Hudson River by foot. Emmet fell through the ice, only to be rescued by Fulton. Freezing water soaked both men, and Fulton developed an acute case of pneumonia. After a brief recovery, he risked his fledgling health again to look over his newest steamboat. Fulton suffered a relapse, lingered briefly, and died on February 23, 1815. With the death of both senior partners, the defense of their monopoly ironically fell to an individual who had just done his best to destroy it.

Conflict over the Western Steamboat Monopoly

After Fulton's death, both the Mississippi River Steam Boat Navigation Company and the Ohio Steam Boat Navigation Company sank slowly into bankruptcy. Problems began in 1811 when Oliver Evans formed a steamboat company in Pittsburgh and petitioned the Kentucky and Tennessee state legislatures for monopoly rights. Evans was a brilliant engineer from Delaware whose power looms had already revolutionized the textile industry. He began construction of a steamboat to run between Natchez and New Orleans but went bankrupt before the vessel could be completed.[92] Meanwhile, Connecticut inventor Daniel French fared somewhat better in his attempts to build a steamboat at Brownsville, Pennsylvania. French had considerable experience in steam power. In 1809, he had secured a federal patent for a steam engine based on an oscillating engine, and he had already constructed a number of steam vessels in New York and Philadelphia. French secured a backer named Samuel Smith to build the *Comet*, an 18-ton steamboat powered by a high-pressure engine and stern-mounted paddle wheel.[93] The *Comet* successfully navigated the Mississippi in February 1814 and made several additional trips between New Orleans and Natchez. French and Smith built on their success and sold stock to wealthy Brownsville residents to incorporate the Monongahela and Ohio Steam Boat Company. Later that year, the company commissioned the twenty-five-ton *Despatch* and the seventy-ton *Enterprize*. French quickly realized, however, that his vessels were neither large enough nor fast enough to successfully compete with Fulton's *New Orleans* and *Vesuvius*. When Fulton threatened legal action, French sold the *Enterprize* to his partner, Captain Henry Miller Shreve, a riverboat trader.[94]

Shreve hailed from a family of New Jersey Quakers. After the death of his father, he worked on riverboats to support his destitute family. Although not a formally trained mechanic, Shreve possessed over ten years of practical experience in the Mississippi River trade. In 1815, he constructed the steamboat *Washington* in Wheeling, Virginia. The *Washington* sported a shallow draft similar to a river barge; a one-hundred-horsepower, high-pressure engine placed above deck to allow more cargo room; and two floors complete with a bar and passenger cabins. In June, most of Wheeling turned out to witness the launch of the *Washington*. A local women's group presented Shreve with a flag embroidered with the figure of Fame and the mottos "Our friends shall not withhold what we have wrested from our enemies" and "Don't give up the ship." These slogans represented none-too-subtle attacks on the Fulton-Livingston interests for their steamboat monopoly on a river defended by American troops at the Battle of New Orleans.[95]

An *Ohio Federalist* editorial likewise warned Shreve to "provide enormous bail at New Orleans and give fees to lawyers, for such we understand, has been the fate of all owners of steam boats in that quarter, who have not obtained Livingston's *sovereign and gracious permission* to navigate within the state of Louisiana." The article attacked the monopoly for controlling a major inland waterway and undercutting the federal patent rights of inventors such as Fitch and Evans.[96] However, despite this auspicious beginning, disaster struck when a boiler on the *Washington* exploded and killed fourteen people just outside of Chillicothe, Missouri. A newspaper account reported, "The whole town was alarmed by the explosion, every physician with a number of citizens went immediately to their relief" to be greeted only "by the screams & groans of the agonizing sufferers, rendering the scene horrible, beyond description."[97]

Undeterred, the riverboat captain attempted a second trip the next fall. Upon Shreve's arrival in New Orleans, Edward Livingston allegedly remarked, "You deserve well of your country, young man but we shall be compelled to beat you if we can."[98] Two-way steamboat service on the Mississippi had become a reality, and within a year, Shreve began to operate a lucrative steamboat service in blatant violation of the Fulton-Livingston monopoly.[99] Public toleration for the Louisiana monopoly crumbled with the success of the *Washington*. An editorial in the *Cincinnati Western Spy* called for "the annihilation of the swindling patent rights." Another article stated, "Our road to market must and will be free; this monopolizing disposition will only arouse the citizens of the West to insist on and obtain recognition of their rights, viz. the privilege of passing, and repassing, unmolested, on the common highway of the West."[100]

83

Public meetings were convened in Cincinnati and Louisville to protest the monopoly. Citizens discussed the possibilities of using state funds to either test the monopoly in federal court or purchase steamboat company stock to be held in public trust. In February 1816, the Ohio state legislature urged its congressional representatives to defeat Fulton and Livingston's patent rights and to hold an inquiry into the constitutionality of the Orleans territorial monopoly grant. The following May, the *Lexington Reporter* quipped, "If it is constitutional for the legislature of Louisiana to grant the exclusive navigation of the Mississippi to an individual, that country might as well have continued a Spanish province." The article continued, "Nor is it less absurd to suppose that a patent right should include all improvements made by others, or prevent the use of them."[101] In January 1817, Senator John M. Breckenridge, who had opposed previous attempts to create a steamboat monopoly in Kentucky, swore to "maintain inviolate by all legitimate means the right of her citizens to navigate said [Mississippi] river, and its tributary streams."[102]

Despite growing public hostility across the nation, the New York and Mississippi steamboat monopolies had proven resistant to attack. Robert Fulton's personal dynamism had played a large role in keeping the monopolies afloat. Although hardly the sole inventor of the American steamboat, he had nevertheless overcome a middling background to become one of the most successful businessmen in early American society. Furthermore, he had conducted the first methodical study of steam technology and combined the works of others to create a truly practical and profitable steam-powered vessel. Fulton's efforts to advertise and expand his steamboat interests had helped him cultivate the reputation of the country's most successful inventor. But an overreliance on his reputation also proved a hindrance, as Fulton's ordeal in Trenton revealed. His confidence shaken, he took refuge in his inventions to the point where such activities effectively cost him his life. The New York monopoly survived the deaths of Fulton and Livingston and continued to dominate local waters throughout the 1810s. The steamboat controversy, however, had attracted powerful interests, such as Aaron Ogden and Thomas Gibbons, who increasingly turned to state and federal courts to contest both their economic interests and their personal rivalries. Ogden and Gibbons would therefore take the rhetoric surrounding monopolies and put the matter to the test in a series of cases that lasted over a decade and culminated in a landmark decision by the U.S. Supreme Court.

CHAPTER 6

Personal Rivalries and Lawsuits

Ungentlemanly Conduct

O N FEBRUARY 23, 1815, Jonathan Dayton reported the repeal of Ogden's New Jersey steamboat monopoly to Thomas Gibbons. "When we took the vote, the disappointment of the Colonel was great, his mortification extreme," gloated Dayton. As Ogden was "governed more by the spirit of prejudice than prescience," he would now certainly negotiate with Gibbons. Dayton concluded, "So much for steam boats, projectors, and proprietors."[1]

The steamboat struggle had become increasingly antagonistic and public. After the death of Fulton, his incipient steamboat empire broke into three separate operations in spring 1815. On the Mississippi River, John and Edward Livingston battled against competitors such as Daniel French and Henry Miller Shreve in their attempts to keep the Mississippi River Steam Boat Navigation Company functioning. In New York, Robert L. Livingston and Edward P. Livingston fought off a series of competitors, including Massachusetts inventor James L. Sullivan and the ever-present John Stevens. On the line from New York City to New Jersey, John R. Livingston, Aaron Ogden, and Thomas Gibbons competed for business. This latter conflict would prove to be the most visible, as Ogden and Gibbons fought not just before state legislatures and in court but also in the press and before the public. Even Thomas Gibbons's family problems played a role in the ongoing struggles to control steam travel along the East Coast. As these conflicts intensified, many realized the intractable nature of the steamboat wars. Over the prior twenty years, informal negotiation reinforced by the threat of legal action had given way to lawsuits, injunctions, and retaliatory state legislation. Ordinary citizens now held town meetings, petitioned legislatures, and demanded that steamboat promoters provide cheaper and more reliable service. When such tactics failed, newspapers began to call for federal intervention to solve the issue of the New York monopoly once and for all.

Problems in Elizabethtown

In addition to feuding over financial concerns, Gibbons, Ogden, and John M. Trumbull fought for social prestige, an important commodity in Elizabethtown, New Jersey. In 1810, Elizabethtown boasted a population of just over three thousand. Traditionally an agrarian area, the town helped link Philadelphia to New York City. By the early 1800s, a younger generation of self-made Democratic-Republicans began to rub shoulders with landholding descendants of the colonial elite. In these environs, family pedigree, personal reputation, and economic success still carried great social weight.[2] Ogden's ancestors had helped settle Elizabethtown in the 1660s, and Trumbull came from a famous Connecticut family of intellectuals, politicians, and soldiers. In contrast, Gibbons's extravagant income, lavish spending habits, and public outbursts sparked the disgust and envy of genteel yet financially vulnerable Elizabethtown elites. The Georgian also carried a Loyalist taint, which contrasted with Ogden's wartime service in the patriot cause. None of this was forgotten in the arguments among the three men, which frequently invoked the language of honor, paternalism, and civic virtue.[3]

Gibbons and Ogden chiefly fought over Elizabethtown Point, a valuable dock facility that provided direct access to New York Harbor. In 1776, British troops had made certain to hold the dock, and George Washington had made a point of visiting it on the way to his inauguration in New York City in 1789. In 1804, Ogden agreed to pay Gibbons an annual rent to use his share of the property. Then, when Gibbons transferred his share of the ferry service to his daughter, Ogden secretly negotiated a significantly cheaper lease agreement.[4] Gibbons confronted Ogden over the incident, and the colonel blasted his rival for buying Elizabethtown Bank stock to influence local credit rates. More seriously, Gibbons had abused Ogden's hospitality and maligned his character through a legislative petition that accused him of robbing Ann Trumbull and her children of their interest in the Elizabethtown ferry business.[5] Gibbons responded, "The obligation in this exchange of civility is on the part of the gentleman who invites, not on him who accepts."[6] While protesting Ogden's petition, Gibbons asked his rival to explain his own character attacks to the state legislature. Gibbons ominously concluded, "I leave this yet open for you to do, with the assurance, that I will never bear an insult, nor an injury remediless at law."[7]

On the advice of attorneys Isaac H. Williamson and Thomas Addis Emmet, Gibbons pressured the Trumbulls to disavow their agreement with Ogden.[8] He also blamed Ogden for "the misfortunes and painful effects which Mrs. Trumbull and her children suffer under" and offered to have the trustees sign a bond with Ogden stating that "all matters between you & the trustees of Mrs. Trumbull may be fairly, justly, and honorably settled."[9] Ogden sputtered, "Nothing has been farther from my mind than to give . . . Mrs. Trumbull any unnecessary trouble." Nevertheless, he stuck by his recent agreement. Barring some form of outside mediation, Ogden concluded, "I believe the time to be fast approaching when I shall be compelled to save myself as far as may be in my power by the means which providentially remain to me."[10]

Two days after Christmas in 1815, Gibbons commenced a scheme to discredit Ogden. He sponsored a town meeting at the Union Hotel, supposedly to discuss plans to dredge the Elizabethtown Creek, build a new drawbridge, and establish a publicly owned steamboat company. A state-chartered bank capitalized at $60,000 would fund these projects. Such a plan would also cripple the Elizabethtown Bank, Ogden's primary source of income and credit.[11] The colonel retaliated in a pamphlet that threatened the Trumbulls with a breach of contract suit. To appear magnanimous, Ogden described Gibbons as "an honest and pleasant man" who had fallen "wholly under the influence of Jon. Dayton." Nevertheless, as a matter of honor, Ogden would resist his foe because "he was and the people thought he was a persecuted man."[12]

In early January, Sheppard Kollock asked John R. Livingston to sell the town a monopoly license. Kollock was a local Continental army veteran, newspaper editor, publisher, and New Jersey common pleas court judge. As a pillar of the Elizabethtown community, he could not be dismissed lightly.[13] Livingston forwarded Kollock's request to Ogden. In a show of civic-mindedness that nevertheless exposed his financial woes, Ogden promised to "promote the benefits of my fellow Citizens which I have so much laboured and so much ventured."[14] However, Ogden consistently avoided signing an agreement. Livingston sided with his fellow monopolist, castigated Kollock for his rashness, and predicted that Elizabethtown could never support its own steamboat service.[15]

Rise of Cutthroat Competition

Commenting that "parsimony in steam boat building is ruinous," Gibbons secured the services of steamboat engineer Daniel Dod and incorporated the Trenton and Philadelphia Steam Boat Company in January 1816. Rejecting attempts by Trumbull to purchase the Elizabethtown Steam Boat Company, Gibbons petitioned the state legislature for a publicly funded road and pier at Elizabethtown Point. Ogden agreed to concede defeat and promised to settle all debts and accept a final separation if his rival would drop the petition.[16] Playing for time, he convened his own town meeting a month later to "remove from the minds of the people in this Town, improper impressions in regard to his private transaction with Thomas Gibbons." When the colonel asked the assembled townsfolk if they intended to challenge his ferry service, he received a chorus of denials.[17] Ogden then rehired Dod to warn the public that Gibbons's steam engine patent rights would not stand up in court. Realizing that "Dod has sold out to A. O.," Gibbons published Ogden's promise to settle all claims with Gibbons and the Trumbulls. The struggle between the former partners thus continued, with no end in sight.[18]

Struggles in the West

As events in Elizabethtown revealed, steamboat monopolies were becoming increasingly unpopular with the public. In December 1814, while British troops entered the Gulf of Mexico, John Livingston cultivated public goodwill by joining forces with his rival Henry Miller Shreve to provide military supplies for the defense of New Orleans. However, Shreve continued to run steamboats on the Mississippi River even after word of the Treaty of Ghent reached the United States. Livingston immediately launched a lawsuit against Shreve in U.S. district court that demanded $5,000 and the forfeiture of his opponent's vessel.[19] Aware of Shreve's popularity, Edward Livingston allowed his rival to conduct business until the matter appeared before a judge.[20] Shreve hired Abner Duncan, a fellow northern migrant of Quaker heritage, to represent him in court. Duncan had been an aide-de-camp to Andrew Jackson during the War of 1812, and he was an acknowledged leader of the New Orleans bar. He argued in court that Shreve possessed a unique steam engine, which he had federally patented in 1809,[21] and that he could not be denied access to a "public highway" such as the Mississippi River. Moreover, Duncan said, the Mississippi River Steam Boat Navigation Company charged exorbitant rates to transport passengers and freight, and ultimately, Congress, not the states, controlled interstate trade.[22] For the defense, Governor Claiborne assembled a committee of leading citizens and steamboat captains to publicly testify that Fulton and Livingston had "provided inestimable benefits to the Mississippi River valley." Furthermore, he pointed out that the partners had "scrupulously maintained the standards of the monopoly."[23]

The committee's report, however, failed to impress the cantankerous federal district court judge Dominick A. Hall. A South Carolina native, Hall spoke fluent French, excelled in maritime law, and had experience as a former Louisiana state supreme court justice. He had proven his tenacity through a writ of habeas corpus issued for a prisoner confined by Andrew Jackson during the siege of New Orleans. Although he himself was briefly imprisoned by the enraged general, Hall quickly gained both his freedom and the respect of the New Orleans Creole community.[24] On May 20, Hall ruled that the New Orleans territorial legislature lacked the authority to grant a steamboat monopoly over the Mississippi River.[25]

Undaunted, the Livingstons filed a second suit in federal district court against Shreve. According to rumor, Edward Livingston had also secretly offered Shreve a full partnership if he would intentionally lose the suit, which would in turn send a powerful warning to other competitors.[26] Shreve apparently declined any such offer, and on April 17, 1817, Justice Hall ruled in *Heirs of Fulton and Livingston v. Henry M. Shreve* that since neither the plaintiffs nor the defendants were Louisiana residents, the court lacked jurisdiction over the case. Edward Livingston appealed to the U.S. Supreme Court but quickly realized the futility of such a move. Displaying characteristic Livingston pragmatism, he accepted defeat and sold the *Vesuvius* and *New Orleans* to cover his losses.[27]

After six years of competition and lawsuits, the Mississippi now bustled with new steamboats such as the *Alabama, Columbus, Constitution, Eagle, Franklin,* and *Governor Shelby.* Local planters tripled the size of their cotton exports and reinvested in new land and slaves.[28] Westerners cheered Shreve as a David who had triumphed

89

New Orleans in 1851. J. Bachman, "Bird's Eye View of New Orleans, 1851," Library of Congress, Prints and Photographs Division, Washington, DC

over a legal Goliath. At a public dinner in his honor, held in Louisville in May 1815, civic leaders praised the riverboat captain for his perseverance and skill. In a spirit of celebration, the participants toasted free trade and the glory of the nation, key topics in future deliberations over steamboat monopolies. Glasses were raised to Robert Fulton ("His name, dear to mankind, is encircled with an unfading halo"), the Ohio and Mississippi rivers ("The high seas of the western country, may they ever be free from patents, restrictive orders, and legislative degrees"), and Captain Shreve ("Who learnt us that the ocean is distant but an eight days journey"). Additional toasts were made to the state of Louisiana ("May she be alive to the policy afforded to the citizens of every part of the Union, equal privileges by granting exclusive monopoly to none") and the Kentucky state legislature ("May they be understood, that commerce, like water, finds its own level and that every community ought, of right, to enjoy the advantages, which can be aligned and upheld by the members of it"). Despite the defeat of the Fulton-Livingston monopoly in the West, the struggle for free navigation continued unabated in the East.[29]

Contracts and Petitions

Robert L. Livingston and Edward P. Livingston grimly received the news that their Mississippi monopoly had fallen. To make matters worse, neither man could sort out the tangle of agreements, contracts, property, loans, and debts left by Chancellor Livingston and Robert Fulton that had kept the New York monopoly afloat. Throughout the fall of 1815, Fulton's friend and former attorney Cadwallader D. Colden sought to create an alliance among those with a stake in the original Fulton-Livingston partnership. He negotiated with Robert L. Livingston and Edward P. Livingston, Albany iron merchants Isaiah and John Townsend, and New York attorneys Thomas Addis Emmet and Dominick Lynch to manage Fulton's steamboats. Harriet Fulton, the inventor's widow and the executrix of his estate, soon joined the cartel, together with her brother-in-law, William Cutting, and her new husband, Charles A. Dale. In April 1817, Colden drew up an agreement on behalf of the stakeholders to create the North River Steam Boat Company and applied to the New York legislature for a grant of incorporation.[30]

From the beginning, the North River Company was an unwieldy alliance among strong-willed individuals. Dale was an English rake whose love for expensive clothes and horse racing was matched only by his short temper. The Townsend brothers were natives of Orange County, New York, who had migrated to Albany in 1799 to become successful iron merchants, bankers, and real estate brokers. Dominick Lynch came from a wealthy Irish Catholic family in Rome, New York. Educated at Georgetown, Lynch became a successful merchant, lived in an upscale home in Greenwich Village, and enjoyed a reputation as "the most fashionable man in New York." Lynch became a patron of the arts and sponsored the first Italian opera company to perform in the Empire State. Although a gregarious individual, Lynch bore little love for the New York court system. In 1805, James Kent had ordered Lynch's father, Dominick Lynch Sr., to pay a former business rival $25,000 in a sensational lawsuit that financially and socially devastated the Lynch family.[31]

91

For the next decade, the Townsends and Lynch struggled to maintain and defend the North River Company, attract customers, pay employees, and placate the headstrong Livingstons, while simultaneously turning a profit.[32] Ironically, both Edward P. Livingston's attempts to dictate company policy and Robert R. Livingston's lack of interest in the monopoly hurt the North River Company. At one point, Lynch complained, "They are obstinate & determined that the affairs of so large a company should be managed in the loose & gentlemanly easy manner."[33] Troubles began in spring 1816, when Edward P. Livingston rallied disgruntled Albany stockholders and ship captains to seize control of the company. One investor cautioned, "A Civil War will break out soon, unless a strong mediation is imposed."[34]

Edward was not the only member of the Livingston family who sought to undercut the North River Company's interests. In early 1817, John R. Livingston, in an attempt to maintain control over steamboat traffic in New York Harbor, subcontracted monopoly licenses to businessmen eager to operate in such a lucrative franchise. Ironically, one such licensee was no lesser light than Daniel D. Tompkins, then the vice president of the United States. The son of working-class farmers from Scarsdale, New York, Tompkins had studied law under Federalists James Kent and Peter Jay Munro but emerged nevertheless as one of the state's most prominent Republicans. Tompkins was a charismatic figure who had served as a New York Supreme Court justice, and as governor he had backed Jefferson's embargo policies. He was eager to become involved in the steamboat trade to provide funds for an upcoming run for the presidency against rival DeWitt Clinton. Livingston, pleased to have such a powerful political ally, quickly granted Tompkins the right to ferry passengers from Manhattan to Staten Island. Adam and Noah Brown, former privateers turned New York City merchants, received similar rights to operate steamboats from the city to ports along the New Jersey coast.[35]

To further solidify their newly established corporate interests, the Livingstons and Ogden negotiated with Harriet Livingston Fulton and William Cutting to share all of Fulton's patents and monopoly rights.[36] In February 1816, Ogden petitioned Congress on behalf of Harriet Fulton and her children for a liberal extension of her husband's steam engine patents. The petition eulogized the inventor and asked, "Ought not the widow and offspring of a man who has planned the means of protecting his country against his enemies be placed above the pressure of embarrassment and the humiliation of dependence?"[37] The Senate commissioned a subcommittee headed by New York senator Rufus King, a firm supporter of the Fulton-Livingston monopoly, to investigate the matter.[38]

The public spectacle of Fulton's widow and children might compel Congress to reaffirm and thus give new life to his long-dormant patent claims. Alarmed by this possibility, Gibbons hired Fernando Fairfax to condemn the petition. Gibbons mused, "Because a man dies insolvent is his widow and family to apply to Government to tax the citizens of America to pay their debts?"[39] As a successful attorney and member of one of Virginia's oldest and wealthiest families, Fairfax sympathized with Gibbons's position. On March 11, he delivered to Congress *A Memorial . . . against the Extension of Patents Granted to Robert Fulton,* in which he depicted Fulton as the usurper of John Fitch's patent claims.[40] Gibbons complained to Congressman John Randolph that Livingston and Ogden "have no merit; they have no claim to useful invention. They are mere locusts and bloodsuckers in this part of the union."[41] Disgusted and alarmed, Gibbons grumbled to Robert G. Harper about several newspapers that were sympathetic to the Fulton cause. Throughout his correspondence, he staunchly denied any ulterior motives and highlighted the need to protect his own family's financial security.[42]

Fragmentation of the Gibbons Family

While the Livingstons and Townsend fought over the future of the North River Company, U.S. Supreme Court justice Brockholst Livingston testified to Congress that Robert Fulton had died heavily in debt. To aid his surviving family, Congress agreed in April 1816 to extend Fulton's patent rights.[43] Gibbons responded badly to the news. When Ann Trumbull confronted her father over inheritance claims, Gibbons snapped, "No living person shall interrogate me about my last will and testament [as] it is the last comfort of a dying man to give his labours the fruits of his industry to those he likes best at the time of his death." Still, his daughter pushed the matter, and in response, Gibbons swore, "Neither she nor Trumbull should have under my Will any part of my Estate."[44]

Furious at this meddling, Gibbons condemned the Trumbulls as "monsters more unnatural they than the Beasts of the fields" and his daughter in particular as "an enemy to the children William and Tom she bore & bred."[45] Ogden joined the fray by having Gibbons arrested on fraud charges over a defunct Bank of Manhattan note the Georgian had endorsed to the colonel several years earlier.

93

Local officials arrested Gibbons, on board the *Sea Horse,* during a return trip from Manhattan. This highly public spectacle on Ogden's own vessel deeply cut Gibbons's pride. He informed Ogden, "To arrest me, and hold me to bail, on the fancied existence of a note, for a paltry sum of $2,000 is conduct unwarrantable in a Gentleman of the Law."[46] Consumed with fury, Gibbons resorted to spying. In July 1816, he wrote to Rev. John McDowell, a Princeton theology professor and Presbyterian minister who had served the Elizabethtown community for over a decade. Gibbons accused Ogden and Trumbull of meeting on the Sabbath to pursue legal strategies. "We ought never to have been connected," wrote Gibbons in reference to Trumbull. "I strove all my power against it. In this life I have never had a curse stick so close to me."[47]

Gibbons's comment proved prophetic, for in late July 1816, Trumbull convinced his mother-in-law to visit Elizabethtown to defend her own interests. But before Ann Gibbons could even unpack her luggage, her enraged husband forced her from the house. She sought sanctuary with the Trumbulls and legal advice from Ogden, and she hired attorney Richard Stockton to initiate divorce proceedings. Stockton was a former Federalist congressman who, like Ogden, had been voted out of office in the wake of the War of 1812 and retreated to a private practice. He had previously been a business partner of John Fitch, but he bore Aaron Ogden and the Livingston family no lingering grudges. Stockton agreed to take Ann Gibbons's case but reassured her estranged husband by promising that he would investigate the matter with "as much delicacy as the just will permit."[48] As legal separations were notoriously rare at the time and required state legislative permission, both Ogden and Stockton realized that any divorce procedure would publicly humiliate Gibbons.

Gibbons now battled on two fronts. Desperate to strike back at Ogden, he turned for advice to New York state senator William A. Duer, who still publicly opposed the monopoly. Duer advised Gibbons to challenge Ogden's monopoly rights in state and federal court rather than risk another round with the New York legislature.[49] Not content merely to sue Ogden in court, Gibbons decided to provoke a physical confrontation with his antagonist. To risk such a confrontation was no easy matter. In the politically turbulent decades of the 1780s and 1790s, duels had served to resolve public disputes, establish reputations, and enforce a measure of discipline among leading citizens in an era before organized party politics. Dueling had declined in the North, however, following the death of former treasury secretary Alexander Hamilton at the hand of U.S. vice president Aaron Burr at Weehawken, New Jersey, in 1804. Northern ministers increasingly condemned dueling as outdated and barbaric, and New York and New Jersey officials began to enforce state antidueling laws. No one understood the dangers of dueling better than Thomas Gibbons. His reputation as a duelist had helped end his political career in Georgia. Yet Ogden had not merely threatened Gibbons's business interests but had publicly challenged his reputation as a gentleman, husband, and father. Gibbons felt that only a similarly public act, such as a duel, could restore his honor. On July 16, 1816, Gibbons approached Ogden's house, armed with a horsewhip. The colonel was not at home, so Gibbons tacked a printed handbill to his front door. The document accused Ogden of plotting on the Sabbath "like Nicanor upon Judas," it labeled the colonel "RASCALLY," and it challenged him to a duel for his interference in Gibbons's family affairs.[50] The fact that Gibbons took the time to print a handbill and waited nearly six weeks before delivering it suggests that he was staging a deliberate spectacle to tarnish Ogden's reputation. For his part, Ogden did not rise to the occasion: instead, he delivered a written apology and filed trespass charges against Gibbons in state court.[51]

Gibbons escaped arrest by taking an impromptu vacation to Saratoga Springs, New York. The serenity of the famous spa town failed to soothe him. He continued on to Boston and channeled his anger into a pamphlet calculated to destroy the reputation of his perceived enemies. The treatise condemned John Trumbull for seducing "the only daughter of the defendant within his walls" and Ann Gibbons Trumbull and Ann Gibbons for supporting Trumbull. It concluded: "Trumbull ought to be hanged for the injustice he has done his children. Amen."[52] Gibbons threatened to distribute fifty copies of the document to family and friends unless his wife promised to drop her divorce suit.[53] Ann Gibbons relented, but Trumbull obtained several of the pamphlets and promptly sued Gibbons for libel in the New York Court of Chancery.[54]

On June 1, 1817, both Ogden and Trumbull separately called on Gibbons and begged him to visit his daughter. Momentarily putting aside his anger, Gibbons found Ann Trumbull dying from a miscarriage. Shortly before her death, Gibbons promised that he would provide for her children.[55] True to his word, in September 1817, he sought custody of William and Thomas Trumbull from the county offices of the New Jersey Orphan's Court. When Trumbull objected, Gibbons claimed he was merely fulfilling Ann Trumbull's dying wishes. "Taking a death bed figure to your aid, you and Aaron Ogden made me make a covenant with death," bellowed Gibbons. "You are now endeavoring to make me disannul that covenant made at the gates of Death; it shall not be so."[56]

Despondent over the deterioration of his family and public attacks on his status as a father and husband, Gibbons focused his rage on Ogden. In late July, former vice president Aaron Burr advised him to challenge Ogden's monopoly rights in court.[57] Not wanting to tie up his steamboats indefinitely in future legislation, Gibbons subcontracted rights from Daniel D. Tompkins and from Adam and Noah Brown to transfer New York passengers from their boats on Staten Island to his vessels before proceeding to New Jersey ports.[58] Gibbons then constructed the Rising Sun Landing near Elizabethtown and purchased a steamboat named the *Stoudinger,* also known as the *Mouse of the Mountain* or more commonly the *Mouse.* More important, he hired a young Cornelius Vanderbilt to captain his vessel. Although already a successful ship captain and merchant, Vanderbilt took the job to learn about steam technology. Vanderbilt and Gibbons developed an effective partnership. Gibbons allowed the captain wide latitude to improve the *Mouse* and made the ferry service more cost effective, and the young ship captain increased the partners' profits substantially. In later years, "Commodore" Vanderbilt would credit his early experience with steamboats as being instrumental in his rise as one of the most successful business magnates of the nineteenth century.[59]

Ogden tried on several occasions to disrupt Gibbons's operations. In October 1817, one of Ogden's captains blocked Gibbons's steamboat at the mouth of the Elizabethtown Creek with a sailboat, for the purpose of "plaguing" the southerner.[60] Isaac Woodruff, an old military colleague of Ogden, advised Gibbons to settle his worldly affairs and meet him on the bluffs of Weehawken, site of the famous Burr-Hamilton duel thirteen years earlier. As Woodruff saw matters, Ogden's "Character, Usefulness in the World, as far outweighs that of yours as a Mill Stone would outweigh a speck of Chaff." He taunted Gibbons to practice with pistols for the duel. Although no record of a duel survives, the fact that both men lived on indicates that some sort of accommodation was reached either on or off the battlefield.[61]

Pamphlets and Public Opinion

While new conflicts erupted between Gibbons and Ogden, Dominick Lynch strove to unite the North River Company.[62] In the fall of 1817, the New York legislature placed a tax on steamboat passengers to help fund the nascent Erie

Canal.[63] Justice Brockholst Livingston considered the law unconstitutional and in any case inapplicable to a private corporation such as the North River Company. When Lynch asked for legal advice, Livingston maintained that in "Washington last winter, they [the Supreme Court justices] had talked it over, and they quite vindicated the idea of the distinction attempted to be drawn by our opponents, between the contract and the remedies." However, the Supreme Court would allow North River Company lawsuits to proceed in any state or federal court the company desired.[64]

In October 1817, John L. Sullivan petitioned the New York legislature to deny an incorporation grant to the North River Company. William Thornton complimented the inventor for his attack against Fulton's "grand inquisition" and asked Sullivan to contribute to a forthcoming pamphlet against the monopoly. The Patent Office chief also criticized Ogden for "selling out to a monopoly he could have beaten in court."[65] To help defend the North River Company, Cadwallader D. Colden authored a biography of his former employer titled *The Life of Robert Fulton*. The New York Society for the Promotion of Manufactures commissioned the work, and the North River Company printed it. The treatise shamelessly described Fulton as a "natural gentleman" and a "zealous, kind, generous, affectionate, and liberal" public benefactor whose "calm constancy, his industry, and that indefatigable patience and perseverance" allowed him to overcome obstacles.[66]

In November 1817, William A. Duer authored *A Letter Addressed to Cadwallader D. Colden, Esq.,* which combined the claims of John Fitch, James Rumsey, and the Albany Steam Boat Company to attack the steamboat monopoly.[67] True to form, Colden counterattacked with *A Vindication by Cadwallader D. Colden,* which further applauded Fulton's scientific talents. Duer shot back with *A Reply to Mr. Colden's Vindication of the Steam-Boat Monopoly.*[68] An anonymously published work labeled *An Examination of Cadwallader D. Colden's Book* also appeared, to "correct some erroneous impressions, which seem to have gone abroad, with regard to the merits of Mr. Fulton."[69] Not to give his opponents the last word, Colden published *A Review of the Letter, Addressed by William Alexander Duer to Cadwallader D. Colden,* in which he defended "the monopoly as a reward for genius."[70] Lynch urged the Townsends to circulate Colden's *Vindication* among new assembly members "who may come to the Legislature, ignorant of the merits of the question, and perhaps with strong prejudices against 'monopolies.'" He further maintained, "It is very popular, to come out as the champion of public rights."[71] These efforts paid off, for in April 1818, the New York state legislature voted unanimously to reincorporate the North River Steam Boat Company.[72]

Gibbons v. Trumbull

While the incorporation debate raged in New York, Gibbons ordered his attorneys, E. Van Ragsdale and Theodore Frelinghuysen, to investigate possible lawsuits against Ogden and Trumbull.[73] Ogden, however, had other problems. Crippling steamboat expenses and business lost to Gibbons forced him to declare bankruptcy and surrender the *Sea Horse* to the Elizabethtown Bank in spring 1818. The bank trustees allowed the former governor to run his boat to pay off debts. Publicly humiliated, Ogden sought revenge in his pending trespass case against Gibbons.[74]

Ogden had good reason to believe that he would receive a favorable ruling. His case was scheduled to appear before New York State Supreme Court justice Ambrose Spencer. The son of a working-class Connecticut ironworker, Spencer attended Yale and Harvard before apprenticing with leading Connecticut attorney Joseph Canfield. Marriage to Canfield's daughter Laura confirmed Spencer's status as a gentleman, which he parlayed into positions as New York assemblyman, senator, attorney general, and member of the Council of Revision, which exercised a veto over state legislation. In 1804, Spencer joined the New York Supreme Court and became known as "the Mansfield of America" for delivering pragmatic opinions similar to those of the legendary eighteenth-century British jurist. After the death of his wife in 1807, Spencer married twice more, both times to sisters of New York governor DeWitt Clinton. In 1811, Spencer had cited personal ties to James Van Ingen's Albany syndicate in declining to rule in *Livingston v. Van Ingen.* Afterward, he invested readily in the North River Steam Boat Company and remained on good social terms with the Livingston family.[75]

In late May, the case of *Gibbons v. Trumbull* appeared before Spencer. In a spacious courtroom thronged with spectators including a "great number of respectable ladies," David B. Ogden, Trumbull's attorney, claimed, "The case was without precedent in the annals of our jurisprudence." If Gibbons's pamphlet were true, then Trumbull had to have been a savage who "deserved the execration of every person in a civilized society."[76] Speaking for Gibbons, Thomas Addis Emmet conceded, "It cannot be concealed, and it will not be denied, that the defendant did wrong" in writing the pamphlet. Yet he stressed that Gibbons was an elderly gentleman who had merely succumbed to righteous anger in lashing out at his opponents.[77] The prosecution countered that Gibbons had deliberately written the pamphlet over a period of weeks, coldly manipulated his wife, and tarnished the honor of his own family.[78] Arguing that "there never was a publication more immoral, indecent, and we may almost say blasphemous, than this," Ogden asked the jury for a harsh verdict that would hurt even a wealthy man like Gibbons. According to a court reporter, Justice Spencer concurred, almost verbatim, that the pamphlet was "a production fraught with so much indecency, immorality, and he might almost add, of blasphemy."[79]

After an hour of deliberation, the jury ruled in Trumbull's favor and demanded that Gibbons pay $15,000 in damages.[80] The *New York Evening Post* reported that the case had "excited an uncommon share of public interest, and that the trial was numerously attended." Although the $15,000 verdict was "the largest in this country," it was also "far beneath public expectation, and one that will not be sensibly felt by the defendant."[81] The *Dedham Gazette* considered the case a warning against further duels. It stated, "High minded and honorable gentlemen may here learn how to resist the bloody combat—how to sustain a character worth a thousand honors of murdering a fellow man. Instead of appealing to the sword, appeal to the laws of the land." Aware of the public opinion now arrayed against him, Gibbons glowered and paid the damages.[82]

Gibbons Challenges Ogden

Having lost to Trumbull, Gibbons again turned his attention to Ogden.[83] In 1818, he ordered Vanderbilt to take the *Bellona* on repeated trips directly to New York City. Gibbons took special delight in the destruction of Ogden's steamboat business and gloated, "I shall continue to run, let the affrighted Colonel slander as he may."[84] The Georgian anticipated that Ogden would seek an injunction from the New York Court of Chancery. Such a response would allow Gibbons to quickly secure appeals to the U.S. circuit court and ultimately the Supreme Court.[85] Daniel D. Tompkins tried to protect his own interests by foiling Gibbons's plans before they were put into action. The vice president urged William Gibbons, Thomas Gibbons's son, to join the New York monopoly and thus bring "all under the lawful banner where it can be done with honor and propriety."[86]

On October 20, 1818, Ogden took Gibbons's bait and filed a motion in the New York Court of Chancery. Chancellor James Kent issued an injunction against Gibbons the next day.[87] To keep his options open, Gibbons secretly dispatched his

99

son to discuss a compromise with Ogden. He remained worried that the agreement with Tompkins only applied to Staten Island routes and not service from Elizabethtown to New York City.[88] The southerner also sought an alliance with John L. Sullivan, stating, "I am willing to restrain that monopoly within due bounds, and will unite in any plan which will effect this purpose."[89] Sullivan responded, "I have been led to believe that while R. [Robert L.] Livingston is in the [state] Senate and until public opinion is more changed, that although I should get a bill through the House, it would stop there."[90] Yet in March 1819, Sullivan nevertheless petitioned the New York state legislature to repeal the steamboat monopoly. As expected, Robert L. Livingston used his legislative allies to defeat Sullivan's memorial.[91]

Gibbons also sought an attorney qualified to argue his case in federal court: he informed attorney William Price, "I want to gallop my case thro the Courts of Chancery & Errors, and I don't care much what their decisions are."[92] Gibbons also told John W. Patterson that he considered "the Court of Chancery and Court of Errors as only step ladders to the Supreme Court of the U. States."[93] However, Price, Patterson, and Martin Van Buren, who was about to be deposed as New York attorney general, declined to take the case.[94] Still hoping to avoid an extended legal battle, John R. Livingston proposed a secret agreement with Gibbons in early April. According to that proposal, Gibbons would receive the right to run the *Bellona* from Staten Island to Elizabethtown, and in return, he would share dock facilities with North River boats, oppose the New York steamboat tax, pay all injunction costs, and keep their arrangement a secret.[95] When Gibbons later demanded a full partnership, Livingston threatened to impose his own injunctions. Gibbons retorted that the state of New York did not control New Jersey waters. He also brandished his agreement with Tompkins and the Brown brothers to run ferries across New York Harbor. Nonetheless, both men still publicly professed a willingness to negotiate on favorable terms.[96]

In May 1819, John R. Livingston made good on his earlier threats. He filed for an injunction in the New York Court of Chancery against Gibbons and, for good measure, Ogden as well. On May 3, Kent rejected an injunction for Ogden and barred Gibbons from "navigating with any boat or vessel propelled by Steam or fire the waters in this Bay of New York or in the Hudson River between Staten Island and Powles Hook." In doing so, however, Kent rejected New York's traditional water rights claims to all of New York Harbor up to the New Jersey shore. Equally important, Kent handed down a decision that would eventually pave the way to bring *Gibbons v. Ogden* before the U.S. Supreme Court.[97]

John R. Livingston's attempts to intimidate Thomas Gibbons into accepting a partnership with the North River Company revealed how desperate the monopolists had become by 1819. In just six short years, popular hostility in the west, combined with the sheer size of the Mississippi River, made enforcement of the Louisiana monopoly virtually impossible. Edward Livingston's defeats to Henry Miller Shreve in federal court thus merely represented the final blows to Robert Fulton's once-grandiose vision of a steamboat empire that stretched from the Great Lakes to the Gulf of Mexico. The heirs of Robert R. Livingston and Robert Fulton retreated to a defense of their New York monopoly. The stockholders of the North River Company gambled that the influence of the Livingston name, support from the New York legislature and state courts, and Fulton's recently renewed patent rights would keep their interests afloat.

Yet opposition to the monopoly continued to grow, primarily from Thomas Gibbons. The former planter was no doubt motivated by the profits that unrestricted navigation of New York Harbor would surely bring to his steamboat business. He also took on the monopoly to destroy the business interests and personal reputation of his chief rival, Aaron Ogden. Over the preceding decade, Ogden had successfully used alliances with Gibbons's in-laws to embarrass the irascible Georgian. Gibbons retaliated by using his vast wealth to hire lawyers who would contest Ogden's steamboat monopoly rights, first in state court and later in federal court. Neither realized that, over time, their personal vendetta would evolve into a monumental constitutional debate over interstate commerce.

The Road to the U.S. Supreme Court

The Growing Importance of Steam Travel

CHANCELLOR KENT'S INJUNCTION provided Ogden with a sorely needed victory. But the spread of steamboats across the United States made the future of the New York monopoly ever more precarious. The steamboat *Henrietta* now plied the Cape Fear River between Fayetteville and Wilmington, North Carolina. Promoters launched the five-hundred-ton *Western Enquirer*, from Noah Brown's Pittsburgh shipyard, to navigate the Ohio and Mississippi rivers. The steamboat *Walk on the Water* offered service on the Great Lakes from Buffalo to Detroit. And the steamboat *Hartford*, complete with a "revolving engine," ferried passengers from New Haven to Boston. Newspaper articles and petitions to the New York legislature repeatedly called for the repeal of the steamboat monopoly.[1]

Yet despite the need for unity, monopoly supporters remained bitterly divided. Edward P. Livingston demanded obedience from the employees and shareholders of the North River Steam Boat Company in much the same way his father-in-law had expected deference from his landed tenants thirty years earlier. When Livingston sued for his share of corporate profits, Chancellor Kent placed the North River Company in receivership and appointed New York merchant

Charles Rhind as manager. Rhind's meticulous record keeping, aggressive public relations work, and strict handling of employee disputes bought time for the beleaguered corporation. In the long run, however, his efforts failed to quell public perceptions that the New York monopoly was a remnant of aristocratic privilege and a barrier to free trade.

Across New York Harbor, John R. Livingston and Aaron Ogden fared little better in their efforts to thwart Thomas Gibbons. Livingston and Ogden secured several injunctions against Gibbons in the hopes of bringing their rival to the bargaining table. Ogden also caught Gibbons off balance with a trespassing suit in the New Jersey Court of Common Pleas. As it turned out, both state and federal judges proved reluctant to rule on the increasingly volatile steamboat issue and urged Gibbons and Ogden to settle their differences privately. But such tactics only furthered Gibbons's desire to pursue his case to Washington, DC, where a final confrontation before the U.S. Supreme Court would finally decide the fate of the New York steamboat monopoly.[2]

The North River Steam Boat Company faced its first major challenge in spring 1819 when Edward P. Livingston tried to forge an alliance with the North River steamboat captains. He ordered the captains to deposit their fares in his private bank accounts. Those skippers who complied would receive a large pay raise; those who refused would lose their jobs. "This is certainly a novel mode of doing business—In one hand a rod, in the other a bribe," Dominick Lynch wryly noted.[3] Livingston also colluded with A. N. Hoffman, a company clerk, to sell dry goods transported on company vessels and pocket the profits. In retaliation, Lynch secured loyalty oaths from the boat captains, fired Hoffman, and spearheaded a corporate resolution to prevent further malfeasance.[4] In early June, Edward P. Livingston reminded Lynch of his inheritance claims to one-fourth of the North River Company. He also cryptically warned that should any stockholders question these claims, "I rely on your candor to furnish me with their Lieutenants, or those of their counsel as frankly as I have done" so that "I may be enabled to decide on the proper course to be pursued."[5]

Struggles for Control

While Dominick Lynch struggled to strengthen the New York monopoly, Thomas Gibbons worked to tear it down. Bound by the terms of his chancery court injunction, Gibbons signed a contract with Daniel D. Tompkins in May

1819 that was designed to circumvent the law. Tompkins's steamboat *Nautilus* would rendezvous with Gibbons's *Bellona* at Great Kills Harbor on Staten Island and exchange passengers and cargo.[6] Although the partners were to split the profits equally, the route from Elizabethtown to Staten Island was far more costly. Gibbons therefore ordered Cornelius Vanderbilt to run the *Bellona* from New Jersey to New York City whenever feasible.[7] Ogden and John R. Livingston quickly learned of Gibbons's plan and demanded that the New York sheriff arrest Gibbons and Vanderbilt for violation of the monopoly. Although Gibbons remained safely out of reach in New Jersey, Vanderbilt kept up a dangerous game of hide-and-seek with New York officials for eight weeks. Antimonopoly sentiment inspired sympathy for Vanderbilt among New Yorkers and New Jerseyites alike and allowed him to operate with relative impunity.[8]

Then, to everyone's surprise, Vanderbilt quietly surrendered to authorities on the New York waterfront on the fourth of June. Escorted under heavy guard to Albany, he appeared before Chancellor Kent to answer contempt charges. Vanderbilt quickly revealed that the entire affair was a public spectacle staged to embarrass Kent and the New York monopolists. Attorneys Abraham Van Vechten and William Henry quickly stepped forward to represent Vanderbilt, and Van Vechten argued that Kent's injunction was too vague to detain his client. Furthermore, it barred only Gibbons and his employees from journeys between Staten Island and Powles Hook: the document made no mention of Manhattan, where Vanderbilt had been captured. For good measure, Vanderbilt produced a signed contract from Daniel D. Tompkins. The document allowed Vanderbilt use of the *Bellona* to travel from Staten Island to New York City every Sunday for the month of June, including the date of the defendant's capture.[9]

Van Vechten's arguments hinged on a strict interpretation of one of Kent's own judicial decrees and the enforceability of contract rights—a legal principle the chancellor had staunchly defended many times throughout his career, most notably in *Livingston v. Van Ingen*. Kent was caught in an embarrassing situation. Seeking to dispose of the matter quickly, he ruled that broadly worded injunctions applied to broadly based actions. New York City obviously formed part of New York Harbor and thus fell under the jurisdiction of the steamboat monopoly. Kent then conceded, "The boat *Bellona*, was, on the day mentioned, the hired boat of D. D. Tompkins, and not in the employment of Gibbons." Therefore, "no fraud or collusion, on purpose to evade the injunction, was averred or suggested." Vanderbilt gained his freedom and revealed the staged nature of the event by publicly forwarding his legal bills to his collaborator, Daniel D. Tompkins.[10]

Promoting the North River Company

No sooner had Kent cleared his desk of *In re Vanderbilt* than he received a thirty-two-page complaint from Edward P. Livingston against the North River Company shareholders for violation of his monopoly rights. The chancellor issued temporary injunctions that barred Captains Samuel WisWall, Arthur Roorbach, and Andrew Bartholomew from operating steamboats in New York.[11] Lynch pessimistically predicted to the North River Company investors, "This measure of Mr. Livingston's will throw the concerns of the company into great confusion, and I fear may stop the boats, as no means are left to meet the current expenses." To ward off disaster, Lynch hired attorneys Chase Graham and William Henry to overturn the injunction, and he negotiated indirectly through Thomas Addis Emmet to buy off Livingston. Robert L. Livingston avoided the matter by refusing to appear in court to defend the monopoly, rendering a pleading *pro confesso* (as confessed) that obligated him to abide by the findings of the court and to obey its decision.[12]

Chancellor Kent handed down a decision in the case of *Livingston v. Cutting* in early August 1819. Kent, not surprisingly, upheld the April 1817 contract between the Livingstons and the Dales as the corporate charter of the North River Company. All subsequent corporate resolutions were thus invalid, as they had not been passed by unanimous consent of the partners under the terms of the original agreement. Kent appointed Charles Rhind to run the company until it conformed to its charter.[13] Rhind's talents were quickly put to the test. In late August 1819, John L. Sullivan announced to Gibbons his intentions to sue the New York monopolists for seizing Connecticut steamboats anchored in New York Harbor. Having outlined his legal strategy, Sullivan asked Gibbons for help with his legal fees.[14] Gibbons responded, "If your case agrees with mine I shall be glad to walk with you, but that each party pays his own expense; mine have been and will continue heavy but I am resolved to go on."[15]

Dominick Lynch learned of Sullivan's plans and consulted two allies, U.S. senator Rufus King and New York City mayor Cadwallader D. Colden, about his options. On their recommendations, Lynch asked Littleton Tazewell of Virginia and William Pinkney of Maryland to take the case should it go before the U.S. Supreme Court. Securing Pinkney's services would be a tremendous asset to the North River Company. As a former congressman, diplomat, minister to Great Britain and Russia, and attorney general to President James Madison, Pinkney was one of the most sought-after attorneys in the nation. Privately, Lynch reasoned that Edward P. Livingston would be willing to help pay for such able legal counsel to keep the company afloat. If not, then his stubbornness might serve as grounds to petition Chancellor Kent for an end to the injunction and receivership against the company.[16]

For the moment, Livingston and Lynch kept up the facade of corporate unity. Both men agreed on the need to protest the steamboat passenger tax law and formally reorganize the North River Company under a New York State incorporation grant. Corporate shareholders cheered when the New York Canal Commission agreed to help repeal the unpopular steamboat passenger tax.[17] An article published in the *New York Daily Advertiser* dismissed the tax as "unconstitutional" and claimed that it "excites public hostility and anger, operates harshly on steamboats which are now great vehicles for traveling in the U.S. The tax hurts and discourages steamboats nationally as well as individually." A tax repeal bill soon passed the state assembly. The North River Company won a bittersweet triumph when the state senate pressured the assembly into revising the bill so as to indefinitely suspend rather than repeal the tax.[18]

In March 1820, the North River Company scored another partial victory with an incorporation grant from the state legislature, which allowed company boats to carry passengers but placed restrictions on the amount of freight they could transport. Rhind immediately launched an aggressive advertising campaign through New York papers, highlighting the speed and safety of company boats. He also made certain that despite ice floes, North River boats were ready for business on the Hudson by mid-March 1820.[19] In addition, Rhind ordered that passenger fares be reduced from $7 to $6 each, and he put his boats at the disposal of the community in highly publicized goodwill gestures. In one incident, he ordered Captain Bunker to ferry passengers to a Methodist camp meeting on Long Island.[20]

Board members, such as Cadwallader D. Colden and Robert L. Livingston, reacted favorably to these recent successes. Edward P. Livingston, however, saw such victories as further proof of his diminishing control over the corporation. Robert L. Livingston reported that his brother-in-law had become "perfectly savage —and talks of taking a house at Albany next winter, with a view of destroying everything, saying he has made up his mind to lose the whole of his interest, rather than succumb." Robert pleaded with Edward, stating that although they could afford to lose the business, bankruptcy would leave Robert Fulton's children penniless.[21] When Edward refused to budge, David Lynch and the Townsends planned for the worst. They persuaded Colden to serve as company president and threatened to reveal inflammatory comments made by Edward P. Livingston about other state senators if he tampered further with the company.[22]

Attempts at Partition

In May 1820, Edward P. Livingston launched a second chancery court lawsuit against the North River Company.[23] After hearing the case, Justice Jonas Platt agreed to write the opinion of the court. As a native of western New York, Platt favored the economic development of the frontier, and he had strongly supported the Erie Canal as a state senator. However, Platt was a lifelong Federalist and a friend of James Kent who shared the chancellor's concerns that rampant democracy and frivolous lawsuits posed a threat to vested property rights. Beyond that, Platt's marriage to Helen Livingston, a cousin of Robert L. and Edward P. Livingston, gave him personal ties to the steamboat monopoly. Not surprisingly, Platt handed down a decision in June that upheld Chancellor Kent's earlier decisions and reaffirmed the legality of the New York monopoly. In particular, he argued that the federal Coasting Act of 1793 merely gave registered vessels an American identity. Moreover, New York's steamboat monopoly laws were not in conflict with federal statutes. In fact, as a state senator, Platt had voted to uphold the New York monopoly eight years earlier in the Van Ingen case. The judge recounted the skill with which Kent and his associates had dealt with the matter. "I have not the vanity to believe that I could add anything to their force or perspicuity," he concluded.[24]

Edward P. Livingston skillfully exploited differences between boat captains and stockholders. Given the restrictions of their incorporation charter, North River captains increased their passenger totals at the expense of transporting freight. In May 1820, they banded together and threatened to petition the state legislature unless the North River Company allowed them to take on more freight. The local postmaster also accused the North River Company captains of delivering letters from Manhattan to Albany without a federal contract, a crime that deprived both the North River Company and the U.S. government of revenue.

Lynch and the Townsends suspected Edward had masterminded the affair, especially when the state senator guaranteed the North River Company captains lifetime employment as long as they remained loyal to him. Lynch grumbled, "It is fortunate that the Chancellor on his deathbed did not insist on all the heirs of the Captains being employed & retained in services until Death."[25] As the company attorney, Lynch waded through Livingston's voluminous lawsuits. Given the limits of his own legal experience, he secured Thomas Addis Emmet to represent the company in chancery court. To save time and expense, Emmet suggested a bench trial rather than a prolonged appearance before a jury. Since such a move would allow Emmet to deploy his formidable oratorical skills against Livingston, the North River investors quickly agreed.[26]

Defending the North River Company in Chancery Court

Throughout summer and fall 1820, Rhind continued to cultivate public goodwill. He directed the company steamboats, *Connecticut* and *Chancellor Livingston,* to tow a U.S. battleship from Albany to the Brooklyn Navy Yard. Crowds flocked to watch the maneuver, and a strategically placed newspaper article hinted at the advantages that steam power could bring in wartime.[27] The next day, New York papers reported that the North River Company's newly constructed luxury boat, the *Robert Fulton,* had navigated the Gulf of Mexico to arrive safely in New Orleans. Rhind printed accolades and testimonials from passengers to advertise the achievement. The *New York Daily Advertiser* remarked that the opening of such a steamboat route "does honor to the citizens of New-York, and from which the citizens of that place, as well as those of Charleston, Havana, and New-Orleans may anticipate the most beneficial results." The article concluded with praise for "the projector of the plan," expressing trust that "he will meet the reward due his enterprise."[28]

In mid-June, Livingston's case against the North River Company reached the New York Court of Chancery. At trial, Livingston's lawyer, William Slosson, struggled to persuade Chancellor Kent of the importance of his client's suit by reading, in their entirety, the morass of suits against the North River Company. In stark contrast to Slosson's zeal, his associate counsel, John Wells, pulled out a pocket watch and indulged in a short nap. A furious Kent adjourned the court for the day. The next morning, the chancellor contemptuously dismissed Livingston's case as frivolous: Edward P. Livingston could hardly bring a lawsuit against a company in which he was himself a stockholder. When Wells claimed that Livingston did not consider himself a stockholder, Chancellor Kent angrily retorted, "If he was so troublesome a man, they [the stockholders] must try to get rid of him."[29]

Emmet seized upon the opportunity presented by Wells to highlight Livingston's lack of leadership in fighting the constant lawsuits leveled against the North River Company. He suggested that since Livingston could not be counted on to act rationally, he should sever ties to the company. Livingston's lawyers expressed shock at the suggestion. Kent, however, warmed to the idea and dismissed the case with a warning to both parties not to return to court unless all hopes at compromise were lost. Slosson and Wells reluctantly offered to discuss the proposal with their client.[30] True to form, Edward P. Livingston rejected all attempts at mediation. As both sides prepared once again for a lengthy court battle, Lynch thwarted an attempt by the North River captains to charge passengers separately, without company approval, for transporting luggage.[31] He railed at the "forwardness & impertinent interference of our Captains with our concerns, as appear by their several advertisements."[32]

Hoping to regain the public trust, Rhind suggested a plan to raise money among the stockholders to help dredge the Hudson River. "All this would amount to a trifle, as the channel could well be cleared in a fortnight," argued Rhind. "And the Company would gain popularity by offering the use of a steamboat— and *entre nous*."[33] Perhaps as an added measure of revenge, Rhind placed Arthur Roorbach in charge of the operation. Known derisively by his coworkers as "the Little Captain," Roorbach had a track record of drunkenness, gambling, and insubordination. When Roorbach snarled that "he would be d__d if he would" clear the channel, Rhind calmly threatened to "find a Captain who would cheerfully do it." Roorbach later apologized, but he received a tongue-lashing from Rhind on the importance of discipline. Rhind privately revealed to John Townsend his growing weariness with the North River Company's problems.[34]

In the meantime, Emmet proceeded to defend the company in chancery court. After he learned of Emmet's skillful defense, Lynch expressed regret at not having opted for an open trial: after all, the Irish attorney's defense left "not a peg to hang a doubt on." Lynch's exuberance, however, quickly turned to despair when Livingston's counsel refused to reply to the suit.[35] "Slosson and Wells are playing the fool with us, we have to take decided steps or they will let the cause be dormant," claimed Lynch. When Livingston's lawyers finally responded to Emmet's argument, Lynch predicted that Chancellor Kent would castigate Livingston and

109

make him pay court costs. "In justice he can do no less," reasoned Lynch. "We have been dragged into a vexatious, costly, and protracted suit to gratify the bad passions of a man, who I think will receive a salutary lesson by making his pocket suffer for the pleasure he has had on disturbing the peace and harmony of others."[36]

Lynch understood the importance of the case. As he remarked to John Townsend, "The question now to be settled by this suit is the keystone of our property in the N.R.S.B. Co. If a decision should be given against us, I would not give five dollars for the whole establishment—witness Mississippi."[37] Lynch also made plans to buy out Edward P. Livingston's interest in the company for between $80,000 and $100,000 should they defeat him in court. Chastising the Townsends for not taking the lawsuit seriously, Lynch observed, "Although we are associated with those who would repose quietly on the banks of the Hudson, until roused by the fire and smoke of the fifty opposition boats which would spring up like mushrooms, it behooves us to devote some attention to the suit."[38]

While Lynch schemed, John R. Livingston and Ogden persuaded Chancellor Kent to issue yet another injunction, this one against Gibbons's new steamboat, the *Olive Branch,* which continued to exchange passengers with Tompkins's *Nautilus* on the run between Elizabethtown and New York City.[39] Kent denied Livingston's motion on the grounds that his 1819 injunction against Gibbons remained in effect.[40] In early September 1820, the chancellor handed down a second decision in the ongoing feud between Edward P. Livingston and the North River Company. He rejected the company's petition for a partition of Edward's interest and cited the authority of the Livingstons' 1817 agreement with the heirs of Robert Fulton. Kent described the Livingstons, shareholders, and employees of the North River Company as "tenants in common," and he gave the interested parties the option either to reach a settlement out of court or to continue to operate under court guidance. Kent also upheld the terms of Chancellor Livingston's will, which granted the steamboat captains of the North River Company lifetime employment.[41]

Lynch and the other North River Company stockholders greeted the chancellor's decree with disgust. Emmet and Colden dismissed the decision as unsound, and they advised their clients to pursue a private settlement with Edward P. Livingston. In the meantime, the North River Company continued its public relations work. In September, Rhind arranged for the company to ferry West Point cadets home from a march. He pointed out to John Townsend the political clout of West Point alumni and the good publicity to be gained from the endeavor. The North River Company also continued to offer extravagant nighttime cruises for wealthy New Yorkers, and it provided cheap fares to passengers on their way to New Haven for commencements at Yale University.[42] In January 1821, Lynch approached Edward P. Livingston with an ultimatum: he could either abide by company regulations or face a petition to Chancellor Kent for a formal partition. As an additional incentive, Robert L. Livingston and the North River shareholders set aside $25,000 to "get rid" of their opponent.[43] To keep the company financially afloat, Lynch suggested a public sale of North River Company stock, perhaps even "attracting influential subscribers to create a confidence in the stock."[44]

As Lynch wrangled with Livingston, state senator Gulian Verplanck seized on popular sentiment to condemn the monopoly. Verplanck was a former Federalist who defected to the Republicans only to become an outspoken critic of New York governor DeWitt Clinton. Verplanck passionately believed in democratic rule, and he lashed out at the steamboat monopoly as "being not only unusual and violent, but also of an arbitrary and unconstitutional aspect." In addition, Verplanck warned, "Although the decisions of our state courts furnish very high authority for the rights of the grantees, yet the principle is still unsettled by the supreme tribunal of the last resort."[45] Repeal of the Fulton-Livingston monopoly would not only free up statewide commerce but also cause the numerous suits against the Fulton-Livingston syndicate to disappear.[46] Lynch warned the stockholders against such a move, which he said could serve only to weaken their interests. He also advised the Townsends that to "keep all we have got, & not cede a point, is our true policy."[47]

Like his uncle in the Van Ingen case, Robert L. Livingston remained cautiously optimistic about the North River Company's chances before the Supreme Court in Washington, DC. "Should we contrary to my expectation lose the suit, we shall have an equitable claim on our Legislature for protection, by taxing all boats coming into our waters propelled by steam," remarked Livingston to the Townsends. "I cannot but think that public sentiment will be in our favour and that a Bill would pass this session laying a tax sufficiently high to prevent any boat from coming into competition with us."[48] Tired of his precarious arrangement with Gibbons, John R. Livingston rediscovered his familial bonds and offered to combine his steamboat services with the North River Company and thus connect New York City with Philadelphia in one continuous route.[49]

A Tenuous Partnership

As the Livingston family closed ranks behind their steamboat monopoly, Gibbons and Ogden formed their own uneasy truce. Gibbons was particularly eager to secure a permanent steamboat line from New York City to New Jersey. His Trenton agent, a sloop and stagecoach owner named Robert Letson, reported, "The Publeck is all inquiring for Steam Boats." If Gibbons could furnish more boats, Letson predicted, "we would have all the travelers, and it would be a great advantage to our line now and hereafter."[50] Throughout summer 1820, Ogden transported passengers on board his vessel *Atalanta* from New York to Elizabethtown, where they transferred to Gibbons's *Bellona* to complete the voyage to New Brunswick. Perhaps due to their mutual distrust, Gibbons and Ogden secured a common agent, William B. Jacques, to collect their profits.

John R. Livingston feared such an alliance and sued Gibbons and Ogden in the New York Court of Chancery. Livingston demanded that, since the New York monopoly granted him navigation rights to the New Jersey shore, Gibbons and Ogden should be enjoined from any further operations.[51] Turning away from several years' worth of his own arguments, Ogden now claimed that the steamboat monopoly applied only to New York, not New Jersey, waterways. Whether some of his partners disembarked in Elizabethtown and then continued on to New Brunswick aboard Gibbons's steamboats was none of his concern. Gibbons brandished a federal coasting license as the only authority he needed to run steamboats in any state. In two separate rulings, Chancellor Kent again upheld the legality of the New York monopoly. Since Livingston was unable to prove a link between Gibbons and Ogden, Kent dismissed charges against Ogden because he still possessed a license from the Fulton-Livingston syndicate. Nevertheless, Kent issued yet another injunction, which barred Gibbons's steamboats from New York waterways.[52]

Gibbons and Ogden in State Court

Even as Gibbons worked with Ogden to defeat Livingston, he secretly prepared his chancery court suit against his former partner. In September 1819, his attorney, William Henry, argued that Ogden's 1815 monopoly license controlled steam travel only from New York City to Elizabethtown Point. Since Gibbons's vessels resupplied at a nearby dock called Halstead's Point, they were not technically in violation of Ogden's contract. More significantly, Gibbons asserted, "His two boats were vessels above the burden of twenty tons, and were duly enrolled and licensed under the laws of the United States, to be employed in carrying on the coasting trade, according to the laws of the United States." For good measure, he reiterated that his agreements with Tompkins and Noah Brown provided subcontracted rights under the New York monopoly to operate his steamboats in New York Harbor.[53] Ogden raced to Albany and joined Abraham Van Vechten to personally refute the charges. The former New Jersey governor argued that if Chancellor Livingston or Robert Fulton had ever enjoyed a monopoly over steam travel in New York, his monopoly license was still valid. Furthermore, his license granted control over all steam travel in the vicinity of Elizabethtown. Therefore, as Gibbons enjoyed limited rights, at best, under the New York monopoly, he could not contest the injunction without the cooperation of his partners, Tompkins and Brown.[54]

On October 6, Chancellor Kent handed down his decision. He first dealt with the thorny issue of Gibbons's federal coasting license. As in *Livingston v. Van Ingen*, Kent maintained that the federal Coasting Act of 1793 merely enrolled American vessels for taxation purposes and therefore did not conflict with the New York monopoly law. Kent buttressed his conclusions by linking the issue of the steamboat monopoly to other, well-established spheres of state control:

> If an individual be, for instance, in possession of any duly patented vehicle, or machine, or vessel, or medicine, or book, must not such property be used, held, or enjoyed, subject to the general laws of the land, such as laws establishing turnpike roads and toll bridges, or the exclusive right to a ferry, or laws for preventing or removing nuisances? Must it not be subject to all other regulations touching the issue and employment of property, which the legislature of the state may deem just and expedient? It appears to me that these questions must be answered in the affirmative.[55]

Accordingly, state power could be limited only if it directly challenged congressional authority granted by the U.S. Constitution: the 1793 Coasting Act contained no such provision. As Congress had not abrogated the New York monopoly while crafting the measure, the monopoly remained valid unless the Supreme Court decided otherwise.[56]

Borrowing a quotation from Virgil's *Aeneid*, Kent concluded that the court must be satisfied that *"Neptunus muros, magnoque emota tridenti, Fundamenta quatit."*[57] As many in the chamber knew, the line, which translates as "Neptune, by the power of his mighty trident, has shaken the walls and foundations [of Troy]," described the role of the gods in the destruction of that ancient city. Kent thus cleverly equated the will of the gods to the supremacy of Congress in the exercise of its enumerated powers. Unless it could be proven that the "gods" of Congress specifically intended to limit state commerce power through the Coasting Act of 1793, Ogden's monopoly license remained valid. Furthermore, Ogden's vested rights could be secured only if he had access to the entire Elizabethtown shore. Therefore, Kent reasoned, "the grant must be so construed as to give it due effect, excluding all contiguous and injurious competition." Since Gibbons's contract with Tompkins and Brown gave no specific rights to transport passengers between Elizabethtown and New York City, Ogden's rights remained completely valid.[58]

Attempts to Manage the North River Company

Despite Ogden's victory, the New York monopolists continued to face internal and external problems. Lynch frequently complained about what he saw as the general lack of organization in the North River Company. He condemned the "officious conduct" of Captain Roorbach, who managed his own private steamboat service from Albany to Greenwich Village. He also criticized Robert L. Livingston for not helping the North River Company overcome its receivership.[59] While Gibbons appealed Ogden's injunction in the New York Court of Appeals in October 1819, the bankrupt colonel petitioned the North River Company to help share the cost of his legal defense. At a shareholders' meeting, Edward P. Livingston and Dominick Lynch, in rare accord, agreed that the company should avoid outside legal expenses unless they were absolutely warranted. Rhind remarked, "It is in my opinion, however, that in the Supreme Court of the United States alone, can this question be satisfactorily settled."[60]

Such unity was short-lived. At a meeting on November 8, Lynch rallied the North River Company shareholders to petition the New York legislature for a new charter as a public corporation. Legal status as a public institution would allow the company to claim that it provided a public service to New York citizens, rather than a private luxury. Edward P. Livingston, who failed to attend the meeting, flew into a rage when he saw his name attached to an announcement in the *Albany Argus* that publicized the North River Company's plans. Livingston claimed that he would personally handle any incorporation plans before the New York state legislature.[61] As tensions between Livingston, the captains, and the stockholders continued to mount, Lynch remarked, "Every day seems to bring forward some new claims, on these premises, which, Mr. E. P. L. ought to fulfill, as he holds them so sacred."[62] The stockholders of the North River Company attempted to maintain a positive public image despite their many problems. In January 1820, the firm placed advertisements in local papers that boasted about the easy access to Connecticut that was available through regularly scheduled trips by Captain Elihu Bunker and the steamboat *Fulton*. However, many local steamboat promoters who could not take their own boats into New York Harbor reacted angrily to the situation. The Connecticut state legislature subsequently began to discuss ways to protest the New York monopoly.[63]

Similarly, in a petition submitted to the New York legislature in late January, a group of Hudson River sloop owners condemned steamboats as a direct threat to their livelihoods. The next week, John L. Sullivan again appeared in Albany and renewed his campaign to repeal the Fulton-Livingston monopoly.[64] In addition, a man named McKorn reported an act to the New York state legislature to incorporate the Lake Erie Steam Boat Company.[65] More ominously, a month later, New Brunswick residents, who felt themselves "injured and insulted by the tributary system practiced upon them by the Citizens of the State of New York," petitioned the New Jersey state legislature to contest the steamboat monopoly. The petitioners also advised New Jersey officials to pass their own retaliatory legislation.[66] Many reacted with surprise when New Jersey governor Isaac H. Williamson publicly criticized Kent's decision in *Livingston v. Ogden and Gibbons*. Under the New Jersey constitution of 1776, governors wielded little political power and deferred to the state legislature on most matters. Yet Williamson also served as chancellor of the New Jersey Court of Appeals, the highest court in the state. This position gave him a formidable voice in any future steamboat cases launched in New Jersey courts. Williamson was respected by Federalists and Republicans alike as a levelheaded public servant who rarely became embroiled in partisan politics. The fact that the normally dispassionate Williamson now urged the New Jersey legislature to take action "against the claims and encroachments of the state of New York" revealed how serious the monopoly issue had become.[67]

Outraged at Kent's decision to enjoin a steam ferry that ran between two New Jersey ports, state legislators in Trenton quickly passed their own monopoly law, on February 25.[68] Under the terms of the New Jersey statute, any New

115

Yorker who issued an injunction against a New Jersey citizen for the operation of a steamboat in New York waters could be sued in New Jersey courts. Those found guilty were liable for triple the damages and were barred from steam travel within New Jersey waters.[69] Under the terms of what many now called the Steamboat Law, Gibbons promptly secured injunctions against both Ogden and John R. Livingston in the New Jersey Court of Chancery.[70] In retaliation, the New York state legislature proposed a bill that prohibited all steamboats from states with monopoly laws injurious to New York from conducting business within state boundaries.[71]

Meanwhile, the North River Company investors had other problems to consider. While on a visit to Washington, DC, Colden stopped by the office of the postmaster general to pick up a copy of a new mail contract, which normally authorized the North River Company to deliver mail from New York City to Albany. Colden was mortified to learn that Postmaster General Return J. Meigs Jr. had already made such an agreement individually with Captain Roorbach. But such a double cross was hardly surprising. Meigs was a former governor and Ohio senator with a penchant for brokering political deals. When Colden learned that Meigs was a kinsman of Captain Bunker, he rationalized the affair as an attempt to defraud the North River Company.[72] While Colden returned to New York City to report his findings, the decisions in the Gibbons and Sullivan cases postponed but failed to resolve the North River Company's problems. Colden lamented the fact that the cases had not been decided on their merits, as he, "Emmet, and Pinkney were decided in their opinions." Since the North River Company remained legally secure, for the moment, Rhind placed announcements in the *New York Evening Post* and the *New York Commercial Advertiser* and offered corporate stock for sale to the public. In particular, Rhind wanted to sell stock out of state in places such as Vermont to give the North River Company more widespread public appeal.[73]

Mail Contracts and Conspiracies

In mid-March, Colden returned to New York City, where he met with the North River Company shareholders. He reported that Sullivan and Gibbons were both soundly defeated and unlikely to trouble the corporation again. Colden also railed against the company's "servants" who had colluded with the postmaster general to deprive the company of its mail contract. As this conspiracy had angered many influential Washington, DC, politicians, Colden promised that a full governmental inquiry would most likely remove Meigs from office. Some stockholders demanded the immediate discharge of Hoffman and Roorbach, but Colden urged caution and stated the need to hear from Washington first in order to "explode the whole conspiracy."[74]

Robert L. Livingston quickly dashed off a letter to President James Monroe to settle the matter. He complained that the collusion between Hoffman, Roorbach, and Meigs was a conspiracy by which "the authority of the federal government is to be brought in direct conflict with the peremptory directions of the statute of the state, and to presume the novel question; whether any contract with a department of the general government is to give exemption to those who without it are amenable to the authority of the state."[75] Finally, Livingston raised the now-familiar specter of Fulton's orphans, who would be left destitute without the income provided by the steamboat monopoly.[76]

Rhind also envisioned a conspiracy orchestrated by Meigs and the North River captains against the North River Company. The agent confidently predicted, "If the whole of this nefarious business is laid properly before the public, it will produce an unanimity in the next election," which would in turn prove "that the people may be beguiled for a time by demagogues but when they see facts like these they will act like freemen."[77] On the orders of President Monroe, the post office suspended all mail contracts to New York steamboat operators until the U.S. Supreme Court could decide the legality of the steamboat monopoly.[78]

The North River Company suffered a tremendous setback when, several days later, Pinkney suffered a fatal stroke while in deliberations before the Supreme Court. Justice Joseph Story lamented to his wife, "Such is human life and such is human fame. If Mr. Pinkney were to die now, in one month it would scarcely excite concern, beyond the bosoms of the few who are his immediate relatives, and those who admire genius, and weep over its ruins." A week later, Pinkney passed away; he was buried in an elaborate funeral attended by many of the Washington, DC, intelligentsia.[79]

Deprived of his ablest legal talent, Rhind rushed to secure a substitute. Former Federalist congressman and New York attorney general Thomas J. Oakley agreed to replace Pinkney on the defense team. Although he lacked his predecessor's reputation and oratorical style, Oakley was nevertheless well known for his keen legal mind, unflappable composure, and ability to deliver logical and meticulous summations in court.[80] And the North River Company desperately needed effective legal counsel, for in early 1822, the people of New Brunswick petitioned the New York state legislature to urge that until New York and New Jersey could reconcile their differences, both states should refrain "from all attempts to forcibly exclude the citizens of the other state from using the waters in dispute, either by the navigation of steam boats or any other vessels."[81] John L. Sullivan also circulated copies of a pamphlet entitled *A Demonstration of the Right to the Navigation of the Waters of New York,* which dismissed the Fulton-Livingston monopoly as unconstitutional.[82] Meanwhile, a group of New York City shipbuilders demanded the right to build steamboats within the state and requested an act to "protect us in the enjoyment of that right, we have ever been led to believe was guaranteed by the constitution of this state and the United States."[83]

In late February 1822, the New York state legislature appointed a special committee to investigate complaints against the state monopoly. John Stevens and William Gibbons testified against the monopoly, and Josiah Ogden Hoffman, who had previously defended Robert Fulton and Robert R. Livingston in *Livingston v. Van Ingen,* represented the North River Company. Faced with such formidable legal talent, Gibbons put on a show of bravado for his father. "In all my life I have never heard such a feeble and fallacious argument from a man of Hoffman's standing as it was. It consisted of declamation and appeal to the feelings, not to the judgment of the committee," the younger Gibbons remarked. Nonetheless, he conceded that such a strategy might actually prevail.[84] This concern proved justified, for several days later, Hoffman and monopoly supporters launched their own petition to the New York state legislature. The petitioners tapped into and redirected public antimonopoly hostility, stating, "As much as a free intercourse between the city of New York and New Jersey was desirable, we wished it, so far as it could be accomplished without a violation of the faith of this State, or the destruction of property and vested rights."[85] With a temporary lull in the conflict, Rhind pushed for an accommodation with both Gibbons and John R. Livingston to prevent future difficulties.[86]

Troubles with Connecticut

One of the most pressing problems faced by the North River Company came from Connecticut. In May 1822, Anthony N. Hoffman, the disgruntled former supplier for the North River Company, testified before the Connecticut state legislature in Hartford about the financial status of his former employers. To strengthen his claims, Hoffman submitted stolen copies of corporate account books, which detailed the feuds between the stockholders, captains, and various members of the Livingston family. Colden denounced Hoffman's credibility before the legislature, but Rhind glumly predicted that North River boats would soon be banned from Connecticut.[87] On May 25, the state senate passed a measure that forbade New York steamboats from Connecticut waters by an eight-to-four vote.[88] Even Rhind now acknowledged that "the grant is in great jeopardy." Although he suggested a negotiation with Ogden to increase ferry services to Rhode Island, which in turn would connect with stage lines to Connecticut, Rhind remained despondent about the future of the North River Company.[89]

Ogden and the Livingstons met to discuss their options. They borrowed from Gibbons's own tactics and threatened to rally Elizabethtown residents to purchase a public steamboat to run between New York City and Elizabethtown if Gibbons did not agree to a partnership.[90] When Gibbons failed to respond, Robert M. Livingston, the hotheaded son of John R. Livingston who served as a junior partner in his father's steamboat business, pressed the matter. He warned Gibbons, "I conceive a strong coalition the only mode to be adopted in order to drive away the swarm of small boats that are now running."[91] To keep his options open, Livingston offered Captain Benjamin Beecher of the steamboat *Connecticut* a partnership in return for access to Connecticut waters.[92] When Beecher agreed, the North River Company stockholders reacted angrily at what they saw as a betrayal.[93] Rhind dismissed Livingston as a "dunce" and a "catspaw" for Beecher and rejoiced when Rhode Island authorities seized Livingston's vessel for lack of proper registration papers.[94]

Determined to defend the monopoly, Rhind petitioned William Cutting and the Fulton Steam Boat Company to join forces against Gibbons. He also urged newspaper editors in New York City and Albany to promote steamboat trips to the Catskill Mountains.[95] In summer 1822, the Fulton Company secured an injunction against Robert M. Livingston in the New York Court of Chancery that prohibited the operation of his steamboat the *Olive Branch* in New York waters.[96] To make matters more complicated, John L. Sullivan courted Albany investors to interest them in his steam-powered towboats. He even petitioned Justice Ambrose Spencer to ask whether the North River Company would object if he ran such steamboats on the Hudson.[97]

Further Conflicts in Chancery Court

While the North River Company continued to face repeated challenges, Ogden carefully amassed affidavits from passengers and members of the *Bellona*'s crew. In November 1819, he asked Chancellor Kent for an injunction against Gibbons, with damages set at $10,000.[98] In a tersely worded decision delivered on December 4, Kent reduced the case to a single legal question: did the collaboration between Gibbons's *Bellona* and Tompkins's *Nautilus* to convey passengers from New Jersey to New York City constitute a violation of Ogden's monopoly rights? Kent defined Ogden's license as an exclusive monopoly "meant to embrace the whole stream of intercourse" between Elizabethtown and New York, which therefore, by its very nature, "excluded all contiguous and injurious competition."[99] Kent admitted that in his previous decision, "it is probable that I may have made observations which misled the defendant." Consequently, he ruled that Gibbons needed only to pay Ogden's legal fees and acknowledge the authority of the previous injunction.[100]

Gibbons interpreted such a lenient decision as weakness on Kent's part and immediately appealed the case once again to the New York Court of Errors.[101] Hoping for a confrontation in federal court, he wrote Daniel Webster and Attorney General William Wirt. Gibbons told Webster, "If that court [the Court of Errors] should decide against me and in favour of the law, I shall carry it before the Supreme Court of the United States at Washington where I shall wish your services associated with W. Wirt the Attorney General."[102] The caliber of legal talent that Gibbons sought to enlist reveals how seriously he took the matter. At thirty-six years of age, Webster already enjoyed a reputation as a dynamic public speaker and successful private attorney. A New Hampshire native and graduate of Dartmouth College, he was known to be an outspoken Federalist congressman. His skills as an orator became legendary following his successful defense of his alma mater in the famous U.S. Supreme Court case *Dartmouth v. Woodward* (1819) and his eulogies to John Adams and Thomas Jefferson in 1826. The attorney general, Wirt, was a Maryland-born son of Swiss immigrants who joined the Virginia bar and became a leading Jeffersonian Republican. Wirt's opposition to the Sedition Acts and his role as prosecutor in the treason trial of Aaron Burr earned him a position as James Monroe's attorney general. Given the sensationalism of the steamboat controversy, not to mention Gibbons's deep pockets, both Webster and Wirt agreed to take the case.[103]

Daniel Webster. James Barton Longacre, *Daniel Webster,* 1850, Stapleton Collection, Bridgeman Art Gallery

William Wirt. James Barton Longacre, *William Wirt,* 1820, Stapleton Collection, Bridgeman Art Gallery

Gibbons was wise to seek legal counsel, for in January 1819, New York sheriff's deputies arrested him in New York City. Released on $3,000 bail, he quickly prepared for his upcoming court date.[104] In April, the court heard arguments in the case of *Gibbons v. Ogden,* which in many ways resembled a rehearing of *Livingston v. Van Ingen.* Gibbons's attorney, William Henry, declared the New York steamboat monopoly to be a violation of both the U.S. Constitution and his client's federal coasting license. If New York could monopolize steam travel, what was there to prevent the Empire State from banning other forms of transportation or even foreign vessels?[105] Josiah Ogden Hoffman responded for the defense. He pointed to the role of the New York monopoly in encouraging steam travel throughout the nation and said that to give Thomas Gibbons's coasting license priority over state law would eviscerate New York's ability to quarantine vessels, prohibit slavery, and license turnpikes. Hoffman cynically concluded, "This case, we supposed, was to be brought here to be argued merely *pro forma,* for the purpose of having the cause carried up to the Supreme Court of the U.S." In response, Henry argued that if Congress could control coastal trade between states, then all state laws to the contrary were unconstitutional. Calling to mind Kent's comments in the New York chancery court case of *Gibbons v. Ogden,* Henry concluded, "We do not call to our aid Neptune with his trident; we invoke only the Goddess Minerva."[106] Kent had called upon the brute power of Neptune to explain the effect of congressional action. Henry, however, hinted that the principle of free trade as symbolized by the goddess of peace and commerce might provide a more equitable solution to the steamboat controversy.

Dueling in the New Jersey State Courts

While Gibbons contested Ogden's monopoly rights in New York, the colonel pursued his four-year-old insult, trespass, and libel case against his former partner in the New Jersey Court of Common Pleas. In response, Gibbons hired William Halsey to represent him in court. With over twenty years of experience before the bar, Halsey was one of the most formidable private attorneys in New Jersey. He was aided by the young assistant, Elias Van Arsdale, who would go on to a successful career as a Democratic state senator and real estate lawyer. Halsey and Van Arsdale soon earned their fees by convincing the court to exonerate Gibbons of the trespass charge. Ogden, however, still insisted on pressing the libel charge.[107]

At trial, the case of *State v. Gibbons* (1818) soon evolved into an extended debate on the barbarity of dueling and the importance of social reputation in early American society. Van Arsdale described Gibbons's behavior as an understandable response to the dishonor of being arrested in a public place over a paltry promissory note. In addition, he contended that Gibbons's inflammatory placard to Ogden was merely a poorly phrased attempt to arrange a meeting with the colonel to discuss their differences.[108] New Jersey attorney general Richard Stockton, demolished Gibbons's claims. He pointed out that Gibbons had approached the Ogdens' house armed with a horsewhip. Moreover, Gibbons's declaration of public hostilities, his announcement of a second, and his attempt to arrange a date for a "meeting" all conformed perfectly to established dueling traditions. Gibbons also had a well-known history of dueling; by contrast, Colonel Ogden "saw the conspiracy against his life, but he met it like a Christian, submitted to the laws of God and the land and appealed to the justice of his country." To make matters worse, Gibbons insisted on personally addressing the jury. For several hours, he ranted about the perceived injustices he had suffered at Ogden's hands. To no one's surprise, the jury returned a decision against Gibbons, with damages set at $5,000.[109]

To save their client from himself, Halsey and Van Arsdale desperately sought a new trial on technical grounds. In February 1819, the New Jersey Court of Appeals rejected the case. Chancellor Samuel L. Southard, who as a private attorney had represented Ogden in his feud with Robert Fulton in Trenton five years earlier, agreed to hear the case. In his decision, Southard asserted that the case not only involved physical damage but also was a matter "of character, of sentiment, of feeling" of a "man who has long filled a respectable rank in the estimation of the public and the honors of his country, and whose connections and influence extend far and operate largely on society." In addition, he stated that Gibbons, as an educated man in "possession of learning, of talents and of influence" who "was once very extensively engaged in the study and the practice of the law," should understand well "the rights of others, and his obligations to respect." Southard also insisted that any decision against Gibbons should be harsh enough to discourage future duels. He warned, "The disposition which prevails among us to staunch our wrongs, real and imaginary, with the blood of our adversaries, has long called but in vain for something sufficiently powerful to repress and control it. It has spurned ridicule, disregarded reproof, and mocked at religion." Gibbons filed several appeals for a new trial until the New Jersey Supreme Court finally reduced the amount to $2,500.[110]

In early April, John R. Livingston launched his own trespass suit for $50,000 against Gibbons in the U.S. District Court for the District of New Jersey.[111] A month later, he also filed suit against Daniel D. Tompkins in the New York Court of Chancery for violating the terms of their 1817 agreement. When the case appeared before Chancellor Kent, Abraham Van Vechten argued for the prosecution that in drafting their agreement three years earlier, Livingston and Tompkins had agreed that if Livingston were ever barred from New Jersey waters, his agreement with Tompkins would be null and void. Thus, since Gibbons had recently secured an injunction against Livingston under the New Jersey Reprisal Law of 1820, the contract was now meaningless. Because Tompkins continued to ferry passengers between Staten Island and Manhattan, he could be prosecuted like any other interloper under the New York monopoly.[112]

Tompkins secured the services of attorney William Henry to defend his monopoly rights. At trial, Henry described his client's request for an injunction as tantamount to a forfeiture of his property rights. Henry blamed Livingston for creating their problems, as he had been the one to prosecute Gibbons in New York state court and thereby prompted the Georgian to petition the New Jersey state legislature for retaliatory legislation against the New York monopoly. For that reason, Henry said, Livingston could not seek a legal redress for a situation he had essentially created. To grant an injunction against the vice president would bankrupt not only Tompkins but also his employees and the turnpikes, ferries, and hotels on Staten Island, which were all financially dependent upon his steamboat.[113]

Chancellor Kent once again reduced a complex case to specific questions. Had the Livingston-Tompkins agreement ceased because of Gibbons's injunction against Livingston? If so, was an injunction against Tompkins the proper remedy?[114] The agreement between Livingston and Tompkins had obviously been breached, for which Livingston most certainly had a right to an injunction. And, Kent added, if the original 1808 monopoly grant claimed too much jurisdiction over too much of New York Harbor, then the state legislature was at fault. As the U.S. Supreme Court ultimately had the responsibility to judge the New Jersey monopoly, Livingston could hardly be accused of creating the circumstances that led to the injunction against him. However, Tompkins had not created the current situation either. Therefore, he said, "considering the great and expensive establishments connected with the enjoyment of the defendant's privilege, an immediate restraint upon its enjoyment would be attended with very injurious consequences."[115]

Suits and Countersuits

Livingston was not the only steamboat operator facing setbacks. Gibbons suffered a similar defeat when Robert M. Livingston, the son of John R. Livingston, seized the *Bellona,* its crew, and Gibbons's son, William, in New York Harbor on a return trip from New York City. The Georgian quickly paid his son's bail and filed replevin suits against Livingston in both U.S. circuit court and the New Jersey Court of Common Pleas. Supreme Court justice Brockholst Livingston forced John R. and Robert M. Livingston to immediately return the *Bellona* or pay a $10,000 fine.[116]

Taking the offensive, Gibbons received an injunction from New Jersey governor Isaac Williamson, acting in his capacity as state chancellor, against Ogden for violation of the New Jersey steamboat law. Robert M. Livingston drafted a letter to Ogden that asked for assistance against Gibbons in court. He also suggested publicly "jesting" Gibbons by using their legal summonses as an excuse to run steamboats full of passengers from Elizabethtown to Trenton on their court dates.[117] When Gibbons and Livingston appeared before Justice Brockholst Livingston in Trenton, the judge refused to grant a permanent injunction against John R. Livingston because Gibbons had regained possession of the *Bellona.* Most important, Justice Livingston also refused to comment on the constitutionality of the New York monopoly grant until the matter was disposed of in state court.[118]

Gibbons and Ogden Return to Court

Since Justice Livingston had again declined to rule on the steamboat monopoly, Gibbons and Ogden prepared for another round of lawsuits. In October 1820, rumors circulated throughout Elizabethtown that Ogden planned to petition the New Jersey state legislature for a repeal of its steamboat monopoly law. A friend of Gibbons, William Hyer, reported, "I have also understood that, Col. Ogden, if taken by an attachment intends to go to Gaol. This is no doubt a scheme of Ogden to excite a clamor among the people in favour of him if he should be imprisoned, which perhaps would aid him in getting the law repealed."[119] Gibbons ignored such rumors and disregarded his increasingly frail health as he prepared to move his case from the New York Court of Errors to the U.S. Supreme Court.[120]

Realizing that their interests remained bound up in Ogden's rights, the North River Company stockholders belatedly agreed to help cover the colonel's legal

125

expenses. They secured the services of Emmet and Colden for $2,000 each. Rhind struck an upbeat note when he observed that "Mr. Colden informed the [stockholders'] meeting that the more he investigated the subject the more he was convinced of success and Mr. Emmet is so sanguine he cannot conceive of a reasonable doubt."[121] Yet even as the North River Company solidified its legal defense, business declined when an early freeze covered the Hudson River and New York Harbor with ice and allowed thousands of pedestrians to walk from New Jersey to New York City.[122]

Gibbons v. Ogden *before the U.S. Supreme Court*

In February 1821, Gibbons's appeal reached the Supreme Court in Washington, DC. Associate Supreme Court justice Joseph Story mentioned the case in a letter to William Fettyplace. "We are to take up, in a few days, another question, whether a State can give to any person an exclusive right to navigate its waters with steamboats, against the rights of a patentee, claimed under the laws of the United States," wrote Story. "The case comes from New York and Mr. Emmet of New York and Mr. Pinkney are on one side; and Mr. Webster, Mr. Ogden of New York, and Mr. Wirt, the Attorney General on the other. The arguments will be very splendid."[123]

This excitement proved premature, as the Court stopped David B. Ogden, one of Gibbons's attorneys, in midargument. It was determined that Chancellor Kent had not entered a final decree in his 1819 chancery court injunction that formed the basis for the current appeal. Although both Gibbons and Ogden had presented evidence and Kent had upheld the monopoly, he had not specifically handed down a final decision on the matter. As a result, the 1819 chancery court case of *Gibbons v. Ogden* was still technically pending, despite the fact that the New York Court for the Correction of Errors had subsequently ruled on the case as well. Thus, under section 25 of the federal Judiciary Act of 1789, the Supreme Court had no jurisdiction over the case. Chief Justice John Marshall declared, "The appeal, in this cause, be, and the same is hereby dismissed, it not appearing from the record that there was a final decree in said Court for the Correction of Errors, and &c. from which an appeal was taken."[124]

A week later, the Supreme Court reached a similar conclusion in the case of *Sullivan v. Fulton Steam Boat Company*. The previous year, Sullivan and several backers from Massachusetts, Connecticut, and Vermont had brought suit in federal circuit court against the Fulton Steam Boat Company in New York City. William Cutting had surprisingly deferred to the bill and allowed it to be brought pro forma to the Supreme Court on appeal.[125] On March 8, the Court heard arguments in the Sullivan case. As he had done previously, Daniel Webster represented the plaintiff. However, no sooner had Webster begun his argument than Chief Justice John Marshall raised another procedural point. Apparently, Webster's legal brief failed to note the state citizenship of his clients. The plaintiffs therefore could not qualify to bring their case before the Supreme Court under the diversity of citizenship clause of the U.S. Constitution.[126]

Despite the Supreme Court's reluctance to rule on the New York steamboat monopoly, Gibbons prepared to bring another case before the High Court as soon as possible.[127] Webster suggested that "the best mode of proceeding, if practicable, would be, that some suit be instituted against you & removed into the Circuit Court, as was intended to be done in the last case." Webster dismissed the idea of making another appeal through the New York Court of Errors as being too slow, but he suggested that since the Supreme Court had ruled the chancery case of *Gibbons v. Ogden* inconclusive, perhaps the subsequent ruling by the New York Court of Errors could still be considered pending and perhaps be resubmitted to the Supreme Court.[128] He also suggested that Sullivan and Gibbons should agree to pursue separate legal strategies so that at least one of them would reach the Supreme Court.[129] In spite of his increasingly poor health, Gibbons vowed to break the monopoly. In a letter to Webster, he declared, "It will ever be painful for me to, to stop here and let the Monopolists of this section of the Union revel in their Monopoly under the laws of New York to the injury of all other persons within the states of New York and New Jersey."[130]

Further Negotiations

Gibbons was not the only one preparing for extended litigation. Ogden gathered testimony from witnesses in Elizabethtown to corroborate the fact that Gibbons had persistently defied the New York monopoly through steamboat trips to New York City. In retaliation, Gibbons dredged up old legal fees Ogden still owed him from the custody battle over Gibbons's grandchildren.[131] Taking no chances, Gibbons also amended his New Jersey chancery court injunction against Ogden for use of the *Atalanta* in New Jersey waters.[132] In early August 1821, Governor Williamson, again serving in his capacity as chancellor of the New Jersey Court of Appeals, ruled the amended injunction against Ogden to be valid.[133] Gibbons quickly had copies of the injunction delivered to Ogden and the crew of the *Atalanta.* When David O. Price attempted to serve Elijah Wilder, the ship's engineer, with papers, Wilder assaulted the courier and called him a "damned rascal, infernal villain, and damned son of a bitch." Wilder also maintained that if it were not for the law, he would "grind Price as fine as powder."[134]

In the meantime, John R. Livingston fought Gibbons's replevin suit in federal circuit court with the argument that he had already returned the *Bellona* to Gibbons and that to ask for additional damages was malicious.[135] In November 1822, Gibbons finally brought suit against Livingston in the New York Marine Court, but he quickly lost. However, Livingston achieved only a token victory, as the jury awarded him damages set at one cent. Meanwhile, Ogden began to distribute handbills throughout Essex County that called for the repeal of the New Jersey steamboat monopoly law. Gibbons countered with his own petition, which demanded that the state legislature stand firm in its defense of New Jersey's sovereign rights.[136]

Since Gibbons presented a formidable threat, representatives of the North River Company attempted to negotiate. As an incentive, Rhind put pressure on John R. Livingston to drop his New York injunctions against the *Bellona.* Rhind observed, "If this is done, Gibbons will aid in support of the New York Grant, and thus a powerful auxiliary will be secured where you have now a powerful enemy."[137] In particular, Rhind wanted Gibbons to buy stock in the company.[138] The owners of North River Company had every reason to hope for a partnership with Gibbons. After all, they had recently concluded an agreement with John Stevens, to whom they gave permission to petition the New York state legislature for a grant to operate steamboats between New York and New Jersey. In November, the New Jersey legislature accordingly incorporated the Hoboken Steam Boat Company under the control of John Stevens and Robert L. Stevens and set specific rates for fares, passengers, and freight.[139]

Final Appeals

Gibbons made no agreements with the North River Company. He had other, more immediate concerns. In December, Ogden informed his rival that he planned to serve notice for further argument in the New Jersey chancery court case of *Gibbons v. Ogden*. Yet he also suggested a meeting with Gibbons to discuss a compromise. When Gibbons failed to respond, the colonel petitioned Governor Williamson for another hearing to dissolve Gibbons's injunction. Williamson granted Ogden ten days to provide additional arguments. The tactic worked, for Elias Van Arsdale approached Ogden on behalf of Gibbons with an offer to negotiate.[140]

In December 1821, the North River Company finally bought out Edward P. Livingston's interest in the company for $25,000. The gleeful stockholders quickly sold off his stock, and Chancellor Kent soon ended the company's receivership.[141] In early January 1822, Lynch informed John Townsend that Gibbons had personally ventured to Albany to once again contest Ogden's injunction against him in the New York Court of Errors. Lynch reported, "Both are willing that it be carried through, that it may be taken this winter to Washington." Gibbons also petitioned the New York state legislature to repeal its steamboat monopoly law. In a strange contrast to his earlier belligerence, Lynch advised a neutral course, stating, "The Company ought not assist the passage nor yet oppose it."[142] Problems continued to develop for the North River Company when Tompkins began to publish inflammatory articles against the New York monopoly in local papers. In late January, Gibbons joined Captains Beecher, Bartholomew, and Roorbach in petitioning the New York state legislature to repeal the steamboat monopoly.[143]

While Gibbons journeyed to Albany to overturn Ogden's New York injunction, the colonel proceeded to Trenton to argue against Gibbons's New Jersey injunction.[144] Gibbons met with defeat in Albany, on January 17, when Chancellor Kent upheld his injunction.[145] Yet he also gained what he had sought, an opportunity to appeal his case on a writ of error to the U.S. Supreme Court. This time, there would be no mistakes. As Gibbons presented his appeal in Washington, DC, the stockholders of the North River Company discreetly inquired into the matter from behind the scenes.[146]

As the North River Company regrouped, Daniel Webster reported to Gibbons that the Supreme Court would hear his appeal in their next judicial term.[147] Gibbons continued to negotiate with James A. Stevens and Robert L. Livingston about the possibility of a partnership, but the men failed to reach a specific agreement.[148] In late February, Webster glumly reported that Ogden had postponed their trial date for at least another year. And because Gibbons had filed his appeal late, Ogden had not been given a full thirty days to mount a defense. The Supreme Court could not compel Ogden to appear in court before the justices adjourned

129

for the season, and Webster predicted the former New Jersey governor would not appear voluntarily. "I see no remedy but patience," he insisted. "I most devoutly wish it were in my power to invent some mode of hastening the trial, but I do not see that it is."[149]

To derail Gibbons's case, Ogden lifted the New York injunction against the *Bellona* and *Mouse* and asked if his opponent still intended to enforce the New Jersey injunctions against the *Sea Horse*.[150] Gibbons responded that he planned to "enjoin as many of the Steam Boats belonging to the monopolists as are required by the laws of N. Jersey, so long as the Citizens of N. Jersey are deprived of their right of freely navigating the waters between the ancient shores of the States of N.Y. & and N.J." As a parting shot, he remarked, "It has always been a matter of astonishment to me that a native Citizen of N.J. should be the only man in the world that interrupts the navigation between N.J. and N. York who has enjoyed her best offices & fed on her crumbs."[151]

Gibbons consulted attorney William Henry as to whether Ogden could dissolve the New York injunction and thus undermine their appeal to the Supreme Court. Henry responded that Ogden might be able to lift the injunction but could not prevent Gibbons from making an appeal before the Supreme Court.[152] Meanwhile, in an attempt to bypass Gibbons, Ogden petitioned New Jersey Governor Williamson to lift Gibbons's injunctions, since his opponent no longer faced injunctions in regard to New York waters. Gibbons responded that only when the New York chancery court guaranteed his right to operate steamboats in New York would he lift his injunction against Ogden in New Jersey.[153]

The New York legislative subcommittee that was created to examine the constitutionality of the steamboat monopoly recommended that the state legislature repeal the measure. Gulian Verplanck led efforts to introduce a repeal bill. Rhind suggested a tactic whereby the bill would proceed to the Senate, where the allies of the monopoly would kill it.[154] He also reported some successes in negotiations with the "Jersey malcontents," John R. Livingston and Gibbons, but he was disheartened that Gibbons still refused to drop his suit against Ogden.[155] In fact, Gibbons solidified a partnership with John Stevens to combine steamboat lines and stagecoach services between New York and Philadelphia.[156] Gibbons also prepared to defend his injunction against Ogden in the New Jersey Court of Chancery at Trenton.[157] He was doubtlessly relieved when, five months later, Governor Williamson refused to overturn the injunction against Ogden.[158] The New York Senate, however, also voted to maintain its own steamboat monopoly.

Threats of a Duel

When Thomas Gibbons refused to engage in negotiations, Robert M. Livingston accosted his son, William Gibbons, on the streets of New York City. The younger Livingston declared that he would challenge the elder Gibbons to a duel if his opponent were not so aged and infirm and certain to sue him in court for making such a statement. Although he acknowledged that "my eyes have failed me" and "the glare of light is injurious to my sight," Thomas Gibbons nevertheless demanded an apology from Livingston—otherwise, he would suffer the consequences.[159] When Livingston refused, Gibbons wrote to him, stating, "I now give you from under my hand, that I ask no exemption from age and that I will take no advantage by Law, and I dare you to pursue your insinuating purposes."[160] Livingston responded that he had not intended to challenge Gibbons to a duel: he had merely wished to warn Gibbons not to draw him into a lawsuit over their steamboat interests. Livingston also stated, "I now desire to know whether I am to consider your letter a challenge or not, for although it may be ridiculous in me to send you an invitation of this kind I shall consider myself bound to accept one if offered."[161]

Gibbons declined to pursue the matter. He instead concentrated on his U.S. Supreme Court appeal set for the 1823 spring term. He again secured the services of William Wirt and Daniel Webster, and he pored over every legal nuance of his rejected appeal from the previous year.[162] In an allusion to the unpopularity of the monopoly, Gibbons lamented the fact that "there is something wrong in our Judiciary, that this important tribunal should convene but once in a year." He urged Webster "to press on the trial, or death will take me from the pleasure of rejoicing with you on the event."[163]

Gibbons had good reason to worry, for the New York monopoly remained a powerful opponent. Dominick Lynch had fought off the threat posed by Edward P. Livingston and gained a charter of incorporation that placed the North River Steam Boat Company upon a solid legal foundation. Charles Rhind had used skillful public relations to portray the North River Company as an efficient corporation committed to the public good. Livingston allies in the New York legislature and state courts had repeatedly upheld the monopoly.

Yet for all of its power, the monopoly could not cultivate the one commodity that mattered most—public goodwill. Gibbons was not the first person to challenge the New York monopoly. For fifteen years, steamboat passengers had weathered high fares and freight costs, frequent disruptions of service, and increasing limitations on out-of-state travel. Repeated petitions, legislative inquiries, and constant lawsuits had left monopoly forces bloodied but unbowed. Many citizens now felt that the monopoly had become so powerful that it was beyond the realm of public accountability. And because the monopoly was seemingly above the law, extraordinary measures were considered justified in opposing it. John L. Sullivan and Thomas Gibbons tapped into this antimonopoly sentiment and began to run steamboats in New York waters with widespread public approval. When the New York state courts repeatedly handed down injunctions against Gibbons, many began to feel that only the federal courts could impartially determine the fate of the steamboat monopoly. The public thus looked with interest to Washington in spring 1823 to see how the U.S. Supreme Court would deal with the "steamboat cause."

CHAPTER 8

Strategies and Deliberations

The Rise of the Marshall Court

ON JUNE 4, 1822, Supreme Court justice Joseph Story wrote his colleague Brockholst Livingston, stating that it was a "matter of regret to me that the constitutionality of the Act of New York is about to come before the Supreme Court." The Supreme Court's reputation had already been maligned by states' rights supporters for the justices' nationalistic decisions in the recent cases of *McCulloch v. Maryland* (1819) and *Cohens v. Virginia* (1821). As a result, Story predicted that "whichever way we decide the Steamboat case, it will create a great sensation—We must content ourselves however in doing our duty & leave to time to decide the consequences."[1] Given his family's long involvement with the steamboat monopoly, Justice Livingston could have sympathized. But a bout of pneumonia kept him more concerned with his own well-being than with the health of the High Court.

Story's trepidation reveals the uneasy situation the Supreme Court faced while deliberating *Gibbons v. Ogden*. Far from developing in isolation, the steamboat controversy remained linked to similar debates over internal improvements, the Second Bank of the United States, and the interstate slave trade. Despite the appearance of an "era of good feelings," federal and states' rights tensions dominated American politics during the late 1810s and early 1820s. Such conflicts sprang from differences in political philosophy, from state pride, and from blatant racism. Whether the federal or state governments maintained the right to control economic development was often a central issue in these controversies. Given the volatility of interstate commerce problems, Chief Justice John Marshall and his brethren would have to proceed delicately if they hoped to settle the "steamboat cause" in a way that minimized risk to the Court's public credibility.

The transportation revolution that had given rise to the New York steamboat monopoly fueled both national economic growth and problems between state and federal governments. By the 1810s, factories had sprung up in New England, Ohio farmers had invested in grain and livestock, and a cotton empire based on slave labor had spread from Georgia to Texas.[2] In 1816, Congressman Henry Clay launched his ambitious "American System," which called for the creation of the Second Bank of the United States, a military buildup, strong tariffs, and internal improvements to be funded by new taxes and western land sales. State legislatures from Massachusetts to South Carolina supported canals and turnpikes, and they sold off public land to investors. Not even the financial panics of 1819 and 1837 could permanently blunt the growth of the American economy.[3]

In addition to governors and legislators, state and federal judges played an important role in the commercial transformation of the United States. Many judges actively reinterpreted communally based English common law to support contractual rights.[4] The process was neither uniform nor conspiratorial. Some judges believed fiercely that law was an instrument to be used in fashioning a new kind of commercial society. Others relied on traditional interpretations of common law principles that protected vested interests against aggressive development. But whatever their jurisprudential leanings, judges navigated unfriendly waters. In an increasingly individualistic society, Americans viewed with suspicion courts that claimed lawmaking powers independent of the legislative process. Given the difficulty of enforcing decrees, judges had to steer a prudent course in the court of public opinion. And no court in the nation was more conscious of its public image than the U.S. Supreme Court.[5]

At its creation in 1789, the federal judiciary was the least powerful branch of an already weak federal government. Under Chief Justices John Jay and Oliver Ellsworth, the Supreme Court had incrementally pursued a reputation as a broker between different individuals, groups, and even states. By 1800, the Supreme Court had arbitrated disputes between citizens of different states in *Chisholm v.*

U.S. Supreme Court chief justice John Marshall.
T. Hamilton Crawford (after Joshua Reynolds), *John Marshall,* c. 1930, Library of Congress, Prints and Photographs Division, Washington, DC

Georgia (1793), enforced U.S. treaty provisions in *Ware v. Hylton* (1796), and upheld federal taxation powers in *Hylton v. United States* (1798). But these decisions were unpopular and were frequently resisted at the local level, particularly in southern and western states.[6]

No one did more to shape the authority and traditions of the early Supreme Court than John Marshall, the fourth chief justice.[7] Marshall was born in 1755 in the northern neck of Virginia to a minor planter family distantly related to Thomas Jefferson. Marshall later recalled that wartime service in the Continental army taught him to consider "America as my country, and Congress as my government. I had imbibed these sentiments so thoroughly that they constituted a part of my being."[8] In particular, the young lieutenant had watched for six years as George Washington argued with local officials to keep his army properly supplied. After the war, Marshall became a leading Virginia Federalist, dedicated to establishing an effective federal government adequately equipped to meet national crises. In 1788, he argued for the appellate power of federal courts at Virginia's ratification debates over the U.S. Constitution. As a representative in the Virginia House of Delegates, Marshall was alienated from most of his neighbors by his support for Alexander Hamilton's plans to assume state debts and create

135

a national bank. In 1800, his brief tenure as John Adams's secretary of state led to a last-minute appointment to the post of chief justice of the U.S. Supreme Court during the tumultuous presidential election that year. As a product of the Revolutionary generation, Marshall understood, perhaps better than anyone else, the tremendous opportunity he and his brethren had to create a new constitutional order from the ground up.[9]

Marshall's closest confidant on the Supreme Court was Justice Joseph Story. Story was the descendant of Massachusetts Puritans, a Harvard graduate, and an insightful legal scholar. Although originally a Jeffersonian Republican appointed to oppose Marshall's Federalist policies, over time Story came to support the chief justice's nationalistic stance in case after case. His expertise in admiralty law also inclined him favorably toward the notion of a central government with formidable powers over commerce.[10] Other members of the Marshall Court represented a variety of legal talents and abilities. Justice Bushrod Washington, the favorite nephew of George Washington, was a loyal Federalist and ardent ally of the chief justice. Justice Gabriel Duvall of Maryland was the oldest member of the Court. Frequently ill and increasingly deaf, Duvall handed down very few majority opinions and consistently voted with Marshall and Story. Justice Thomas Todd, from Kentucky, likewise frequently deferred to Marshall.[11]

Justice William Johnson of South Carolina was a notable exception in terms of Marshall's influence over his colleagues. Johnson was the son of a South Carolina blacksmith and had been a state assemblyman and a Patriot leader during the American Revolution. The future justice excelled academically at Princeton and quickly became one of the most successful lawyers and state representatives in South Carolina. Marriage to Sarah Bennett, the daughter of a local rice planter and lumber baron, brought wealth and inclusion into the ranks of the Charleston gentry. Like Joseph Story, he was appointed to the Court by President Thomas Jefferson in 1804 as a counterbalance to the nationalistic tendencies of John Marshall. Unlike Story, Johnson proved to be an effective critic of Marshall. Yet as his actions in *Gibbons v. Ogden* reveal, the South Carolinian was quite capable of disagreeing with Jefferson too when he felt the circumstances warranted it.[12]

Dangerous Precedents

During Marshall's time as chief justice, the Supreme Court justices lived together in the same Washington, DC, boardinghouse. These close accommodations encouraged debate and a free exchange of ideas, and it increased their solidarity in controversial cases.[13] As a result, the Marshall Court handed down a number of landmark decisions that promoted nationalism and economic development. In *Fletcher v. Peck* (1810), for instance, Marshall ruled that a land deal tainted by bribery struck between New England real estate companies and the Georgia state legislature still represented a valid contract. Furthermore, in *Martin v. Hunter's Lessee* (1816), the Marshall Court upheld British land claims in the face of Virginia confiscation laws.[14] And in *Trustees of Dartmouth College v. Woodward* (1819), the Court declared that Dartmouth's charter with New Hampshire was a contract immune to state legislative interference.[15]

The Marshall Court faced one of its greatest challenges with the case of *McCulloch v. Maryland* (1819). In the wake of the panic of 1819, the Maryland state legislature levied a heavy tax on the Baltimore branch of the Second Bank of the United States. When the bank director sued Maryland, Chief Justice Marshall and his colleagues ruled that under the necessary and proper clause of the U.S. Constitution, Congress could establish a national bank to help gather taxes and regulate commerce. Since "the power to tax was the power to destroy," Maryland could not interfere with a bank commissioned by Congress. In one of the most frequently cited lines in American jurisprudence, Marshall defended a broad construction of the Constitution with the maxim "Let the end be legitimate, let it be within the scope of the constitution, and all means which are appropriate, which are plainly adapted to that end, which are not prohibited, but consist with the letter and spirit of the constitution, are constitutional."[16]

Marshall's McCulloch decision sparked widespread public criticism throughout the West and the South. The loudest outcry came from Marshall's home state of Virginia. Like many southern states, the Old Dominion had economically suffered during the Panic of 1819, and for many Virginians, attempts by the Second Bank of the United States to call in loans and raise interest rates compounded local economic downturns. The defense of the hated bank by Marshall, a fellow Virginian, in *McCulloch v. Maryland* seemed to add insult to injury. The leaders of the Richmond Junto, a powerful group of Republican reactionaries, tapped into this public sentiment. Throughout spring and summer 1819, Virginia General Court judge William Brockenbrough, *Richmond Enquirer* editor Thomas Ritchie, and Virginia Court of Appeals chief justice Spencer Roane published anonymous diatribes in Virginia newspapers. These editorials attacked the Marshall Court for undermining states' rights and subverting the U.S. Constitution in the McCulloch case. Writing under the pseudonym Hampden, Roane accused the Court of instituting "a judicial coup de main; to give a general letter of attorney to the future legislators of the Union; and to tread under foot all those parts and articles of the Constitution which had been, heretofore, deemed to set limits to the power of the federal legislature."[17] An infuriated Marshall set aside his usual sense of judicial restraint and penned a series of responses. He argued that the U.S. Constitution looked to the American people, not the states, for its authority. The federal government was a limited body but sovereign within its sphere of influence. If advocates of states' rights were to prevail, he said, "the government of the whole will be prostrated at the feet of its members; and that grand effort of wisdom, virtue, and patriotism, which produced it, will be totally defeated."[18]

A public dispute over the Second Bank of the United States was one matter. But when the debate over federalism became intertwined with the issue of slavery in the Missouri Crisis of 1820 to 1821, the results proved explosive. Since the Philadelphia Convention of 1787, northerners and southerners had realized that disagreements over the issue of slavery could lead to civil war. To mollify South Carolina and Georgia delegates, the framers had provided in the Constitution for slaves to be counted as a portion of the southern population for the purpose of apportioning representation in Congress and for the return of fugitive slaves to their owners. Many northern delegates uncomfortable with slavery accepted the compromise in the hope that slavery might be phased out as the young nation expanded westward. Yet the expansion of the "cotton kingdom" across the South in the early 1800s served only to strengthen the institution of slavery. Accordingly, when Missouri sought to enter the Union as a slave state in 1818, New York congressman James Tallmadge suggested that, as a condition for statehood, a "further introduction of slavery or involuntary servitude" should be banned from Missouri. Furthermore, he stated that "all children born within the said State, after the admission thereof into the Union, shall be free at the age of twenty-five Years."[19] Southern political leaders threatened secession if Missouri were not allowed to enter the United States on its own terms. Although the Missouri Compromise fundamentally represented a debate on the evils of slavery, it touched upon the issue of whether Congress or the southern states held the right to control the interstate slave trade. In 1821, Congressman Henry Clay of Kentucky helped broker a compromise under which Missouri entered the Union as a slave state, Maine became a free state, and the western frontier was divided at the 36°30' parallel into free and slave territories. This sectional accommodation allowed the crisis to pass, but it failed to resolve the issue of slavery.[20]

Sectional tensions over the Missouri issue were still evident a year later when the Supreme Court agreed to hear the case of *Cohens v. Virginia* (1821).[21] The case evolved from an attempt by two brothers, Philip and Mendes Cohen, to sell tickets in Virginia for a lottery licensed by Congress. When arrested by Virginia authorities for violating a state antigambling law, the Cohens appealed their case to the federal courts under section 25 of the Judiciary Act of 1789, which allowed the U.S. Supreme Court to hear cases on appeal from state supreme courts. Virginia asserted that under the Eleventh Amendment, by which states could not be parties to lawsuits without their permission, the Supreme Court had no jurisdiction over the matter. In any case, it was argued, section 25 violated the sovereignty of state courts and was therefore unconstitutional. In a unanimous vote, the Marshall Court stated that regardless of the Eleventh Amendment, Article III of the Constitution gave the Supreme Court clear appellate power in all cases involving federal laws. Federal jurisdiction depended upon the nature of the case, not the status of the court from which the decision was appealed. In a famous expression of nationalism, Marshall maintained, "In war, we are one people. In making peace, we are one people. In all commercial regulations, we are one and the same people. In many other respects, the American people are one, and the government, which is alone capable of controlling and managing their interests in all these respects, is the government of the Union."[22]

Any state laws that conflicted with the Constitution or federal statutes were accordingly null and void. After delivering this stirring defense of nationalism, Marshall turned to the merits of the case. He found that when Congress authorized the lottery, it had done so merely for the District of Columbia and not for the nation at large. Virginia could thus restrict lotteries as it saw fit, and its conviction of the Cohens was perfectly legal.

Although Virginia's attorneys technically had won their case, states' rights advocates condemned the Cohens decision. Spencer Roane lamented that under Marshall's conception of federalism, "there is no common arbiter of their rights but the people. If this power of decision is once conceded to either party, the equilibrium established by the constitution is destroyed, and the compact exists thereafter, but in name."[23] John Taylor of Caroline was an eccentric Virginia senator and Old Republican named after his sprawling estate in order to distinguish him from other John Taylors prominent in Virginia politics. He condemned Marshall's decision for attempting "to enrich a local capitalist interest at the expense of the people; to create corporations for abridging states' rights; to make roads and canals; and finally to empower a complete negative over state laws and judgments, and an affirmative power as to federal laws."[24] Even former president Thomas Jefferson published an editorial arguing that the federal and state governments had separate spheres of power in which they were entirely supreme. When problems of conflicting interests occurred, he stated, a constitutional convention, rather than Congress or the Supreme Court, should solve the matter.[25]

With the death of Spencer Roane in spring 1822, the hostility of states' rights proponents toward the Marshall Court subsided somewhat. Yet the Court became embroiled in another controversy when Justice Brockholst Livingston died on March 18, 1823. Charles Rhind took a grimly pragmatic view of the matter, speculating, "So we have another year and the addition of a Judge who will be in our favor." Rhind, like many New Yorkers, expected President James Monroe to replace Livingston with one of their own.[26] Monroe informally offered the position to Smith Thompson, a former New York Supreme Court justice, the current secretary of the navy, and a loyal Republican. As a state judge, Thompson had upheld the steamboat monopoly in *Livingston v. Van Ingen,* and so, he was more than acceptable to the Livingstons and their allies. Thompson, however, had his sights set on the presidency, and he equivocated on Monroe's offer.

Sensing Thompson's reluctance, New York senator Rufus King, a political ally of the North River Company, and Attorney General William Wirt actively petitioned Monroe to offer James Kent the position.[27] Appalled at the thought of appointing a strong Federalist to the bench, Monroe retorted that he had to "look to the good of *the whole country, to their great and permanent interests* and not to the ephemeral whining and exacerbating of the day" when selecting judges.[28] By summer 1823, even Supreme Court members were showing signs of exasperation. Story wrote to Marshall in June 1823, "I feel deep anxiety as to the successor of our lamented friend, Judge Livingston. I have heard strange rumors on the subject. If the President does not make a very excellent appointment, he is utterly without apology, for there was never a more enlightened Bar, from which to make the best selection."[29] Realizing he lacked the national political support to run for president, Thompson finally agreed to take the position in December. Yet he would play no role in the steamboat monopoly case. The untimely death of his daughter delayed his admittance to the Court until several months after *Gibbons v. Ogden* had been decided.

While Thompson dealt with political aspirations and personal tragedy, Justice William Johnson grappled with a constitutional crisis brewing in his home state of South Carolina. In August 1823, Johnson handed down a decision in the controversial circuit court case of *Elkison v. Deliesseline* (1823), which had strong repercussions for *Gibbons v. Ogden*. The case occurred in the wake of an attempted slave revolt led by Denmark Vesey, an African American carpenter and minister, in Charleston in 1822. White authorities crushed the uprising before it could come to fruition. Convinced that free blacks serving in the British navy had inspired Vesey and his followers to rebel, the South Carolina legislature had passed the Negro Seaman Act under which black sailors were to be quarantined aboard their ships while in port. In 1823, the Charleston sheriff arrested Henry Elkison, a Jamaican-born, free black British subject. In court, Elkison's lawyer dismissed the South Carolina statute as a violation of the commerce clause of the U.S. Constitution and federal trade treaties with Great Britain. Opposing counsel retorted that South Carolina had merely acted on its reserved police powers to keep the public peace. In his decision, Johnson criticized South Carolina's states' rights stance as "altogether irreconcilable with the powers of the general government," which would lead "to a dissolution of the Union, and implies a direct attack upon the sovereignty of the United States." If South Carolina could flout one federal law, then "it may be done as to all; and, like the old confederation, the Union becomes a mere rope of sand."[30]

White South Carolinians loudly criticized the Elkison decision in the local press. One critic, writing under the pseudonym Zeno, considered Johnson's decision "adapted to the Northern feeling on the slave system, and northern jealousy towards the south." Zeno also asserted that unless the Supreme Court overturned Johnson's ruling, "the Constitution of the United States must be altered, or it must be violated."[31] In another editorial, a writer identified as Caroliniensis deplored that under the Elkison decision, "the President and Senate may permit the brigands of St. Domingo to come here freely and securely, with their cargoes, and that we must quietly and tamely submit, because 'the State gave up to Congress the right to regulate commerce.'"[32] Johnson responded under the name Philonimus, stating, "My decision goes no further than to sustain the power of the General Government to open a Commerce with what nation they please, & to deny to a State the power to restrict that right to nations of white men." Far from undermining states' rights, he said, his decision "expressly recognizes the State power, as to every exercise of it within those limits, over its own population."[33]

John Marshall watched events develop in Charleston with a bemused concern. He remarked wryly to Story, "Our brother Johnson, I perceive, has hung himself on a democratic snag in a hedge composed entirely of thorny states' rights in South Carolina, and will find some difficulty, I fear, in getting off onto smooth open ground."[34] The chief justice had, in fact, faced a similar situation three years earlier in the circuit court case *The Wilson v. United States* (1820), which dealt with a Virginia law that prevented ships from importing free or enslaved blacks. Rather than confront the issue directly, Marshall defined black sailors as employees rather than cargo and therefore not "imports."[35] As he related to Story, "I might have considered its constitutionality had I chosen to do so; but it was not absolutely necessary, &, as I am not fond of butting against a wall in sport, I escaped on the construction of the act."[36]

Preparing for Opening Arguments

Against this backdrop of hostility toward the Supreme Court, Thomas Gibbons pushed his case forward. In New York, Charles Rhind remarked, "I have no doubt but Messrs. Emmet and Oakley would do real justice to that cause, and I have ever been sanguine that the decision would be in our favor." He nevertheless cautioned that "the oppositionists will use every exertion out of doors to bias the [Supreme Court] Members."[37] John Townsend likewise noted, "The great cause will of course come on for trial. I saw Colden today, he is less than sanguine."[38] William Wirt confided in his colleague Judge Dabney Carr, "Tomorrow begin my toils in the Supreme Court, and about tomorrow week will come on the great Steamboat question from New York. Emmet on one side, Webster and myself on the other." He urged Carr to hear the case, stressing the tempting prospect of watching Emmet in action: "Emmett's whole soul is in the cause and he will stretch out all his powers." Wirt also drew from Greek and Roman history to describe the high-profile attorneys involved with the case. He compared Thomas Oakley to Phocion, a Greek statesman who, in the sixth century BCE, had tried to warn his fellow Athenians of the dangers of decadence and remind them of the need for frugal living. Thomas Addis Emmet took on the role of Themistocles, a shrewd general who had convinced the Greeks to build a navy and engage the Persians at the Battle of Salamis in 480 BCE. Not surprisingly, Wirt described Daniel Webster as "ambitious as Caesar" and insisted, "He will not be outdone by any man, if it is within the compass of his power to avoid it."[39]

Webster's Arguments

On the morning of February 4, 1824, spectators crowded into the Supreme Court chambers in the basement of the U.S. Capitol. Seated at a table near the front of the courtroom were Senator Daniel Webster and Attorney General William Wirt, counsel for Thomas Gibbons. Aaron Ogden's attorneys, former New York State attorneys general Thomas Addis Emmet and Thomas Oakley, sat at a second table near their opponents. The crowd fell silent as Chief Justice Marshall led five other Supreme Court justices into the courtroom. Marshall and his fellow justices Gabriel Duvall, William Johnson, Joseph Story, Thomas Todd, and Bushrod Washington took their places behind a row of mahogany desks. At precisely eleven o'clock in the morning, a U.S. marshal cried out, "God save the United States and this honorable Court!"[40]

Daniel Webster, as lead counsel for Gibbons, began arguments by acknowledging New York's longtime support for the steamboat monopoly. He pointed out that as a court of appeals, the Supreme Court certainly had jurisdiction to hear state court cases, especially ones that dealt with the complex issue of commerce regulation. Did the New York state legislature have the authority to create the steamboat monopoly? If so, did such a grant conflict with the U.S. Constitution and federal laws?[41] Having laid out these questions, Webster launched into a discussion of the various state monopoly laws and their implications for federal commerce powers. He observed, "Nothing was more complex than commerce; and in an age such as this, no words embrace a wider field than commercial regulation."[42] The steamboat law was obviously a monopoly, he contended, and the framers had never meant to allow the states to retain the power to create monopolies.[43] Webster cited the Annapolis Convention, called in 1785 to discuss commercial rivalries between the states, and New York's own ratifying debates to reveal that the framers had sought a stronger central government in no small part to prevent regional economic conflicts. The founders had never meant to give the states concurrent regulatory powers, he said, and to adopt them now would lead to endless confusion and danger.[44]

Certainly, states could pass pilot, health, and quarantine laws as public health measures, Webster continued. The steamboat monopoly, however, was not a health or inspection law but a money-making venture that saddled New Yorkers with high fares and unreliable service. He concluded, "The people of New York have a right to be protected against this monopoly."[45] Webster affirmed Thomas Gibbons's right to navigate steam-powered vessels in New York under the federal Coasting Act of 1793, but he dismissed defense claims that such a license only registered vessels as American, that is, the property of American citizens. Coasting licenses also gave ship captains full access to American ports and discounted rates on tonnage duties.[46] The monopoly thus interfered with congressional powers to set tonnage duties, collect shipping fees, and grant monopolies. After Webster concluded his two and a half hours of argument, Thomas J. Oakley rose to defend the New York monopoly on behalf of Aaron Ogden.[47]

Oakley's Arguments

Oakley's meticulous nature showed through in a thorough defense of the New York monopoly that began on February 4 and carried over into the next evening. He began with a broad defense of states' rights. As sovereign entities, the American states had erected, in 1787, a limited federal government of expressly delegated powers, some of which were shared concurrently with the states.[48] Under the Tenth Amendment, only state laws that were "absolutely and totally contradictory and repugnant" to federal interests could be struck down.[49] The steamboat monopoly violated neither federal patent nor commerce powers. Federal patents applied only to specific inventions and for limited periods of time. Because Congress had not regulated patent rights in many areas, Oakley argued that states could continue to do so until the federal government declared otherwise.

Since Congress represented a limited government of enumerated powers, he continued, it could not create patent rights but only protect common-law patent rights.[50] Knowing full well that Fulton had repeatedly claimed to be the inventor of the steamboat, Oakley now attempted to argue that Fulton and Chancellor Livingston had merely imported such technology from Europe and that they deserved the right to exclusively enjoy it under New York law. In any event, Oakley said, Gibbons never claimed any patent rights, and therefore the issue was moot.[51] According to Oakley, commerce was a major area in which the states and the federal government wielded concurrent power. As a matter of sovereignty, states could regulate commerce within their borders unless such efforts directly conflicted with federal laws. and they could make temporary commercial agreements for turnpike, toll bridge, stagecoach, and ferry monopolies.[52]

Oakley gave his own account of the nation's founding, one that maintained that the framers had sought to regulate trade for taxation purposes and not to control travel between states. Under all other circumstances, he argued, states wielded the sovereign power to regulate their internal commerce.[53] To illustrate his legal position, Oakley portrayed the steamboat monopoly not as a commercial regulation but rather as a navigation law akin to New York's quarantine, inspection, and licensing laws. Although the federal government frequently taxed interstate trade, states retained the right to establish toll roads and ferries. In fact, Oakley cunningly cited federal law that required states to provide open access to their waterways as proof that the federal government, in effect, conceded some state powers to regulate commerce.[54] The term *commerce,* he said, thus had to be narrowly construed as the "transportation and sale of commodities." Since Gibbons carried passengers and not cargo on his ships, he was not involved in the coasting trade. The New York monopoly was accordingly valid.[55]

Emmet's Arguments

On the afternoon of February 7, Thomas Addis Emmet followed Oakley with a skillfully constructed defense of the steamboat monopoly, concluding on Monday, February 9. Emmet insisted that if Thomas Gibbons wished to strike down the New York monopoly, he had to show how the law specifically injured him. Like Oakley, Emmet pointed to the consistent validation of the steamboat monopoly by New York courts. He also cited similar monopoly grants in Massachusetts, New Hampshire, Pennsylvania, Georgia, and Tennessee. Could the Constitution consider all of these laws invalid?[56]

Emmet then denied that the steamboat monopoly conflicted with either federal commerce or patent powers. He cited both the journals of the Constitutional Convention and the Tenth Amendment to argue that the framers had granted Congress broad commerce powers precisely to maintain concurrent state jurisdiction.[57] In fact, he argued, "the expression, concurrent powers, is objected to, as if it implied equality in the rights vested in Congress and the States. It is only a verbal criticism, that it would be more correct if the term used was co-ordinate."[58] Emmet narrowly defined commerce as "the exchange of one thing for another; the interchange of commodities; trade or traffic."[59] He conceded federal authority to regulate import duties and foreign or interstate trade. To grant Congress broad

145

powers over inland trade, however, would jeopardize state control over harbors and canals, most notably the Erie Canal, and undermine internal improvement projects.[60]

In a similar vein, Emmet admitted that although the federal government wielded admiralty jurisdiction over cases in international waters, New York could still quarantine ships in New York Harbor. Echoing Oakley, he pointed to congressional acceptance of a wide variety of state taxation and inspection laws linked to interstate commerce. Emmet defended concurrent regulation as being not only constitutional but also practical, in order to accommodate local interests. Even the Mandarin rulers of China, he said, allowed provincial authorities to adapt commercial regulations to local circumstances. "With us," he stated, "the peculiar nature and principles of our free and federative government make the existence of such subordinate legislation more prudent and politic."[61]

Emmet insisted that the founders had understood the necessity of balancing state and federal interests. They had accordingly granted Congress broad commerce powers and left local economic matters to the states. Emmet concluded with a discussion of America's glorious past but troubled future. He remarked, "The thirteen original States were a band of brothers, who suffered, fought, bled, and triumphed together; they might, perhaps, have safely confided each his separate interest to the general will." But he warned that "if ever the day should come, when representatives from beyond the Rocky Mountains shall sit in this capitol; if ever a numerous and inland delegation shall wield the exclusive power of making regulations for our foreign commerce, without community of interest or knowledge of our local circumstances, the Union will not stand; it cannot stand; it cannot be the ordinance of God or nature, that it should stand."[62]

Not content merely to link the fate of the United States to futuristic commercial squabbles, Emmet also raised the subject of slavery, a topic on many Americans' minds following the Missouri Crisis and the Denmark Vesey conspiracy. If Congress could control the interstate slave trade, Emmet argued, it had to concede to the states the power to regulate such commerce. Congress had allowed northern state bans on slavery to continue despite constitutional guarantees not to regulate the international slave trade for twenty years, which proved, he said, that states still held rights to regulate commerce.[63] Federal recognition of state quarantine laws, piloting licenses, inspection standards, state-funded lighthouses, and state agreements with Native American tribes likewise showed that even Congress acknowledged the rights of states to regulate commerce.[64]

To answer the charge that the steamboat monopoly could lead to restrictions on other types of vessels, Emmet replied on practical grounds. The New York monopoly did not prohibit steamboats from New York waters, he said; it only banned the operation of their steam engines while inside state boundaries.[65] Emmet humorously illustrated his arguments through an imaginary dialogue between a sober-minded New York customs official and an offended English steamboat captain. Upon being informed of the New York monopoly law, the captain blustered, "I insist upon my right of entering your waters as I please; and if your State authorities, or any one acting under them, should prevent me, the King, my master, will know how to enforce the rights of his subjects." Emmet's customs inspector soothingly responded, "Patience, good Captain, patience. . . . Let your head and your boiler cool; no one means to prevent your entering into our waters. Only stop your machinery, and hoist those sails you have carried twenty times between this [port] and Liverpool, and, I'll answer for it."[66]

Almost as an aside, Emmet turned to a brief discussion of federal patent powers. Congress was a limited government of exclusive powers, he submitted, and it could not create patent rights but only protect preexisting common-law patent rights. Like Oakley, he pointed out that Gibbons had never claimed any federal patent rights. Even if he had, New York could still prohibit any form of property, even patented property such as steamboats, from its waters under its sovereign rights to regulate commerce.[67] Emmet concluded with a passionate account of the progress the New York monopoly had brought to the state and the nation in general. He trumpeted the New York monopoly and the wisdom of the New York legislature as the keys to Fulton's success. With a nod to Chancellor Kent, who had invoked Virgil's *Aeneid* in *Livingston v. Van Ingen,* Emmet concluded that New York

> may proudly raise her head, and cast her eyes over the whole civilized world; she there may see its countless waters bearing on their surface countless offsprings of her munificence and wisdom. She may fondly calculate on their speedy extension in every direction, and through every region, from Archangel to Calcutta; and justly arrogating to herself the labours of the man she cherished, and, conscious of the value of her own good works, she may turn the mournful exclamation of Aeneas into an expression of triumph, and exultingly ask, *"Quae regio in terris, nostri non plena laboris?"*[68]

In concluding his defense, Emmet thus continued the literary debate begun by Kent and Henry thirteen years earlier. He drew his audience to the by now

147

148 familiar scene in which Aeneas, observed paintings in the palace of Carthage depicting the destruction of his Troy and cried, "What country of the world is not full of our travails?" Whereas Aeneas used the phrase to lament that the entire ancient world had heard of the fall of Troy, Emmet sought to remind his audience that countries around the globe had witnessed American successes in steam power. It was a literary allusion that Emmet soon regretted.[69]

Wirt's Arguments

On the afternoon of February 9, William Wirt answered Emmet's emotionally charged arguments with a barrage from the parapets of the commerce clause. Unlike Oakley, who had offered exhaustive arguments, or Emmet, with his colorful orations, Wirt "delights and convinces, and no man hears him without understanding his arguments—a sure indication of a clear head and a logical mind," noted a reporter for the *New York Statesman.*[70] Another article was less complimentary, observing that Wirt's "argument thus far has been almost entirely in reply to that of Mr. Oakley; to unravel the knotty points of which, literally caused the attorney general to perspire freely."[71]

Wirt described the steamboat monopoly as unconstitutional because it conflicted with federal commerce and patent powers. Even if New York enjoyed concurrent regulatory powers, he said, the monopoly still interfered with congressional authority and was therefore void. Wirt first accepted the defense's argument that the framers had granted Congress broad commerce powers to allow the federal and state governments to wield concurrent jurisdiction. But why had the framers given the federal government any commerce powers at all? He answered, "They were all created by the Constitution, because they are to be wielded by the whole Union over the whole Union, which no state could previously do."[72]

Likewise, he asked, if state patent rights were sovereign, why should the federal government be given patent rights at all? In the 1780s, the framers created the Constitution in part to protect the economic and scientific potential of the United States. Wirt paraphrased an argument first raised in Brockholst Livingston's 1811 district court decision in *Livingston v. Van Ingen*—namely, if New York could monopolize steam power, "why should it not be done equally with all the other elements, such as gravitation, magnetism, galvanism, electricity, and others?"[73]

He then rejected the claim that the New York monopoly represented a reward for importing steam technology. Fulton's frequent claims to be the inventor of the steamboat were well documented, he pointed out, and to now claim to be a mere possessor of new technology was only a ruse to avoid federal patent law. Furthermore, the New York monopoly was obviously not a public safety measure, nor had the New York legislature ever claimed that it was.[74] Of course states had the right to pass public health laws as part of their police powers, he observed. But they had surrendered control of interstate trade to the federal government with the passage of the U.S. Constitution. Both the Constitution and the federal Coasting Act of 1793 sought to regulate commerce as it moved across state borders or between sovereign nations.[75]

Despite his precisely crafted attack on the steamboat monopoly, Wirt ended his summation on an emotional note. He took issue with Emmet's quotation of the *Aeneid*, insisting that his colleague had only repeated part of the quote. Wirt reminded the justices that the primary significance of Aeneas's statement hinged on the fact that it was not made in a moment of triumph but in a moment of despair, during which the protagonist contemplated the fall of Troy in a civil war that pitted Trojans against their distant Achaean cousins. Wirt juxtaposed this mournful scene of fratricide with the current interstate rivalries over the issue of steam travel. He warned, "If the spirit of hostility, which already exists in three of our States, is to catch by contagion, and spread among the rest, as, from the progress of the human passions, and the unavoidable conflict of interests, it will too surely do, what are we to expect?" He warned that "civil wars have often arisen from far inferior causes, and have desolated some of the fairest provinces of the earth."[76]

Perhaps to subtly mock Emmet's emotion-laden summation, Wirt delivered his own melodramatic closing. He raised the possibility of future state and constitutional conflicts that might destroy the American experiment and undermine the cause of republicanism across the world. Wirt mournfully concluded, "Then, sir, when New-York shall look upon this scene of ruin, if she have the generous feelings which I believe her to have, it will not be with her head aloft, in the pride of conscious triumph—'her rapt soul sitting in her eyes;' no, sir, no: dejected, with shame and confusion—drooping under the weight of her sorrow, with a voice suffocated with despair, well may she then exclaim, '*Quis jam locus, Quae regio in terris nostri non plena laboris!*'"[77]

149

Reactions in the Press

Newspapers in Washington, DC, and throughout the United States provided coverage of the arguments in *Gibbons v. Ogden*. Such attention ranged from brief editorials to detailed accounts of the arguments and personalities involved with the affair. The *Washington Daily Intelligencer*, for instance, described the events of each day and printed portions of the attorneys' arguments.[78] The *Richmond Enquirer* provided elaborate coverage of the case and printed a letter from a trial observer to a friend in Richmond. "The Supreme Court has seldom, if ever, exhibited a greater display of legal learning, ability and eloquence, than in the argument of this question," the writer announced. "Vast research and ingenuity were manifested by each member of the counsel, but the great contest seemed reserved for Mr. Emmet and the Attorney General, who counseled the case on their respective sides." In particular, Webster's final statement was "truly thrilling and affecting—and I never witnessed such an effect from any burst of eloquence—every face was filled with the fine transport and prophetic fury of the orator, and all united in applauding the peroration, as affording for matter, diction, happy application, and striking effect, the most powerful oratory that they ever witnessed."[79] New York papers paid particular attention to the steamboat monopoly case. The *New York Evening Post* reported, "Perhaps there has never been a more elaborate argument before the Supreme Court than this; certainly not a more important question. It has been placed upon constitutional grounds, and is a conflict between federal and states' rights."[80]

Over four days of extensive deliberations, Gibbons and Ogden's able attorneys had laid out every major argument surrounding steam travel and interstate commerce that had been articulated since John Fitch's experiments in the 1780s. They had done so in an atmosphere charged with public fears over economic downturns, aggressive states' rights advocacy, the consolidation of federal power, the expansion of slavery, slave uprisings, disunion, and civil war. For over twenty years, John Marshall and his followers had sought to use the influence of the Supreme Court to inspire national economic and cultural nationalism. Yet intense public reactions to the panic of 1819, the Missouri Crisis, and the McCulloch and Cohens decisions had sparked a resurgence of states' rights fervor, which the High Court now had to deal with when contemplating the facts in *Gibbons v. Ogden*.

The attorneys who argued the steamboat monopoly case were well aware of these background factors, and they alluded to them in their arguments. Webster and Wirt had produced a logical series of arguments that portrayed Congress as the historical and practical choice of governmental bodies with which to control trade between the states. Emmet and Oakley, however, had crafted an emotionally appealing and well-documented defense of the New York monopoly as a cornerstone of states' rights. In contrast to Spencer Roane's bombastic states' rights defenses, Emmet more subtly invoked the *Aeneid* to depict both Robert Fulton and New York in noble strokes that accentuated their commitment to the cultivation of science and generosity in sharing its bounty with the several states. Webster summoned the same metaphor to warn of a future in which unchecked state rivalries dissolved of the Union. As Aeneas lamented, after all, Troy fell; so could the United States. With these two alternatives in mind, Americans across the nation waited to see what decision the Marshall Court would produce.

The Gibbons Decision
and Popular Reaction

Rumors and Speculation

THE ARGUMENTS IN *Gibbons v. Ogden* had been masterful and the drama intense. Charles Rhind stoically informed the Townsends, "The battle is begun and we must patiently await the result."[1] William Wirt took a different approach and optimistically informed his brother that "the Steam Boat cause is finished—and we are triumphant I hope—not as to the decision of the cause for that is not yet settled, But as to the argument."[2] Daniel Webster likewise bragged, "There is no doubt but that the decision will be against the New York Monopoly; at least as far as respects Vessels going from Other states to New York—which is the present case. Be assured the result was certain."[3]

Behind such bravado, however, lay a kernel of doubt that Chief Justice Marshall would uphold Gibbons's federal license but allow the North River Company to continue operations in New York. In fact, during their arguments, Colden and Emmet had spent as much time defending state police powers in general as they did justifying the monopoly. They presumably sought to carve out a fallback position for their client in the event of an unfavorable court decision. If Ogden and his New York allies were forced to abandon their New Jersey-to-New York operations, they could at least retain the lucrative Hudson River trade, which lay entirely within the borders of the Empire State. This proved to be a wise strategy, for as Ohio congressman James Thomson, a colleague of the Townsends who witnessed the trial, noted, "Bets are laid on both sides and speculation is afloat. Sober minded men of the Law however have come to the conclusion after studying the question that the court will protect the State right but will open the Waters between State & State."[4] In similar fashion, Webster maintained, "I have no doubt the Court will decide, that so far as respects commerce between different states (which is this case) the law of N. York is inoperative." In a rare moment of doubt, he conceded, "Possibly the navigation of the N. York waters between port & port, in her own territory, may be subject to a different consideration."[5] New York state senator John A. King, on the other hand, felt that a Gibbons victory would completely rout the monopoly forces. King commented to his father, Senator Rufus King (a key monopoly supporter), "It is difficult to understand in what manner the other question [i.e., congressional control over interstate commerce] can be decided without virtually having the strongest leaning on their monopoly. If boats can under this decision, go from port to port of different states why not from port to port in the same states?"[6]

In early February, attorney David Bayard Ogden wrote to his cousin, Aaron Ogden, with the bitter news that he had "not seen a man who heard the argument, and the Court room was crowded," who still entertained "a doubt about the unconstitutionality of the laws."[7] William Gibbons confidently informed his father that there were now no hopes for the monopoly. Webster boasted to Gibbons of news from an inside source that when *Gibbons v. Ogden* first came before the Court, "a majority of the justices had considered the case to merely involve a conflict between state and federal laws. But after hearing the argument they have changed that opinion & consider it more than collision, that is a broad constitutional question upon which scarcely any doubt exists." Although optimistic about getting a favorable outcome from the Supreme Court, William Gibbons remained distrustful of Webster. The younger Gibbons even speculated, "It would not be a matter of surprise to me if he [Webster] had the opinion of the Judges in his possession & meant to delay it until the matter of fees was settled."[8]

As gossip over *Gibbons v. Ogden* reached a feverish pitch, however, the Supreme Court justices announced that their decision would be postponed. On February 19, after returning from a dinner at the White House, the chief justice had slipped and fallen on a patch of ice, briefly lost consciousness, and dislocated his shoulder. He reported to his wife, Polly, "Although I feel no pain when perfectly still, yet I cannot get up and move about without difficulty & cannot put on my coat."

The Gibbons Decision and Popular Reaction

Marshall also said, "Of course I cannot go to court."[9] The judge remained bed-ridden for two weeks, which led to rumors that Joseph Story had actually crafted the Gibbons decision.[10] Within a week, however, Marshall returned to work, and the Supreme Court announced that it would hand down its decision on the steamboat monopoly case on March 2.

The Decision of the Supreme Court

Newspaper accounts revealed that there was a fair amount of public anticipation over the Gibbons decision. The *New York Statesman* reported, "Inquiries are hourly made respecting the anxiously-looked-for decision of the Supreme Court in this important case."[11] On March 2, the *New York Commercial Advertiser* noted, "This morning, his honor, Chief Justice Marshall appeared for the first time since his confinement . . . and took his seat on the bench. . . . The courtroom was thronged at an early hour in anticipation of what has taken place—the reading of the opinion of the Court in the great *Steamboat Case.*"[12]

After he took his seat before a filled courtroom, the chief justice handed down one of the most significant decisions of his celebrated judicial career. In reading his decision, Marshall employed a rhetorical strategy of which he had frequently made good use. As Benjamin Henry Latrobe had noted years earlier, Marshall's technique involved "placing his case in that point of view suited to the purpose he aims at, throwing a blazing light upon it, and keeping the attention of his hearers fixed upon the object to which he originally directed it."[13] In this case, Marshall transfixed his audience with the grand subject of commerce. He began with an acknowledgment that the monopoly had been "supported by great names—by names which have all the titles to consideration that virtue, intelligence, and office, can bestow." However, he reminded his audience of the Supreme Court's duty to render decisions independently, as the people of the United States expected them to do.[14]

The chief justice then laid out a broad interpretation of the Constitution. Although states were initially sovereign after the American Revolution, he said, they subordinated part of their independence to the federal government through the adoption of the Constitution. The Constitution by necessity granted broad powers to the federal government. To deny Congress powers not specifically listed in the Constitution "would cripple the government, and render it unequal to the object, for which it is declared to be instituted, and to which the powers given, as fairly understood, render it competent."[15] As a former ratifier of the U.S. Constitution, Marshall insisted that "the enlightened patriots who formed our constitution, and the people who adopted it," employed plain words to clearly express their ideas toward government.[16] The commerce clause of the U.S. Constitution clearly gave Congress the "power to regulate commerce with foreign nations, and among the several states, and with the Indian tribes." He broke the clause down into its constituent parts. The phrase "commerce," he said, referred to the purchase or sale of commodities. However, he added, "commerce, undoubtedly, is traffic, but it is something more; it is intercourse." Under Marshall's definition, intercourse included trade between nations and between different parts of the same nation. The chief justice wryly commented, "The mind can scarcely conceive a system for regulating commerce between nations, which shall exclude all laws concerning navigation, which shall be silent on the admission of vessels of the one nation into the ports of the other, and be confined to prescribing rules for the conduct of individuals, in the actual employment of buying and selling, or of barter."[17]

Since its inception, Congress had frequently wielded power over navigation as well as commerce, Marshall said. Both the framers and the American public in 1787 had understood that commerce necessarily included navigation. If Congress could show no favoritism to one American port at the expense of another, then the legislative branch obviously had powers to regulate both commerce and navigation. The ability of the federal government to impose embargoes further belied formidable powers to regulate commerce and navigation in both wartime and peacetime. Even New Englanders who had opposed President Jefferson's embargoes twenty years earlier had conceded the point.[18]

Having defined commerce, the chief justice then upheld Congress's authority to regulate commerce with foreign nations and "among the several states." Marshall argued that the word "among" meant "intermingled with." He further elaborated, "A thing, which is among others, is intermingled with them. Commerce among the States, cannot stop at the external boundary line of each State, but may be introduced into the interior."[19] States retained exclusive power only over internal trade solely within their borders.[20] Congressional commerce power, however, did not end at state boundaries but included "the deep streams which penetrate our country in every direction, pass thorough the interior of almost every state in the Union." The federal government could, therefore, regulate commerce within state boundaries: because many states shared common borders, interstate commerce necessarily included trade across state lines.[21]

Having completed his exhaustive analyses of the commerce clause, Marshall affirmed that congressional commerce power was limited but supreme over foreign and interstate trade.[22] For instance, both the federal and state governments could levy import and export duties on foreign goods. But such power did not grant states the ability to regulate foreign or interstate commerce in general. The federal government derived the power to establish import duties from its taxation power. Congressional authority to regulate trade, however, flowed from the commerce clause. Although import duties might influence commerce, they were still fundamentally taxes. The framers thus kept federal taxation and commerce powers separate under the Constitution.[23]

In a similar vein, he argued that states could enact inspection, quarantine, and health laws under their police powers.[24] Yet although both the states and the federal government could concurrently regulate commerce, states could not exercise powers reserved for the federal government or vice versa. Federal laws that ordered customs officials to abide by state inspection laws acknowledged only state police powers.[25] Federal regulatory powers, which banned the importation of foreign-born slaves into free states, similarly confirmed state commerce powers. Although the Constitution's initial twenty-year ban on federal legislation to prohibit the slave trade had allowed states to regulate the importation of foreign slaves in the interim, this temporary abeyance of federal authority only proved the general rule that Congress could trump state regulatory schemes under normal circumstances. Even federal statutes that required pilots to abide by state regulations did not presuppose concurrent commerce powers. They merely gave state safety laws the force of federal law when needed.[26]

The chief justice next addressed Webster's adoption of the phrase "to regulate" as an implication that congressional power over interstate commerce excluded all forms of state regulation. Marshall asserted, "There is great force in this argument, and the court is not satisfied that it has been refuted."[27] In any event, the central issue remained whether the New York steamboat monopoly violated federal law, not whether the monopoly sprang from state police or commerce powers. He concluded, "In one case and the other, the acts of New-York must yield to the law of Congress; and the decision sustaining the privilege they confer, against a right given by the law of the Union, must be erroneous."[28]

Marshall agreed that the right of interstate trade was a natural one that predated the Constitution. In fact, the framers had recognized this right and had given Congress the power to regulate it. Congress, in turn, had used such authority to produce the Coasting Act of 1793. The act thus conveyed to ship captains who applied for a license under its power both privileges in docking fees and the broader right to travel from port to port in separate states. Consequently, Marshall stated, "it would be contrary to all reason, and to the course of human affairs, to say . . . that a state is unable to strip a vessel of the particular privileges attendant on the exercise of a right, and yet may annul the right itself." In short, it was absurd to argue that the state of New York could not prevent an enrolled and licensed vessel from traveling from its port to a New Jersey port but could shut up that same vessel within one of its own ports.[29]

Having laid down the legal framework for his decision, Marshall proceeded to examine the specifics of the Gibbons-Ogden conflict. He noted that the federal coasting law gave only enrolled vessels the right to trade in American ports.[30] The phrase "coasting trade" was, he said, a perfectly intelligible, well-understood term that obviously included trade between different states.[31] Federal laws made no distinction between sailing ships that bore cargo and those that bore passengers. Many ships, in fact, carried both cargo and passengers and were completely subject to federal regulation. Marshall cited an 1819 federal law that provided for the comfort and safety of passenger ships but made no regulations regarding whether such ships had to carry persons or cargo; not even the New York steamboat monopoly laws or injunctions issued against Gibbons distinguished between passengers and cargo. Likewise, federal regulatory laws rarely considered the principles by which vessels were powered.[32]

Marshall concluded with a stern lecture to states' rights advocates, presumably meaning James Kent and the leaders of the Richmond Junto. The chief justice defended his extended commentary as tedious but unavoidable. In fact, he said, "the conclusion to which we have come, depends upon a train of principles which it was necessary to prove unbroken." Furthermore, he noted that "although some of them were thought nearly self-evident, the magnitude of the question, the weight of the character belonging to those whose judgment we dissent, and the argument and the bar, determined that we should assume nothing."[33] Marshall also warned against "powerful and ingenious minds, taking, as postulates, that the powers expressly granted to the government of the Union, are to be contracted by construction, into the narrowest possible compass." Such states' rights advocates would, he continued,

> explain away the constitution of our country, and leave it, a magnificent structure, indeed, to look at, but totally unfit for use. They may so entangle and perplex the understanding, as to obscure principles, which were before thought

157

quite plain, and induce doubts where, if the mind were to pursue its own course, none would be perceived. In such a case, it is peculiarly necessary to recur to safe and fundamental principles to sustain those principles, and, when sustained, to make them the tests of the arguments to be examined.[34]

Johnson's Concurring Opinion

Despite the fact that there was a unanimous vote by the Supreme Court in the Gibbons case, Justice William Johnson insisted on delivering a concurring opinion. This was not unusual, for Johnson had gained a reputation as a contrarian on the Court.[35] Furthermore, the South Carolinian had long disliked the New York monopoly. In a speech delivered to the Literary and Philosophical Society of Charleston in 1815, for example, he had applauded internal improvements but warned against the dangers of state-granted monopolies such as the New York steamboat monopoly. Johnson concluded, "It is to be hoped, that we shall not be tempted to the adoption of that short-sided [sic] policy which renders a whole community liable to be severely accessed by the cupidity of a few individuals."[36] Johnson apparently maintained an active interest in the steamboat controversy, for three years later, on a voyage from New York to New Haven, future president John Quincy Adams witnessed the associate justice "avidly philosophizing with another of the passengers upon the construction of the steamboat and the conflicting pretensions of Fulton and Fitch."[37] In addition to these factors, Johnson felt the need to defend his strong nationalist stance in *Elkison v. Deliesseline.*

Johnson accordingly began his concurring opinion in *Gibbons* with an expression of support for Marshall's decision. But he then maintained that "having adopted my conclusions on views of the subject materially different from those of my brethren, I feel it incumbent on me to express those views."[38] Starting on a moderate note, he dismissed both broad and strict constitutional construction as misleading. "The simple, classical, yet precise comprehensive language, in which it [the Constitution] is couched, leaves, at most, but very little latitude for construction," he stated.[39] When the extent and meaning of the Constitution were determined, all that remained was to fulfill the guidelines of the document in the most efficient manner possible. The purpose of the Constitution, he added, "was to unite this mass of wealth and power, for the protection of the humblest individual; his rights, civil and political, his interests and prosperity, are the sole end; the rest are nothing but the means."[40]

Although Johnson acknowledged the broad powers reserved to the states, he pointed to the economic rivalries of the confederation era and the subsequent intent of the framers to promote uniform commerce regulation.[41] As a matter of practicality, Congress never "permitted" certain types of commerce, except to strike down state prohibitions on free trade. Congressional commerce powers were, therefore, broadly based and exclusive. Having established his general points, Johnson proceeded to discuss the constitutionality of the steamboat monopoly. He completely dismissed any difference between the principles of navigation and commerce.[42] Individuals who built ships, transported goods, and hired and supervised sailors were important parts of commercial prosperity. If the federal government could not regulate such subjects, it could not claim to regulate commerce at all.[43]

The constitutional clause, which forbade congressional obstruction of the international slave trade, argued Johnson, implicitly recognized the rights of the federal government to control immigration and even tax individuals about to enter the United States. The Constitution gave Congress the power to strike down state laws that forced American vessels to pay port duties.[44] It was thus a self-evident proposition that "the sense of mankind, the practice of the world, the contemporaneous assumption, and continued exercise of the power, and universal acquiescence" clearly gave Congress control "over navigation, and the transportation of both men and their goods."[45] Not even New York distinguished between navigation and commerce in its control of internal steamboat traffic.

Since Congress wielded sole authority over interstate trade, the federal Coasting Act of 1793 was of dubious significance in Johnson's estimation: if the Coasting Act were repealed tomorrow, Gibbons would still have the right to ply New York waters with a steamboat due to the authority of the commerce clause.[46] Johnson argued that, in fact, "one half the doubts in life arise from the defects of language" and that Gibbons's license would more appropriately be called an exemption. The purpose of the Coasting Act was not to give enrolled vessels an American designation but to give American ships taxation and trading advantages over foreign vessels and thus promote domestic commerce.[47] Gibbons's federal coasting license therefore invalidated any attempts at concurrent commercial jurisdiction.[48] Furthermore, the Coasting Act applied equally to wind-powered and steam-powered boats.[49] Although states could pass health and inspection laws

159

as part of their police powers, the federal government maintained broad control over state inspection laws through Article I, Section 10, of the Constitution.[50]

Johnson admitted that state and federal commerce powers overlapped in some instances. and he compared those instances to a thief who robbed the federal mail and then stole a horse in order to escape. In such a situation, both state and federal governments could legitimately charge the offender, even if their powers to do so conflicted. But one authority would eventually have to give way to the other. Johnson concluded, "Wherever the powers of the respective governments are frankly exercised, with a distinct view to the ends of such powers, they may act upon the same object, or use the same means, and yet the powers be kept perfectly distinct." Having dismissed the New York monopoly based upon a broad reading of the commerce clause, Johnson declined to address the question of whether the New York monopoly violated federal patent powers. Such an approach also served to underscore the contention that *only* the commerce clause was necessary to invalidate the monopoly.[51]

When Johnson concluded, Marshall handed down the decree of the Supreme Court. First, he reviewed the facts of the case and the decision of the Court. He then declared that the Coasting Act of 1793 gave Gibbons the right to participate in coastal trade and that any state law to the contrary was void. With a strong endorsement of federal commerce power, the chief justice struck down the New York steamboat monopoly as "erroneous," saying that it "ought to be reversed, and the same is hereby reversed and annulled: and this Court doth further DIRECT, ORDER, and DECREE, that the bill of the said Aaron Ogden be dismissed, and this same is hereby dismissed accordingly."[52]

Reactions to the Gibbons Decision

Both litigants and the general public reacted heatedly to the outcome of the case. The chief justice was pleased with his decision, and in response to requests for copies of it, he stated that he had "not the slightest objection to its publication." He furthermore believed that the Court had no reservations except to prefer that a final copy of the decision be printed instead of a rough draft.[53] Other Washington luminaries were less enthusiastic, however. One staunch critic of the Gibbons decision was Virginia congressman John Randolph of Roanoke. Randolph was born into a family of wealthy Virginia tobacco planters, and he embraced the lifestyle of a country gentleman. He spent much of his adult life in Congress as an enthusiastic Democratic-Republican and as chair of the powerful Ways and Means Committee. In 1806, he broke with his mentor, Thomas Jefferson, to form a splinter faction of so-called Old Republicans, who militantly opposed any increases in federal power. One court reporter noted that Randolph had attended many of the court sessions in *Gibbons v. Ogden.*[54] The Virginian had shown particular approval of Emmet's arguments and "nodded eloquent assent to all his leading positions. A great stickler himself for States' rights, the unyielding tenacity of EMMET pleased him."[55] As a result, Marshall's decision in the Gibbons case came as a disappointment to Randolph. The Old Republican confided to a friend, "It is the fashion to praise the Chief Justice's opinion in the case of Ogden against Gibbons. But you know I am not a fashionable man; I think it is unworthy of him." Furthermore, he observed, the decision "contains a great deal that has no business there, or indeed anywhere." In fact, "a judicial opinion should decide nothing and embrace nothing that is not before the Court." The old Republican further quipped, "Since the case of *Cohen v. Virginia,* I am done with the Supreme Court."[56]

Former president Thomas Jefferson also decried the Gibbons decision. Although in poor health, he wrote to his friend William Branch Giles on the dangers of a powerful federal government. "I see, as you do, and with the deepest affliction, the rapid strides with which the federal branch of our government is advancing towards the usurpation of all the rights reserved to the States," he observed: "Consolidation in itself of all powers, foreign and domestic; and that, too, by constructions which, if legitimate, leave no limits to their power." In particular, Jefferson argued that "under the power to regulate commerce, they assume indefinitely that also over agriculture and manufactures, and call it regulation to take the earnings of one of these branches of industry, and that too the most depressed, and put them into the pockets of the other, the most flourishing of all."[57]

The stockholders and employees of the North River Steam Boat Company also bitterly accepted the Gibbons decision. Yet Rhind and his partners remained more concerned with practical business matters than abstract constitutional theories. Captain Samuel Wiswall wrote to John Townsend, "The agony is over, all is gone by the board." Competitors had seven boats ready in anticipation of the Supreme Court's decision and now merely waited for the ice to clear on the Hudson River to begin business.[58] As news that the Gibbons decision was at hand reached Albany, Charles Rhind confided, "The decision has not yet come down but will doubtless be here tomorrow although there is a hope left, it is but a small one for I fear the License will in some way or another open a door for evasion." Like Wiswall, Rhind warned stockholders that soon "every old Basket of a Boat will be put in requisition" for service on the Hudson.[59]

Gibbons v. Ogden *in the National Press*

The Gibbons decision created an instant media sensation and generated coverage ranging from reprints of the Supreme Court decision to lengthy articles on the implications of the case. A number of New York papers reacted favorably to the decision. The *New York Commercial Advertiser* reported that Marshall's arguments presented "one of the most powerful effects of the human mind that has ever been displayed from the bench of any Court."[60] The *New York Spectator* asserted that the Gibbons decision should "command the assent of every impartial mind competent to embrace such a subject" and represented "the strongest document in support of the powers of the Federal Government that has ever issued from the same authority."[61] The *New York Daily Advertiser* speculated, "Perhaps there has never been a more elaborate argument before the Supreme Court than this; certainly not a more important question. It has been placed upon constitutional grounds, and is a conflict between federal and states' rights."[62] The *New York Evening Post* concluded, "Many passages indicate a profoundness and a forecast, in relation to the destiny of our confederacy, peculiar to the great man who acted as the organ of our court. The Steam Boat grant is at an end."[63]

New England papers widely applauded the Gibbons decision. The *Connecticut Courant* reported, "The waters are now free, and those who heretofore held with an iron grasp, and exercised with unfeeling perverseness, their precarious power will now perhaps lament, when it is too late, the rashness and severity which has involved them in embarrassment, if not ruin."[64] Striking a note of fear, the *Courant* warned, "If the States should once embrace a feeling of hostility or even jealousy toward the National councils, it is to be feared those ties which bind us together will be dissolved."[65] The *Norwich Courier* adopted a more legalistic approach and noted, "From these principles thus laid down, it would seem that a steam-boat having a coasting license from any Custom-house in the Union, may go and ply wherever a coasting vessel can sail, either from one State to another, or from port to port, in the same state." Although admitting that "perhaps the latter position may hereafter be contested," the paper stated that "certainly the opinion of the Supreme Court plainly implies this doctrine." The *Courier* nevertheless concluded, "In one word then, the grant of the State of New-York to Livingston and Fulton is decided to be UNCONSTITUTIONAL."[66]

Other northern papers were similarly supportive of the decision. The *Elizabethtown Gazette* of Elizabethtown, New Jersey, heaped praise on Thomas Gibbons, stating, "Scarcely another throughout the United States could have been found of talents, courage, perseverance and resources, equal to the successful accomplishment of so great an object." The article concluded on a conciliatory note with the prediction that "New Yorkers themselves will, in no distant day, unite in gratitude to that man, and that high tribunal, who have been so instrumental in doing them a great good."[67] The *United States Gazette* of Philadelphia similarly applauded the Gibbons decision: "We have rarely read a decision which we thought marked with more plain sense and sterling truth than this. The privileges of the individual states, and the rights of the general government, respecting commerce, are clearly and luminously pointed out." To be certain, the paper continued, "individuals at New York, will, we are aware suffer by this decision, but monopoly will receive a deserved check. [Yet] whatever may be our regret that a few enterprising individuals should be disappointed in their entrepreneurial games, we must heartily rejoice that the rights of the whole are ascertained and defined!!!"[68]

Although they were in the midst of the public controversy over the steamboat monopoly, newspapers in Washington, DC, remained surprisingly detached from the controversy.[69] The Washington-based *Daily National Intelligencer* provided day-to-day trial coverage but comparatively little insight into the details of the case. One article commented on "the high importance, as well as reputed ability and conclusiveness of the Opinion of the Supreme Court, yesterday declared; in the case of the celebrated Steam Boat controversy." Yet the author merely concluded, "It is of considerable length, and is decisive against the right of the state of New York to constitute the Steam Boat monopoly."[70] The *National Gazette* provided perhaps the most specific comment on the Gibbons decision. It asserted, "The constitutional law which is so thoroughly expounded in this masterpiece of judicial reasoning concerns every citizen. . . . It is a matter for general complacency that unlimited scope is now afforded to enterprise and capital in steam navigation."[71]

163

Because *Gibbons v. Ogden* held serious implications for states' rights and the interstate slave trade, southerners and southern papers followed the proceedings of the case with interest. The *Charleston Courier* stated that "the interest excited by the decision, of the Supreme Court, in the Steam boat controversy, has induced us to give the following brief and imperfect view of the Opinion delivered, to gratify our readers."[72] The *Charleston City Gazette* remarked, "By this decision it would appear that the sovereignty of a State under the Federal Constitution is not unlimited. A principle of greatest magnitude is thus settled in the United States, and consequences of material interest in every part of the Republic will flow from its decision."[73]

Perhaps out of deference to the Gibbons family, the Georgia press published a variety of positive editorials on the outcome of the steamboat monopoly case. The *Augusta Chronicle,* for instance, stated, "The principle settled, in the Steam Boat question recently before the Supreme Court of the U. States is one of such vast interest and importance to our country, that we deem it a duty to lay the entire opinion of the court, long as it is, to our readers." Strongly in support of the Marshall Court, the article expressed doubted that the Gibbons decision would "be unacceptable to any portion of the American population, who have not an interest in wishing that a question of this magnitude has been brought to a different result."[74] The *Savannah Daily Georgian* commented, "The important Steam Boat Question was decided in the Supreme Court of the United States as Washington on the 2nd . . . . The opinion, which was delivered by Chief Justice Marshall is said to be able and conclusive against the right of the state of New York to contain the Steam Boat monopoly."[75] Even the *Georgia Patriot,* which normally favored states' rights, concluded, "The exercise of the power of the U.S. Courts, in matters of this kind, cannot but be interesting to the individual states into its bearing on the independence of their legislation. Having no original jurisdiction, the Supreme Court is the standard to which all disputed rights, and authorities must be brought for test and determination."[76]

Gulf state papers contained several articles that discussed the Gibbons decision. The *New Orleans Courier* observed that the decision "will deeply affect the interest of the North River Steam Boat Company, who it is believed, has a capital employed, of something like six hundred thousand dollars." The article also conceded, "At any rate, about that sum has been employed since the experiments in navigating by steam were commenced; a considerable part of which was sunk, in bringing the invention to perfection, and reducing it to practice."[77] More optimistically, the

Mobile Commercial Register announced, "We rejoice at the decision of the Supreme Court of the United States, against the right of States to grant monopolies on public highways." Furthermore, the paper stated, "the patent navigation of Boats and Stages, on Rivers and Roads, will no longer find themselves beyond the reach of fair competition, they will find themselves unable in the future to close the door of enterprise, even under the authority of legislative sanction."[78]

Although westerners had a long history of animosity to the monopoly, papers headquartered on the more remote parts of the frontier contained only scanty references to the Gibbons case. The *Kentucky Reporter* and the *St. Louis Enquirer* reprinted the entire Supreme Court decision but provided no editorial comment. The *Kentucky Gazette* noted briefly, "The Supreme Court of the United States has decided the case in which the rights of the state of New York to legislate over her own waters is involved. It is called the steam boat case; and it is decided against the right of the state to pass such laws."[79] More conclusively, the *Louisville Public Advertiser* stated, "We not only believe the opinion of the Court to be correct, but we feel confident that, had the same case been tried by any competent tribunal not within the State of New York, the result would have been the same."[80] The *Missouri Republican* noted that "some of the New Yorkers show themselves a little restive under the late decision of the U.S. Supreme Court on the subject of the steam boat monopoly." The editor then gloated, "They may rest assured that it is a decision approved of in their sister States, who can see no propriety in the claim of New York to domineer over the waters which form the means of intercourse between that State and others, and over the intercourse itself."[81]

Gibbons v. Ogden met resistance from some quarters. Many New Yorkers held interests in the North River Steam Boat Company and vented their anger in the popular press. For instance, a *New York Evening Post* article warned that "in entire conformity with the decision at Washington, the Fulton grant, so far as relates to the cities of New York and Albany, and all intermediate ports or places on the North River, is, we repeat, untouched, directly or indirectly, and no person can interfere with that grant, but at their peril."[82] Another article complained, "Some of the rules of construction [in the Gibbons decision] appear to be inadmissible and dangerous, and the opinion appears to have been hastily drawn, and in language not very remarkable for delicacy or respect towards the claims and pretensions of this state."[83] One critic even called for a verbatim account of the Gibbons decision to "judge whether the decree goes beyond the decision. This can hardly be supposed; but if it does it is certainly void."[84]

A *New York National Advertiser* article warned that regardless of its constitutionality, the Gibbons decision, with its strong defense of federal commerce regulation, would antagonize states' rights interests. Although the article's author proclaimed respect for the High Court, he predicted such decisions would only lead to the consolidation of states' rights under federal supremacy. To prevent such a calamity, he urged that "the SENATE OF THE UNITED STATES SHOULD BE CONSTITUTED A COURT OF ERRORS AND APPEALS IN ALL QUESTIONS TOUCHING THE RIGHTS OF STATES; and that an amendment to the Constitution, to this effect, should be made forthwith."[85] To give the Senate an equal role in constitutional interpretation, the author suggested, would allow Congress to act in a manner similar to the New York Court of Errors, in which state supreme court justices and state senators combined to form a court of last appeal for controversial issues such as the steamboat monopoly.[86] This suggestion sparked an angry response from the *New York Evening Post,* which warned, "Whatever we do, for God's sake let us abstain from the damnable political heresy of blending judicial with legislative powers." In an allusion to the partisanship of the court of errors, the article concluded that such a checkered history was "amply sufficient to deter every considerate man from listening for a moment to a proposition so largely pregnant with momentous mischief."[87]

Nor was such criticism limited to New York papers. Not surprisingly, the *Richmond Enquirer* took particular exception to *Gibbons v. Ogden.* One contributor commented on Marshall's statement in *Gibbons* that loose construction would leave the Constitution "a magnificent structure, indeed, to look at, but totally unfit to use." The critic responded, "And suppose we fly to the opposite extreme. . . . Suppose we stretch the power of the Government by a most liberal construction, suppose we consider 'necessary' to be synonymous with 'convenient,' what would be then the state of the case?" Under such circumstances, he continued, "the state Governments would moulder into ruins, upon which would rise up one powerful, gigantic and threatening edifice." The author concluded, "To which of these extremes the steam of decisions from the Supreme Court is sweeping, we refer to the case of *McCullough* and the case of the *Cohens.*"[88]

Despite dissenting opinions in certain quarters, Marshall's decision met with overwhelming support across the nation and seemed to put the complex issue of interstate commerce to rest. The Supreme Court had recovered from the bad publicity of its McCulloch and Cohens decisions. Marshall had successfully put the Court on the popular side in the debate over steam power and social progress.

But articles such as those published in the *New York National Advertiser* and the *Richmond Enquirer* revealed the deep antagonisms that were still unresolved between the advocates of nationalism and the supporters of states' rights, especially in regard to the complex issue of commerce. Many states' rights supporters believed that Marshall's broad decision gave states a sphere in which to regulate commerce. These groups would continue to argue even as the issue of the New York steamboat monopoly returned to state court in summer 1824.[89]

The Decline of the New York Steamboat Monopoly

New Competitors

IN THE WAKE of the Gibbons decision, the North River Steam Boat Company lost its most powerful weapon—the ability to legally enjoin out-of-state competitors from running steamboats in New York waters. Marshall, however, had primarily addressed congressional control of interstate commerce in his decision. Many monopoly supporters thus believed they might still control steamboat traffic that operated solely on the Hudson River. And even a limited monopoly could give the North River Company an edge in the lucrative Hudson River steamboat trade. Even if the monopoly failed in the long run, profits could still be made for the foreseeable future. At any rate, after a decade of struggle to preserve the monopoly, the employees and stockholders of the North River Company were not about to give in without a fight.

In short order, more than twenty new steamboat lines sprang up in and around New York State. The day Marshall handed down his decision, former New York chancellor John Lansing and his business partner, Thomas Thayer, incorporated the Hudson River Steam Boat Company. In an obvious jab at the monopoly, the partners promised not to infringe on the rights of others to operate steamboats in state waters.[1] On March 8, Captain Elihu Bunker, now employed by the Connecticut Steam Boat Company, piloted the *United States* into New York Harbor with streamers flying, and he was greeted with an enthusiastic response by local crowds.[2] The Connecticut Company then commenced regular steamboat service between New York City and New Haven, with fares at $3 per passenger.[3] A group of Connecticut businessmen meanwhile refurbished the steamboat *Henry Eckford* and negotiated to run stagecoaches from Providence to New Haven, where passengers would then embark by steamboat for New York City.[4] The Fulton Steam Boat Company of New York City also resumed service to Providence, Rhode Island, and to New London and New Haven, Connecticut.[5] Thomas Gibbons's elegant new steamboat, the *Thistle*, churned the waters between New Brunswick and New York City, despite the fact that several bystanders were injured when a cannon used to salute the voyage exploded. Competition quickly induced Gibbons to lower fares to 12.5¢ per passenger and to provide free onboard meals to attract customers.[6]

Defending Intrastate Commerce

Gibbons v. Ogden resulted in renewed public pressure on New York authorities to repeal the steamboat monopoly. The Livingston family still wielded considerable influence in Albany, but state politics had changed drastically since the days of Robert R. Livingston. In 1817, DeWitt Clinton used his support for the Erie Canal to win a special election and become New York governor. Clinton had initially been a political friend of the Livingston family, but his removal of Brockholst Livingston from the New York Council of Appointment in 1806 had shattered their alliance. Clinton now harbored no affection for Robert L. Livingston and Edward P. Livingston, or for their monopoly. He proved to be a popular governor, but his use of political patronage and his obsession to complete his "big ditch" created enemies within his own party. Tammany Hall, a charitable organization in New York City that morphed into a political machine, quickly turned on Clinton. Similarly, State Senator Martin Van Buren helped form a statewide political coalition called the Bucktails to oppose the governor. Van Buren and the leaders of the Bucktails soon became known as the Albany Regency. In 1820, Tammany and Bucktail leaders called for the creation of a new state constitution that would limit gubernatorial powers and provide for universal suffrage for white males. Clinton allied with New York's remaining Federalists to oppose the measure. Chancellor Kent strongly opposed an extension of the vote, stating: "The men of no property, together with the crowds of dependents connected with great manufacturing and commercial establishments, and the motley and undefinable population of crowded ports, may, perhaps, at some future day, under skillful management, predominate in the assembly; and yet we should be perfectly safe if no laws could pass without the free consent of the owners of the soil. That security we at present enjoy; and it is that security which I wish to retain."[7]

Despite the chancellor's best efforts, in January 1822, New York voters, by a decisive majority, adopted a new constitution that limited terms for governors, abolished the councils of appointment and revision, removed property requirements for white men, and extended limited voting rights to free black citizens. Sensing the winds of political change, Kent retired a year later.[8]

Constitutional changes to the New York government did not bode well for the future of the steamboat monopoly. In April 1824, the New York state legislature asked Attorney General Samuel A. Talcott for an official opinion on the legal implications of the *Gibbons* precedent for the steamboat monopoly. Talcott was an ambitious politician who, at the age of thirty-five, was already one of the leading voices of the Albany Regency. It therefore came as no surprise when, on April 12, he reported, "The reasoning of the court in the case alluded to, would extend to protect steam vessels navigating the waters of the Hudson, between New York and Albany, or any other port upon the river, under regular coasting licenses." Consequently, "it would be immaterial whether they should be engaged in carrying passengers or not."[9]

An angry *New York Evening Post* rebuttal by "Causidicus" dismissed Talcott's claims as legally meaningless, a distortion of the Gibbons decision. Unless the Supreme Court ruled otherwise, Causidicus opined, states still controlled internal commerce. Above all, the Fulton-Livingston monopoly was "completely in consonance with the definitions of the license."[10] Rhind likewise dismissed Talcott's report as irrelevant to the North Company's upcoming chancery court case. Although he insisted that Chancellor Nathan Sanford had a duty to support state laws, Rhind sounded somewhat worried when he mused, "I cannot think that the first *Legal* Office of our State will be ready to abandon our sovereignty at once." "But," the agent continued, "laws are but cobwebs—and Lawyers are Men—and men are subject to error, corruption, prejudice, etc. etc. so that until a thing is decided I value no man's opinion for in general it may be purchased, or *warped* by prejudice which is the same thing."[11]

As the New York state legislature proved reluctant to strengthen the steamboat monopoly through additional legislation, North River Company supporters once again turned to the state courts to protect whatever remained of their rights. They did not have to wait long for a legal challenge. In May, John R. Livingston, who had entered into secret negotiations with Thomas Gibbons, ran his steamboat the *Olive Branch* between New York City and Albany. In the course of such voyages, Livingston briefly stopped at Jersey City to exchange passengers and cargo and to maintain the status of "interstate commerce."[12] Although licensed under the New York monopoly to carry out trade between New York City and New Jersey, Livingston had been required through agreements with Chancellor Livingston and Fulton to stay out of the lucrative Hudson River trade. Livingston now seized upon *Gibbons v. Ogden* to procure a federal coasting license and make periodic trips to Albany. In response, Rhind hired a battery of lawyers to defend the monopoly. Thomas Addis Emmet and Thomas Oakley, already well acquainted with the facts of the case, agreed to represent the monopoly. While the two attorneys discussed legal strategies, New York Supreme Court justice Ambrose Spencer, a North River Company investor, promised to launch an appeal in the New York Court of Chancery for an injunction against Livingston's *Olive Branch*.[13]

North River Steam Boat Company v. John R. Livingston

In mid-April, officials of the North River Company filed suit against John R. Livingston for fraud and infringement of their monopoly rights. This move was a risky one, for James Kent's replacement as chancellor was Nathan Sanford. Whereas Kent had represented an earlier generation of legal scholars and gentlemen, Sanford was indisputably a modern politician. He was a clever, career-minded Republican who had served as a U.S. district attorney, New York congressman, and U.S. senator. Having lost a bid to become vice president in 1824, Sanford now sought to rejuvenate his political career at the local level. Most of the attorneys present at the trial were veterans of previous steamboat monopoly cases. Emmet and Oakley represented the North River Company, and Albany attorney Edward Haines joined veteran counselors William Henry and Abraham Van Vechten to defend Livingston.[14]

The prosecution launched a strong attack, which combined familiar states' rights arguments with newly crafted appeals to state pride and economic development. Oakley began by noting that the New York state courts had upheld the steamboat monopoly many times. Despite the Gibbons decision, the monopoly still applied to steam-powered voyages that began and ended in state waters. The

172

Olive Branch had made only a pretense of stopping in New Jersey, Oakley argued, and such a detour was not interstate commerce but merely an attempt to circumvent the monopoly.[15]

Haines responded that steamboats enrolled under the federal Coasting Act could navigate fully between separate states or different destinations in the same state. "The city of New York is becoming to this continent what London is to the other," he asserted. "It may be a great object for coasting vessels to bring cargoes to the city of New York, land them there, and then proceed to Albany, Troy, or elsewhere within our waters to take other cargoes."[16] He pointed out that Congress had regulated commerce on the Hudson for thirty years with the full compliance of the New York government.[17] And beyond that, the plain language of *Gibbons* bound the actions of all lower courts: New York state courts could not interpret Supreme Court decisions on their own terms. John R. Livingston's motives for traveling to Jersey City were irrelevant, as such a voyage constituted a legitimate participation in the coasting trade. In any event, even if the Gibbons decision was flawed, Haines argued, "it must still be followed, else there is an end of all security and of all subordination." Further, he observed, if the public feared congressional interference in state affairs, "the remedy is not in State pride or jealousy, but in frequent elections, and the spirit of public liberty, which cannot fail to be a protection."[18]

Van Vechten elaborated on Henry's arguments in a succinct conclusion for the defense. Drawing from his previous experience with the steamboat monopoly, he cited Chancellor Kent's comment in *Livingston v. Van Ingen* that in the case of conflict between federal and state laws, state authority must yield to federal concerns. Under both the federal Coasting Act and the Gibbons decision, he said, the coasting trade applied to both New York Harbor and the Hudson River, and New York state courts could neither narrow a Supreme Court decision nor issue an injunction where the constitutionality of *Gibbons* lay in doubt. John R. Livingston could thus navigate the Hudson with the *Olive Branch* until the Supreme Court determined otherwise.[19]

In response to such an all-out assault by the attorneys of a former ally of the North River Company, Emmet launched a final spirited defense of the steamboat monopoly. He accused the opposition of inflaming state pride against the monopoly. In contrast, Emmet invoked the issue of federal consolidation, warning, "If some of the principles laid down by the chief justice in the case of *Gibbons v. Ogden* are not overruled in twenty years, the Constitution will before then have verged towards a form of government which many good men dread, and which assuredly the people never chose."[20] As *Gibbons* had only dealt with interstate commerce, the New York monopoly could still control intrastate trade. Emmet concluded with a strong defense of states' rights, which he declared to be "the bulwarks of individual and personal liberty [and] the outposts of the Constitution." Cautioning that "consolidation will be the euthanasia of our Constitution," he declared, "Make that consolidated government as democratic and free as you please; make its base as broad and its principles as liberal as philanthropy and philosophy can devise; it will still be single government over a vast extent of territory; it will follow . . . the course of all governments of ancient times and modern Europe, which began with elective rights and free institutions, but have silently sunk into despotisms."[21]

On May 14, Chancellor Sanford retired to contemplate the controversy. Local gossip buzzed about the anticipated decision. Charles Rhind made plans "to be ready to have one or two thousand copies printed & circulated without a moment's delay" in case of a favorable decision.[22] However, Rhind became despondent after a discussion with James Kent. The retired chancellor voiced concern that Sanford was "wavering" in his commitment to states' rights and considered the future of the monopoly "doubtful."[23]

Local newspapers provided periodic updates on the progress of the case.[24] One article in the *New York Evening Post* commented, "It is now some fifteen years since the controversy on the constitutionality of the New York laws commenced. Public opinion has been agitated, state hostility has been produced." The article concluded, "If another appeal is to be made to the Supreme Court at Washington, it is to be hoped that years and years will not transpire ere that appeal will meet with a final decision."[25]

The Aetna *Disaster*

Public interest in the case increased due to the *Aetna* disaster, one of the most tragic steamboat accidents in American history. On Saturday, May 15, 1824, the boilers on the steamboat *Aetna,* en route from Washington, New Jersey, exploded less than six miles offshore from Washington, DC. Thirteen people, mostly passengers, were killed by shrapnel or scalding water. Captain Benjamin Beecher and the steamboat *United States* rescued the survivors. Many observers

173

blamed the accident on the *Aetna*'s captain, who, it was maintained, had kept the boat's boilers on high pressure to increase speed. The *Aetna* incident was reported widely and fomented a national debate on the dangers of high-pressure steam engines and the necessity of regulating commerce in order to provide for the public safety.[26]

For instance, the *New York Evening Post* noted the large numbers of passengers on steamboats and asserted, "This shows that laws are necessary to restrain people from putting at hazard their lives. We again appeal to the corporation to interfere, and interdict our waters to high pressure steam boats."[27] The *Charleston Courier* remarked that North River Company boats constructed by Fulton had navigated the Hudson for a decade with no accidents, and it said that steamboat operators would do well to remember that "safe and solid construction and careful management, will secure to them a more substantial and enduring monopoly, than any that the law can give."[28]

Given the public outcry over the *Aetna* disaster, Congress debated a law that called for the inspection of all steamboats in the United States to ensure that they ran on low-pressure boilers. Although the measure failed to pass, such arguments revealed the growing public concerns over the possible dangers as well as the benefits of steam travel.[29] Charles Rhind moved quickly to turn the *Aetna* disaster to the North River Company's advantage. He ordered North River Company captains to keep their engines strictly on low pressure and refrain from races with other steamboats. Rhind also urged the Townsends to publish news of these new regulations "for so many female lives have been lost the Ladies are *in terrorem* at the very idea of any Steamboat." Rhind also insisted, "It is therefore absolutely necessary that we should keep the public in mind that the *Fulton* Boats are always safe—& that all these *high* Steam & *low* priced opposition Boats are dangerous." Two days later, New York papers began to publish testimonials as to the safety and efficiency of North River boats.[30] Not to be undone, William Gibbons published a heroic account of Captain Beecher's rescue of the *Aetna* survivors, and he issued a check to reimburse the skipper for the cost of their safe delivery to New Brunswick. In a gesture equally magnanimous and well-publicized, Captain Beecher virtuously declined any payment for his services.[31]

Against the backdrop of busting boilers and congressional debates, Chancellor Sanford handed down his decision in the North River Steam Boat Company case on June 14, 1824. The decree cleverly echoed the arguments of Emmet and Oakley, yet Sanford nevertheless refused to grant an injunction against

Livingston. He understood the need to appeal to state pride, and so, he denounced *Gibbons v. Ogden* throughout his opinion.[32] He asserted that complex laws such as the federal Coasting Act, which qualified as both taxation and commercial regulation, should be interpreted as narrowly as possible. Since both Congress and the states indisputably wielded taxation powers, some form of concurrent regulation over intrastate trade was permissible. To argue that a federal license conferred an absolute right to navigate in New York waters free from state laws, he emphasized, was to imply a right not specifically stated in either the act or the Gibbons case.[33] Having laid the blame for the Gibbons decision squarely at the feet of the federal government, Sanford nevertheless accepted it as binding precedent. Furthermore, since John R. Livingston's Jersey City trips constituted "a case of navigation from State to State, according to the sense and spirit of that decision which has determined that a license for the coasting trade confers a right to navigate from one state to another," the chancellor refused to grant an injunction. As a result, the New York monopoly suffered a tremendous defeat from which it would never recover.[34]

The Fate of the Steamboat Monopoly

Like the decision in *Gibbons v. Ogden,* Chancellor Sanford's decision sparked media coverage and public attention. An article in the *New York Daily Advertiser* criticized the chancellor for failing to uphold states' rights. By contrast, a reporter for the *New York Evening Post* described the decision as "entitled to great credit, whether we regard the precision and gravity of its style, or the chasteness of the literary tastes that provides it . . . *Final Justicia* is our motto."[35] Another article maintained, "We have always understood it was a legal axiom that, '*fraud vitiates everything it touches.*' Can the Chancellor be supposed to controvert so well established a doctrine? Certainly not for one moment."[36]

Newspapers across the nation, however, declared the steamboat monopoly controversy to be decisively settled.[37] Several days after Chancellor Sanford's decree, the *Olive Branch* triumphantly entered Albany before an enthusiastic crowd of six hundred spectators.[38] A month later, the *Norwich Courier* reported toasts given at a local Fourth of July celebration, one of which contained an obvious reference to the steamboat monopoly case: "The Constitution of the United States—May the Chief Engineer and all others employed, so faithfully perform their part, that the pistons be kept playing and the wheels revolving, and although we move on the high pressure principle, may we never limit our boilers."[39]

The North River Company stockholders greeted the decision with dismay. Charles Rhind dismissed it as a "petty thing" and claimed, "I cannot divine the object of this man's postponing the question if he never meant to give an Injunction."[40] He noted that "the present unhinged state of things is very injurious to the company," and he glumly concluded, "This time—in the Spring no—Boat will be ready & the indignation of the public will be extreme."[41] Rhind also accused Chancellor Sanford of collusion with Tammany Hall politicians. In a final note of disgust, he stated, "It is enough to make a man turn Aristocrat at once."[42]

Despite his private consternation, Rhind struggled to keep the North River Company in business. Although he acknowledged that "the public laugh[s] at us," he reduced fares on North River boats from $6 to $5. Rhind and Robert L. Livingston also threatened John R. Livingston with another lawsuit.[43] Their estranged associate responded that he would run his boats wherever he wished and charge whatever he pleased.[44] The North River Company received a congenial letter from Thomas Gibbons, who crowed about his recent Supreme Court victory but promised to keep off the Hudson unless he received the company's consent. Rhind and Gibbons then agreed to coordinate their steamboat schedules and fares for the run between New York City and Albany.[45]

The North River Company also attempted to attract business through an aggressive public relations campaigned designed to coincide with Gilbert du Motier, marquis de Lafayette's much-anticipated visit to the United States in summer 1824. As a venerated war hero, Lafayette had commenced a goodwill tour throughout the United States as a prelude to the Republic's silver jubilee in 1826. His visit proved a huge media sensation. On the advice of Robert L. Livingston, Rhind stocked the steamboats *Chancellor Livingston* and *James Kent* with a bountiful supply of provisions and alcohol for the pleasure of Lafayette and his entourage. While conceding the publicity value of such a gesture, Rhind condemned the drain on the company's already stretched resources. He confided in John Townsend, "It is a mistaken policy—as regards the Interest of the Co.—and it is *mean*."[46]

In August, Lafayette arrived in New York City aboard the navy frigate *Constitution*. Steamboat promoters put aside their rivalries to volunteer for the festivities. In addition to the North River Company's boats, the Connecticut Steam Boat Company's *Oliver Ellsworth* and *Connecticut,* Daniel D. Tompkins's *Nautilus,* and Thomas Gibbons's *Bellona* joined in a parade across New York Harbor to the lower Manhattan docks. A twenty-one-gun salute, New York state dignitaries decked out in full dress, and thousands of onlookers greeted the flotilla. After several days in New York City, Lafayette boarded the *James Kent* for passage to Albany. A committee responsible for the organization of the voyage publicly offered Commodore Wiswall, captain of the *James Kent,* and Charles Rhind "the warmest mead of praise for their conduct, and the politeness and attention with which the guests are treated throughout."[47]

Capitalizing upon the newly acquired patriotic image, Rhind prepared an appeal to the New York Court for the Correction of Errors to overturn the *North River Steamboat Company* verdict. He again hired Emmet and Oakley to represent the North River Company, and Livingston deployed Henry and Van Vechten to defend his interests. By this point, however, even Emmet doubted the ability of state laws to resist federal commerce authority. In fall 1824, New York governor DeWitt Clinton asked Emmet and Oakley whether the *Gibbons* precedent might allow Congress to tax canal barges on the soon-to-be-completed Erie Canal. Emmet professed his state loyalties but quickly added, "I do not think we can question the right of Congress to tax anything in the Union that it may consider a fit subject of taxation." He concluded, "I should regret securing this state embarked in such an opposition."[48] In contrast, Oakley maintained a defiant states' rights outlook and insisted, "The trouble is that Congress, in legislating another subject of the coasting trade, has lost sight of the distinctions, between 'commerce among the States' and the 'internal commerce' of any State."[49]

In late January 1825, the New York Supreme Court and the New York Senate convened to form the New York Court of Errors and hear arguments in the second case of *North River Steam Boat Company v. John R. Livingston.* Emmet and Oakley hoped only to secure an injunction against Livingston. Henry and Van Vechten, however, successfully urged the court to consider the legality of the entire steamboat monopoly. Emmet then accused Livingston of stopping in Jersey City only to further the illusion of interstate trade. Oakley also pointed out that since Chancellor Sanford's decision, Livingston had often dispensed with trips to the Jersey City wharves altogether and now sailed directly from New York City to Albany. Henry and Van Vechten countered that Livingston's federal coasting license gave him access to the Hudson. Furthermore, they contended, the New York monopoly was an outmoded and inefficient piece of legislation, which should be finally laid to rest.[50]

177

Rhind held out the bleak hope that a victory in court might salvage the monopoly. He noted, however, that steamboat promoters from Albany and Troy packed the courtroom and had been "feasting the [New York state] Senators at a great rate," which would "have more effect than Emmet's logic."[51] However, Rhind's hopes were dashed on February 28, when Chief Justice John Savage handed down a majority opinion for the New York Court of Errors. Like Sanford, Savage was a Republican, a former district attorney, and a former member of Congress. Savage was well aware of the need to assuage wounded state pride while simultaneously dealing with the fate of the unpopular steamboat monopoly. Newspaper accounts described a courtroom packed by members of the bar as well as ordinary New Yorkers. Facing a crowded gallery, Savage reviewed the history of the case and ruled in favor of Livingston.[52] He strongly insisted that federal law trumped state law in all cases where the two collided. As *Gibbons v. Ogden* revealed, there could be no concurrent commerce regulation shared by Congress and the states. The opinion held that for federal coasting license holders to enjoy their rights to participate in the coasting trade, they had to be given complete access to both New York Harbor and the Hudson River, which, like other major rivers throughout the nation, constituted "arms of the sea." Although states still had a right to control internal commerce, the federal Coasting Act of 1793 and the Gibbons decision totally invalidated the New York monopoly.[53]

In the spirit of Chancellor Sanford's recent decision, Judge Savage concluded with a bow to the inevitability of the Gibbons precedent, a warning about the dangers of concentrated federal power, and an appeal to state sentiment. He noted that even if he were to grant an injunction against Livingston, it would do no good, for

> [t]he citizens of other states, with their steam-boats, have full right to navigate our waters, and carry on a profitable business, commencing or terminating their voyage in their own state; while our own citizens must stand with their arms folded and look on, unless they too terminate their voyages without the state. If this deplorable state of things necessarily results from the constitution and laws of our country, it must be submitted to with what grace we can; but is it not a powerful argument to prove that the reasoning which leads to such a result is unsound?[54]

In a conclusive vote, Savage and twenty-eight state senators defeated two state supreme court justices and seven senators to deny the injunction.[55]

Given their most recent defeat, Rhind and the Livingstons discussed plans to petition the New York legislature for the tonnage and impost duties the company had paid to the state for the previous thirty years. As the New York courts had upheld the constitutionality of the federal Coasting Act and as North River boats had always maintained such licenses, the North River Company directors speculated that the state had no right to tax them. Rhind optimistically hoped for a refund of between $80,000 and $90,000.[56] Yet public hostility to the monopoly squelched any such prospects.

Aftermath and Dissolution

In March 1825, the *Albany Argus* reported, "Since the late decision of the court of errors, steam boats on our rivers have become 'thick as blackberries.' The *Henry Eckford, Bristol, Chief Justice Marshall, Olive-Branch,* and how many more we cannot tell, together with the boats of the old line, are now in successful operation, or nearly so." The article also reported that even though fares currently stood at $4, by the end of the year, customers could expect free passage and possibly free meals and wine with their voyages. Such was certainly the case for many state legislators and lobbyists who, after the decision in the North River case, received a free jaunt aboard the steamboat *Chief Justice Marshall* complete with food and drink, sponsored by a group of grateful steamboat promoters from Troy.[57] The *New York Statesman* also reported, "The regular lines, old and new, of steam-boats, have commenced running to Albany, to Providence, to Hartford, etc. and promise more cheap, speedy and frequent communication with our sister states, than has been recognized." The article concluded, "To what an astonishing state of things has the genius of Fulton exhibited in this country!"[58]

By late 1825, increased competition and disagreement among the Livingston family and stockholders caused the North River Company to descend into bankruptcy the following year. Boats, engines, and docks were auctioned off to the highest bidders. After twenty-five years of domination over the waters of New York, the steamboat monopoly was finally dead.[59] At first glance, the attempts by the North River Company to defend the monopoly in the wake of the Gibbons decision may have appeared hopeless, but there was good reason at the time to believe that at least some portion of the monopoly might be preserved. After all, the monopoly had survived repeated challenges for over twenty years, and state monopolies over bridges, public roads, and stagecoach services continued

179

to flourish throughout the nation. Furthermore, the Livingstons, Rhind, and their formidable attorneys could use state pride to rally support in defense of the monopoly. The doctrine of states' rights was a potent force in early America, and no one knew how to deploy that issue more effectively than the Livingston clan and Thomas Addis Emmet. Yet the leaders of the Richmond Junto could use economic hardships and the declining power of Virginia in national politics to attract followers to their cause. In contrast, New York could boast a growing population and a resurging economy fueled by the twin wonders of the Erie Canal and steam power. Social elites saw steamboats as lucrative investment opportunities, farmers hoped they would bring crops to market faster, merchants viewed steam power as a means of expanding markets, and expansionists predicted that such inventions would promote western settlement. Even those at the margins of power in New York, such as backcountry farmers, immigrant laborers, women, and free blacks, appeared to benefit from the greater geographical mobility offered by steam travel. Local citizens across class lines could embrace John Marshall's vision of a strong nation supported by strong economy, with little risk to their identity as New Yorkers.

Gibbons v. Ogden as Historical Precedent

Consequences of the Gibbons Decision

G IBBONS V. OGDEN was a conflict that bordered at times on melo-
drama. Nonetheless, it was not merely the story of powerful families, public campaigns, and private intrigue. The steamboat monopoly case found
its origins in a new age of experimentation, in the efforts of John Fitch and James
Rumsey to secure federal patents and state monopolies over new forms of steam
travel. Over the next thirty-five years, the matter escalated from a dispute between rival inventors into a conflict fought by the ruling elites of New York and
New Jersey. By 1824, the "steamboat cause" had become a national debate over
whether states or Congress had the right to regulate commercial and technological development in the early United States.

There were winners and losers in this struggle. Many of the New York monopolists and their allies sank into insolvency. Not surprisingly, they often railed
against the dangers of unchecked capitalism to any who would listen. On the
other hand, those who had been prudent enough to cut their ties to the Fulton-
Livingston cartel prospered in the thriving steamboat and railroad industries
of the 1830s and 1840s. Their personal success stories lent credibility to the kind of

federal regulation *Gibbons v. Ogden* permitted. But the case's landmark status is founded on more than just the pragmatic economic outcome of ending the monopoly. The durability of Marshall's opinion owes much to its complexity and nuance, which lend the case great plasticity as a legal precedent. In future years, groups ranging from businessmen to temperance supporters, from stockyard owners to opponents of child labor, and from segregationists to civil rights workers would invoke *Gibbons* as a precedent for federal regulation of both economic and social issues. Their efforts would keep generations of jurists and lawyers busy fleshing out the broad guidelines for commerce regulation laid down by Chief Justice John Marshall in 1824.

One individual who benefited directly from Marshall's decision was John R. Livingston, the former privateer who had allied himself at various times with Chancellor Livingston, John Stevens, Robert Fulton, Aaron Ogden, and Thomas Gibbons. Such shrewdness allowed Livingston to prosper in the steamboat business, and he died a wealthy man at the venerable age of ninety-three. His brother Edward Livingston quit the Mississippi steamboat trade to become a Louisiana state representative, a member of Congress, and a senator. He also authored a popular treatise on American civil law and served as Andrew Jackson's secretary of state and U.S. minister to France.[1] Those in other branches of the Livingston clan were not so fortunate. Divided over matters of inheritance and the failure of the North River Company, the Livingstons of Clermont lost both wealth and influence. Robert L. Livingston remained an amiable landowner and amateur scholar who loaned money freely and sold off large portions of his manorial estate in a futile bid to maintain his family's social status. Edward P. Livingston enjoyed only moderate political success as lieutenant governor of New York and president of the Electoral College. Both men suffered financially in the panic of 1837, died in 1843, and left meager inheritances for their children.[2]

The heirs of Robert Fulton were similarly unfortunate. Harriet Livingston Fulton Dale and her husband Charles traveled extensively in Europe, invested heavily in the North River Company, attempted to charter a bank, and went broke in 1825. When Harriet died the following year, she was mourned as the wife of a great inventor. Her obituary ironically reported, "When Fulton was worn down with exertions in bringing his steam power into practical use," his wife had "soothed his wounded feelings, and encouraged him to go on with alacrity, and cheered him with the brightest visions of triumphant success—and her faith has been fully rewarded."[3] Charles Dale married a woman named Margaret Greenleaf but quickly descended into alcoholism and depression; he was arrested for as-

New York City in 1859. J. Bachman, "Bird's Eye View of the City of New York, 1859," Library of Congress, Prints and Photographs Division, Washington, DC

saulting his new wife and committed suicide in prison in 1832. In 1836, the Fulton children petitioned the federal government for aid in consideration of their father's assistance in the defense of New Orleans during the War of 1812. After a decade of debate, Congress in 1847 awarded $76,000 to the surviving members of the Fulton family.[4]

The destruction of the unpopular monopoly and the completion of the Erie Canal in October 1825 led to a boom in the steamboat business along the Hudson River and in New York Harbor. In November 1825, some 43 steamboats competed for customers in New York waters. By 1838, 150 steamboats were ferrying more than 2 million passengers a year throughout the region. Cornelius Vanderbilt purchased the *Bellona* in 1828, styled himself "commodore," and shuttled passengers between Peekskill, New York, and New York City. He soon encountered competition from the Stevens family, which had purchased many of the North River Company's boats and dominated the Hudson River trade. A vicious price war ensued until Vanderbilt allowed Stevens to buy him out in 1834. Vanderbilt then invested heavily in ocean steamers and railroads to become one of the greatest robber barons of the nineteenth century.[5]

Steamboats also flourished on the Mississippi River. When Judge Hall struck down the Louisiana steamboat monopoly in 1817, only 17 steamboats operated along western rivers. But within three years, 69 vessels churned the Mississippi and Ohio rivers, and by 1855, 727 riverboats ranged across the Mississippi River valley from Montana to New Orleans. Henry Miller Shreve made a vast fortune from his steamboat ventures, used steam-powered snagboats to clear a logjam on the Red River, and lent his name to the thriving river town of Shreveport, Louisiana. In 1828, Congress made Shreve the superintendent of western rivers, a position he maintained for thirteen years.[6]

Steamboats in the 1820s helped pave the way for other forms of transportation. In August 1825, Robert Stevens successfully returned his family's name to financial and social prominence by demonstrating the economic potential of the British-made steam locomotive *John Bull* and soon afterward started a train service from Perth Amboy to Camden, New Jersey. The first major American railway, the Baltimore and Ohio Railroad, appeared in 1828. By the 1860s, more than thirty thousand miles of track crisscrossed the young nation and linked heavily populated eastern cities to the frontier.[7] Although *Gibbons v. Ogden* destroyed a particularly unpopular monopoly, federal, state, and local governments continued to incorporate transportation companies, dredge rivers, donate land for railroad tracks, sanction lotteries to support transportation initiatives, and occasionally run steamboat or rail service directly. Even the federal government granted more than $6 million in western lands to fund railroads. *Gibbons v. Ogden* marked an end to state-granted steamboat monopolies but not to governmental support for transportation projects in general.[8]

Thomas Gibbons, the cantankerous planter and businessman who had taken on the New York monopoly, could boast with pride of his achievements in 1824. His victory proved short-lived. Less than two years later, Gibbons succumbed to diabetes, and his bitterness toward Ogden and the Trumbulls lasted to the very end of his life. He stipulated in his will that none of "the children of the said John M. Trumbull, or John M. Trumbull himself, or any of his or their descendants" should ever "acquire or inherit one cent of my estate."[9] Although he died a wealthy man, Gibbons remained estranged from most of his family and the American public in general.

Aaron Ogden, by contrast, never emerged from the financial debt of his steamboat ventures but still retained his status as a gentleman. After surviving for several years on the charity of friends, he was given a congressional appointment as customs collector for the port of Jersey City in 1829. Nonetheless, New York authorities arrested the former governor four years later for his outstanding debts. A lengthy jail term ultimately generated sympathy for Ogden's cause, as former comrades in arms came to visit him. Childhood friend Aaron Burr Jr. secured passage of a state law that forbade the imprisonment of Revolutionary War veterans for insolvency. Ogden's status as a gentleman with connections thus kept his creditors at bay. He returned to Jersey City, served as president of the Society of the Cincinnati, and helped keep alive the memory of the Revolutionary generation. In 1839, he died peacefully at home, surrounded by family and friends.[10]

Gibbons v. Ogden *in Historical Memory*

As the United States moved forward into the age of steam, *Gibbons v. Ogden* became a popular precedent. Marshall's broad decision gave states' rights supporters hope that they too had a sphere in which to regulate commerce. Not surprisingly, many early commerce clause cases to appear before the Supreme Court involved the rights of state legislatures to regulate commerce under their taxation and police powers in the absence of federal regulation. A mere three years after the Gibbons decision, the Marshall Court examined the constitutionality of a Maryland law designed to tax goods imported across state lines in the case of *Brown v. Maryland*. Marshall responded with what became known as the "original package" doctrine, which stated that Congress controlled goods being shipped across state lines as part of a single commercial transaction but that such merchandise became subject to state taxation when it was sold. Two years later, in *Willson v. Black Bird Creek Marsh Company*, the Marshall Court retreated even further from its nationalistic stance in *Gibbons* to rule that a dam constructed over a navigable branch of the Delaware River did not constitute a barrier to interstate commerce.[11]

In 1828 former war hero, Indian fighter, and land speculator Andrew Jackson of Tennessee gained the presidency with promises of reducing the size of the federal government and returning power to the states. When John Marshall died in 1835, Jackson appointed Roger Brooke Taney of Maryland, a loyal Jacksonian, as chief justice. Taney did not seek to overturn the nationalistic precedents laid down by his predecessor but significantly narrowed their scope. The Taney Court frequently deferred to state legislatures on the issue of commerce regulation, particularly as it applied to the interstate slave trade. Subsequently, in *Groves v. Slaughter* (1841), the Court used a technicality to avoid defense attorney Daniel Webster's argument that a clause in the Mississippi state constitution that banned the importation of slaves violated federal control of interstate trade.[12] Six years later, in the *License Cases,* the Taney Court considered the constitutionality of several state prohibition laws. Taney upheld the acts on grounds that *Gibbons* "establishes the doctrine that a State may, in the execution of its powers of internal police, make regulations of foreign commerce; and that such regulations are valid, unless they come into collision with a law of Congress."[13]

But two years later, in the *Passenger Cases,* the Supreme Court struck down state laws that authorized the inspection, taxation, and expulsion of foreign immigrants as violations of the commerce clause. In a divided majority opinion, Justice James Wayne asserted that *Gibbons v. Ogden* "will always be a high and honorable proof of the eminence of the American bar of that day, and of the talents and distinguished ability of the judges who were then in the places which we now occupy."[14] To resolve such differences, the Taney Court ruled in the case of *Cooley v. Board of Wardens* (1852) that Congress controlled national commerce but that states could regulate trade issues on which the federal government had not spoken. With several variations, the "Cooley doctrine" provided a baseline for determining federal commerce clause cases from the 1850s to the 1930s.[15]

Although the Unites States had few prominent legal scholars before the Civil War, many keen minds—some with personal ties to the case—discussed the merits of *Gibbons v. Ogden.* In 1826, James Kent, in his seminal *Commentaries on American Law,* quipped that if Congress had meant for coasting licenses to invalidate state commerce regulations, "it was supposed they would have said so in plain and intelligible language, and not have left their claim of supremacy to be hidden from the observation and knowledge of the state governments, in the unpretending and harmless shape of a coasting license."[16] Overall, Kent felt that "the decree of the Supreme Court seems to be broader than the facts in the case would warrant" and that its "language was too general and comprehensive for the case."[17]

Other voices rallied to the defense of the Gibbons decision. In his own *Commentaries on the Constitution of the United States,* published in 1833, Joseph Story broadly defended federal commerce authority as "vital to the prosperity of the Union," without which "the government would scarcely deserve the name of a national government; and would soon sink into discredit and imbecility."[18] Two decades later judicial biographer George Van Santvoord agreed, describing *Gibbons v. Ogden* as "a most brilliant passage of arms." The case accordingly required "no small degree of moral courage and firmness on the part of the Supreme Court" to "lop off, with a keen edge of the Constitutional axe, a branch of state sovereignty, which by the growth of years had become so firmly engrafted as to be scarcely distinguishable from the parent trunk."[19] In his autobiography, Daniel Webster brashly took credit for the Gibbons decision, asserting that Marshall had taken in his arguments "as a baby takes in its mother's milk" and that "the opinion of the court, as rendered by the chief justice, was little else than a recital of my argument."[20]

The late nineteenth and early twentieth centuries witnessed rapid industrial growth that had important repercussions for interstate commerce. With *Gibbons* as a precedent, the Supreme Court upheld federal commerce power to regulate railroad freight rates across state lines in *Wabash Railway v. Illinois* (1886). Under the leadership of Chief Justice Melville Fuller, however, the court more often sought to maintain the balance struck between state and federal commerce regulation in *Cooley*. In *United States v. E. C. Knight Co.* (1895), the Fuller Court distinguished between manufacturing monopolies, which could be prosecuted under the Sherman Anti-Trust Act, and agricultural firms, which could not. The court likewise struck down another attempt to regulate business in *Lochner v. New York* (1905), invalidating a New York law regulating the number of hours bakers could work as a violation of the freedom to contract guaranteed by the Fourteenth Amendment. The following year, however, the Supreme Court ruled that a stockyard could be prosecuted for price fixing under the Sherman Anti-Trust Act in *Swift v. United States*. Finally, in *Hammer v. Dagenhart* (1918), the court struck down the Keating-Owen child labor law passed under the authority of the commerce clause as a violation of state rights to control local labor standards.[21]

Like their nineteenth-century counterparts, many progressive era academics viewed *Gibbons v. Ogden* as a triumph for American commercial development.

Former U.S. assistant attorney general and law professor Charles Warren depicted the case as "the emancipation proclamation of American commerce."[22] In their study of American railroads, Harvard economist Eliot Jones and business professor Homer B. Vanderblue applauded Marshall's "powerful blow for free enterprise," which "had a long and profound impact on both economic and legal affairs."[23] And historian Samuel Eliot Morison, in his influential *Oxford History of the United States*, called *Gibbons* the "most luminous and far reaching" of Marshall's opinions, one that "not only smashed a State-chartered monopoly of Steamboat traffic, but mapped out the course that Congress would follow for a century in regulating interstate commerce."[24]

Despite these accolades, *Gibbons* faced criticism in some circles. Legal scholar Frederick H. Cooke dismissed the case as a "judicial fetish, regarded with little less than superstitious veneration and awe."[25] Substantively, Cooke criticized Marshall's decision for its lack of originality and its vagueness in defining specific congressional commerce powers. In his work *John Marshall and the Constitution*, constitutional historian Edwin S. Corwin conceded that Marshall's opinion in *Gibbons v. Ogden* was "in some respects a great intellectual performance" but added that it did not equal *McCulloch v. Maryland* "in those qualities of form which attract the amateur and stir the admiration of posterity." Corwin argued that Marshall had, in true Hamiltonian style, handed down a decision designed to portray the Supreme Court as the champion of early American business interests.[26]

The Great Depression paved the way for the election of Franklin Delano Roosevelt as president and for the emergence of strong Democratic majorities in Congress. These developments, in turn, brought about drastic changes for federal-state relations and the legal significance of *Gibbons v. Ogden*. During Roosevelt's first term, Congress attempted to broaden the concept of interstate commerce to embrace federal regulation of industry, agriculture, mining, and labor unions. Over the next four years, however, a group of four conservative Supreme Court justices—James Clark McReynolds, George Sutherland, Willis Van Devanter, and Pierce Butler—dubbed the "four horsemen" by the media of the day, would lead efforts to strike down key pieces of New Deal legislation such as the National Industrial Recovery Act in *Schechter Poultry Corp. v. United States* (1935), the Agricultural Adjustment Act in *United States v. Butler* (1936), and the Coal Mining Act in *Carter v. Carter Coal Company* (1936).[27]

Roosevelt interpreted his reelection in 1936 and the addition of even more Democrats to Congress as a mandate for judicial change. The following year, he proposed increasing the number of Supreme Court justices and introducing mandatory retirement for court members. This court-packing plan proved unpopular and even unnecessary, as the Supreme Court had already begun to show signs of accepting a broader definition of interstate commerce. Whatever the reasons for the Court's change of heart, it meant a return to the fundamentals of *Gibbons v. Ogden*—the proposition that Congress held the primary role in defining the scope of interstate commerce. In cases such as *National Labor Relations Board v. Jones & Laughlin Steel Corp.* (1937), the High Court signaled a new deference to congressional constitutional interpretation.[28]

Scholars sympathetic to the New Deal quickly seized upon *Gibbons v. Ogden* as a harbinger for the rise of a regulatory state. This was hardly a new development. As early as 1911, Columbia University political science professor and leading reformer Frank J. Goodnow had expressed the hope that the broad nationalism espoused in the Gibbons decision would help make the commerce clause "a means for the reconstitution of our political system in accordance with changing economic needs."[29] In 1937, two years before his appointment to the Supreme Court, Felix Frankfurter gave new life to Goodnow's argument in his work *The Commerce Clause under Marshall, Taney, and Waite*. Frankfurter suggested that John Marshall's Gibbons decision had tentatively promoted the doctrine that "the commerce clause, by its own force and without national legislation, puts it into the power of the Court to place limits on state authority," which in turn reinforced the notion that "though we are a federation of states we are also a nation."[30] In that same year, Pulitzer Prize–winning historian Burton J. Hendrick asserted that after the Gibbons decision, "America, so far as its rivers and harbors and navigation were concerned, had become a nation."[31] In addition, he observed that "the vast enhancement of trade and navigation that followed *Gibbons v. Ogden* demonstrated its effect in unlocking the resources and enterprises of the American people." Depicting the Gibbons decision as a pivotal event in the life of the young nation, Hendrick concluded, "It was a time in which the principles of localism could not possibly endure. This year of the commerce decision, 1824, may be taken as the dividing line between the old and the new."[32]

One scholar even took the novel approach of asserting that Marshall had not gone far enough in upholding congressional powers over interstate commerce in *Gibbons v. Ogden*. According to progressive law professor William Crosskey, Marshall had undercut the true potential of the commerce clause through an ambiguous decision in *Gibbons* that aimed to prevent dissension on the court.

189

The result of the decision "was undeniably to narrow ostensibly and quite *unwarrantedly*, the power of Congress over commerce."[33]

Frankfurter's and Hendrick's interpretations of *Gibbons v. Ogden* helped justify the further expansion of congressional commerce power in a variety of areas. In *United States v. Carolene Products Co.* (1938), Justice Harlan Fiske Stone drew from *Gibbons* to assert that Congress could ban products (in this case, filled or skimmed milk) from traveling across state lines when the public health was at stake. Stone's decision was also significant for its fourth footnote, which called for "more exacting judicial scrutiny" in examining future cases in which "prejudice against *discrete and insular minorities* may be a special condition." Although its import was not immediately apparent, footnote four would play a key role in future civil rights cases.[34]

After Stone's elevation to chief justice in 1941, the High Court further elaborated on the legacy of *Gibbons*. In *Wickard v. Filburn* (1942), Justice Robert Jackson upheld the 1938 Agricultural Adjustment Act on the precedent of *Gibbons*. Noting that Marshall had attributed to Congress broad commerce powers under *Gibbons*, Jackson conceded that for half a century the federal government had left most economic affairs in state hands. However, the expansion of federal commerce power through legislation such as the Interstate Commerce Act (1887) and the Sherman Anti-Trust Act (1903) had created a need for "new phases of adjudication, which required the Court to approach the interpretation of the Commerce Clause in the light of an actual exercise by Congress."[35] The Supreme Court had theretofore been reluctant to follow this trend. Nevertheless, "other cases called forth broader interpretations of the Commerce Clause destined to supersede the earlier ones, and to bring about a return to the principles first enunciated by Chief Justice Marshall in *Gibbons v. Ogden*."[36] The "principles" Jackson spoke of included the need for courts to defer to legislatures on determining the definition and scope of commerce regulation.

Writing in the wake of *Carolene* and *Wickard*, academics in the late 1940s and 1950s generally interpreted *Gibbons v. Ogden* as an early legal precedent that condoned broad Congressional regulation of commerce. In 1947, C. Perry Patterson, a professor of government at the University of Texas, described the case as "a shockingly nationalistic opinion" that "began the spiral of nationalism which has drawn into its vortex practically the complete industrial and agricultural life of the nation."[37] James Willard Hurst's *Law and the Conditions of Freedom in the Nineteenth-Century United States* claimed that *Gibbons v. Ogden* "blueprinted an active role for Congress in defining and protecting national free trade." *Gibbons* thus made the Supreme Court an "active agent in federal policy" that would, in the future, "set aside state legislation, which in its judgment might unduly confine the play of economic energy."[38]

In 1954, the U.S. Supreme Court under the leadership of Chief Justice Earl Warren used the concept of strict scrutiny suggested in footnote four of *Carolene* to strike down a school segregation law in the landmark case of *Brown v. Board of Education of Topeka, Kansas.* This decision gave momentum to the burgeoning civil rights movement but prompted southern political leaders to invoke state powers to protect public safety as a means of avoiding desegregation. Through passage of the Civil Rights Act of 1964 and Voting Rights Act of 1965, Congress insisted that the Bill of Rights in conjunction with the equal protection clause of the Fourteenth Amendment and other constitutional provisions, such as the commerce clause, trumped state police powers. Because these laws were based in part on the authority of the commerce clause, civil rights attorneys were quick to argue that *Gibbons v. Ogden* provided a broad interpretation of federal commerce power which could and should be used to combat segregation.[39]

An early opportunity to test this theory came in *Heart of Atlanta Motel, Inc., v. United States* (1964), in which Justice Thomas Campbell Clark adopted a broad interpretation of *Gibbons* to strike down segregation laws in hotels that served interstate traffic. Clark ruled, "Although the principles which we apply today are those first formulated by Chief Justice Marshall in *Gibbons v. Ogden,* the conditions of transportation and commerce have changed dramatically, and we must apply those principles to the present state of commerce." Increases in interstate traffic, Clark found, made segregation laws an undue burden on interstate commerce. The same year, the Warren Court ruled in *Katzenbach v. McClung* that federal authorities could desegregate Ollie's Barbeque, a popular eatery in Birmingham, Alabama, which prepared and sold food that had been shipped across state lines.[40]

Ironically, while civil rights attorneys and federal judges were putting *Gibbons v. Ogden* to work to promote social justice, historians proved more interested in the case's relationship to the emergence of a national market economy in the early nineteenth century. No less a figure than New Left historian William Appleman Williams, in his influential *Contours of American History,* described John Marshall as a "firm mercantilist" committed to an activist state whose Gibbons decision bore "a striking resemblance to the key struggles in England to open up the system created by mercantilism and yet at the same time prevent any one element from

191

destroying the balance of the political economy."[41] Lawrence M. Friedman's *History of American Law,* published in 1973, similarly emphasized *Gibbons's* role in striking down state commerce powers to help create an integrated national market.[42] With the rise of cultural history in the 1980s, historian G. Edward White depicted the steamboat monopoly case as a symbolic conflict pitting "economic privilege against free competition, the few against the many, the resistors against the defenders of progress." But he also concluded that Marshall's Gibbons decision was "highly inconclusive," which "For all the fanfare with which it was received, settled very little and that in an awkward fashion."[43]

The legacy of *Gibbons* did not long remain solely an academic matter. Beginning in the 1990s, the Rehnquist Court launched a substantive attempt to sharply limit congressional commerce authority. Observers dubbed this trend the "New Federalism." In *United States v. Lopez* (1995), the Supreme Court struck down a federal statute based on the notion that the possession of guns near public schools, if repeated throughout the nation, could have a negative impact on interstate trade.[44] Five years later, in *United States v. Morrison,* the Court invalidated a portion of the Violence against Women Act that provided for federal civil suits for victims of gender-motivated violence, based on the contention that violence against women inhibited travel and commerce across state lines.[45] In both cases, the Rehnquist Court held that state laws already provided gun control and rape prevention, making federal laws based on the commerce clause unnecessary. Yet even the New Federalism appeared to have limits, for in *Gonzales v. Raich* (2005) the Court upheld a federal controlled substances act that made it illegal to transport marijuana, even for medical purposes, across state lines.[46]

By the dawn of the twenty-first century, jurists and academics were no closer to reaching a consensus on the meaning of *Gibbons v. Ogden* than they were in 1824. Yet this was a state of affairs that John Marshall presumably would have understood. For the early Republic was a time of paradoxes. Rising groups of inventors and businessmen sought alliances with an older generation of elites, and these same landowners called for the regulation of steam travel in order to preserve their traditional wealth and status. State and federal judges navigated treacherous waters when such issues came before their courts, and they were mindful of the public support they would require to legitimate their decisions. When viewed from this perspective, the language of commerce and nationalism that Marshall deployed in *Gibbons v. Ogden* makes sense. It was not a clever attempt to sidestep the thorny issue of interstate commerce. Rather, Marshall had sensibly struck down an unpopular monopoly on narrow grounds and left the politically sensitive issue of regulation for future cases.

After all, Marshall had seen in *Livingston v. Van Ingen* and *Elkison v. Deliesseline* the problems that either a strong states' rights or a strong nationalistic stance on commerce regulation might cause. He also understood the weakness of the state and federal courts in the early Republic. The power of such institutions lay not in their ability to hand down binding precedent but in their power to convince a majority of Americans—northerners, southerners, westerners, farmers, planters, merchants, and mechanics—that each had a vested interest in the future technological and commercial development of the young United States. *Gibbons* was not just one in a series of state and federal commerce cases, but a complex debate over the modernization of American society. It was negotiated both through the courts and in newspapers, private letters, public advertisements, and steamboat races. Its participants were not only those who were directly implicated in the monopoly but also the thousands of Americans who daily opted to travel on steamboats. Marshall's broad decision was calculated to spark discussions of commerce that would be settled not only through future litigation but also in the court of public opinion. It is therefore not surprising that *Gibbons* continues to resonate. Its issues of technological change, commerce, and social upheaval are as relevant today as they were when Robert Fulton's *North River Steam Boat* first traversed the waterways of New York nearly two centuries ago.

NOTES

Preface

1. *Elizabethtown Gazette,* March 15, 1824, reprinted in the *Savannah Daily Georgian,* March 31, 1824, p. 2, cols. 4–5.

2. Albert J. Beveridge, *The Life of John Marshall,* vol. 4, *The Building of the Nation, 1815–1835* (Boston: Houghton Mifflin, 1919), 430; Charles Warren, *The Supreme Court in United States History* (Boston: Little, Brown, 1922); Charles Haines, *The Supreme Court in American Government and Politics, 1789–1835* (Berkeley: University of California Press, 1944); G. Edward White, *The Marshall Court and Cultural Change, 1815–1835* (New York: Oxford University Press, 1991); Maurice Baxter, *The Steamboat Monopoly: Gibbons v. Ogden, 1824* (New York: Alfred A. Knopf, 1972), quote on v. See also John A. Garraty, *Quarrels That Have Shaped the Constitution,* rev. ed. (New York: Harper & Row, 1987).

3. Charles Sellers, *The Market Revolution: Jacksonian America, 1815–1846* (New York: Oxford University Press, 1991), Melvyn Stokes and Stephen Conway, eds., *The Market Revolution in America: Social, Political, and Religious Expressions, 1800–1880* (Charlottesville: University Press of Virginia, 1996), and Scott C. Martin, *Cultural Change and the Market Revolution in America, 1789–1860* (Lanham, MD: Rowman and Littlefield, 2005) provide the fullest discussion of the market revolution thesis. For alternative viewpoints, see Daniel Feller, *The Jacksonian Promise: America, 1815–1840* (Baltimore, MD: Johns Hopkins University Press, 1995); Daniel Feller, "The Market Revolution Ate My Homework," *Reviews in American History* 25 (September 1997): 408–15; Laura Rigal, *The American Manufactory: Art, Labor and the World of Things in the Early Republic* (Princeton, NJ: Princeton University Press, 1998), 55–88; and Daniel Walker Howe, *What Hath God Wrought: The Transformation of America, 1815–1848* (New York: Oxford University Press, 2007). For the role of technology in antebellum society, see John Kasson, *Civilizing the Machine: Technology and Republican Values in America, 1776–1900* (New York: Viking, 1976); Maury Klein, *The Power Makers: Steam, Electricity, and the Men Who Invented Modern America* (London: Bloomsbury, 2008); Leo Marx, *The Machine in the Garden: Technology and the Pastoral Ideal in America* (New York: Oxford University Press, 1967); Judith A. McGraw, *Early American Technology: Making and Doing Things from the Colonial Era to 1850* (Chapel Hill: University of North Carolina Press, 1994); and David R. Meyer, *Networked Machinists: High-Technology Industries in Antebellum America* (Baltimore, MD: Johns Hopkins University Press, 2006).

Chapter 1: Steam Power and Patent Law Development in the Eighteenth Century

1. John Fitch, *The Autobiography of John Fitch,* ed. Frank D. Prager (Philadelphia: American Philosophical Society, 1976), 178–79; Thomas Boyd, *Poor John Fitch, Inventor of the Steamboat* (New York: G. P. Putnam's Sons, 1935), 179–81.

2. Edward C. Walterscheid, "To Promote the Progress of Science and Useful Arts: The Background and Origin of the Intellectual Property Clause of the United States Constitution," *Journal of Intellectual Property Law* 2 (Fall 1994): 45–54. See also Walterscheid, *The Nature of the Intellectual Property Clause: A Study in Historical Perspective* (Buffalo, NY: W. S. Hein, 2002), and *To Promote the Progress of Useful Arts: American Patent Law and Administration, 1798–1836* (Littleton, CO: F. B. Rothman, 1998).

3. Scholars have long acknowledged the connections between science and law, but they have disagreed as to the nature of the relationship. Many nineteenth-century works on steamboat development argued that American inventive genius created economic and legal systems that rewarded individual risk taking, which in turn produced steamboats and fueled western development. Over time, these narratives gave way to twentieth-century accounts that stressed the role of technology

in shaping historical change. Although such monographs revealed the importance of steam power in creating an industrial state, they often portrayed historical actors as the prisoners of overwhelming historical forces. The current debate over these trends is summarized in Merritt Roe Smith and Leo Marx, eds., *Does Technology Drive History? The Dilemma of Technological Determinism* (Cambridge, MA: MIT Press, 1994), 3–24. For general histories of steam power, see R. A. Fletcher, *Steam-Ships: The Story of Their Development to the Present Day* (London: Sidgwick and Jackson, 1910), 4–9; John Kennedy, *The History of Steam Navigation* (Liverpool, England: Charles, Birchall, 1903), 1–6; Andrea S. Sutcliffe, *Steam: The Untold Story of America's First Great Invention* (New York: Palgrave Macmillan, 2004), 1–16; and James Thomas Flexner, *Steamboats Come True: American Inventors in Action* (New York: Fordham University Press, 1944, 1992), 348–63. The development of steam power in America is chronicled in Louis C. Hunter, *Steamboats on the Western Rivers: An Economic and Technological History* (New York: Octagon Books, 1969), and George R. Taylor, *The Transportation Revolution, 1815–1860* (New York: Holt, Rinehart, 1951).

4. Christine MacLeod, *Inventing the Industrial Revolution: The English Patent System, 1660–1800* (Cambridge: Cambridge University Press, 1988), 150–99; Walterscheid, "To Promote the Progress," 5–7.

5. E. Wyndham Hulme, "The History of the Patent System under the Prerogative and at Common Law," *Law Quarterly Review* 46 (April 1896): 141–54; Hulme, "On the Consideration of the Patent Grant, Past and Present," *Law Quarterly Review* 51 (July 1897): 313–18. These dated yet thorough accounts of the early English patent system can be found at http://www.myoutbox.net/polist.htm (accessed March 10, 2009).

6. Copyright Act, 1709, 8 Anne c. 19; J. R. Harris, *Industrial Espionage and Technology Transfer: Britain and France in the Eighteenth Century* (Aldershot, England: Ashgate, 1998), 350–55.

7. *Millar v. Taylor*, 4 Burr. 2303, 98 Eng. Rep. 201 (1769); *Donaldson v. Beckett*, 4 Burr. 2408, 98 Eng. Rep. 257 (1774); Edward C. Walterscheid, "Inherent or Created Rights: Early Views on the Intellectual Property Clause," *Hamline Law Review* 19 (Fall 1995): 81–98.

8. Ronald R. Kline, *Consumers in the Country: Technology and Social Change in Rural America* (Baltimore, MD: Johns Hopkins University Press, 2000), 7–36; Jonathan Prude, "Capitalism, Industrialization, and the Factory in Post-Revolutionary America," in *Wages of Independence: Capitalism in the Early American Republic*, ed. Paul A. Gilje (Madison, WI: Madison House, 1997), 81–100.

9. John Kennedy, *History of Steam Navigation*, 1–6.

10. Charles Sellers, *The Market Revolution: Jacksonian America, 1815–1846* (New York: Oxford University Press, 1991), 41–44, 131–47.

11. Neil Longley York, *Mechanical Metamorphosis: Technological Change in Revolutionary America* (Westport, CT: Greenwood, 1985), 183–94; Dolores Greenberg, "Reassessing the Power Patterns of the Industrial Revolution: An Anglo-American Comparison," *American Historical Review* 87 (December 1982): 1246–47.

12. Eric H. Robinson, "The Early Diffusion of Steam Power," *Journal of Economic History* 34 (March 1974): 96–98.

13. *Pennsylvania Gazette*, August 3, 1774, p. 1; searchable copies of the *Pennsylvania Gazette* are available through http://www.accessible.com/accessible/preLog (accessed March 10, 2009). Also see Deborah Epstein Popper, "Poor Christopher Colles: An Innovator's Obstacles in Early America," *Journal of American Culture* 28 (June 2005): 180–81, and Thompson Westcott, *The Life of John Fitch: The Inventor of the Steamboat* (Philadelphia: J. B. Lippincott, 1857), 153–59.

14. John Fitch, "Notes on Petition to the Pennsylvania General Assembly," n.d., John Fitch Papers, Library of Congress, 148–54.

15. Fitch, *Autobiography*, 19–41; Francis Jordan Jr., *The Life of William Henry of Lancaster, Pennsylvania, 1729–1786* (Lancaster, PA: New Era Printing, 1910), 34–52.

16. See the biographical essay in James Rumsey, "Letters of James Rumsey, Inventor of the Steamboat," *William and Mary Quarterly*, 1st ser., 24 (January 1916): 154–56.

17. George Washington to James Rumsey, September 7, 1784; James Rumsey to George Washington, October 18, 1784; James Rumsey to George Washington, March 10, 1785; George Wash-

ington to James Rumsey, June 5, 1785; James Rumsey to George Washington, September 19, 1786, in George Washington Papers at the Library of Congress, http://memory.loc.gov/ammem/mtjhtml/mtjres.html (accessed March 21, 2003); Ella May Turner, *James Rumsey, Pioneer in Steam Navigation* (Scottdale, PA: Mennonite Publishing House, 1930), 27–75; Emory Kemp, "James Rumsey and His Role in the Improvements Movement," special issue, *West Virginia History* 48 (1989): 1–6.

18. Worthington C. Ford et al., eds., *Journals of the Continental Congress, 1774–1789*, vol. 27 (Washington, DC: Government Printing Office, 1928), 24, 411, 432–34; Brooke Hindle, *Emulation and Invention* (New York: New York University Press, 1981), 33. See also "Articles of Agreement between James McMechen and James Rumsey," September 7, 1784, in James Rumsey, "Letters of James Rumsey: Inventor of the Steamboat," 169.

19. George Washington to Hugh Williamson, March 15, 1785, George Washington Papers at the Library of Congress; Thomas Jefferson, "Autobiography Draft Fragment," July 27, 1821, Thomas Jefferson Papers, Library of Congress, http://memory.loc.gov/ammem/mtjhtml/mtjres.html (accessed March 21, 2003).

20. Worthington C. Ford et al., eds., *Journals of the Continental Congress, 1774–1789*, vol. 29 (Washington, DC: Government Printing Office, 1933), 349–50.

21. Frank D. Prager, "The Steamboat Pioneers before the Founding Fathers," *Journal of the Patent Office Society* 37 (July 1955): 493–95.

22. Worthington C. Ford et al., eds., *Journals of the Continental Congress, 1774–1789*, vol. 30 (Washington, DC: Government Printing Office, 1934), 669–70.

23. Fitch, *Autobiography*, 154.

24. George Washington, *The Diaries of George Washington*, ed. Donald Jackson and Dorothy Twohig, vol. 4 (Charlottesville: University Press of Virginia, 1978), 218; Fitch, *Autobiography*, 154–57, 204.

25. Hindle, *Emulation and Invention*, 65–69.

26. Prager, "Steamboat Pioneers before the Founding Fathers," 511–13. See also John Fitch, "Petition to the New York State Legislature," February 27, 1787, Thomas Jefferson Papers, Library of Congress.

27. John Fitch, "Petition to the Pennsylvania General Assembly," March 23, 1786, Thomas Jefferson Papers, Library of Congress; Fitch, *Autobiography*, 154–59.

28. Arthur Donaldson, "Petition to the Pennsylvania General Assembly," March 18, 1786, Thomas Jefferson Papers, Library of Congress; Fitch, *Autobiography*, 164–65; *Pennsylvania Gazette*, May 10, 1786, p. 2, col. 1, June 14, 1786, p. 2, col. 1, November 15, 1786, p. 2, col. 1, and December 6, 1786, p. 2, col. 1.

29. Caleb S. Riggs to John Fitch, March 15, 1787, Thomas Jefferson Papers, Library of Congress.

30. Fitch, *Autobiography*, 164–65; *Pennsylvania Gazette*, May 10, 1786, p. 2, col. 1, June 14, 1786, p. 2, col. 1, November 15, 1786, p. 2, col. 1, and December 6, 1786, p. 2, col. 1.

31. *Columbian Magazine*, December 1786 and January 1787, cited in Prager, "Steamboat Pioneers before the Founding Fathers," 515; John Fitch, "Petition to the Honorable James Madison," August 11, 1787, Thomas Jefferson Papers, Library of Congress; Act of March 26, 1784, 1784 S.C. Acts 618.

32. Walterscheid, "To Promote the Progress of Science," 40–46; Patent to Joseph Jenkes by the Massachusetts General Court at Boston, March 6, 1646, copy at http://www.whipple.org/joanne/firstpatent.html (accessed March 10, 2009).

33. Tench Coxe, *An Address to an Assembly of the Friends of American Manufactures . . .* (Philadelphia: R. Aitken, 1787), 1–30, cited in Walterscheid, "To Promote the Progress of Science," 40–41; Jacob E. Cooke, *Tench Coxe and the Early Republic* (Chapel Hill: University of North Carolina Press, 1978).

34. Max Farrand, *The Records of the Federal Convention of 1787* (New Haven, CT: Yale University Press, 1911), 3:248–56, 321–33, 447–56; Prager, "Steamboat Pioneers before the Founding Fathers," 515–20.

35. Walterscheid, "To Promote the Progress of Science," 40–41; Irah Donner, "The Copyright Clause of the U.S. Constitution: Why Did the Framers Include It with Unanimous Approval?" *American Journal of Legal History* 36 (October 1992): 361–67. See also Albert S. Abel, "The Commerce Clause in the Constitutional Convention and Contemporary Comment," *Minnesota Law Review* 25, no. 4 (1941): 432–93.

36. Jonathan Elliot, ed., *The Debates in the Several State Conventions on the Adoption of the Federal Constitution, as Recommended by the General Convention at Philadelphia in 1787*, 2nd ed. (Philadelphia: J. B. Lippincott, 1859), 5:440, 5:511, 5:560–61, cited in Walterscheid, "To Promote the Progress of Science," 56–57.

37. James Madison, "Powers Delegated to the General Government: III," in *The Federalist Papers: The Famous Papers on the Principles of American Government,* ed. Benjamin F. Wright (New York: Metrobooks, 2002), 309.

38. United States, House of Representatives, Representatives of James Rumsey, Report No. 403, March 5, 1846, 7–15; George M. Beltzhoover Jr., *James Rumsey, the Inventor of the Steamboat* (Wheeling: West Virginia Historical and Antiquarian Society's Publication, 1900), 5–27. This celebratory work overstates Rumsey's abilities but provides an insightful account of his steamboat trials based on primary sources.

39. James Rumsey, *A Short Treatise on the Application of Steam* . . . (Philadelphia: Joseph James, 1788).

40. John Fitch, *The Original Steam-Boat Supported* . . . (Philadelphia: Zachariah Poulson, 1788).

41. Joseph Barnes, *Remarks on Mr. John Fitch's Reply to Mr. James Rumsey's Pamphlet* (Philadelphia: Joseph James, 1788).

42. Hindle, *Emulation and Invention,* 40–41.

43. Ibid., 41–42.

44. Thomas Jefferson to James Rumsey, October 14, 1789, Thomas Jefferson Papers, Library of Congress.

45. Edwin T. Layton Jr., "James Rumsey: Pioneer Technologist," special issue, *West Virginia History* 48 (1989): 15.

46. Eric H. Robinson, "The Early Diffusion of Steam Power," *Journal of Economic History* 34 (March 1974): 104–5. Layton and Robinson differ in their interpretations of the meeting between Rumsey, Boulton, and Watt. Layton maintains that Rumsey refused to abandon his followers in the Rumseian Society and rejected offers to take a Boulton and Watt engine abroad. Robinson, however, argues that Boulton and Watt terminated the negotiations when Rumsey threatened to take one of their engines to Ireland for further experiments. See also Brooke Hindle, "James Rumsey and the Rise of Steamboating in the United States," special issue *West Virginia History* 48 (1989): 33–42.

47. James Rumsey to Charles Morrow, August 4, 1789, reprinted in James Rumsey, "Letters of James Rumsey: Inventor of the Steamboat (Concluded)," *William and Mary Quarterly,* 1st ser., 25 (July 1916): 31.

48. James Rumsey to Charles Morrow, January 5, August 23, and September 12, 1791, reprinted in "Letters of James Rumsey (Concluded)," 239–51.

49. Fitch, *Autobiography,* 182–84; Westcott, *Life of John Fitch,* 302–3.

50. William Thornton, *Papers of William Thornton,* ed. C. M. Harris, vol. 1 (Charlottesville: University Press of Virginia, 1995), xxxi–iii; "Fitch's Steamboat," *Scientific American* 2 (October 17, 1846): 1. See also Gordon S. Brown, *Incidental Architect: William Thornton and the Cultural Life of Early Washington DC, 1794–1828* (Athens: Ohio University Press, 2009).

51. Linda Grant De Pauw, Charlene Bangs Bickford, Kenneth R. Bowling, LaVonne Marlene Siegel, and Helen E. Veit, eds., *Documentary History of the First Federal Congress of the United States* (Washington, DC: Government Printing Office, 1982), 6:1626–32; Patent Act of 1790, 1 Stat. 109.

52. Thomas Jefferson, "Bill on Useful Arts, Copyright," December 1, 1791, Thomas Jefferson Papers, Library of Congress.

53. Edward C. Walterscheid, "Patents and the Jeffersonian Mythology," *John Marshall Law Review* 29 (Fall 1995): 283–86.

54. De Pauw, Bickford, Bowling, Siegel, and Veit, *Documentary History,* 6:1644, cited in E. C. Walterscheid, "Thomas Jefferson and the Patent Act of 1793," *Essays in History* 40 (July 1998): 5.

55. Joseph Barnes, *Treatise on Justice, Policy, and Utility of Establishing an Effectual System of Promoting the Progress of Useful Arts . . .* (Philadelphia: Francis Bailey, 1792), cited in Walterscheid, "Patents and the Jeffersonian Mythology," 316–18.

56. Fitch, *Autobiography,* 244–46.

57. Patent Act of 1790, 1 Stat. 109. See also Thomas Jefferson to Hugh Williamson, November 13, 1791, William Short to Thomas Jefferson, February 29, 1792, and William Short to Thomas Jefferson, July 26, 1792, Thomas Jefferson Papers, Library of Congress.

58. Daniel Preston, "The Administration and Reform of the U.S. Patent Office, 1790–1836," *Journal of the Early Republic* 5 (Fall 1985): 331–53; Leonard D. White, *The Federalists: A Study in Administrative History, 1789–1801* (New York: Macmillan, 1954), 163–69.

59. Walterscheid, "Thomas Jefferson and the Patent Act of 1793," 9–10.

60. Boyd, *Poor John Fitch,* 283–91.

61. Ibid.

62. Ibid.

Chapter 2: Origins of the Fulton-Livingston Monopoly

1. *New York Columbian,* January 26, 1820, p. 2, cols. 1–3.

2. David Maldwyn Ellis, *New York: City and State* (Ithaca, NY: Cornell University Press, 1979), 96–97; Robert G. Albion, *Rise of New York Port* (New York: Charles Scribners' Sons, 1939), 55–75.

3. Ellis, *New York: City and State,* 96–116; Joyce Appleby, *Inheriting the Revolution: The First Generation of Americans* (Cambridge, MA: Belknap, 2000); Timothy Breen, *The Marketplace of Revolution: How Consumer Politics Shaped American Independence* (New York: Oxford University Press, 2004); Paul A. Gilje, "The Rise of Capitalism in the Early Republic," in *Wages of Independence: Capitalism in the Early American Republic,* ed. Paul A. Gilje (Madison, WI: Madison House, 1997), 5–10; John Lauritz Larson, *Internal Improvement: National Public Works and the Promise of Popular Government in the Early United States* (Chapel Hill: University of North Carolina Press, 2001), 9–37; Cathy D. Matson, "Capitalizing Hope: Economic Thought and the Early National Economy," in Gilje, *Wages of Independence,* 116–30; George Rogers Taylor, *The Transportation Revolution, 1815–1860* (New York: Rinehart, 1951), 6–32.

4. Carol Sheriff, *The Artificial River: The Erie Canal and the Paradox of Progress, 1817–1862* (New York: Hill and Wang, 1996), 24–26; Ronald E. Shaw, *Erie Water West: A History of the Erie Canal, 1792–1854* (Lexington: University of Kentucky Press, 1966), 12–17. Leading biographies on DeWitt Clinton include Evan Cornog, *The Birth of Empire: DeWitt Clinton and American Experience, 1769–1828* (New York: Oxford University Press, 1998), and Craig Hanyan and Mary L. Hanyan, *De Witt Clinton and the Rise of the People's Men* (Ottawa: McGill-Queens University Press, 1996).

5. Allan Kulikoff, "The Transition to Capitalism in Rural America," *William and Mary Quarterly,* 3rd ser., 46 (January 1989): 120–44; Cathy Matson and Peter S. Onuf, "Toward a Republican Empire: Interest and Ideology in Revolutionary America," *American Quarterly* 37 (Fall 1985): 496–531; Gordon S. Wood, "The Enemy Is Us: Democratic Capitalism in the Early Republic," in Gilje, *Wages of Independence,* 137–53; and Wood, *Radicalism of the American Revolution* (New York: Alfred A. Knopf, 1991). The literature on early American economic development is extensive. Important works on precapitalist culture include James Henretta, "Families and Farms: *Mentalité* in Pre-industrial America," *William and Mary Quarterly,* 3rd ser., 35 (January 1978): 3–32, and Richard B. Sheriden, "The Domestic Economy," in *Colonial British America: Essays in the New History of the Early Modern Era,* ed. Jack Greene and J. R. Pole (Baltimore, MD: Johns Hopkins University Press, 1984), 43–85. The transition from subsistence to commercial farming is detailed in Christopher Clark, *Roots of Rural Capitalism* (Ithaca, NY: Cornell University Press, 1990), and Alan Kulikoff, *The Agrarian Origins of American Capitalism* (Charlottesville: University Press of Virginia, 1992). Jonathan Prude,

199

The Coming of Industrial Order: Town and Factory Life in Massachusetts, 1810–1860 (New York: Cambridge University Press, 1983), and Sean Wilentz, *Chants Democratic: New York City and the Rise of the American Working Class, 1788–1850* (New York: Oxford University Press, 1986), examine the transformation of urban areas and the decline of artisan culture. Works such as Deborah A. Rosen, *Courts and Commerce: Gender, Law, and the Market Economy in Colonial New York* (Columbus: Ohio State University Press, 1997), and Martin Bruegel, *Farm, Shop, Landing: The Rise of a Market Society in the Hudson Valley, 1780–1860* (Durham, NC: Duke University Press, 2002), discuss New York's economic development throughout the colonial period and early Republic.

6. George Dangerfield, *Chancellor Robert R. Livingston of New York, 1746–1813* (New York: Harcourt, Brace, 1960), 7, 1–29, 186–92.

7. Ibid., 44–58; Cynthia A. Kierner, *Traders and Gentlefolk: The Livingstons of New York, 1675–1790* (Ithaca, NY: Cornell University Press, 1992), 208–50; Clare Brandt, *An American Aristocracy: The Livingstons* (Garden City, NY: Doubleday, 1986), 9–50; Sung Bok Kim, "Robert Livingston and Moral Judgment," *Hudson Valley Regional Review* 4 (March 1987): 1–7; Edwin Brockholst Livingston, *The Livingstons of Livingston Manor* (New York: Knickerbocker Press, 1910), 353–92.

8. Clare Brandt, "Robert R. Livingston, Jr., the Reluctant Revolutionary," *Hudson Valley Regional Review* 4 (March 1987): 8–20; Edward Countryman, "Consolidating Power in Revolutionary America: The Case of New York, 1775–1783," *Journal of Interdisciplinary History* 6 (Spring 1976): 645–77; David Hackett Fisher, *The Revolution of American Conservatism: The Federalist Party in the Era of Jeffersonian Democracy* (New York: Harper & Row, 1965), 3–35; Peter J. Galie, *Ordered Liberty: A Constitutional History of New York* (New York: Fordham University Press, 1996), 36–55.

9. Robert R. Livingston to Charles De Witt, June 25, 1784, Robert R. Livingston Papers, New-York Historical Society.

10. Dangerfield, *Chancellor Robert R. Livingston*, 186.

11. Robert R. Livingston to George Washington, February 4, 1795, George Washington to Robert R. Livingston, February 16, 1795, Walter Livingston, "Calculations on the Advantages of the Mohawk Navigation," 1792, Robert R. Livingston Papers, New-York Historical Society.

12. Archibald Douglas Turnbull, *John Stevens: An American Record* (New York: Century, 1928), 35–58.

13. John Stevens to Robert R. Livingston, December 3, 1788, Randall LeBoeuf Collection, New-York Historical Society; John Stevens to Robert R. Livingston, August 6, 1794, Robert R. Livingston Papers, New-York Historical Society; Robert R. Livingston to John Stevens, August 30, 1795, Stevens Family Papers, New Jersey Historical Society, reprinted in Turnbull, *John Stevens*, 122–24.

14. John Stevens to Robert R. Livingston, July 20, 1789, "Articles of Agreement between John Stevens and Mary Stevens Livingston in Regards to the Estate of John Stevens," May 10, 1792, Robert R. Livingston, "Agreement with John Stevens Regarding Debts from His Father's Estate," February 22, 1798, Robert R. Livingston Papers, New-York Historical Society. See also Cynthia Owen Philip, "Robert R. Livingston: Enthusiastic Inventor, Prudent Entrepreneur," *Hudson Valley Regional Review* 4 (March 1987): 74–80.

15. John Stevens to Robert R. Livingston, January 4, 1789, Robert R. Livingston Papers, New-York Historical Society.

16. John Stevens to James Rumsey, September 4, 1789, John Stevens, "Plan for a Steam Engine Certified by John Watts," February 2, 1791, Randall LeBoeuf Collection, New-York Historical Society; "Petition to New York for Exclusive Rights to Steamship Operation," Stevens Family Papers, New Jersey Historical Society, cited in Turnbull, *John Stevens*, 106–7.

17. G. H. Preble, *A Chronological History of the Origin and Development of Steam Navigation* (Philadelphia: L. R. Hamersly, 1895), 46–52.

18. Robert R. Livingston to Nicholas Roosevelt, February 22, 1797, December 8, 1797, and December 14, 1797, Robert Fulton Papers, New-York Historical Society.

19. Turnbull, *John Stevens*, 33–43.

20. Charles Stoudinger to Nicholas Roosevelt, December 18, 1797, Robert R. Livingston to Nicholas Roosevelt, December 22, 1797, and Charles Stoudinger to Nicholas Roosevelt, December 29, 1797, Robert Fulton Papers, New-York Historical Society.

21. Robert R. Livingston to Nicholas Roosevelt, August 17, 1798, Robert Fulton Papers, New-York Historical Society.

22. Nicholas Roosevelt to Robert R. Livingston, August 27, 1807, Robert Fulton Papers, New-York Historical Society.

23. Dangerfield, *Chancellor Robert R. Livingston*, 288.

24. Robert R. Livingston to James Watt, November 4, 1799, Robert R. Livingston to Nicholas Roosevelt, April 6, 1798, and August 27, 1798, Robert Fulton Papers, New-York Historical Society; John Stevens to Robert R. Livingston, October 27, 1798, March 8, 1799, April 12, 1799, January 8, 1800, and July 4, 1800, Robert R. Livingston Papers, New-York Historical Society.

25. Robert R. Livingston to Nicholas Roosevelt, January 12, 1798, January 23, 1798, February 20, 1798, March 18, 1798, August 22, 1798, August 30, 1798, September 1, 1798, September 10, 1798, and September 18, 1798, Nicholas Roosevelt to Robert R. Livingston, August 27, 1798, September 6, 1798, September 10, 1798, and October 21, 1798, Robert Fulton Papers, New-York Historical Society; Robert R. Livingston to James Watt, November 4, 1799, Robert R. Livingston Papers, New-York Historical Society.

26. Joseph J. Ellis, *American Sphinx: The Character of Thomas Jefferson* (New York: Alfred A. Knopf, 1997), 204–8; Willard Sterne Randall, *Thomas Jefferson: A Life* (New York: Henry Holt, 1993), 566–67.

27. Kirkpatrick Sale, *The Fire of His Genius: Robert Fulton and the American Dream* (New York: Free Press, 2001), 82–83; Alice Crary Sutcliffe, *Robert Fulton* (New York: Macmillan, 1915), 37–72.

28. Cynthia Owen Philip, *Robert Fulton: A Biography* (New York: Franklin Watts, 1985), 3–13.

29. Robert Fulton to Charles Mahon, Third Earl of Stanhope, April 10, 1798, and April 14, 1798, Gilder Lehrman Collection, New-York Historical Society. See also Philip, *Robert Fulton*, 26–36, 54–56.

30. A. E. Musson and E. Robinson, "The Early Growth of Steam Power," *Economic History Review* 11 (April 1959): 429–39; Donald Sheehan, "The Manchester Literary and Philosophical Society," *Isis* 33 (December 1941): 519–23.

31. Sale, *Fire of His Genius*, 56–60. For views of science and social progress popular among Fulton's generation, see Thomas Bender, *New York Intellect: A History of Intellectual Life in New York City from 1750 to the Beginnings of Our Own Time* (New York: Alfred A. Knopf, 1987), 121–30.

32. Robert Fulton, *Treatise on the Improvement of Canal Navigation* (London: I. and J. Taylor, 1796), 12. See also Robert Fulton, July 28, 1796, and Fulton, *Report on the Proposed Canal between the Rivers Heyl and Helford*, November 24, 1796, Gilder Lehrman Collection, New-York Historical Society.

33. Sale, *Fire of His Genius*, 53–54.

34. Michael Broers, *Europe under Napoleon, 1799–1815* (London: Hadder Arnold, 1996), 99–143.

35. James Woodress, *A Yankee's Odyssey: The Life of Joel Barlow* (Philadelphia: J. B. Lippincott, 1958), 216–20. See also Esther Morris Douty, *Hasty Pudding and Barbary Pirates: A Life of Joel Barlow* (Westminster, England: Westminster Press, 1975), and Charles Burr Todd, *Life and Letters of Joel Barlow: Poet, Statesman, Philosopher* (New York: DaCapo, 1970).

36. Robert Fulton, "Essay to the Friends of Mankind on the Advantages of Free Trade," Robert Fulton Papers, New-York Historical Society, 5.

37. Philip, "Robert R. Livingston," 76–78.

38. Ibid., 78–80.

39. Ibid., 80–83.

40. Robert R. Livingston to Thomas Tillotson, November 12, 1802, Robert R. Livingston Papers, New-York Historical Society.

41. Thomas Tillotson to Robert R. Livingston, March 4, 1803, Robert R. Livingston Papers, New-York Historical Society.

42. Dangerfield, *Chancellor Robert R. Livingston*, 366–71.

43. Robert Fulton to William Constable, November 4, 1798, Gilder Lehrman Collection, New-York Historical Society; M. J. Breckin and Jennifer Tamm, "The International Diffusion of the Watt Engine, 1775–1825," *Economic History Review* 31 (November 1978): 541–64.

44. Robert Fulton to the Conservancy of Arts and Trades, January 24, 1803, cited in H. W. Dickinson, *Robert Fulton, Engineer and Artist: His Life and Works* (London: John Lane, 1913), 151.

201

45. Philip, *Robert Fulton,* 150.

46. *Washington National Intelligencer,* January 16, 1807, p. 2, col. 2, cited in Sale, *Fire of His Genius,* 115–17.

47. Sale, *Fire of His Genius,* 115–17.

48. Jeffersonian notions of the frontier have inspired a variety of scholarly debates, a trend that intensified with the bicentennial of Jefferson's administration and the Louisiana Purchase. See James P. Ronda, *Jefferson's West: A Journey with Lewis and Clark* (Chapel Hill: University of North Carolina Press, 2002); M. R. Montgomery, *Jefferson and the Gunmen: How the West Was Almost Lost* (New York: Crown, 2000); Ellis, *American Sphinx;* and Randall, *Thomas Jefferson.*

49. John Kasson, *Civilizing the Machine: Technology and Republican Values in America, 1776–1900* (New York: Viking, 1976), 22–29, 140–80.

50. Robert Fulton to Henry Dearborn, January 13, 1807, Gilder Lehrman Collection, New-York Historical Society.

51. Philip, *Robert Fulton,* 188–89; Dangerfield, *Chancellor Robert R. Livingston,* 411–22.

52. Robert Fulton to Robert R. Livingston, January 12, 1806, Livingston Family Papers, Clermont State Historical Site; Robert R. Livingston to Robert Fulton, March 10, 1807, Historical Society of Pennsylvania, cited in Philip, *Robert Fulton,* 188–89.

53. Philip, *Robert Fulton,* 295–302.

54. Ibid.

55. Sale, *Fire of His Genius,* 5–8.

56. Celebratory accounts of the maiden voyage of the *North River Steam Boat* include Cadwallader D. Colden, *The Life of Robert Fulton* (New York: Kirk and Mercein, 1817), 170; James Thomas Flexner, *Steamboats Come True: American Inventors in Action* (New York: Fordham University Press, 1992), 319; and J. Frank Reigart, *The Life of Robert Fulton* (Philadelphia: G. C. Henderson, 1856), 1–5. These accounts are evaluated in Donald C. Ringwald, "First Steamboat to Albany," *American Neptune* 23 (July 1964): 157–71.

Chapter 3: Corporate Negotiations

1. Robert Fulton to Joel Barlow, n.d., in *Life and Letters of Joel Barlow: Poet, Statesman, Philosopher,* ed. Charles B. Todd (1886; reprint New York: DaCapo, 1970), 233; Alice Crary Sutcliffe, *Robert Fulton and the "Clermont"* (New York: Century, 1909), 235.

2. Meyer Weinberg, *A Short History of American Capitalism* (Amherst, MA: Meyer Weinberg, 2002), 101–6; Edward Pessen, "The Business Elite of Antebellum New York City: Diversity, Continuity, Standing," in *An Emerging Independent American Economy, 1815–1875,* ed. Joseph R. Frese and Jacob Judd (Tarrytown, NY: Sleepy Hollow Press, 1980), 163–65; Pessen, "Who Has Power in the Democratic Capitalistic Community? Reflections on Antebellum New York City," *New York History* 58 (April 1977): 136–39; L. Ray Gunn, *The Decline of Authority: Public Economic Policy and Political Development in New York, 1800–1860* (Ithaca, NY: Cornell University Press, 1988), 57–73.

3. Martin Bruegel, *Farm, Shop, Landing: The Rise of a Market Society in the Hudson Valley, 1780–1860* (Durham, NC: Duke University Press, 2002), 64–89, and Carol Sheriff, *The Artificial River: The Erie Canal and the Paradox of Progress, 1817–1862* (New York: Hill and Wang, 1996), 110–36, discuss the various rationales early New Yorkers used to fund economic development in the early 1800s. Carter Goodrich, *Government Promotion of American Canals and Railroads, 1800–1890* (New York: Columbia University Press, 1960), 54–73, and Louis Hartz, *Economic Policy and Democratic Thought: Pennsylvania, 1776–1860* (Cambridge, MA: Harvard University Press, 1948), 40–46, provide seminal accounts of early national economic development.

4. Edward J. Balleisen, *Navigating Failure: Bankruptcy and Commercial Society in Antebellum America* (Chapel Hill: University of North Carolina Press, 2001); Joanne B. Freeman, *Affairs of Honor: National Politics in the Early Republic* (New Haven, CT: Yale University Press, 2001); Naomi R. Lamoreaux, Daniel M. G. Raff, and Peter Temin, "Beyond Markets and Hierarchies: Towards a New Synthesis of American Business History," *American Historical Review* 108 (April 2003):

404–33; Naomi R. Lamoreaux, *Insider Lending: Banks, Personal Connections, and Economic Development in Industrial New England* (New York: Cambridge University Press, 1994); Bertram Wyatt-Brown, *Southern Honor: Ethics and Behavior in the Old South* (Oxford: Oxford University Press, 1983). For the limitations of judicial power in the early Republic, see William E. Nelson, *The Americanization of the Common Law: The Impact of Legal Change on Massachusetts Society, 1760–1830* (Cambridge, MA: Harvard University Press, 1975).

5. Sutcliffe, *Robert Fulton and the Clermont*, 66–80.

6. Peter Augustus Jay to John Jay, August 21, 1807, John Jay to Peter Augustus Jay, September 2, 1807, John Jay Papers, Columbia University Library.

7. Cynthia Owen Philip, "Robert R. Livingston: Enthusiastic Inventor, Prudent Entrepreneur," *Hudson Valley Regional Review* 4 (March 1987): 74–80; Brooke Hindle, *Emulation and Invention* (New York: New York University Press, 1981), 25–83.

8. Robert Fulton to Robert R. Livingston, October 18, 1807, Gilder Lehrman Collection, New-York Historical Society; Robert Fulton to Robert R. Livingston, November 6, 1807, Robert Fulton to Robert R. Livingston, December 1, 1807, Livingston Family Papers, Clermont State Historical Site, cited in Cynthia Owen Philip, *Robert Fulton: A Biography* (New York: Franklin Watts, 1985), 210–11.

9. Fulton's attempts to interest the federal government in his steamboat proposals can be found in Robert Fulton to Thomas Jefferson, December 3, 1807, Thomas Jefferson to Robert Fulton, December 10, 1807, Thomas Jefferson Papers, Library of Congress. See also Philip, *Robert Fulton*, 68–77, 228–29.

10. William Thornton to Robert Fulton, December 16, 1807, William Thornton Papers, Library of Congress.

11. John Stevens to Robert R. Livingston, December 28, 1807, Stevens Family Papers, New Jersey Historical Society.

12. Ibid.

13. Robert R. Livingston to John Stevens, January 18, 1808, Stevens Family Papers, New Jersey Historical Society.

14. Robert R. Livingston and Robert Fulton to John Stevens, January 18, 1808, Stevens Family Papers, New Jersey Historical Society, cited in Roy Louis DuBois, "John Stevens: Transportation Pioneer" (PhD diss., New York University, 1973), 234–35.

15. Robert R. Livingston and Robert Fulton to John Stevens, January 18, 1808, Stevens Family Papers, New Jersey Historical Society.

16. Mary Stevens Livingston to Robert R. Livingston, March 20, 1807, John Stevens to Robert R. Livingston, March 20, 1808, Stevens Family Papers, New Jersey Historical Society, cited in DuBois, "John Stevens," 187.

17. John Stevens to Robert R. Livingston and Robert Fulton, February 13, 1808, Draft of Letter to Robert R. Livingston and Robert Fulton, n.d., Stevens Family Papers, New Jersey Historical Society, cited in DuBois, "John Stevens," 180.

18. Act of April 11, 1808, 1808 N.Y. Laws 617.

19. Mary Stevens Livingston to Robert R. Livingston, April 21, 1808, John Stevens to Robert R. Livingston, April 21, 1808, Stevens Family Papers, New Jersey Historical Society, cited in DuBois, "John Stevens," 187–88.

20. Robert R. Livingston to John Stevens, May 9, 1808, John Stevens to Robert R. Livingston, May 11, 1808, Robert R. Livingston to John Stevens, May 11, 1808, Stevens Family Papers, New Jersey Historical Society, cited in DuBois, "John Stevens," 189–91.

21. Robert Fulton to Charles Wilson Peale, June 11, 1808, Gilder Lehrman Collection, New-York Historical Society.

22. Robert Fulton to Robert R. Livingston, July 12, 1807, John Stevens to Robert R. Livingston and Robert Fulton, July 23, 1808, Stevens Family Papers, New Jersey Historical Society, cited in DuBois, "John Stevens," 181, 238.

23. Robert Fulton to Robert R. Livingston, August 2, 1808, Robert Fulton Papers, Gilbert Montague Collection, New York Public Library.

24. John Stevens to Richard Harison, July 29, 1808, Stevens Family Papers, New Jersey Historical Society, cited in DuBois, "John Stevens," 181.

25. Ibid.

26. Contract between Robert R. Livingston and Robert Fulton and John R. Livingston, August 20, 1808, Robert Fulton Papers, Gilbert Montague Collection, New York Public Library. Additional copies can be found in File BM-0-109, New York Chancery Court Papers, New York County Clerk's Office. For details on John R. Livingston, see Lorna Skaaren, "John R. Livingston and the American Revolution," *Hudson Valley Regional Review* 4 (March 1987): 311–20.

27. John Stevens, Broadside Announcing Steamboat Lines, Stevens Family Papers, New Jersey Historical Society, cited in DuBois, "John Stevens," 194.

28. Robert R. Livingston to John Stevens, October 10, 1808, Robert R. Livingston Papers, New-York Historical Society.

29. "A Friend to Useful Invention and Justice," *American Citizen,* October 27, 1808, p. 2, col. 1. See also rough draft titled "Fair Play," n.d., Robert R. Livingston Papers, New-York Historical Society.

30. Robert Fulton to John Stevens, October 28, 1808, Robert Fulton Papers, Gilbert Montague Collection, New York Public Library.

31. Thornton also mentioned to Stevens that he had invented a steamboat far superior to Fulton's vessel. When patented, this new steamboat would give Thornton sufficient leverage to overturn Fulton and Livingston's steamboat monopoly. Thornton also wrote an ally, William Brown, in New Orleans with a request to mount a public campaign against Fulton and Livingston should they attempt to secure a monopoly through the territorial legislature. William Thornton to John Stevens, October 11, 1808, William Thornton to William Brown, October 28, 1808, William Thornton Papers, Library of Congress.

32. John Stevens to William Thornton, October 28, 1808, William Thornton to John Stevens, November 2, 1808, and William Thornton to John Stevens, January 23, 1809, William Thornton Papers, Library of Congress.

33. John Stevens, Draft of Reply to "A Friend to Useful Inventions and Justice," November 1811, Stevens Family Papers, New Jersey Historical Society, cited in DuBois, "John Stevens," 243.

34. Robert R. Livingston to Mary Stevens Livingston, November 19, 1808, Robert R. Livingston Papers, New-York Historical Society.

35. Robert Fulton to John Stevens, December 6, 1808, Robert Fulton Papers, Gilbert Montague Collection, New York Public Library.

36. Horace Birney to John Stevens, February 19, 1809, Stevens Family Papers, New Jersey Historical Society, cited in DuBois, "John Stevens," 244.

37. Benjamin Henry Latrobe to Robert Fulton, February 7, 1809, Benjamin Henry Latrobe Papers, Library of Congress; Talbot Hamlin, *Benjamin Henry Latrobe* (New York: Oxford University Press, 1955).

38. Benjamin Henry Latrobe to Nicholas Roosevelt, February 7, 1809, Benjamin Henry Latrobe Papers, Library of Congress.

39. John R. Livingston to John Stevens, May 8, 1809, Stevens Family Papers, New Jersey Historical Society, cited in DuBois, "John Stevens," 195.

40. John Stevens to Robert Fulton, May 8, 1809, Robert Fulton to John Stevens, May 8, 1809, and John Stevens to Robert Fulton, May 9, 1809, Stevens Family Papers, New Jersey Historical Society, cited in DuBois, "John Stevens," 245–46, Robert Fulton to William Thornton, May 9, 1809, William Thornton Papers, Library of Congress.

41. Robert Fulton, "Plan for Mississippi Steamboat Company," n.d., Robert Fulton Papers, Gilbert Montague Collection, New York Public Library.

42. Benjamin Henry Latrobe to Nicholas Roosevelt, February 7, 1809, and Benjamin Henry Latrobe to Robert Fulton, February 7, 1809, in Benjamin Henry Latrobe, *The Correspondence and Miscellaneous Papers of Benjamin Henry Latrobe,* ed. John C. Van Horne and Lee W. Formwalt, vol. 2 (New Haven, CT: Yale University Press, 1987), 421–23; Benjamin Henry Latrobe to Lydia Latrobe Roosevelt, May 11, 1809, Benjamin Henry Latrobe Papers, Library of Congress.

43. Benjamin Henry Latrobe to Lydia Latrobe Roosevelt, May 11, 1809, Benjamin Henry Latrobe Papers, Library of Congress.

44. Benjamin Henry Latrobe to Nicholas Roosevelt, June 23, 1809, Benjamin Henry Latrobe Papers, Library of Congress; John H. B. Latrobe, *The First Steamboat Voyage on the Western Waters* (Baltimore: Maryland Historical Society, 1871), 4–28.

45. Latrobe, *First Steamboat Voyage*, 29–33.

46. Benjamin Henry Latrobe to Nicholas Roosevelt, January 23, 1810, Benjamin Henry Latrobe Papers, Library of Congress; Nicholas Roosevelt, "Denunciation of Claim by Nicholas Roosevelt and John Stevens," n.d., Gilder Lehrman Collection, New-York Historical Society.

47. Kirkpatrick Sale, *The Fire of His Genius: Robert Fulton and the American Dream* (New York: Free Press, 2001), 135–38.

48. Henry Voight to William Thornton, June 9, 1809, Henry Voight, Signed Affidavit, June 21, 1809, William Thornton to John Stevens, July 8, 1809, William Thornton Papers, Library of Congress; John Stevens to Horace Birney, August 7, 1809, Stevens Family Papers, New Jersey Historical Society, cited in DuBois, "John Stevens," 218.

49. Robert Fulton to Charles Browne, August 1, 1809, Robert Fulton Papers, Gilbert Montague Collection, New York Public Library; Robert R. Livingston to John Stevens, November 11, 1809, Stevens Family Papers, New Jersey Historical Society, cited in DuBois, "John Stevens," 247; Robert Fulton to John Stevens, November 11, 1809, Robert Fulton Papers, Gilbert Montague Collection, New York Public Library.

50. John Stevens to Robert R. Livingston and Robert Fulton, November 25, 1809, Stevens Family Papers, New Jersey Historical Society, cited in DuBois, "John Stevens," 247–48.

51. Robert Fulton to John Stevens, November 25, 1809, Stevens Family Papers, New Jersey Historical Society, cited in DuBois, "John Stevens," 248–49.

52. Robert Fulton to John Stevens, November 29, 1809, Stevens Family Papers, New Jersey Historical Society, cited in DuBois, "John Stevens," 249.

53. Memorandum of an Agreement between Robert R. Livingston and Robert Fulton with John Stevens, Robert Fulton Papers, New Jersey Historical Society, cited in DuBois, "John Stevens," 212.

54. John Stevens to Robert R. Livingston, n.d., Robert R. Livingston Papers, New-York Historical Society.

55. David Waldstreicher, *In the Midst of Perpetual Fetes: The Making of American Nationalism, 1776–1820* (Chapel Hill: University of North Carolina Press, 1997), 246–47, 269–71, 271–93. For an overview of works on western identity, see Richard White, "Western History" in *The New American History*, ed. Eric Foner, rev. ed. (Philadelphia: Temple University Press, 1997), 203–30; Andrew R. L. Cayton, *The Frontier Republic: Ideology and Politics in the Ohio Country, 1780–1825* (Kent, OH: Kent State University Press, 1986), 76–77; Cayton and Peter Onuf, *The Midwest and the Nation* (Bloomington: Indiana University Press, 1990), 21–25; Francis S. Philbrick, *The Rise of the West, 1754–1830* (New York: HarperCollins, 1965), 6–17; and Henry Nash Smith, *Virgin Land: The American West as Symbol and Myth* (Cambridge, MA: Harvard University Press, 1950), 13–30.

56. Cayton and Onuf, *Midwest and the Nation*, 24–25.

57. Robert R. Livingston and Robert Fulton to the Governor of the Upper Michigan Territory, August 20, 1810, Robert R. Livingston Papers, New-York Historical Society; H. Dora Stecker, "Constructing a Navigation System in the West," *Ohio Archaeology and Historical Society Publications* 22 (January 1913): 18–21. See also William J. Petersen, *Steamboating on the Upper Mississippi* (Iowa City: State Historical Society of Iowa, 1937), 44.

58. Stecker, "Constructing a Navigation System," 18–20.

59. Kimberly S. Hanger, *A Medley of Cultures: Louisiana Culture at the Cabildo* (New Orleans: Louisiana Museum Foundation, 1996), 69–88; Light T. Cummins, "Anglo Merchants and Capital Migration in Spanish Colonial New Orleans, 1763–1803" *Gulf Coast Historical Review* 4 (Fall 1988): 7–28; William W. Chenault and Robert C. Reinders, "The Northern Born Community of New Orleans in the 1850s," *Journal of American History* 51 (September 1964): 232–47; Joseph G. Treagle Jr., "Early New Orleans Society: A Reappraisal," *Journal of Southern History* 18 (February 1952): 20–36.

206

60. Nathaniel Herbert Claiborne, *Notes on the War in the South: With Biographical Sketches of the Lives of Montgomery Jackson, Sevier, the Late Gov. Claiborne and Others* (Richmond, VA: William Ramsay, 1819), 91–112; Joseph T. Hatfield, *William Claiborne: Jeffersonian Centurion in the American Southwest* (Lafayette: University of Southwestern Louisiana, 1976), 136–62; Randall R. Couch, "William Charles Cole Claiborne: An Historiographical Review," *Louisiana History* 36 (Fall 1995): 453–65; John D. Winters, "William C. C. Claiborne: Profile of a Democrat," *Louisiana History* 10 (Summer 1969): 189–210.

61. Mark F. Fernandez, "Local Justice in the Territory of Orleans: W. C. C. Claiborne's Courts, Judges, and Justices of the Peace," in *A Law unto Itself? Essays in the New Louisiana Legal History,* ed. Warren M. Billings and Mark F. Fernandez (Baton Rouge: Louisiana State University Press, 2001), 9–28.

62. Joseph T. Hatfield, *William Claiborne,* 190–92; William B. Hatcher, *Edward Livingston: Jeffersonian Republican and Jacksonian Democrat* (Baton Rouge: Louisiana State University Press, 1940), 108–38, 413–64; Louise Livingston Hunt, *Memoir of Mrs. Edward Livingston* (New York: Harper and Brothers, 1886), 31–32; W. O. Hart, "Mrs. Louise Livingston, Wife of Edward Living-ston," *Louisiana Historical Quarterly* 5 (July 1922): 352–56; William B. Hatcher, "Edward Livingston's View of the Nature of the Union," *Louisiana Historical Quarterly* 24, no. 3 (1941): 698–728.

63. Robert R. Livingston to Edward Livingston, September 6, 1810, Livingston Family Papers, Clermont State Historical Site. Evidence of Claiborne's expensive tastes can be found in W. C. C. Claiborne to Albert Gallatin, June 21, 1809, Albert Gallatin Papers, New-York Historical Society. Claiborne's relationship with Fulton and Chancellor Livingston is revealed in W. C. C. Claiborne to Robert R. Livingston, July 26, 1811, Official Letterbooks of W. C. C. Claiborne, Mississippi State Archives.

Chapter 4: Defending the Monopoly

1. *New York Times,* July 9, 1911, p. 11, col. 3; Stefan Belinski, "James Van Ingen," *New York State Museum,* http://www.nysm.nysed.gov/albany/bios/vi/javingen6426.html (accessed May 28, 2008); David M. Ellis, "Yankee-Dutch Confrontation in the Albany Area," *New England Quarterly* 45 (June 1972): 262–70.

2. Thomas P. Robinson, "The Life of Thomas Addis Emmet" (PhD diss., New York University, 1955); Thomas Addis Emmet, "Opinion for Robert R. Livingston and Robert Fulton Relative to Their Patent Rights for Operating Steamboats," January 19, 1811, Gilder Lehrman Collection, New-York Historical Society. An additional copy can be found in the Thomas Addis Emmet Papers, New York Public Library.

3. Robert Fulton to Lord Stanhope, April 10, 1811, Gilder Lehrman Collection, New-York Historical Society.

4. Act of April 9, 1811, 1811 N.Y. Laws 368.

5. W. C. C. Claiborne, *Message to the Louisiana Legislative Council and House of Representatives,* March 19, 1811, Official Letterbooks of W. C. C. Claiborne, Mississippi State Archives.

6. W. C. C. Claiborne to Robert R. Livingston, March 26, 1811, Official Letterbooks of W. C. C. Claiborne, Mississippi State Archives.

7. Chapter 26 of the Second Session, Third Legislature, Territory of New Orleans 1811, 112; W. C. C. Claiborne to Robert Fulton, April 26, 1811, Official Letterbooks of W. C. C. Claiborne, Mississippi State Archives.

8. *Pittsburgh Gazette,* October 18, 1811, p. 1, col. 1, and October 25, 1811, p. 1, col. 1. An anecdotal yet insightful account of the voyage of the *New Orleans* can be found in Mary Helen Dohan, *Mr. Roosevelt's Steamboat: The First Steamboat to Travel the Mississippi* (New York: Dodd, Mead, 1981), 1–22. For eastern newspaper promotions and accounts regarding the *New Orleans,* see the *New York Gazette and General Advertiser,* September 25, 1811, p. 2, col. 1; *New York Spectator,* September 29, 1811, p. 1, col. 1; *Washington National Intelligencer,* November 2, 1811, p. 3, col. 2; and *New York Evening Post,* November 15, 1811, p. 2, col. 1.

9. *Western Sun* (Vincennes, IN), November 30, 1811, p. 1, col. 1, cited in Louis C. Hunter, *Steamboats on the Western Rivers: An Economic and Technological History* (New York: Octagon Books, 1969), 10–11; *New York Columbian*, December 23, 1811, p. 2, col. 2.

10. W. C. C. Claiborne to Robert R. Livingston, December 11, 1811, Official Letterbooks of W. C. C. Claiborne, Mississippi State Archives.

11. *Louisiana Monitor*, January 14, 1812, p. 1, col. 1; *Louisiana Gazette and Daily Advertiser*, January 18, 1812; John H. B. Latrobe, *The First Steamboat Voyage on the Western Waters* (Baltimore: Maryland Historical Society, 1871), 4–28.

12. W. C. C. Claiborne to Robert R. Livingston, January 26, 1812, Official Letterbooks of W. C. C. Claiborne, Mississippi State Archives; "Report of Commissioners appointed by Governor Claiborne whether the steamboat New Orleans met the conditions of the Act," Randall LeBoeuf Collection, New-York Historical Society; Robert Fulton, "Plan for Mississippi Steamboat Company," n.d., and "Proposals for Two Steamboats on Mississippi," August 12, 1812, Gilder Lehrman Collection, New-York Historical Society; *Louisiana Gazette*, January 16, 1812, p. 2, col. 3, January 21, 1812, p. 2, col. 4, and January 23, p. 3, col. 4; Alfred R. Maass, "The Right of Unrestricted Navigation on the Mississippi, 1812–1818," *American Neptune* 60 (January 2000): 51–52.

13. Robert Fulton to Joel Barlow, April 19, 1812, cited in Alice Crary Sutcliffe, *Robert Fulton and the "Clermont"* (New York: Century, 1909), 221.

14. George Dangerfield, *Chancellor Robert R. Livingston of New York, 1746–1813* (New York: Harcourt, Brace, 1960), 418–19.

15. Gerald T. Dunne, "Brockholst Livingston," in *The Justices of the United States Supreme Court, 1789–1969: Their Lives and Major Opinions,* ed. Leon Friedman and Fred L. Israel (New York: Chelsea House, 1969), 1:23–47.

16. Ibid.

17. Clare Brandt, *An American Aristocracy: The Livingstons* (Garden City, NY: Doubleday, 1986), 146–47.

18. *New York Evening Post,* June 28, 1811, p. 2, col. 5.

19. *New York Columbian,* June 22, 1811, p. 2, col. 4.

20. *New York Evening Post,* June 28, 1811, p. 2, col. 5.

21. Robert Fulton to Joel Barlow, June 28, 1811, Gilder Lehrman Collection, New-York Historical Society.

22. *New York Evening Post,* July 31, 1811, p. 3, col. 2; *New York Spectator,* August 4, 1811, p. 2, cols. 4–5.

23. *New York Spectator,* August 4, 1811, p. 2, cols. 4–5.

24. Ibid.; Elihu Bunker went to great lengths to maintain an image of public respectability in order to counter public perceptions of riverboat captains as unsavory characters. One observer noted that Bunker "seemed to be a plain, religious sort of man. He had more the look of parson than sailor, and had posted a list of regulations at the cabin-door, which, if properly enforced, were well calculated to keep his passengers in good order." See Franklin Ellis, *History of Columbia County, New York* (Philadelphia: Everts and Ensign, 1878), 162–63.

25. Paul David Nelson, "Cadwallader D. Colden," in *American National Biography,* ed. John A. Garraty and Mark C. Carnes (New York: Oxford University Press, 1999), 5:200; Edwin R. Purple, "Notes Biographical and Genealogical of the Colden Family," *New York Genealogical and Biographical Record* 4 (1873): 161–83; Philip Ranlet, *The New York Loyalists* (Knoxville: University of Tennessee Press, 1986), 53–55. George F. McFarland, "The Old Stone Mill at Morley," *St. Lawrence County Historical Association Quarterly* 36 (Fall 1991): 1–5, contains information on Richard Harison. See C. E. Fitch, *Encyclopedia of Biography of New York,* vol. 1 (New York: American Historical Society, 1916), 285, for information on Josiah Ogden Hoffman. Biographical information on John T. Harrison can be found at *Political Graveyard: A Database of Historic Cemeteries,* http://politicalgraveyard.com/index.html (accessed March 21, 2003).

26. L. B. Proctor, "Abraham Van Vechten, the Founder of the Bar of the State of New York," *Albany Law Journal* 58 (July 30, 1898): 60–69; *New York Spectator,* January 13, 1827, p. 2, col. 1; Dixon Ryan Fox, *The Decline of Aristocracy in the Politics of New York* (New York: Columbia University Press,

1919), 1–34; Donald M. Roper, "The Elite of the New York Bar as Seen from the Bench: James Kent's Necrologics," New York Historical Society Quarterly 36 (July 1947): 199–237; "David A. Ogden," in *Biographical Directory of the United States Congress, 1774–1996*, ed. Joel D. Treese (Washington, DC: Congressional Quarterly Press, 1996), 87–88; "Edmund Henry Pendleton," in Treese, *Biographical Directory,* 87–88; *National Advocate,* September 12, 1823, p. 2, cols. 1–2.

27. *Livingston v. Van Ingen,* 15 F. Cas. 697 (C.C.D.N.Y. 1811) (No. 8,420).

28. Ibid.

29. Ibid.

30. Ibid., 697–98.

31. Ibid., 700–701.

32. Ibid.; *New York Columbian,* August 1, 1811, p. 3, col. 1, reprinted in the *New York Spectator,* August 4, 1811, p. 2, cols. 4–5, and the *New York Evening Post,* August 6, 1811, p. 2, col. 4.

33. Robert Fulton to John Gales, August 10, 1811, John Gales to Robert Fulton, August 14, 1811, and Robert Fulton to John Gales, August 20, 1811, Robert R. Livingston Papers, New-York Historical Society.

34. Andrew Bartholomew to Robert R. Livingston, August 17, 1811, Robert R. Livingston Papers, New-York Historical Society. See also *New York Columbian,* August 10, 1811, p. 3, col. 2.

35. *New York Columbian,* August 10, 1811, p.3, col. 2.

36. *New York Evening Post,* September 3, 1811, p. 3, cols. 1–2.

37. *New York Evening Post,* September 5, 1811, p. 2, col. 1.

38. *New York Spectator,* September 28, 1811, p. 1, col. 1.

39. *New York Evening Post,* October 24, 1811, p. 3, col. 1.

40. *New York Evening Post,* November 8, 1811, p. 3, cols. 1–2.

41. Ibid.

42. *New York Evening Post,* November 8, 1811, p. 3, cols. 4–5.

43. Cynthia Owen Philip, *Robert Fulton: A Biography,* (New York: Franklin Watts, 267–68.

44. "John Lansing," in *American National Biography,* ed. John A. Garraty and Mark C. Carnes (New York: Oxford University Press, 1999), 13:180–81. See also Lucien Brock Proctor, "Chancellors Livingston, Lansing, and Kent," *Albany Law Journal* 45 (January–July 1892): 17–22.

45. John Lansing to William Thornton, August 4, 1810, William Thornton to John Lansing, August 18, 1810, James Van Ingen to William Thornton, November 20, 1810, William Thornton to James Van Ingen, December 2, 1810, and William Thornton to James Van Ingen, December 14, 1810, William Thornton Papers, Library of Congress.

46. *Livingston v. Van Ingen,* 9 Johns. 507 (1811). Lansing's opinion begins on page 514 in the Court of Error records. Chancery court opinions were not recorded separately until 1814.

47. Robert R. Livingston to Edward Livingston, November 11, 1811, Robert R. Livingston Papers, New-York Historical Society, cited in Philip, *Robert Fulton,* 268.

48. *Livingston v. Van Ingen,* 9 Johns. at 516.

49. Ibid., 514–17.

50. Ibid., 514–20.

51. Ibid., 520.

52. Ibid., 520–21.

53. Robert Fulton to William Thornton, November 29, 1811, Randall LeBoeuf Collection, New-York Historical Society.

54. Robert Fulton to James Monroe, February 13, 1812, Robert Fulton Papers, New York State Library.

55. *New York Columbian,* November 23, 1811, p. 2, col. 4; *New York Evening Post,* December 3, 1811, p. 3, col. 2; Robert Fulton to William Thornton, November 29, 1811, Robert Fulton to Oliver Evans, January 30, 1812, Randall LeBoeuf Collection, New-York Historical Society.

56. *New York Columbian,* November 21, 1811, p. 2, col. 4.

57. *New York Columbian,* November 23, 1811, p. 2, col. 4.

58. *New York Evening Post,* December 2, 1811, p. 3, col. 2.

59. Robert R. Livingston to Arthur Roorbach, February 23, 1812, Gilder Lehrman Collection, New-York Historical Society.

60. James Kent to Simeon Baldwin, September 7, 1787, James Kent to Thomas Washington, October 6, 1828, Kent Family Papers, Columbia University Library. See also Thomas Campbell, "Chancellor Kent, Chief Justice Marshall, and the Steamboat Cases," *Syracuse Law Review* 25, no. 2 (1974): 497–513, and John T. Horton, *James Kent: A Study in Conservatism, 1763–1847* (New York: D. Appleton-Century, 1939).

61. *Livingston v. Van Ingen,* 9 Johns. at 532.

62. Ibid., 536.

63. Ibid., 539.

64. Ibid., 542–45.

65. Ibid., 553.

66. Ibid., 554–58.

67. Ibid., 558.

68. Ibid., 557–63.

69. Spencer's decision to recuse himself contrasted sharply with Brockholst Livingston's decision several weeks earlier to hear the same case in which his own family's interests were involved. See ibid., 562.

70. Ibid., 563–70.

71. Ibid., 573.

72. Ibid., 574.

73. Ibid., 576–77.

74. Ibid., 579–80.

75. Ibid., 589.

76. Robert R. Livingston to Robert Fulton, March 24, 1812, Robert R. Livingston Papers, New-York Historical Society, cited in Philip, *Robert Fulton,* 276.

77. Robert Fulton to Joel Barlow, April 19, 1812, Harvard University Library, cited in Philip, *Robert Fulton,* 276.

78. Dangerfield, *Chancellor Robert R. Livingston,* 421–22.

79. Robert Fulton to Cadwallader D. Colden, April 14, 1812, Randall LeBoeuf Collection, New-York Historical Society.

80. Robert Fulton, "Purchase of Hope," December 11, 1812, Randall LeBoeuf Collection, New-York Historical Society.

81. Edwin L. Dunbaugh, *Night Boat to New England, 1815–1900* (New York: Greenwood, 1992), 1–6.

82. *New York Spectator,* June 3, 1812, p. 1, col. 2.

Chapter 5: Interstate Competition

1. Robert Fulton to Thomas Law, April 4, 1812, Robert Fulton Papers, Gilbert Montague Collection, New York Public Library.

2. Brian J. Cudahy, *Over and Back: The History of Ferryboats in New York Harbor* (New York: Fordham University Press, 1990), 20–42; Robert G. Albion, *The Rise of New York Port, 1815–1860* (New York: Scribners' Sons, 1939), 143–49.

3. Robert Fulton, Property Deed, January 1, 1813, Robert Fulton Papers, Columbia University Library; Robert Fulton to Daniel Beach, January 28, 1813, Robert Fulton Papers, Randall LeBoeuf Collection, New-York Historical Society; Nathaniel S. Prime, *Long Island, from Its First Settlement by Europeans to the Year 1845* (New York: Robert Carter, 1845), 376–80.

4. Robert Fulton, "Considerations Concerning North River Steam Boats," November 27, 1813, Robert Fulton Papers, Gilbert Montague Collection, New York Public Library, cited in Cadwallader D. Colden, *The Life of Robert Fulton* (New York: Kirk and Mercein, 1817), 274–75, and

Kirkpatrick Sale, *The Fire of His Genius: Robert Fulton and the American Dream* (New York: Free Press, 2001), 152–53.

5. Robert Fulton to Edward Livingston, June 15, 1812, Robert Fulton Papers, Gilbert Montague Collection, New York Public Library.

6. Benjamin Henry Latrobe to Henry S. B. Latrobe, May 3, 1812, Latrobe to Robert Fulton, May 3, 1812, Benjamin Henry Latrobe to Henry S. B. Latrobe, June 1, 1812, in Benjamin Henry Latrobe, *The Correspondence and Miscellaneous Papers of Benjamin Henry Latrobe*, ed. John C. Van Horne and Lee W. Formwalt, vol. 3 (New Haven, CT: Yale University Press, 1988), 758–71.

7. Agreement between Robert Fulton and John Livingston, July 1811, Robert Fulton Papers, Gilbert Montague Collection, New York Public Library; Robert Fulton to John Livingston, April 12, 1812, Robert Fulton to John Livingston, May 30, 1812, Randall LeBoeuf Collection, New-York Historical Society.

8. Robert Fulton to Benjamin Henry Latrobe, August 18, 1812, Benjamin Henry Latrobe to Robert Fulton, April 20, 1812, Benjamin Henry Latrobe to Henry S. B. Latrobe, May 3, 1812, Benjamin Henry Latrobe to Robert Fulton, May 3, 1812, and Benjamin Henry Latrobe to Henry S. B. Latrobe, June 1, 1812, cited in Latrobe, *Correspondence and Miscellaneous Papers*, 3:278–79, 287–89, and 363–66.

9. Benjamin Henry Latrobe to Robert Fulton, January 18, 1815, Latrobe to Robert Fulton, May 3, 1812, and Benjamin Henry Latrobe to Henry S. B. Latrobe, June 1, 1812, cited in Latrobe, *Correspondence and Miscellaneous Papers*, 3:611–12.

10. Robert Fulton to Benjamin Henry Latrobe, October 26, 1814, Randall LeBoeuf Collection, New-York Historical Society.

11. Benjamin Henry Latrobe to William Thornton, February 13, 1815, cited in Latrobe, *Correspondence and Miscellaneous Papers*, 3:618–19. See also Robert Fulton to David Cooke, November 4, 1814, Randall LeBoeuf Collection, New-York Historical Society.

12. Robert Fulton, Grant of Power of Attorney to John Devereaux Delacy, February 1, 1813, Robert Fulton Papers, Gilbert Montague Collection, New York Public Library. Fulton gave Delacy the right to establish steamboat navigation companies on all waterways south of Baltimore and in Georgia and Florida except on rivers where Fulton had already established operations. For background on Delacy, see John H. B. Latrobe, *A Lost Chapter in the History of the Steamboat* (Baltimore: Maryland Historical Society, 1871), 1–5.

13. Benjamin Henry Latrobe to Robert Fulton, November 12, 1812, and January 18, 1815, in Latrobe, *Correspondence and Miscellaneous Papers*, 3:181–82, 388–89, 611–13; Robert Fulton to Benjamin West, July 12, 1813, Robert Fulton Papers, Randall LeBoeuf Collection, New-York Historical Society, cited in Sale, *Fire of His Genius*, 154.

14. Sale, *Fire of His Genius*, 149–52.

15. Harriet Fulton to Robert R. Livingston, July 29, 1812, Livingston Family Papers, Clermont State Historical Site.

16. Cynthia Owen Philip, *Robert Fulton: A Biography* (New York: Franklin Watts, 1985), 334.

17. John Stevens to the Speaker of the General Assembly of North Carolina, November 9, 1813, Robert R. Livingston Papers, New-York Historical Society.

18. Robert Fulton to John Stevens, October 23, 1812, Robert Fulton Papers, Randall LeBoeuf Collection, New-York Historical Society; Robert Fulton to John Stevens, October 27 and October 29, 1812, Stevens Family Papers, New Jersey Historical Society, cited in Roy Louis DuBois, "John Stevens: Transportation Pioneer" (PhD diss., New York University, 1973), 251.

19. John Devereaux Delacy, Petition to the North Carolina State Legislature, February 23, 1813, Robert Fulton, Affidavit to the North Carolina State Legislature, March 23, 1813, Robert R. Livingston Papers, New-York Historical Society.

20. John Stevens, "Petition to the Virginia State Legislature," December 9 and December 22, 1812; Stevens Family Papers, New Jersey Historical Society, cited in DuBois, "John Stevens," 229; North Carolina State Legislature Grant to John Stevens, December 24, 1812, Stevens Family Papers, New Jersey Historical Society, cited in DuBois, "John Stevens," 231; Thomas Henderson to

John Stevens, December 18, 1813, John Stevens to Cadwallader D. Colden, March 5, 1813, Robert R. Livingston Papers, New-York Historical Society.

21. John Stevens to Cadwallader D. Colden, April 2, 1813, Stevens Family Papers, New Jersey Historical Society, cited in DuBois, "John Stevens," 263.

22. Ibid.

23. John Stevens to Robert R. Livingston, May 5, 1813, Robert R. Livingston Papers, New-York Historical Society, cited in DuBois, "John Stevens," 263–64.

24. Drafts of agreements between Robert Fulton, the heirs of Robert R. Livingston, and John Stevens, May 15 and May 27, 1813, Robert R. Livingston Papers, New-York Historical Society, cited in DuBois, "John Stevens," 263–64.

25. John Stevens to Robert Fulton, June 12, 1813, Robert Fulton Papers, New-York Historical Society; John Stevens to Robert Fulton, June 15, 1813, Cadwallader D. Colden to John Stevens, June 16, 1813, cited in DuBois, "John Stevens," 264.

26. John Stevens to Robert L. Stevens, July 18, 1813, Stevens Family Papers, New Jersey Historical Society, cited in DuBois, "John Stevens," 265.

27. John Stevens to Robert L. Stevens, August 3, 1813, Stevens Family Papers, New Jersey Historical Society, cited in DuBois, "John Stevens," 212.

28. William Thornton to Federal Judiciary Committee, December 30, 1812, William Thornton Papers, Library of Congress.

29. Robert Fulton to Benjamin Henry Latrobe, November 23, 1812, in Latrobe, *Correspondence and Miscellaneous Papers,* 3:391–94.

30. Robert Fulton to John Livingston, March 3, 1813, Robert Fulton Papers, Randall LeBoeuf Collection, New-York Historical Society.

31. Philip, *Robert Fulton,* 291–92.

32. Ibid.; Clare Brandt, *An American Aristocracy: The Livingstons* (Garden City, NY: Doubleday, 1986) 147–48, 173–76.

33. Robert Fulton to Edward P. Livingston, n.d., Robert Fulton Papers, Gilbert Montague Collection, New York Public Library.

34. Robert Fulton to Thomas Jefferson, April 13, 1813, and June 29, 1813, Thomas Jefferson Papers, Library of Congress, cited in Philip, *Robert Fulton,* 292; Robert Fulton to General Lewis, April 14, 1813, Robert Fulton to Benjamin Henry Latrobe, April 22, 1813, Robert Fulton Papers, Randall LeBoeuf Collection, New-York Historical Society; Memorandum of an Agreement between Robert Fulton and Samuel Swartwout, July 22, 1813, Robert Fulton Papers, Gilbert Montague Collection, New York Public Library.

35. Robert Fulton, Considerations Concerning North River Steam Boats, November 27, 1813, and Robert Fulton to Robert L. Livingston, December 1, 1813, Robert Fulton Papers, Gilbert Montague Collection, New York Public Library.

36. Robert Fulton to Robert L. Livingston, December 16, 1813, Robert Fulton Papers, Gilbert Montague Collection, New York Public Library.

37. Robert Fulton to John Livingston, August 8, 1814, Gilder Lehrman Collection, New-York Historical Society.

38. *Louisiana Gazette,* May 3, 1815, p. 2, col. 1; Agreements between Robert Fulton, Robert L. Livingston, and Edward P. Livingston, June 14, 1814, and July 25, 1814, Livingston Family Papers, Clermont State Historical Site.

39. Benjamin Henry Latrobe to William Thornton, November 8, 1812, and James Langdon Sullivan to William Thornton, December 1, 1813, William Thornton Papers, Library of Congress. See also P. J. Federico, "Early Interferences and the Case of *Robert Fulton v. John L. Sullivan," Journal of the Patent Office Society* 19 (August 1937): 761 66.

40. Reported in Robert Fulton to James Langdon Sullivan, July 7, 1814, Robert Fulton Papers, New-York Historical Society.

41. John Langdon Sullivan, "Patent for Steam Tow Boat and Warping Windlass, April 2, 1814," http://www.myoutbox.net/poinvtrs.htm (accessed March 10, 2009).

42. Benjamin Henry Latrobe, Petition of Robert Fulton to James Monroe, May 24, 1813, printed in William Alexander Duer, *A Reply to Mr Colden's Vindication of the Steam-Boat Monopoly* (Albany, NY: E. and E. Hosford, 1819), xxv–xxvi.

43. Don C. Skemer, "The Institutio Legalis and Legal Education in New Jersey: 1783–1817," *New Jersey History* 96 (Autumn/Winter 1978): 123–33.

44. Richard A. Harrison, *Princetonians, 1769–1775: A Biographical Dictionary* (Princeton, NJ: Princeton University Press, 1980), 328–34; Aaron Ogden to George Washington, April 6, 1783, and Jonathan Trumbull Jr. to Aaron Ogden, April 12, 1783, George Washington Papers, Library of Congress; Theodore Thayer, *As We Were: The Story of Old Elizabethtown* (Elizabeth, NJ: Grassman, 1964), 162–68; Aaron Ogden, *Autobiography of Col. Aaron Ogden of Elizabethtown* (Paterson, NJ: Printing Press and Publishing, 1893), 17–19; Carl E. Prince, *New Jersey's Jeffersonian Republicans: The Genesis of an Early Party Machine, 1789–1817* (Chapel Hill: University of North Carolina Press, 1964), 69–157; William Livingston, *The Papers of William Livingston*, ed. Carl E. Prince, Dennis P. Ryan, Pamela B. Schafler, and Donald W. White, vol. 5 (New Brunswick, NJ: Rutgers University Press, 1988), 573.

45. Jonathan Dayton and Aaron Ogden to the Honorable Mayor and Corporation of the City of New York, August 20, 1800, Aaron Ogden to William Coxe, July 22, 1808, and Aaron Ogden Papers, New Jersey Historical Society; Aaron Ogden to Jonathan Dayton, January 25, 1805, Jonathan Dayton Papers, New Jersey Historical Society; Lucius Q. C. Elmer, *Reminiscences of the Bench and Bar during More Than Half a Century* (Newark, NJ: Martin R. Dennis, 1872), 152–55.

46. George Lamplugh, "'Up from the Depths': The Career of Thomas Gibbons, 1783–1789," *Atlanta Historical Journal* 25, no. 3 (1981): 38–43.

47. Complaint, *Aaron Ogden and Thomas Gibbons v. Walter Rutherford*, unreported case (1803), New Jersey Court of Chancery, copy on file at the New Jersey State Archives; Thomas Gamble, *Savannah Duels and Duelists, 1733–1877* (Savannah, GA: Review Publishing and Printing, 1923), 67–69; Gibbons Family Papers, Drew University Library; George Lamplugh, *Politics on the Periphery: Factions and Politics in Georgia, 1783–1806* (Newark: University of Delaware Press, 1986), 32–56, 145–58; Lamplugh, "Up from the Depths," 38; "Whitehall Plantation," pt. 1, *Georgia Historical Quarterly* 25 (December 1941): 341–62, and pt. 2, *Georgia Historical Quarterly* 26 (March 1942): 40–64.

48. *Trenton Federalist*, May 23, 1823, p. 2, col. 5; David W. Thomson, "The Great Steamboat Monopolies: Part II, The Hudson," *American Neptune* 16 (Winter 1956): 274.

49. Act of January 25, 1811, 1811 N.J. Laws 298, reprinted in John Ward, ed., "An Account of the Steamboat Controversy," *Proceedings of the New Jersey Historical Society*, vol. 9, *1860–1864* (Newark: New Jersey Historical Society, 1864), 5–6.

50. Wheaton J. Lane, *From Indian Trail to Iron Horse: Travel and Transportation in New Jersey, 1620–1860* (Princeton, NJ: Princeton University Press, 1939), 185; Daniel Dod, Patent for Steam Engine, May 12, 1812, http://www.myoutbox.net/http://www.myoutbox.net/poinvtrs.htm (accessed March 10, 2009).

51. Lane, *From Indian Trail to Iron Horse*, 185–87; George Johnson to Thomas Gibbons, April 17, 1812, Thomas Gibbons to George Johnson, May 1, 1812, George Johnson to Aaron Ogden, May 23, 1812, and George Johnson to Thomas Gibbons, May 24, 1812, Gibbons Family Papers, Drew University Library.

52. Act of January 25, 1811, 1811 N.J. Laws 298; Act of February 12, 1813, 1813 N.J. Laws 564; "The Memorial of Aaron Ogden," December 23, 1811; and "The Memorial and Petition of Aaron Ogden," October 29, 1813, all reprinted in "Concerning Steamboats: Documents without Comments," in Ward, "Account of the Steamboat Controversy," 3–4, 8–9.

53. *New York Evening Post*, August 20, 1814, p. 2, col. 3; David M. Roth, *Connecticut's War Governor: Jonathan Trumbull* (Chester, CT: Pequot, 1974).

54. George Johnson to Thomas Gibbons, March 2, 1812, Gibbons Family Papers, Drew University Library. The origins of the feud between Gibbons and the Trumbulls can be found in George Johnson to Thomas Gibbons, May 28, 1812, George Johnson to Thomas Gibbons, May 29, 1812, and Thomas Gibbons to Jonathan Dayton, June 23, 1812, Gibbons Family Papers, Drew University Library.

55. Thomas Gibbons to George Johnson, c. March, 1813, and George Johnson to Thomas Gibbons, Gibbons Family Papers, Drew University Library.

56. George Johnson to Thomas Gibbons, March 13 and March 25, 1813, Gibbons Family Papers, Drew University Library.

57. Aaron Ogden to Daniel D. Coit, October 5, 1813, Gibbons Family Papers, Drew University Library.

58. Joseph Trumbull to Daniel W. Coit, November 1, 1813, Joseph Trumbull to Daniel W. Coit, November 8, 1813, and Daniel W. Coit to Aaron Ogden, November 15, 1813, Gibbons Family Papers, Drew University Library.

59. Thomas Gibbons to George Johnson, August 4, 1814, Thomas Gibbons to Daniel W. Coit, August 9, 1814, Daniel W. Coit to Joseph Trumbull, August 13, 1814, Joseph Trumbull to Thomas Gibbons, September 17, 1814, Aaron Ogden to Thomas Gibbons, September 21 and September 24, 1814, Thomas Gibbons to Aaron Ogden, September 25, 1814, William Gibbons to Thomas Gibbons, September 26, 1814, Aaron Ogden to Daniel W. Coit, October 5, 1814, and Jonathan Dayton to Thomas Gibbons, December 15, 1814, Gibbons Family Papers, Drew University Library.

60. Aaron Ogden, *Petition of Aaron Ogden to the New York State Assembly*, 1814, printed in William Alexander Duer, *A Letter, Addressed to Cadwallader D. Colden, Esquire, in Answer to the Strictures Contained in His "Life of Fulton," upon the Report of the Select Committee, to Whom Was Referred a Memorial Relative to Steam Navigation . . .* (Albany, NY: E. and E. Hosford, 1817), 94–97.

61. Autobiographical material on William A. Duer can be found in William A. Duer, *New-York as It Was, during the Latter Part of the Last Century* (New York: Stanford and Swords, 1849).

62. Colden, *Life of Fulton*, 250–51.

63. Robert Fulton to Aaron Ogden, 1815, n.d., Robert Fulton Papers, New-York Historical Society; Joseph Trumbull to Thomas Gibbons, November 8, 1814, Gibbons Family Papers, Drew University Library.

64. New York State Legislature, *Report of the Committee to Whom Was Referred the Memorial and Petition of Aaron Ogden* (Albany, NY: n.p., 1814), 1–27.

65. Ibid., 24–27.

66. Broadside titled *An Act to Repeal the Several Acts Therein Mentioned, Concerning Steamboats*, March 25, 1814, Randall LeBoeuf Collection, New-York Historical Society.

67. Robert Fulton to Cadwallader D. Colden, April 2, 1814, Randall LeBoeuf Collection, New-York Historical Society.

68. Philip, *Robert Fulton*, 335–38.

69. John R. Livingston to Mahlon Dickerson, November 17 and December 14, 1813, Mahlon Dickerson to Robert Fulton, November 29, 1813, Mahlon Dickerson Papers, New Jersey Historical Society, cited in Michael Birkner, "Samuel L. Southard and the Origins of *Gibbons v. Ogden*," *Princeton University Library Chronicle* 40 (Winter 1979): 171–82.

70. John R. Livingston to John Stevens, November 22 and December 20, 1813, Stevens Family Papers, New Jersey Historical Society, cited in DuBois, "John Stevens," 270–71.

71. Robert Fulton to Thomas Addis Emmet, December 6, 1813, Robert Fulton Papers, Gilbert Montague Collection, New York Public Library.

72. DeWitt Clinton, "Two Depositions Regarding the Length of Service of Andrew Bartholomew and Arthur Roorbach," December 13, 1813, Gilder Lehrman Collection, New-York Historical Society.

73. Robert Fulton to John Trumbull[?], c. 1814, Robert Fulton Papers, Gilbert Montague Collection, New York Public Library.

74. The Petition of John R. Livingston and Robert J. Livingston to the Legislature of New Jersey Respecting Steam-Boats, in Ward, "Account of the Steamboat Controversy," 1–30.

75. Ibid., 12.

76. Ibid., 186.

77. Robert Fulton to James Monroe, December 27, 1814, and James Monroe to William Thornton, December 27, 1814, cited in Philip, *Robert Fulton*, 338.

78. William Thornton to James Monroe, January 19, 1815, William Thornton to Richard Rush, January 19, 1815, and William Thornton Papers, Library of Congress; William Thornton, *A Short Account of the Origins of Steamboats* (Washington, DC: Eliot's Patent Press, 1814).

79. For instance, Greenleaf poured through all of Fitch's papers at the Library Company of Philadelphia, only to inform Thornton that his old friend was "crazy." Robert Fulton to William Thornton, n.d., Robert Fulton Papers, Gilbert Montague Collection, New York Public Library; James Greenleaf to William Thornton, December 13, 1814, Nathaniel Cutting to Fernando Fairfax, July 31, 1813, Sworn Testimony of Oliver Evans, December 16, 1814, and Fernando Fairfax to William Thornton, February 1, 1815, William Thornton Papers, Library of Congress.

80. Birkner, "Samuel L. Southard," 175–76.

81. Burton Alva Konkle, *Joseph Hopkinson, 1770–1842, Jurist-Scholar-Inspirer of the Arts: Author of Hail Columbia* (Philadelphia: University of Pennsylvania Press, 1931).

82. Lucius Horatio Stockton, *A History of the Steamboat Case, Lately Discussed by Counsel before the Legislature of New Jersey, Comprised in a Letter to a Gentleman at Washington* (Trenton, NJ: Privately printed, 1815), 3–4; *National Advocate,* February 1, 1815, p. 2, col. 5.

83. Stockton, *History of the Steamboat Case,* 7–8.

84. Ibid., 9–11.

85. Ibid., 13–15.

86. Ibid., 15–16.

87. Robert Fulton to Aaron Ogden, n.d., reprinted in "Concerning Steamboats: Documents without Comments," in Ward, "Account of the Steamboat Controversy," 19–20.

88. Ibid.

89. Robert Fulton to Thomas Cutting, January 28, 1814, and Robert Fulton to Walter Jones, January 28, 1814, Robert Fulton Papers, Gilbert Montague Collection, New York Public Library.

90. The Petition of John R. Livingston and Robert J. Livingston to the Legislature of New Jersey Respecting Steam-Boats, in Ward, "Account of the Steamboat Controversy," 1–42.

91. "Copy of Articles of Agreement between John R. Livingston and Aaron Ogden," May 5, 1815, reprinted in "Concerning Steamboats: Documents without Comments," in Ward, "Account of the Steamboat Controversy," 24–25.

92. Greville Bathe and Dorothy Bathe, *Oliver Evan: A Chronicle of Early American Engineering* (Philadelphia: Historical Society of Pennsylvania, 1935), 190, 265.

93. Alfred R. Maass, "Daniel French and the Western Steamboat Engine," *American Neptune* 56 (Winter 1996): 29–44.

94. Ibid., 29–35. Information on the *Vesuvius* can be found in "Mississippi and Ohio Steam Boat Vesuvius: or, The Information of the Public," c. 1812, Robert Fulton Papers, Gilbert Montague Collection, New York Public Library.

95. Edith McCall, *Conquering the Rivers: Henry Miller Shreve and the Navigation of America's Inland Waterways* (Baton Rouge: Louisiana State University Press, 1984), 34–65; Florence L. Dorsey, *Master of the Mississippi: Henry Miller Shreve and the Conquest of the Mississippi* (New York: Literary Classics, 1941), 67–139; Caroline Pfaff, "Henry Miller Shreve: A Biography," *Louisiana Historical Quarterly* 10 (April 1927): 192–239. Also, article for the *Ohio Federalist,* June 6, 1816, reprinted in the *Louisiana Gazette,* July 3, 1816, p. 2, cols. 1–2. See also *Louisiana Gazette,* May 20, 1816, p. 2, col. 1.

96. *Louisiana Gazette,* May 15, 1816, p. 2, col. 2.

97. *Louisiana Gazette,* July 3, 1816, p. 2, cols. 1–2.

98. Caroline S. Pfaff noted that Edward Livingston's quote was cited in several sources but could not be confirmed. See Pfaff, "Henry Miller Shreve: A Biography," 203.

99. Louis C. Hunter, "The Invention of the Western Steamboat," *Journal of Economic History* 3 (November 1943): 201–20; McCall, *Conquering the Rivers,* 87–88.

100. *Cincinnati Western Spy,* March 29, 1816; *Cincinnati Gazette,* November 15, 1816, cited in Louis C. Hunter, *Steamboats on the Western Rivers: An Economic and Technological History* (New York: Octagon Books, 1969), 10–11.

101. Article from the *Lexington Reporter,* reprinted in *Louisiana Gazette,* May 8, 1816, p. 2, col. 3.

102. *Louisiana Gazette*, January 18, 1817, p. 3, col. 2; H. Dora Stecker, "Constructing a Navigation System in the West," *Ohio Archaeology and Historical Society Publications* 22 (January 1913): 22–24.

Chapter 6: Personal Rivalries and Lawsuits

1. Jonathan Dayton to Thomas Gibbons, February 23, 1815, Gibbons Family Papers, Drew University Library.

2. Population data for Elizabethtown can be found at http://www.library.uu.nl/wesp/populstat/Americas/usas-njt.htm (accessed March 13, 2003). See also Theodore Thayer, *As We Were: The Story of Old Elizabethtown* (Elizabeth, NJ: Grassman, 1964), 206–29.

3. George Lamplugh, *Politics on the Periphery: Factions and Politics in Georgia, 1783–1806* (Newark: University of Delaware Press, 1986), 31–69; William Ogden Wheeler, *The Ogden Family in America, Elizabethtown Branch, and Their English Ancestry* (Philadelphia: J. B. Lippincott, 1907), 3–12. See also John W. Ifkovic, *Connecticut's Nationalist Revolutionary* (Hartford: American Revolution Bicentennial Commission of Connecticut, 1977).

4. Thayer, *As We Were*, 120–25, 223–25.

5. Aaron Ogden to Thomas Gibbons, August 7, September 6, and October 12, 1815, Gibbons Family Papers, Drew University Library.

6. Thomas Gibbons to Aaron Ogden, September 4, 1815, Gibbons Family Papers, Drew University Library.

7. Jonathan Dayton to Thomas Gibbons, May 14, 1815, and Thomas Gibbons to Aaron Ogden, September 4 and September 9, 1815, Gibbons Family Papers, Drew University Library.

8. Thomas Gibbons, "For the Opinion of Counsel, the Case of Mrs. Trumbull and Her Children," July 28, 1815, Isaac H. Williamson, "The Opinion of Isaac H. Williamson, Esq.," August 2, 1815, Aaron Ogden to the Trustees of Mrs. Trumbull, Joseph Trumbull, D. W. Coit, and William Gibbons, October 26, 1815, William Gibbons to Thomas Gibbons, November 1815, Thomas Gibbons to J. W. Coit, November 13, 1815, D. W. Coit to Aaron Ogden, November 21, 1815, John M. Trumbull to Aaron Ogden, January 2, 1816, and Thomas Gibbons to John M. Trumbull, January 4, 1816, Aaron Ogden to John M. Trumbull, November 12, 1815, Aaron Ogden to D. W. Coit, November 29, 1815, William Gibbons to Aaron Ogden, November 30, 1815, and Aaron Ogden to Thomas Gibbons, December 3, 1815, Gibbons Family Papers, Drew University Library.

9. Thomas Gibbons to Aaron Ogden, December 13, 1815, Gibbons Family Papers, Drew University Library.

10. Thomas Gibbons to William Gibbons, December 14, 1815, Aaron Ogden to Thomas Gibbons, December 21 and December 23, 1815, Thomas Gibbons to D. W. Coit, December 22, 1815, and Aaron Ogden to Thomas Gibbons, December 23, 1815, Gibbons Family Papers, Drew University Library.

11. Thomas Gibbons to Aaron Ogden, December 26, 1815, *Resolutions of the Elizabeth Town Meeting, to the Legislature of the State of New Jersey: The Memorial and Petition of the Subscribers, Inhabitants of Elizabeth Town and Its Vicinity in the County of Essex Respectfully Showeth . . . ,* December 27, 1815, Gibbons Family Papers, Drew University Library.

12. J. Montgomery Livingston, Conversation with Aaron Ogden, December 28, 1815, Special Collections, Dartmouth University Library.

13. Shepherd Kollock to John R. Livingston, January 2 and January 4, 1816, Gibbons Family Papers, Drew University Library; Thayer, *As We Were*, 154–57.

14. Aaron Ogden to Sheppard Kollack, January 6, 1816, Gibbons Family Papers, Drew University Library.

15. John R. Livingston to Sheppard Kollack, January 10, 1816, Gibbons Family Papers, Drew University Library.

16. Thomas Gibbons to General Elliot Tucker, January 3, 1816, and John M. Trumbull to Thomas Gibbons, January 10, January 22, January 24, and January 26, 1816, Gibbons Family Papers, Drew University Library.

17. Affidavit of William Shute and William R. Williamson, New Jersey, Borough of Eliza-beth, February 3, 1816, Gibbons Family Papers, Drew University Library.

18. Thomas Gibbons to Jonathan Dayton, January 14, 1817, Thomas Gibbons to General Elliot Tucker, February 17, 1816, and Silas Ward to Daniel Dod, March 3, 1816, Gibbons Family Papers, Drew University Library.

19. Alfred R. Maass, "The Right of Unrestricted Navigation on the Mississippi, 1812–1818," *American Neptune* 60 (January 2000): 53–54.

20. Doctors Hunter and Bryant and Captain Rinker, Affidavit Sworn to before the Deputy Clerk, United States District Court in New Orleans, Appraising Value of the Enterprize, May 3, 1815, Randall LeBoeuf Collection, New-York Historical Society.

21. Daniel French, Affidavit Attesting to the Ownership of a Federal Steamboat Patent and Ownership of the *Enterprize,* September 4, 1815, Randall LeBoeuf Collection, New-York Historical Society.

22. Abner L. Duncan, "Outline of argument for counsel in *Livingston v. Shreve* (1816)"; Dun-can, "Answer to charges filed against Henry Miller Shreve, January 22, 1816"; and Duncan, "Sup-plemental answer regarding 1811 New Orleans territorial monopoly," February 14, 1816, Randall LeBoeuf Collection, New-York Historical Society.

23. Biographical information on Abner L. Duncan can be found in William Preston Johnston, *The Johnstons of Salisbury: With a Brief Comment on the Hancock, Strother, and Preston Families* (New Orleans, LA: I. Graham and Son, 1897), 122; Memo of testimony of seven witnesses swearing that freight rates of the steamboat *Vesuvius* were in accordance with the rates set by the Orleans legislature, March 18, 1816; Memo of testimony of a Mr. Talman [or Falman] swearing that freight rates for Mississippi Steam Boat Navigation Company were in accordance with the rates set by the Orleans legislature, April 4, 1816; and Report filed on May 4, 1816, Randall LeBoeuf Collection, New-York Historical Society.

24. "Dominick Augustin Hall," in *Dictionary of American Biography,* ed. Dumas Malone, vol. 4 (New York: Charles Scribner's Sons, 1931), 123–24.

25. *Louisiana Gazette,* April 29, 1817, p. 2, cols. 1–2.

26. *Heirs of Fulton and Livingston v. Henry M. Shreve* (1817), accession 70A-006, file 1003, box 449452, Federal Records Center, Fort Worth, TX, copy in Randall LeBoeuf Collection, New-York Historical Society.

27. Ibid.; Contract between Jasper Lynch and Sam Postlethwaite, November 5, 1816, and Pe-tition to United States District Court, Louisiana District, November 26, 1816, Randall LeBoeuf Collection, New-York Historical Society.

28. *Louisiana Monitor,* July 19, 1817, p. 1, col. 3; *Louisiana Gazette,* July 19, 1817, p. 1, col. 1, March 25, 1818, p. 1, col. 2, August 14, 1819, p. 1, col. 1, April 17, 1819, p. 1, col. 2, August 12, 1816, p. 2, col. 2, August 26, 1816, p. 2, col. 3, and November 4, 1816, p. 2, cols. 3–4.

29. *Louisiana Gazette,* May 6, 1817, p. 2, cols. 1–2.

30. Dominick Lynch to Townsend, December 24, 1815, and copy of New York Court of Chancery decision in *Livingston v. Cutting,* August 8, 1819, Townsend Family Papers, New York Public Library.

31. D. Lynch to Townsend, April 24, 1819, Townsend Family Papers, New York Public Library; *Lehigh Herald,* July 20, 1832, reprinted in *Rhode Island Republican,* August 7, 1832, p. 2, cols. 4–5; *Pittsfield Sun,* August 31, 1854, p. 3, col. 5; *Southern Patriot,* February 27, 1838, p. 2, col. 5; "Dominick Lynch and His Family," in *The Journal of the American-Irish Historical Society,* ed. Thomas Bonaventure Lawler and Thomas Hamilton Murray (Boston: American-Irish Historical Society, 1907), 36–38.

32. *New York Evening Post,* December 19, 1815, p. 4, col. 2.

33. Dominick Lynch to Isaiah Townsend, June 1, 1816, Townsend Family Papers, New York Public Library.

34. William Cutting to John Townsend, March 28, 1816, Dominick Lynch to Isaiah Townsend, April 14, May 3, and June 29, 1816, Samuel Lockwood to Isaiah Townsend, S. Wiswall to North River Steamboat Co., April 12, 1817, C. Jenkins to Isaiah Townsend, June 28, 1816, Townsend Family Papers, New York Public Library.

35. Agreement between John R. Livingston and Daniel David Tompkins, January 8, 1817, Gibbons Family Papers, Drew University Library. See also Ray Watkins Irwin, *Daniel D. Tompkins: Governor of New York and Vice President of the United States* (New York: New-York Historical Society, 1968), 132–68.

36. An Indenture between Edward P. Livingston and Robert L. Livingston, first part; Harriet Fulton and William Cutting, second part; Aaron Ogden and Thomas Morris, third part, December 29, 1815, Robert R. Livingston Papers, New-York Historical Society; *John Lawrence v. Harriet Fulton*, BM-346 (1816), New York Chancery Court Papers, New York County Clerk's Office; Thomas Gibbons to Alfred Cuthbert, Esq., March 6, 1816, Gibbons Family Papers, Drew University Library.

37. Extension of a Patent Right, February 27, 1816, in *American State Papers: Miscellaneous,* ed. Walter Lowrie and Walter S. Franklin (Washington, DC: Gales and Seaton, 1834), 2:292–93.

38. Ibid.

39. Thomas Gibbons to Fernando Fairfax, March 16 and March 22, 1816, Gibbons Family Papers, Drew University Library.

40. Fernando Fairfax, *Memorial of Fernando Fairfax against the Extension of the Patents Granted to Robert Fulton for Improvements in Propelling Vessels by Steam* (Washington, DC: Edward De Krafft, 1816).

41. Thomas Gibbons to Thomas Spaulding, March 18, 1816, and Thomas Gibbons to John Randolph, March 20, 1816, Gibbons Family Papers, Drew University Library.

42. *Senate Journal,* 14th Cong., 1st sess., March 11, 1816, 277; Thomas Gibbons to Thomas Spaulding, March 18, 1816, Thomas Gibbons to John Randolph, March 20, 1816, and Thomas Gibbons to Robert G. Harper, March 24, 1816, Gibbons Family Papers, Drew University Library.

43. Thomas Gibbons to Fernando Fairfax, April 13, 1816, Gibbons Family Papers, Drew University Library.

44. Thomas Gibbons to John Trumbull, April 18, 1816, Gibbons Family Papers, Drew University Library.

45. Thomas Gibbons to Ann Gibbons, May 13, 1816, Gibbons Family Papers, Drew University Library.

46. Thomas Gibbons to David B. Ogden, June 1, 1816, Gibbons Family Papers, Drew University Library.

47. Thomas Gibbons to Reverend John McDowell, July 24, 1816, Gibbons Family Papers, Drew University Library.

48. Thomas Gibbons to Richard Stockton, July 26, 1816, Gibbons Family Papers, Drew University Library; Richard Stockton to Thomas Gibbons, July 29, 1816, Walter Dormitzer Collection, New Jersey Historical Society.

49. Opinion of William A. Duer, July 14, 1816, Thomas Gibbons Papers, Museum of American Finance, cited in Herbert A. Johnson, *"Gibbons v. Ogden* before Marshall," in *Courts and Law in Early New York: Selected Essays,* ed. Leo Hershkowitz abd Milton M. Klein (Port Washington, NY: Kennikat Press, 1978), 107, 147.

50. Thomas Gibbons to Aaron Ogden, May 30, July 25, and July 26, 1816, in Unpublished Handbill, July 16, 1816, Gibbons Family Papers, Drew University Library; Thayer, *As We Were,* 230.

51. Thayer, *As We Were,* 230.

52. Thomas Gibbons, untitled pamphlet, quoted in New York State, "Report of a Trial for a Libel . . . on the 24th and 25th Days of June, 1818 . . . *John M. Trumbull, v. Thomas Gibbons,"* *New York City Hall Recorder* 7 (July 1818): 97–112.

53. Ibid., 101–2.

54. Thomas Gibbons to Mrs. Thomas Gibbons, November 7, 1816, Gibbons Family Papers, Drew University Library.

55. Gibbons Family Genealogy, 12, and Thomas Gibbons to John M. Trumbull, September 23, 1817, Gibbons Family Papers, Drew University Library.

56. *New York Spectator,* June 7, 1817, p. 1, col. 6; Thomas Gibbons to John M. Trumbull, September 23, 1817, Gibbons Family Papers, Drew University Library.

217

57. Opinion of Aaron Burr, July 31, 1817, Thomas Gibbons Papers, Museum of American Finance, cited in Johnson, *"Gibbons v. Ogden* before Marshall," 108, 147.

58. Thomas Gibbons, Memorandum, June 14, 1817, and Agreement between Daniel D. Tompkins and Adam and Noah Brown, October 11, 1817, Miscellaneous Manuscripts, New-York Historical Society.

59. Memorandum of Agreement Made by Thomas Gibbons and Cornelius Vanderbilt, June 26, 1818, Gibbons Family Papers, Drew University Library; Meade Minnigerode, *Certain Rich Men* (New York: G. P. Putnam's Sons, 1927), 103–33; Edward J. Renehan, Jr. *Commodore: The Life of Cornelius Vanderbilt* (New York: Basic Books, 2007), 91–104.

60. Isaac Woodruff to Thomas Gibbons, July 20, 1817, Gibbons Family Papers, Drew University Library.

61. Thomas Gibbons to Aaron Ogden, October 31, 1817, Gibbons Family Papers, Drew University Library.

62. Dominick Lynch to Isaiah Townsend, December 2 and December 6, 1817, Townsend Family Papers, New York Public Library.

63. Ronald E. Shaw, *Erie Water West: A History of the Erie Canal, 1792–1854* (Lexington: University of Kentucky Press, 1966), 71–80.

64. Dominick Lynch to John and Isaiah Townsend, April 25, 1817, Townsend Family Papers, New York Public Library.

65. William Thornton to John L. Sullivan, October 9, 1817, William Stockton to William Thornton, March 25 and June 9, 1818, William Thornton Papers, Library of Congress.

66. Cadwallader D. Colden, *The Life of Robert Fulton* (New York: Kirk and Mercein, 1817), 179, 257–59. For popular reaction to *The Life of Robert Fulton*, see "The Life of Robert Fulton," *American Monthly Magazine and Critical Review* 1 (August 1817): 250–57, and 2 (January 1818): 233.

67. William A. Duer, *A Letter, Addressed to Cadwallader D. Colden, Esquire, in Answer to the Strictures, Contained in His "Life of Robert Fulton"* . . . (Albany, NY: E. and E. Hosford, 1817); Cadwallader D. Colden, *A Vindication by Cadwallader D. Colden, of the Steam Boat Right Granted by the State of New York* . . . (New York: W. A. Mercein, 1818).

68. William A. Duer, *A Reply to Mr. Colden's Vindication of the Steam-Boat Monopoly* (New York: E. and E. Hosford, 1817), 8.

69. Anon., *An Examination of Cadwallader D. Colden's Book, Entitled, "A Life of Robert Fulton,"* by *a Friend of John Fitch, Deceased* (London: n.p., 1818), 3. Fairfax or Thornton may have written this tract.

70. Cadwallader D. Colden, *A Review of the Letter Addressed by William Alexander Duer, to Cadwallader Colden in Answer to Strictures Contained in His "Life of Robert Fulton"* . . . (New York: Kirk and Mercein, 1818), 3.

71. Dominick Lynch to John Townsend, March 5, 1818, Townsend Family Papers, New York Public Library.

72. Dominick Lynch to John Townsend, March 11, 1818, Dominick Lynch to Townsend, April 9, 1818, Townsend Family Papers, New York Public Library.

73. William Gibbons to E. Van Arsdale and Theodore Frelinghuysen, Esqs., December 17, 1817, Gibbons Family Papers, Drew University Library.

74. Subpoena for Samuel Burtt, Elias P. Dayton, and Peter Coriel, May 1818, Affidavit of Joseph Williams, May 1818, Affidavit of Isabella Post, May 9, 1818, Affidavit of Joseph Periam, May 9, 1818, Affidavit from Joseph Williams, and Subpoena for John M. Trumbull, May 9, 1818, Gibbons Family Papers, Drew University Library. See also *Thomas Gibbons v. John M. Trumbull*, May 29, 1818, In the Court for the Treatment of Small Essex County Causes before Aaron Munn, Esq., One of the Justices of the Peace for the County of Essex, State of New Jersey, Gibbons Family Papers, Drew University Library.

75. Daniel D. Barnard, *A Discourse on the Life, Character, and Public Services of Ambrose Spencer* (Albany, NY: J. Munsell, 1849).

76. *Gibbons v. Trumbull*, 98–100; *Dedham Gazette*, October 23, 1818, p. 1, cols. 4–5.

77. *Gibbons v. Trumbull*, 107–8.

78. Ibid., 108–10.

79. Ibid.

80. Ibid., 110–12.

81. *New York Evening Times* article reprinted in *Niles' Register,* July 4, 1818, p. 325, cols. 1–2.

82. *Dedham Gazette,* October 23, 1818, p. 1, cols. 4–5; *New York Daily Advertiser,* June 26, 1818, p. 2, col. 2;

83. William Gibbons to Aaron Ogden, August 31, 1818, William Gibbons to John M. Trumbull, Thomas Gibbons to Aaron Ogden, September 3, 1818, Subpoena for John Rutherford, Aaron Ogden, and Jonathan Dayton, September 3 and September 10, 1818, Thomas Gibbons to William Coleman, September 22, 1818, and William Coleman to Thomas Gibbons, September 24, 1818, Gibbons Family Papers, Drew University Library.

84. Thomas Gibbons to Peter Jay Munro, October 3, 1818, Gibbons Family Papers, Drew University Library.

85. Johnson, *"Gibbons v. Ogden* before Marshall," 108–10.

86. Daniel D. Tompkins to Edward P. Livingston, October 5, 1818, Gibbons Family Papers, Drew University Library.

87. *Gibbons v. Ogden,* unreported case (1818), New York Chancery Court Papers, New York County Clerk's Office.

88. Thomas Gibbons to Aaron Ogden, December 10, 1818, William Gibbons, Memorandum Concerning Aaron Ogden, December 11, 1818, Thomas Gibbons to P. J. Munro, December 27, 1818, and January 22, 1819, and P. J. Munro to Thomas Gibbons, January 5, January 18, and January 29, 1819, Gibbons Family Papers, Drew University Library.

89. Thomas Gibbons to John L. Sullivan, January 1, 1819, Gibbons Family Papers, Drew University Library.

90. John L. Sullivan to Thomas Gibbons, January 1, 1819, Gibbons Family Papers, Drew University Library.

91. Robert L. Livingston to Messrs. Isaiah and John Townsend, March 6, 1819, Townsend Family Papers, New York Public Library.

92. Thomas Gibbons to Wm. Price, March 1, 1819, Gibbons Family Papers, Drew University Library.

93. William M. Price to Thomas Gibbons, March 15, 1819, and Thomas Gibbons to John W. Patterson, March 18, 1819, Gibbons Family Papers, Drew University Library.

94. J. W. Patterson to Thomas Gibbons, April 2, 1819, Gibbons Family Papers, Drew University Library.

95. List of Propositions for an Agreement between Thomas Gibbons and J. R. Livingston, April 1, 1819, Gibbons Family Papers, Drew University Library.

96. John R. Livingston to Thomas Gibbons, April 21, 1819, and Thomas Gibbons to John R. Livingston, April 22, 1819, Gibbons Family Papers, Drew University Library.

97. James Kent, Court of Chancery Decree, May 3, 1819, Gibbons Family Papers, Drew University Library.

Chapter 7: The Road to the U.S. Supreme Court

1. *New York Daily Advertiser,* May 8, 1819, p. 2, col. 3, May 12, 1819, p. 2, col. 1, and July 3, 1819, p. 2, col. 4; *New York Spectator,* June 25, 1819, p. 2, col. 4, and June 29, 1819, p. 2, col. 4; article from the *Connecticut Mirror* reprinted in the *New York Spectator,* July 20, 1819, p. 3, col. 4.

2. See, for instance, Robert G. Albion, *The Rise of New York Port* (New York: Charles Scribners' Sons, 1939), 143–64; Edwin F. Hatfield, *History of Elizabeth, New Jersey: Including the Early History of Union County* (New York: Carlton and Lanahan, 1868), 554 64; Herbert A. Johnson, *"Gibbons v. Ogden* before Marshall," in *Courts and Law in Early New York: Selected Essays,* ed. Leo Hershkowitz and Milton M. Klein (Port Washington, NY: Kennikat, 1978), 105–13; Theodore Thayer, *As We Were: The Story of Old Elizabethtown* (Elizabeth, NJ: Grassman, 1964), 230–43.

3. Dominick Lynch to John Townsend, May 13, 1819, Townsend Family Papers, New York Public Library.

4. Dominick Lynch to Townsend, May 20 and May 24, 1819, and Dominick Lynch to John Townsend, May 27, 1819, Townsend Family Papers, New York Public Library.

5. Dominick Lynch to Townsend, Edward P. Livingston to Dominick Lynch, June 5, 1819, Townsend Family Papers, New York Public Library.

6. Agreement between the Richmond Turnpike Company and Thomas Gibbons, May 13, 1819, Livingston Family Papers, Clermont State Historical Site; Agreement between T. Gibbons and Daniel D. Tompkins, May 13, 1819, and Daniel D. Tompkins to William Gibbons, June 15, 1819, Gibbons Family Papers, Drew University Library.

7. Copy of Injunction in New York Chancery Court Case *Ogden v. Gibbons,* June 21, 1819, Gibbons Family Papers, Drew University Library.

8. Wheaton J. Lane, *Cornelius Vanderbilt: An Epic of the Steam Age* (New York: Alfred A. Knopf, 1942), 33–37.

9. *In re Vanderbilt,* 4 Johns. Ch. 57 (1819); Lane, *Cornelius Vanderbilt,* 34–35.

10. *In re Vanderbilt,* 4 Johns. Ch. at 59–60; Lane, *Cornelius Vanderbilt,* 35.

11. *Livingston v. Cutting,* unreported case, L126 Joo87-82 (1819), New York Chancery Court Miscellaneous Files, New York State Archives.

12. Dominick Lynch to Isaiah and John Townsend, July 23 and July 31, 1819, Townsend Family Papers, New York Public Library; *New York Daily Advertiser,* August 3, 1819, p. 2, col. 3.

13. Copy of New York Chancery Court decision in *Livingston v. Cutting,* August 8, 1819, and Dominick Lynch to Townsend, August 18, 1819, Townsend Family Papers, New York Public Library.

14. John L. Sullivan to Thomas Gibbons, August 17, 1819, Gibbons Family Papers, Drew University Library.

15. Thomas Gibbons to John L. Sullivan, September 8, 1819, Gibbons Family Papers, Drew University Library.

16. Dominick Lynch to John Townsend, August 21 and August 23, 1819, and Dominick Lynch to Townsend, September 15, 1819, Townsend Family Papers, New York Public Library; Robert Ireland, *The Legal Career of William Pinkney, 1764–1822* (New York: Garland, 1986).

17. Committee of the Canal Fund Commissioners to the President and Directors of the New York State and Mechanics and Farmers Bank, New York, February 5, 1820, Townsend Family Papers, New York Public Library.

18. *New York Daily Advertiser,* March 18, 1820, p. 2, col. 3, and April 3, 1820, p. 2, col. 2.

19. *New York Daily Advertiser,* March 30, 1820, p. 2, col. 5; Charles Rhind to Isaiah and John Townsend, March 14, 1820, Townsend Family Papers, New York Public Library.

20. *New York Daily Advertiser,* March 30, 1820, p. 2, col. 2, and April 22, 1820, p. 2, col. 3.

21. Dominick Lynch to John Townsend, April 1, 1820, Townsend Family Papers, New York Public Library.

22. Ibid.

23. *Livingston v. Cutting,* L126 Joo71 (1820), New York Chancery Court, Miscellaneous Files, New York State Archives. See also Dominick Lynch to Isaiah and John Townsend, April 6, 1819, and Dominick Lynch to Townsend, May 10, 1820, Townsend Family Papers, New York Public Library.

24. *Gibbons v. Ogden,* 17 Johns. 488, 510 (1820); D. E. Wager, "Whitesboro's Golden Age," in *Transactions of the Oneida Historical Society, at Utica,* ed. Warren C. Rowley, Alexander Seward, and Rees G. Williams (Utica, NY: Ellis H. Roberts, 1881), 83–90.

25. Dominick Lynch to John Townsend, May 20, 1820, May 22, 1820, Townsend Family Papers, New York Public Library.

26. Dominick Lynch to John Townsend, May 25, 1820, and Dominick Lynch to Townsend, June 7, 1820, Townsend Family Papers, New York Public Library.

27. *New York Columbian,* June 5, 1820, p. 2, col. 2.

28. *New York Columbian,* June 6, 1820, p. 2, col. 3; *New York Daily Advertiser,* June 16, 1820, p. 2, cols. 4–5, and July 7, 1820, p. 2, col. 3.

29. *Edward P. Livingston v. Robert L. Livingston,* L596 Joo70 (1820), New York Chancery Court Miscellaneous Files, New York State Archives; Dominick Lynch to Townsend, June 18, 1820, Townsend Family Papers, New York Public Library.

30. Dominick Lynch to Townsend, June 18, 1820, Townsend Family Papers, New York Public Library.

31. *New York Columbian,* June 27, 1820, p. 2, col. 3.

32. Dominick Lynch to John Townsend, July 5, 1820, Townsend Family Papers, New York Public Library.

33. Charles Rhind to John Townsend, July 7, 1820, Townsend Family Papers, New York Public Library. The French term *entre nous* translates as "between us," and its use here perhaps represented a desire on Rhind's part to keep confidential the plans to dredge the Hudson River and thus create goodwill for the North River Company.

34. Charles Rhind to John Townsend, July 14, 1820, and Charles Rhind to John Townsend, August, 1820, Townsend Family Papers, New York Public Library; *New York Columbian,* August 8, 1820, p. 2, col. 4.

35. Dominick Lynch to Townsend, July 25, 1820, Townsend Family Papers, New York Public Library.

36. Dominick Lynch to John Townsend, August 20, 1820, Townsend Family Papers, New York Public Library.

37. Ibid.

38. Ibid.

39. Copy of the Order of Chancellor Kent on Petition of *Aaron Ogden v. Thomas Gibbons,* August 28, 1820, Gibbons Family Papers, Drew University Library.

40. *Livingston v. Gibbons,* 4 Johns. Ch. 571 (1820).

41. *Livingston v. Cutting,* L126 J0071 (1820), New York Chancery Court Miscellaneous Files, New York State Archives.

42. Dominick Lynch to Townsend, September 14, 1820, Charles Rhind to John Townsend, September 1, 1820, and Dominick Lynch to John Townsend, September 15, 1820, Townsend Family Papers, New York Public Library; *New York Daily Advertiser,* August 29, 1820, p. 2, col. 4, and September 9, 1820, p. 2, col. 2.; *New York Columbian,* September 13, 1820, p. 2, col. 1.

43. Dominick Lynch to John Townsend, October 21, 1820, Townsend Family Papers, New York Public Library.

44. Dominick Lynch to Townsend, January 24, 1821, Townsend Family Papers, New York Public Library.

45. Ibid.

46. Robert William July, *The Essential New Yorker, Gulian C. Verplanck* (Durham, NC: Duke University Press, 1951), 80–81.

47. Dominick Lynch to Townsend, February 2, 1821, Townsend Family Papers, New York Public Library.

48. Robert L. Livingston to Isaiah and John Townsend, February 6, 1821, Townsend Family Papers, New York Public Library.

49. Charles Rhind to John Townsend, February 18, 1821, North River Steam Boat Company Papers, Rutgers University Library.

50. Robert Letson to Thomas Gibbons, February 17, 1821, Gibbons Family Papers, Drew University Library.

51. *Livingston v. Ogden and Gibbons,* 4 Johns. Ch. 48 (1819).

52. *Livingston v. Ogden and Gibbons,* 4 Johns. Ch. 95 (1819).

53. *Gibbons v. Ogden,* 17 Johns. 488 (1820); Report of Argument in Gibbons against Ogden, September 27–28, 1819, Gibbons Family Papers, Drew University Library.

54. *Gibbons v. Ogden,* 17 Johns. at 488–93.

55. Ibid., 493–95.

56. Ibid., 495–96.

57. Ibid., 496.

58. Ibid., 496–510.

59. Dominick Lynch to John Townsend, October 13, 1819, Townsend Family Papers, New York Public Library.

60. Charles Rhind to John Townsend, October 24, 1819, Charles Rhind to Isaiah and John Townsend, October 28, 1819, and Dominick Lynch to John Townsend, October 29, 1819, Townsend Family Papers, New York Public Library.

61. Livingston may also have been preoccupied by the latest in a series of tenant uprisings on Livingston lands and attacks in the press that accused the Livingston family, Judge Josiah Odgen Hoffman, and Martin Van Buren of political corruption. *New York Columbian*, December 3, 1819, p. 2, cols. 1–2.

62. Dominick Lynch to Townsend, November and November 27, 1819, Townsend Family Papers, New York Public Library.

63. *New York Daily Advertiser*, January 17, 1820, p. 2, cols. 4–5; *New York Spectator*, January 18, 1820, p. 2, col. 2; *New York Columbian*, January 19, 1820, p. 2, cols. 3–4.

64. Charles Rhind to Isaiah and John Townsend, January 31, 1820, Townsend Family Papers, New York Public Library.

65. *New York Daily Advertiser*, February 1, 1820, p. 2, col. 3.

66. *Copy of Petition of the People of New Brunswick to the Honorable the Legislature of the State of New Jersey*, January 1, 1820, Gibbons Family Papers, Drew University Library.

67. *New York Columbian*, February 1, 1820, p. 2, col. 3; Frank J. Esposito, "Isaac H. Williamson," in *The Governors of New Jersey: Biographical Essays, 1664–1974*, ed. Paul A. Stellhorn and Michael J. Birkner (Trenton: New Jersey Historical Commission, 1982), 96–98.

68. Act of February 25, 1820, 1820 N.J. Laws 689; *New York Daily Advertiser*, February 2, 1820, p. 2, cols. 4–5.

69. Act of February 25, 1820, 1820 N.J. Laws 689. A copy of the New Jersey steamboat monopoly law is reprinted in *Livingston v. Tompkins*, 4 Johns. Ch. 415, 418–19 (1820).

70. The injunctions against Livingston and Ogden are recounted in *Livingston v. Tompkins*, 4 Johns. Ch. at 421–23, and *Gibbons v. Ogden*, 6 N.J.L. 285 (1822).

71. *New York Daily Advertiser*, March 1, 1820, p. 2, col. 4.

72. Cadwallader D. Colden to Isaiah and John Townsend, March 8, 1821, Townsend Family Papers, New York Public Library.

73. Charles Rhind to John Townsend, March 12, 1821, and Charles Rhind to Isaiah Townsend, April 25, 1821, Townsend Family Papers, New York Public Library; George Wood to Thomas Gibbons, March 14, 1821, Gibbons Family Papers, Drew University Library.

74. Charles Rhind to John Townsend, March 14, 1821, Townsend Family Papers, New York Public Library.

75. Robert L. Livingston to James Monroe, March 18, 1821, James Monroe Papers, Library of Congress.

76. Ibid.

77. Charles Rhind to John Townsend, March 22, 1822, Townsend Family Papers, New York Public Library.

78. Return J. Meigs to John Townsend, March 26, 1821, and Return J. Meigs to Anthony Hoffman, March 26, 1821, Townsend Family Papers, New York Public Library.

79. Joseph Story to Mrs. Joseph Story, February 21 and February 28, 1822, in *The Life and Letters of Joseph Story*, ed. William Wetmore Story (Freeport, NY: Books for Libraries Press, 1971), 2:414–15.

80. Charles Rhind to John Townsend, March 23 and March 30, 1824, Townsend Family Papers, New York Public Library; Robert Ludlow Fowler, "Constitutional and Legal History of New York in the Nineteenth Century," in *The Memorial History of the City of New York: From Its First Settlement to the Year 1892*, ed. James Grant Wilson, vol. 3 (New York: New-York History, 1893), 654.

81. *Of the Inhabitants of New-Brunswick, N.J. Respecting Steam Boat Laws, to the Honorable the Legislature of the State of New York*, January 30, 1822, a Petition of the Mayor, Alderman, and Common Council of the City of New-Brunswick on the Subject of Steam-Boat Navigation, February 6, 1822, Gibbons Family Papers, Drew University Library.

82. *Memorial of John Stevens to the Legislature of the State of New York*, February 11, 1822, Gibbons Family Papers, Drew University Library; John Langdon Sullivan, *A Demonstration of the Right to the Navigation of the Waters of New York* (Cambridge, MA: Hilliard and Metcalf, 1821).

83. *Petition of the Ship-Builders of the City of New-York to the Honorable the New York State Legislature,* February 7, 1822, Gibbons Family Papers, Drew University Library.

84. William Gibbons to Thomas Gibbons, February 27, 1822, Gibbons Family Papers, Drew University Library.

85. *Recantation of Sundry Citizens of the City of New-York, Petitioners for, Modification of the Steam Boat Laws: To the Honorable the Legislature of the State of New York,* February 27, 1822, Gibbons Family Papers, Drew University Library.

86. Charles Rhind to John Townsend, March 7 and March 8, 1824, North River Steam Boat Company Papers, Rutgers University Library.

87. Charles Rhind to John Townsend, May 18, 1822, North River Steam Boat Company Papers, Rutgers University Library.

88. Dominick Lynch to John Townsend, May 18, 1822, and Charles Rhind to John Townsend, May 23 and May 25, 1822, North River Steam Boat Company Papers, Rutgers University Library.

89. Charles Rhind to John Townsend, May 31 and June 6, 1822, North River Steam Boat Company Papers, Rutgers University Library.

90. Robert M. Livingston[?] to Thomas Gibbons, June 14, 1822, Statement Signed by Isaac Brown, June 21, 1822, Gibbons Family Papers, Drew University Library.

91. Robert M. Livingston to Thomas Gibbons, June 27, 1822, Gibbons Family Papers, Drew University Library.

92. Robert M. Livingston to Captain B. Beecher, July 12, 1822, Gibbons Family Papers, Drew University Library.

93. Charles Rhind to John Townsend, July 17, 1822, North River Steam Boat Company Papers, Rutgers University Library.

94. Charles Rhind to John Townsend, July 17, 18, and 24, 1822, North River Steam Boat Company Papers, Rutgers University Library.

95. Charles Rhind to John Townsend, July 24, 1822, North River Steam Boat Company Papers, Rutgers University Library.

96. *Fulton Steamboat Co. v. Livingston,* L456 Joo70 (1822), New York Chancery Court Miscellaneous Files, New York State Archives; Robert L. Livingston to John Townsend, December 13, 1822, North River Steam Boat Company Papers, Rutgers University Library.

97. Charles Rhind to John Townsend, August 8, 1822, North River Steam Boat Company Papers, Rutgers University Library; John L. Sullivan to Judge Ambrose Spencer, August 10, 1822, Townsend Family Papers, New York Public Library.

98. *Ogden v. Gibbons,* 4 Johns. Ch. 174 (1819).

99. Ibid., 179.

100. Ibid., 180–82.

101. Thomas Gibbons to Daniel D. Tompkins, December 4, 1819, Gibbons Family Papers, Drew University Library.

102. Thomas Gibbons to Daniel Webster, December 13, 1819, Gibbons Family Papers, Drew University Library.

103. Signed Receipt, William Wirt to Thomas Gibbons, February 27, 1821, and Signed Receipt, Daniel Webster to Thomas Gibbons, February 28, 1821, Gibbons Family Papers, Drew University Library. The literature on Webster and Wirt is extensive. Key works on Webster include Irving H. Bartlett, *Daniel Webster* (New York: W. W. Norton, 1978); Maurice G. Baxter, *One and Inseparable: Daniel Webster and the Union* (Cambridge, MA: Harvard University Press, 1984); Merrill D. Peterson, *The Great Triumvirate: Webster, Clay, and Calhoun* (New York: Oxford University Press, 1988); Robert Remini, *Daniel Webster: The Man and His Time* (New York: W. W. Norton, 1997); and Kenneth E. Shewmaker, ed., *Daniel Webster, "The Completest Man"* (Hanover, NH: University Press of New England, 1990). Wirt's life and career are chronicled in Joseph Charles Burke, "William Wirt: Attorney General and Constitutional Lawyer" (PhD diss., Indiana University, 1965); Anya Jabour, *Marriage in the Early Republic: Elizabeth and William Wirt and the Companionate Ideal* (Baltimore, MD: Johns Hopkins University Press, 1998); and John Pendleton Kennedy, *Memoirs of the Life of William Wirt, Attorney General of the United States,* 2 vols. (Philadelphia: Lea and Blanchard, 1849).

104. Writ in the Case of *Ogden v. Gibbons,* New York State Supreme Court, November 26, 1819, and Bail Agreement in the Case of *Ogden v. Gibbons,* January 6, 1819, Gibbons Family Papers, Drew University Library.

105. *Gibbons v. Ogden,* 17 Johns. 488 (1820).

106. Ibid., 488–501.

107. *Boston Daily Atlas,* August 19, 1843, p. 2, cols. 4–5; *Trenton State Gazette,* January 30, 1854, p. 2., col. 3.

108. *State v. Gibbons,* 4 N.J.L. 45 (1818); *State v. Dayton,* 4 N.J.L. 64 (1818).

109. *State v. Gibbons,* 4 N.J.L. at 64–83.

110. *Ogden v. Gibbons,* 5 N.J.L. 612 (1819); *New York Columbian,* June 2, 1820, p. 2, col. 4; Thayer, *As We Were,* 230–32; D. Kendall, "Mr. Gibbons and Colonel Ogden," *Michigan State Bar Journal* 26 (February 1947): 23–24.

111. U.S. Supreme Court chief justice John Marshall personally signed an arrest warrant for Gibbons. Notice in Third Circuit Court of the United States, New Jersey District, *Livingston v. Gibbons,* April 1, 1820, Gibbons Family Papers, Drew University Library.

112. *Livingston v. Tompkins,* 4 Johns. Ch. 415 (1820).

113. Ibid., 416–24.

114. Ibid., 416–18.

115. Ibid., 418–24.

116. Copy of Injunction in *Gibbons v. Livingston,* September 1, 1820, Copy of Replevin Suit in *Gibbons v. Livingston,* New Jersey Court of Common Pleas, September 12, 1820, Copy of Bond with Federal Marshall's Office, September 25, 1820, and Affidavit of Thomas Gibbons concerning the *Bellona,* September 27, 1820, Gibbons Family Papers, Drew University Library.

117. Robert M. Livingston to Aaron Ogden, October 3, 1820, Aaron Ogden Papers, Rutgers University Library.

118. Opinion of His Honour Brockholst Livingston in the case of Thomas Gibbons v. John R. Livingston, October 8, 1820, Gibbons Family Papers, Drew University Library.

119. William Hyer to Thomas Gibbons, October 23, 1820, Gibbons Family Papers, Drew University Library.

120. Thomas Gibbons to Cornelius Vanderbilt, January 25, 1821, Thomas Gibbons to Commodore Lewis, February 8, 1821, and Elias Van Arsdale to Thomas Gibbons, February 10, 14, 15, and 22, 1821, Gibbons Family Papers, Drew University Library.

121. Charles Rhind to John Townsend, January 25, 1821, Townsend Family Papers, New York Public Library.

122. Charles Rhind to John Townsend, January 26, 1821, North River Steam Boat Company Papers, Rutgers University Library.

123. Joseph Story to William Fettyplace, February 28, 1821, in Joseph Story, *The Life and Letters of Joseph Story,* ed. William Wetmore Story (Freeport, NY: Books for Libraries Press, 1971), 2:396–97; *Gibbons v. Ogden,* 19 U.S. (6 Wheat.) 448 (1821).

124. *Gibbons v. Ogden,* 19 U.S. at 488.

125. *Sullivan v. Fulton Steam Boat Co.,* 19 U.S. (6 Wheat.) 450 (1821).

126. Ibid., 450.

127. Thomas Gibbons to Daniel Webster, April 2, 1821, Thomas Gibbons to William Heyer, April 30, 1821, Gibbons Family Papers, Drew University Library.

128. Daniel Webster to Thomas Gibbons, May 9, 1821, Gibbons Family Papers, Drew University Library.

129. Ibid.

130. Thomas Gibbons to William Wirt, May 14, 1821, Gibbons Family Papers, Drew University Library.

131. Elias Van Arsdale to Thomas Gibbons, June 9, 1821, and George Wood to Thomas Gibbons, June 18, 20, 22, and 26, 1821, Gibbons Family Papers, Drew University Library.

132. Copy of injunction in New Jersey Chancery Court as a result of an amended bill, July 7, 1821, Thomas Gibbons to George Wood, July 13, 1821, and George Wood to Thomas Gibbons,

July 14, 1821, Gibbons Family Papers, Drew University Library; Charles Rhind to John Townsend, July 18, 1821, North River Steam Boat Company Papers, Rutgers University Library; George Wood to Thomas Gibbons, July 19, 1821, and Affidavit of Abraham Baneker, July 22, 1821, Gibbons Family Papers, Drew University Library.

133. Elias Van Arsdale to Thomas Gibbons, August 11, 1821, Gibbons Family Papers, Drew University Library.

134. Memorandum of David O. Prince's service of injunction, September 26, 1821, and Affidavit of David O. Price in *Gibbons v. Ogden*, October 12, 1821, Gibbons Family Papers, Drew University Library.

135. Thomas Gibbons to Theodore Frelinghuysen, August 26, 1821, Gibbons Family Papers, Drew University Library.

136. *To the Honourable Legislature of the State of New Jersey, a Petition and Remonstrance of the Subscribers, Residents of the County of Essex, and Citizens of the State of New Jersey . . . ,* October 31, 1821, Gibbons Family Papers, Drew University Library. See also Thayer, *As We Were,* 240.

137. Charles Rhind to John Townsend, November 1, 1821, North River Steam Boat Company Papers, Rutgers University Library.

138. Charles Rhind to John Townsend, November 13, 1821, North River Steam Boat Company Papers, Rutgers University Library.

139. Roy Louis DuBois, "John Stevens: Transportation Pioneer" (PhD diss., New York University, 1973), 266–67; Act of November 3, 1821, 1821 N.J. Laws 9; copy in Clements-DeGolyer Collection, Southern Methodist University Library.

140. Elias Van Arsdale to Thomas Gibbons, December 6, 10, 11, and 12, 1821, Gibbons Family Papers, Drew University Library.

141. Cadwallader D. Colden to John Townsend, December 25, 1821, Townsend Family Papers, New York Public Library.

142. David Lynch to John Townsend, January 3, 1822, North River Steam Boat Company Papers, Rutgers University Library; Thomas Gibbons, *To the Honorable Chancellor James Kent of the State of New York,* 1822, New York Chancery Court Papers, New York County Clerk's Office; *James P. Allaire, to the Honorable the Legislature of the State of New York,* January 10, 1822, Gibbons Family Papers, Drew University Library.

143. Charles Rhind to John Townsend, January 18, 21, 1822, North River Steam Boat Company Papers, Rutgers University Library.

144. Elias Van Arsdale to Thomas Gibbons, January 3, 10, 1822, Gibbons Family Papers, Drew University Library.

145. Copy of Chancellor Kent's Decree, January 17, 1822, Gibbons Family Papers, Drew University Library.

146. Charles Rhind to John Townsend, January 24, 1822, North River Steam Boat Company Papers, Rutgers University Library.

147. Daniel Webster to Thomas Gibbons, February 2, 1822, Gibbons Family Papers, Drew University Library.

148. James A. Stevens to Thomas Gibbons, February 12 and February 14, 1822, Gibbons Family Papers, Drew University Library.

149. Daniel Webster to Thomas Gibbons, February 21, 1822, Gibbons Family Papers, Drew University Library. Rules for attorneys arguing before the United States Supreme Court were drawn from English and state court precedents and codified in 1790, with an updated version appearing in 1801. See Maeva Marcus and James R. Perry, eds., *The Documentary History of the Supreme Court of the United States, 1789–1800,* vol. 1 (New York: Columbia University Press, 1985), 177.

150. Aaron Ogden to Thomas Gibbons, March 22, 1822, Gibbons Family Papers, Drew University Library.

151. Thomas Gibbons to Aaron Ogden [Rough Draft], March 22, 1822, Gibbons Family Papers, Drew University Library.

152. William Gibbons to Thomas Gibbons, March 25, 1822, Miscellaneous Manuscripts, New Jersey Historical Society.

153. Elias Van Arsdale to Thomas Gibbons, March 27, 1822, and Thomas Gibbons to Aaron Ogden, March 30, 1822, Gibbons Family Papers, Drew University Library.

154. Charles Rhind to John Townsend, April 4, 1822, North River Steam Boat Company Papers, Rutgers University Library.

155. Charles Rhind to John Townsend, April 9, 1822, North River Steam Boat Company Papers, Rutgers University Library.

156. Agreements between Steamboats Bellona & Philadelphia and the Union Line of Stages, April 22, 1822, Gibbons Family Papers, Drew University Library.

157. Seth P. Staples to Thomas Gibbons, May 9, 1822, and Elias Van Arsdale to Thomas Gibbons, June 10, 1822, Gibbons Family Papers, Drew University Library.

158. Elias Van Arsdale to Thomas Gibbons, October 16, 19, 1822, Gibbons Family Papers, Drew University Library.

159. Thomas Gibbons to Samuel Parkman, August 8, 1822[?], Gibbons Family Papers, Drew University Library.

160. Thomas Gibbons to Robert M. Livingston, August 26, 1822, Gibbons Family Papers, Drew University Library.

161. Robert M. Livingston to Thomas Gibbons, August 31, 1822, Gibbons Family Papers, Drew University Library.

162. William Wirt to Thomas Gibbons, December 21, 1822, Gibbons Family Papers, Drew University Library.

163. Thomas Gibbons to Daniel Webster, January 14, 1823, Gibbons Family Papers, Drew University Library.

Chapter 8: Strategies and Deliberations

1. Joseph Story to Brockholst Livingston, June 4, 1822, Joseph Story Papers, Massachusetts Historical Society, cited in Gerald T. Dunne, *Justice Joseph Story and the Rise of the Supreme Court* (New York: Simon and Schuster, 1971), 214. See also George Dangerfield, *The Era of Good Feelings* (New York: Harcourt, Brace, and Smith, 1952), 309–24.

2. Albert S. Abel, "Commerce Regulation before *Gibbons v. Ogden:* Interstate Transportation Facilities," *North Carolina Law Review* 25, no. 2 (1947): 121–71; Elisha P. Douglass, *The Coming of Age of American Business: Three Centuries of Enterprise, 1600–1900* (Chapel Hill: University of North Carolina Press, 1971), 97–110; Wallace Mendelson, "New Light on *Fletcher v. Peck* and *Gibbons v. Ogden,*" Yale Law Journal 58 (March, 1949): 567–73; Douglass C. North, *The Economic Growth of the United States, 1790–1860* (Englewood Cliffs, NJ: Prentice-Hall, 1961), 165–79; Lewis Perry, *Boats against the Current: American Culture between Revolution and Modernity, 1820–1860* (New York: Oxford University Press, 1993), 16–18.

3. Robert Sobel, *Panic on Wall Street: A History of America's Financial Disasters* (Frederick, MD: Beard Books, 1999), 32–76.

4. Maxwell Bloomfield, *American Lawyer in a Changing Society* (Cambridge, MA: Harvard University Press, 1976); Richard E. Ellis, *Jeffersonian Crisis: Courts and Politics in the Young Republic* (New York: Oxford University Press, 1971); J. Willard Hurst, *Law and the Conditions of Freedom in the Nineteenth-Century United States* (Madison: University of Wisconsin Press, 1956); Morton Horwitz, *The Transformation of American Law, 1780–1860* (Cambridge, MA: Harvard University Press, 1977); Horwitz, *The Transformation of American Law, 1870–1960: The Crisis of Legal Orthodoxy* (New York: Oxford University Press, 1992); William E. Nelson, *The Americanization of the Common Law: The Impact of Legal Change on Massachusetts Society, 1760–1830* (Cambridge, MA: Harvard University Press, 1975); William J. Novak, *The People's Welfare: Law and Regulation in Nineteenth-Century America* (Chapel Hill: University of North Carolina Press, 1996).

5. Peter Karsten, *Heart versus Head: Judge-Made Law in Nineteenth-Century America* (Chapel Hill: University of North Carolina Press, 1997); Barbara Young Welke, *Recasting American Liberty:*

Gender, Race, Law, and the Railroad Revolution, 1865–1920 (Cambridge: Cambridge University Press, 2001).

6. Recent works on this subject include William R. Casto, *Supreme Court in the Early Republic: The Chief Justiceships of John Jay and Oliver Ellsworth* (Columbia: University of South Carolina Press, 1995); Scott Douglas Gerber, *Seriatim: The Supreme Court before John Marshall* (New York: New York University Press, 1998); James F. Simon, *What Kind of a Nation: Thomas Jefferson, John Marshall, and the Epic Struggle to Create a United States* (New York: Simon and Schuster, 2002); and G. Edward White, *The Marshall Court and Cultural Change, 1815–1835* (New York: Oxford University Press, 1991).

7. Albert J. Beveridge, *The Life of John Marshall*, vols. 1–4 (Boston: Houghton Mifflin, 1916–19); R. Kent Newmyer, *John Marshall and the Heroic Age of the Supreme Court* (Baton Rouge: Louisiana State University Press, 2001).

8. John Marshall, *An Autobiographical Sketch* (Ann Arbor: University of Michigan Press, 1937), 9–10.

9. Herbert A. Johnson, *The Chief Justiceship of John Marshall, 1801–1835* (Columbia: University of South Carolina Press, 1997); David Scott Robarge, *A Chief Justice's Progress: John Marshall from Revolutionary Virginia to the Supreme Court* (Westport, CT: Greenwood, 2000); Jean Edward Smith, *John Marshall: Definer of a Nation* (New York: Henry Holt, 1996).

10. Dunne, *Justice Joseph Story;* R. Kent Newmyer, *Supreme Court Justice Joseph Story: Statesman of the Old Republic* (Chapel Hill: University of North Carolina Press, 1986).

11. Irving Dilliard, "Gabriel Duvall," in *The Justices of the United States Supreme Court, 1789–1995: Their Lives and Major Opinions,* ed. Leon Friedman and Fred L. Israel (New York: Chelsea House Publishers, 1995), 419–29; Fred L. Israel, "Thomas Todd," in Friedman and Israel, *Justices of the United States Supreme Court,* 407–16; David L. Annis, "Mr. Bushrod Washington, Supreme Court Justice on the Marshall Court" (PhD diss., University of Notre Dame, 1974); Albert P. Blaustein and Roy M. Mersky, "Bushrod Washington," in Friedman and Israel, *Justices of the United States Supreme Court,* 243–66.

12. Donald G. Morgan, *Justice William Johnson: The First Dissenter* (Columbia: University of South Carolina Press, 1954).

13. White, *Marshall Court and Cultural Change,* 157–200.

14. *Fairfax's Devisee v. Hunter's Lessee,* 11 U.S. (7 Cranch) 603 (1813); *Martin v. Hunter's Lessee,* 14 U.S. (1 Wheat.) 304 (1816).

15. *Trustees of Dartmouth College v. Woodward,* 17 U.S. (4 Wheat.) 518 (1819).

16. *McCulloch v. Maryland,* 17 U.S. (4 Wheat.) 316 (1819). See also Richard E. Ellis, *Aggressive Nationalism: McCulloch v. Maryland and the Foundation of Federal Authority in the Young Republic* (New York: Oxford University Press, 2007).

17. Gerald Gunther, comp., *John Marshall's Defense of* McCulloch v. Maryland (Palo Alto, CA: Stanford University Press, 1969), 110.

18. Ibid., 214.

19. *House Journal,* 15th Cong., 2nd sess., February 16, 1819, 272.

20. Donald Fehrenbacher, *The South and Three Sectional Crises* (Baton Rouge: Louisiana State University Press, 1995); Paul Finkelman, *Slavery and the Founders: Race and Liberty in the Age of Jefferson* (Armonk, NY: M. E. Sharpe, 2001); Robert Pierce Forbes, *The Missouri Compromise and Its Aftermath: Slavery and the Meaning of America* (Chapel Hill: University of North Carolina Press, 2007).

21. *Cohens v. Virginia,* 19 U.S. (6 Wheat.) 264 (1821).

22. Ibid., 414.

23. *Richmond Enquirer,* May 25, 1821, reprinted in *The John P. Branch Historical Papers of Randolph-Macon College,* ed. William E. Dodd, vol. 2 (Richmond, VA: Taylor and Taylor Printing, 1902), 80.

24. John Taylor, *New Views of the Constitution of the United States* (Washington, DC: Way and Gideon, 1823), 156.

25. *Richmond Enquirer,* July 17, 1821, p. 1, cols. 1–5.

26. Charles Rhind to John Townsend, March 7 and March 22, 1823, North River Steam Boat Company Papers, Rutgers University Library.

27. Rufus King to James Monroe, April 3, 1823, Rufus King Papers, New-York Historical Society.

28. William Wirt to James Monroe, May 5, 1823, William Wirt Papers, Maryland Historical Society. Copies are also available at the Library of Congress.

29. Joseph Story to John Marshall, June 22, 1823, in Charles Warren, "The Story-Marshall Correspondence (1819–1831)," *William and Mary Quarterly*, 2nd ser., 21 (January 1941): 1–26; Donald M. Roper, *Mr. Justice Thompson and the Constitution* (New York: Garland Press, 1987).

30. *Elkison v. Deliesseline*, 8 Fed. Cas. 493, 493–94 (C.C.S.C. 1823) (No. 4366).

31. *Charleston Courier*, September 5, 1823, p. 2, cols. 5–6.

32. *Charleston Mercury*, September 6, 1823, p. 2, cols. 1–3.

33. Ibid., October 6, 1823, p. 2, col. 1.

34. John Marshall to Joseph Story, September 26, 1823, in *The Papers of John Marshall*, vol. 9, ed. Charles F. Hobson (Chapel Hill: University of North Carolina Press, 1998), 338–39.

35. *The Wilson v. United States*, 30 F. Cas. 239 (C.C.D. Va. 1820) (No. 17,846).

36. John Marshall to Joseph Story, September 26, 1823, in Hobson, *Papers of John Marshall*, 9:339.

37. Charles Rhind to John Townsend, January 24, 1824, Townsend Family Papers, New York Public Library.

38. John Townsend to Isaiah Townsend, January 30, 1824, Townsend Family Papers, New York Public Library.

39. William Wirt to Judge Dabney Carr, February 1, 1824, William Wirt Papers, Maryland Historical Society. Interestingly, in a rough draft of his letter to Carr, Wirt initially wrote that Webster was as ambitious as Lucifer.

40. *Richmond Enquirer*, February 26, 1824, p. 4, col. 4; *Washington Daily National Intelligencer*, March 3, 1824, p. 3, cols. 1–2; *New York Evening Post*, March 3, 1824, p. 2, cols. 3–4.

41. *Gibbons v. Ogden*, 22 U.S. (9 Wheat.) 1, 1–11 (1824).

42. Ibid., 9.

43. Ibid., 9–11.

44. Ibid., 11–18.

45. Ibid., 18–25.

46. Ibid., 25–32.

47. Ibid., 32–33.

48. Ibid., 33–44.

49. Ibid., 38.

50. Ibid., 44–57.

51. Ibid., 51–58.

52. Ibid., 58–63.

53. Ibid., 63–71.

54. Ibid., 71–76.

55. Ibid., 76–79.

56. Ibid., 79–83.

57. Ibid., 83–88.

58. Ibid., 88.

59. Ibid., 89.

60. Ibid., 89–91.

61. Ibid., 91–101.

62. Ibid., 101–3.

63. Ibid., 103–12.

64. Ibid., 112–23.

65. Ibid., 123–39.

66. Ibid., 139–41.

67. Ibid., 141–57.

68. Ibid., 157–59.

69. The quote comes from the *Aeneid*, bk.1, line 460.

70. Article from the *New York Statesman,* reprinted in the *Richmond Enquirer,* March 9, 1824, p. 4, cols. 2–3.

71. Article from the *New York Statesman,* reprinted in the *New London Gazette,* February 18, 1824, p. 3, col. 3.

72. *Gibbons v. Ogden,* 22 U.S. at 159–62.

73. Ibid., 162–70.

74. Ibid., 170–76.

75. Ibid., 176–83.

76. Ibid., 183–84.

77. Ibid., 184–86.

78. *Washington Daily National Intelligencer,* February 4, 1824, p. 3, col. 4, February 6, 1824, p. 3, col. 1, and February 10, 1824, p. 3, col. 5; *Washington Gazette,* February 4, 1824, p. 2, col. 5, and February 5, 1824, p. 3, col. 2.

79. *Richmond Enquirer,* March 2, 1824, p. 3, cols. 1–2.

80. *New York Evening Post,* February 13, 1824, p. 2, cols. 3–6.

Chapter 9: The Gibbons Decision and Popular Reaction

1. Charles Rhind to John Townsend, February 8, 1824, Townsend Family Papers, New York Public Library.

2. William Wirt to E. Wirt, February 11, 1824, William Wirt Papers, Maryland Historical Society.

3. Daniel Webster to Joseph Hopkinson, February 14, 1824, in *The Papers of Daniel Webster: Correspondence,* vol. 1, *1798–1824,* ed. Charles M. Wiltse and Harold Moser (Hanover, NH: University Press of New England, 1974), 353–54.

4. James Thomson to John Townsend, February 17, 1824, Townsend Family Papers, New York Public Library.

5. Daniel Webster to Jeremiah Mason, February 18, 1824, in Wiltse and Moser, *Papers of Daniel Webster,* 353–54.

6. John A. King to Rufus King, February 19, 1824, Rufus King Papers, New-York Historical Society.

7. David B. Ogden to Aaron Ogden, February 9, 1824, Robert Fulton Papers, New-York Historical Society.

8. William Gibbons to Thomas Gibbons, February 23, 1824, Gibbons Family Papers, Drew University Library.

9. John Marshall to Mary W. Marshall, February 23, 1823, in John Marshall, *The Papers of John Marshall,* vol. 10, ed. Charles F. Hobson (Chapel Hill: University of North Carolina Press, 1998), 4–5.

10. Jean Edward Smith, *John Marshall: Definer of a Nation* (New York: Henry Holt, 1996), 473–74.

11. *New York Statesman,* March 5, 1824, p. 3, cols. 1–2.

12. *New York Commercial Advertiser,* March 3, 1824, p. 3, col. 1.

13. Letter of Benjamin H. Latrobe, May 31, 1796, in John E. Semmes, *John H. B. Latrobe and His Times* (Baltimore, MD: Norman, Remington, 1917), 7–9.

14. *Gibbons v. Ogden,* 22 U.S. (9 Wheat.) 1, 186–87 (1824).

15. Ibid., 187–88.

16. Ibid., 188–89.

17. Ibid., 189–91.

18. Ibid., 191–93.

19. Ibid., 193–94.

20. Ibid., 194–95.

21. Ibid., 195–96.

22. Ibid., 196–97.

23. Ibid., 197–203.

24. Ibid., 203–4.

25. Ibid., 204–6.

26. Ibid., 206–9.

27. Ibid., 209.

28. Ibid., 209–10.

29. Ibid., 210–12.

30. Ibid., 212–13.

31. Ibid., 213–15.

32. Ibid., 215–20.

33. Ibid., 220–22.

34. Ibid., 222.

35. Donald G. Morgan, *Justice William Johnson: The First Dissenter* (Columbia: University of South Carolina Press, 1954), 57–58, 153–88.

36. William Johnson, *Nugae Georgicae: An Essay, Delivered to the Literary and Philosophical Society of Charleston, South Carolina, October 14, 1815* (Charleston, SC: J. Hoff, 1815), 37–40, cited in Morgan, *Justice William Johnson,* 102–3.

37. John Quincy Adams, September 2, 1818, in *Memoirs of John Quincy Adams, Comprising Portions of His Diary from 1795 to 1848,* ed. Charles Francis Adams, vol. 4 (Philadelphia: J. B. Lippincott, 1875), 128–29, cited in Morgan, *Justice William Johnson,* 105.

38. *Gibbons v. Ogden,* 22 U.S. at 222–23.

39. Ibid., 223.

40. Ibid.

41. Ibid., 223–26.

42. Ibid., 226–29.

43. Ibid., 229–30.

44. Ibid., 230.

45. Ibid., 230–31.

46. Ibid., 231–32.

47. Ibid., 232.

48. Ibid., 232–34.

49. Ibid., 234–35.

50. Ibid., 235–38.

51. Ibid., 238–39.

52. Ibid., 239–40.

53. John Marshall to Gales and Seaton, March 3, 1824, in Hobson, *Papers of John Marshall,* 10:35.

54. Kirk Russell, *Randolph of Roanoke: A Study in Conservative Thought* (Chicago: University of Chicago Press, 1951)

55. *Richmond Enquirer,* February 26, 1824, p. 4, col. 4.

56. John Randolph to Dr. John Brockenbrough, March 3, 1824, in Hugh Garland, ed., *The Life of John Randolph of Roanoke* (New York: D. Appleton, 1851), 2:212.

57. Thomas Jefferson to William Branch Giles, December 26, 1825, Thomas Jefferson Papers, Library of Congress.

58. Samuel Wiswall to John Townsend, March 5, 1824, Townsend Family Papers, New York Public Library.

59. Charles Rhind to John Townsend, March 6, 1824, Townsend Family Papers, New York Public Library.

60. *New York Commercial Advertiser,* March 12, 1824, cited in Charles Warren, *The Supreme Court in United States History* (Boston: Little, Brown, 1922), 613.

61. *New York Spectator,* March 8, 1824, cited in Warren, *Supreme Court in United States History,* 613.

62. *New York Daily Advertiser,* February 18, 1824, p. 2, col. 6.

63. *New York Evening Post,* March 5, 1824, p. 2, cols. 2–3.

64. *Connecticut Courant,* March 9, 1824, cited in Warren, *Supreme Court in United States History,* 620.

65. Ibid.

66. *Norwich Courier,* March 10, 1824, p. 3, col. 3.

67. *Elizabethtown Gazette,* March 15, 1824, reprinted in the *Savannah Daily Georgian,* March 31, 1824, p. 2, cols. 4–5.

68. *United States Gazette,* March 9, 1824, p. 2, col. 1.

69. The proximity of Washingtonians to the deliberations in *Gibbons v. Ogden* may have made extensive newspaper coverage of the case redundant.

70. *Washington Daily National Intelligencer,* March 3, 1824, p. 3, cols. 1–5.

71. *National Gazette,* March 9, 1824, cited in Warren, *Supreme Court in United States History,* 613.

72. *Charleston Courier,* March 13, 1824, p. 2, col. 4.

73. *Charleston City Gazette,* March 10, 1824, cited in Warren, *Supreme Court in United States History,* 618.

74. *Augusta Chronicle,* March 17, 1824, p. 2, cols. 1–5.

75. *Savannah Daily Georgian,* March 11, 1824, p. 2, col. 1.

76. *Georgia Patriot,* April 26, 1824, p. 2, col. 2.

77. *New Orleans Courier,* April 13, 1824, p. 1, col. 3.

78. *Mobile Commercial Register,* March 30, 1824, p. 2, col. 1.

79. *Kentucky Gazette,* March 18, 1824, p. 3, col. 1.

80. *Louisville Public Advertiser,* March 28, 1824, cited in Warren, *Supreme Court in United States History,* 614.

81. *Missouri Republican* (St. Louis), April 26, 1824, cited in Warren, *Supreme Court in United States History,* 614–15.

82. *New York Evening Post,* March 16, 1824, p. 2, col. 1.

83. *New York Evening Post,* March 26, 1824, p. 2, cols. 1–3.

84. *New York Evening Post,* April 1, 1824, p. 2, col. 3.

85. *New York National Advertiser,* March 8, 1824, reprinted in *Washington (GA) News,* March 27, 1824, p. 2, col. 4.

86. Ibid.

87. *New York Evening Post,* March 8, 1824, p. 2, cols. 3–4.

88. *Richmond Enquirer,* March 16, 1824, cited in Warren, *Supreme Court in United States History,* 618.

89. Gerald Gunther, *John Marshall's Defense of* McCulloch v. Maryland (Palo Alto, CA: Stanford University Press, 1969), 63–64, 80–85, 205–6.

Chapter 10: The Decline of the New York Steamboat Monopoly

1. *New York Evening Post,* March 3, 1824, p. 2, cols. 3–4.

2. *New York National Union,* March 19, 1824, *Connecticut Courant,* March 9, 1824, and *Albany Argus,* March 9, 1824, cited in Charles Warren, *The Supreme Court in United States History* (Boston: Little, Brown, 1922), 615.

3. *New York Evening Post,* March 13, 1824, p. 2, col. 2.

4. *Norwich Courier,* April 21, 1824, p. 2, col. 6.

5. *Washington (GA) Gazette,* April 1, 1824, p. 3, col. 3; *Washington Daily National Intelligencer,* April 22, 1824, p. 3, col. 4, and April 27, 1824 p. 3, col. 4.

6. *New York Evening Post,* April 23, 1824, p. 2, col. 2; *Norwich Courier,* June 9, 1824, p. 2, cols. 2–3.

7. James Kent, "Chancellor Kent on Universal Suffrage," in *Readings in American Constitutional History, 1776–1876,* ed. Allen Johnson (New York: Houghton Mifflin, 1912), 358.

8. Peter Galie, *Ordered Liberty: A Constitutional History of New York* (New York: Fordham University Press, 1996), 71–94.

9. *New York Evening Post,* April 12, 1824, p. 2, cols. 3–4; *Washington Daily National Intelligencer,* April 13, 1824, p. 2, cols. 3–4; Alden Chester, *Legal and Judicial History of New York* (New York: National Americana Society, 1911), 3:235–36.

10. *New York Evening Post,* April 26, 1824, p. 2, col. 3.

11. Charles Rhind to John Townsend, April 13, 1824, Townsend Family Papers, New York Public Library.

12. *New York Spectator* [n.d.], reprinted in the *Norwich Courier,* May 5, 1824, p. 2, col. 6.

13. Charles Rhind to John Townsend, March 23 and March 30, 1824, Townsend Family Papers, New York Public Library; Robert Ludlow Fowler, "Constitutional and Legal History of New York in the Nineteenth Century," in *The Memorial History of the City of New York: From Its First Settlement to the Year 1892,* ed. James Grant Wilson, vol. 3 (New York: New-York History, 1893), 654.

14. *New York Spectator,* October 22, 1838, p. 2, col. 4; *Connecticut Courant,* October 27, 1838, p. 3, col. 3; *North River Steam Boat Co. v. Livingston,* 1 Hopk. Ch. 149 (1824).

15. *North River Steam Boat Co. v. Livingston,* 1 Hopk. Ch. at 150–55.

16. Ibid., 164.

17. Ibid., 164–71.

18. Ibid., 180.

19. Ibid., 180–88.

20. Ibid., 188.

21. Ibid., 197.

22. Charles Rhind to John Townsend, May 14, 1824, Townsend Family Papers, New York Public Library.

23. Charles Rhind to John Townsend, May 14, 27, and 28 and June 14 and 16, 1824, Townsend Family Papers, New York Public Library.

24. *New York Evening Post,* May 5, 1824, p. 2, col. 1, and May 12, 1824, p. 2, col. 1; *Charleston Courier,* May 21, 1824, p. 2, col. 2.

25. *New York Evening Post,* May 6, 1824, p. 2, col. 1.

26. *Washington Daily National Advertiser,* May 20, 1824, p. 3, col. 5; *Augusta Chronicle,* May 29, 1824, p. 3, col. 3; *Richmond Enquirer,* May 26, 1824, p. 4, cols. 2–3; *Maryland Gazette,* May 27, 1824, p. 3, col. 3; and *Kentucky Gazette,* June 3, 1824, p. 3, col. 2. The debate over federal regulation of steamboat safety would continue well into the nineteenth century. See John G. Burke, "Bursting Boilers and the Federal Power," *Technology and Culture* 7 (Winter 1966): 1–23; and Harlan I. Halsey, "The Choice between High-Pressure and Low-Pressure Steam Power in America in the Early Nineteenth Century," *Journal of Economic History* 41 (December 1981): 723–41.

27. *New York Evening Post,* May 26, 1824, p. 2, col. 2.

28. *Charleston Courier,* May 26, 1824, p. 2, col. 3.

29. *House Journal,* 18th Cong., 1st sess. May 25, 1824, 579.

30. Charles Rhind to John Townsend, May 17, 1824, p. 2, cols. 1–2; *New York Evening Post,* May 18, 1824, p. 2, cols. 1–2.

31. *New York Daily Advertiser,* reprinted in the *Savannah Daily Georgian,* June 8, 1824, p. 2, col. 6.

32. *North River Steam Boat Co. v. Livingston,* 1 Hopk. Ch. at 197–205.

33. Ibid., 206–9.

34. Ibid., 210–11.

35. *New York Evening Post,* June 19, 1824, p. 2, col. 5.

36. *New York Evening Post,* June 23, 1824, p. 2, col. 4.

37. *Washington (GA) Gazette,* June 22, 1824, p. 2, col. 4.; *United States Gazette,* June 22, 1824, p. 1, col. 4, and July 6, 1824, p. 4, col. 4; *Niles' Register,* June 26, 1824, p. 267, col. 1; *Savannah Daily Georgian,* July 3, 1824, p. 2, col. 3; and *Kentucky Gazette,* July 8, 1824, p. 3, col. 2.

38. *Savannah Daily Georgian,* July 24, 1824, p. 2, col. 2.

39. *Norwich Courier,* July 7, 1824, p. 3, cols. 1–3.

40. Charles Rhind to John Townsend, June 24, 1824, Townsend Family Papers, New York Public Library.

41. Charles Rhind to John Townsend, July 8, 1824, Townsend Family Papers, New York Public Library.

42. Charles Rhind to John Townsend, July 9, 1824, Townsend Family Papers, New York Public Library.

43. Charles Rhind to John Townsend, July 16, 1824, Townsend Family Papers, New York Public Library.

44. Charles Rhind to John Townsend, August 8, 1824, Townsend Family Papers, New York Public Library.

45. Charles Rhind to John Townsend, August 11, 1824, Townsend Family Papers, New York Public Library.

46. Charles Rhind to John Townsend, August 25, 1824, and January 1, 1825, Townsend Family Papers, New York Public Library.

47. *United States Gazette,* September 25, 1824, p. 4, col. 3. Lafayette's visit to the United States is chronicled in Andrew Burstein, *America's Jubilee* (New York: Alfred A. Knopf, 2001), 11–30.

48. Thomas Addis Emmet to DeWitt Clinton, December 11, 1824, De Witt Clinton Papers, Columbia University Library.

49. Thomas Oakley to DeWitt Clinton, November 18, 1824, De Witt Clinton Papers, Columbia University Library.

50. *North River Steam Boat Co. v. Livingston,* 3 Cow. 713, 713–15 (1825).

51. Charles Rhind to John Townsend, January 28, 1825, Townsend Family Papers, New York Public Library.

52. *New York Evening Post,* March 3, 1825, p. 2, col. 3, March 15, 1825, p. 2, col. 1, and March 16, 1825, p. 2, cols. 1–2; *United States Gazette,* March 11, 1825, p. 2, col. 3; *Niles' Register,* March 19, 1825, p. 35, col. 2.

53. *North River Steam Boat Company v. Livingston,* 3 Cow. 713 at 717–56, quote at 748.

54. Ibid., 756.

55. Ibid.

56. Charles Rhind to John Townsend, March 3, 1825, and Robert L. Livingston to John Townsend, March 3, 1825, Townsend Family Papers, New York Public Library.

57. *Albany Argus* [n.d.], reprinted in the *New York Evening Post,* March 15, 1825, p. 2, cols. 1–3.

58. *New York Statesman* [n.d.], reprinted in *United States Gazette,* March 11, 1825, p. 2, col. 3.

59. *Connecticut Courant,* September 18, 1826, p. 4, col. 3; Robert G. Albion, *The Rise of New York Port* (New York: Charles Scribners' Sons, 1939), 153; Clare Brandt, *An American Aristocracy: The Livingstons* (Garden City, NY: Doubleday, 1986), 178–79.

Conclusion: *Gibbons v. Ogden* as Historical Precedent

1. Clare Brandt, *An American Aristocracy: The Livingstons* (Garden City, NY: Doubleday, 1986), 178–79.

2. Ibid., 174–83.

3. *Boston Commercial Gazette,* April 3, 1826, p. 2, col. 5.

4. *Lehigh Herald,* July 20, 1832, reprinted in the *Rhode Island Republican,* August 7, 1832, p. 2, cols. 4–5; *Senate Journal,* 24th Cong., 1st sess., April 13, 286–87, 29th Cong., 1st sess., July 20, 425–28, and 29th Cong., 1st sess., August 7, 490–96; Cynthia Owen Philip, *Robert Fulton: A Biography* (New York: Franklin Watts, 1985), 350–53; Kirkpatrick Sale, *The Fire of His Genius: Robert Fulton and the American Dream* (New York: Free Press, 2001), 177–79.

5. Sale, *Fire of His Genius,* 181–87.

6. George Rogers Taylor, *The Transportation Revolution, 1815–1860* (New York: Rinehart, 1951), 63–67; Charles Sellers, *The Market Revolution: Jacksonian America, 1815–1846* (New York: Oxford University Press, 1991), 131–32, 146–57.

7. Taylor, *Transportation Revolution,* 74–86; Sellers, *Market Revolution,* 380–92.

233

8. Taylor, *Transportation Revolution*, 86–103.

9. Thomas Gibbons, Will of Thomas Gibbons, October 26, 1825, Gibbons Family Papers, Drew University Library, additional copy on file in Miscellaneous Manuscripts, New-York Historical Society; *Boston Daily Advertiser,* September 12, 1823 p. 2, col. 2.

10. *Connecticut Courant,* April 27, 1839, p. 3 col. 2; Theodore Thayer, *As We Were: The Story of Old Elizabethtown* (Elizabeth, NJ: Grassman, 1964), 232–42.

11. *Willson v. Blackbird Creek Marsh Co.,* 27 U.S. 245 (1829).

12. *Groves v. Slaughter,* 40 U.S. 449 (1841).

13. *License Cases,* 46 U.S. 504, 581 (1847).

14. *Passenger Cases,* 48 U.S. 283, 437 (1849). See also Peter Harvey, *Reminiscences and Anecdotes of Daniel Webster* (Boston: Little, Brown, 1877), 143.

15. *Cooley v. Bd. of Wardens of the Port of Philadelphia,* 53 U.S. 299 (1852).

16. James Kent, *Commentaries on American Law,* vol. 2 (New York: O. Halstead, 1827), 408.

17. Ibid., 408–9.

18. Joseph Story, *Commentaries on the Constitution of the United States,* vol. 2 (Boston: Hilliard, Gray, 1833), section 1053.

19. George Van Santvoord, *Sketches of the Lives and Judicial Services of the Chief-Justices of the Supreme Court of the United States* (New York: Charles Scribner, 1854), 412–17.

20. Harvey, *Reminiscences and Anecdotes of Daniel Webster,* 142.

21. *Wabash, St. Louis, & Pacific Ry. Co. v. Illinois,* 118 U.S. 557 (1886); *Swift v. United States,* 196 U.S. 375 (1904); *United States v. E. C. Knight Co.,* 156 U.S. 1 (1895); *Hammer v. Dagenhart,* 247 U.S. 251 (1918). See also Paul W. MacAvoy, *The Economic Effects of Regulation: The Trunk-Line Railroad Cartels and the Interstate Commerce Commission before 1900* (Cambridge, MA: MIT Press, 1965).

22. Charles Warren, *The Supreme Court in United States History* (Boston: Little, Brown, 1922), 2:76. See also William E. Church, "A Forgotten Episode—*Gibbons v. Ogden,*" *Illinois Law Review* 4, no. 6 (1910): 420–24.

23. Eliot Jones and Homer B. Vanderblue, *Railroads: Cases and Selections* (New York: Macmillan, 1925), 106–7.

24. Samuel Eliot Morison, *The Oxford History of the United States, 1783–1917* (Oxford: Oxford University Press, 1927), 1:317–18.

25. Frederick H. Cooke, "The *Gibbons v. Ogden* Fetish," *Michigan Law Review* 9 (1911): 324–33.

26. Edwin S. Corwin, *John Marshall and the Constitution: A Chronicle of the Supreme Court* (New Haven, CT: Yale University Press, 1919), 130–31.

27. *Schechter Poultry Corp. v. United States,* 295 U.S. 495 (1935); *United States v. Butler,* 297 U.S. 1 (1936); *Carter v. Carter Coal Co.,* 298 U.S. 238 (1936).

28. *National Labor Relations Board v. Jones & Laughlin Steel Corp.,* 301 U.S. 1 (1937); Barry Cushman, *Rethinking the New Deal Court: The Structure of a Constitutional Revolution* (New York: Oxford University Press, 1998); William E. Leuchtenburg, *The Supreme Court Reborn: The Constitutional Revolution in the Age of Roosevelt* (New York: Oxford University Press, 1995).

29. Frank J. Goodnow, *Social Reform and the Constitution* (New York: Macmillan, 1911), 35–36.

30. Felix Frankfurter, *The Commerce Clause under Marshall, Taney, and Waite* (Chapel Hill: University of North Carolina Press, 1937), 18–19.

31. Burton J. Hendrick, *Bulwark of the Republic: A Biography of the Constitution* (Boston: Little, Brown, 1937), 202–3.

32. Ibid.

33. William W. Crosskey, *Politics and the Constitution in the History of the United States,* vol. 1 (Chicago: University of Chicago Press, 1953), 8–11. Crosskey formulated many of his theories in the 1930s but did not publish his major works until the early 1950s.

34. *United States v. Carolene Prods. Co.,* 304 U.S. 144, 152 (1938).

35. *Wickard v. Filburn,* 317 U.S. 111, 121 (1942).

36. Ibid., 122.

37. C. Perry Patterson, *Presidential Government in the United States: The Unwritten Constitution* (Chapel Hill: University of North Carolina Press, 1947), 20.

38. J. Willard Hurst, *Law and the Conditions of Freedom in the Nineteenth-Century United States* (Madison: University of Wisconsin Press, 1956), 44–46.

39. *Brown v. Bd. of Educ. of Topeka,* 347 U.S. 483 (1954); Civil Rights Act of 1964, Pub. L. 88-352, 78 Stat. 244; Voting Rights Act of 1965, Pub. L. 89-110, 79 Stat. 437. See also Taylor Branch, *Pillar of Fire: America in the King Years, 1963–65* (New York: Simon and Schuster, 1999).

40. *Heart of Atlanta Motel v. United States,* 379 U.S. 241, 251 (1964); *Katzenbach v. McClung,* 379 U.S. 294 (1964).

41. William Appleman Williams, *The Contours of American History* (Cleveland, OH: World Publishing, 1961), 213.

42. Lawrence M. Friedman, *A History of American Law* (New York: Simon and Schuster, 1973).

43. G. Edward White, *The Marshall Court and Cultural Change, 1815–1835* (New York: Oxford University Press, 1991), 578–79.

44. *United States v. Lopez,* 514 U.S. 549 (1995).

45. *United States v. Morrison,* 529 U.S. 598 (2000).

46. *Gonzales v. Raich,* 545 U.S. 1 (2005).

BIBLIOGRAPHY

Primary Sources

Manuscript Collections

Claiborne, William Charles Cole. Official Letterbooks. Mississippi State Archives
Clements-DeGolyer Collection. Southern Methodist University
Clinton, De Witt. Papers. Columbia University Library
Dayton, Jonathan. Papers. New Jersey Historical Society
Dickerson, Mahlon. Papers. New Jersey Historical Society
Dormitzer, Walter. Collection. New Jersey Historical Society
Emmet, Thomas Addis. Papers. New York Public Library
Fitch, John. Papers. Library of Congress
Fulton, Robert. Papers. Gilbert Montague Collection. New York Public Library
———. Papers. New-York Historical Society
———. Papers. New York State Library
Gallatin, Albert. Papers. New-York Historical Society
Gibbons, Thomas. Papers. Museum of American Finance
———. Papers. New-York State Archives
Gibbons Family Papers. Drew University Library
Gilder Lehrman Collection. New-York Historical Society
Jay, John. Papers. Columbia University Library
Jefferson, Thomas. Papers. Library of Congress
Kent Family Papers. Columbia University Library
King, Rufus. Papers. New-York Historical Society
Latrobe, Benjamin Henry. Papers. Library of Congress
LeBoeuf, Randall. Collection. New-York Historical Society
Livingston, Robert R., Papers. New-York Historical Society
Livingston Family Papers. Clermont State Historical Site
Miscellaneous Manuscripts. Harvard University Law Library
Miscellaneous Manuscripts. New-York Historical Society
Monroe, James. Papers. Library of Congress
New York Chancery Court. Miscellaneous Files. New York State Archives
———. Papers. New York County Clerk's Office
———. Papers. New York State Archives
North River Steam Boat Company. Papers. Rutgers University Library
Ogden, Aaron. Papers. New Jersey Historical Society
Ogden, Aaron. Papers. Rutgers University Library
Seligman, R. A., Papers. Columbia University Library
Special Collections, Dartmouth University Library
Stevens Family Papers. New Jersey Historical Society
Thornton, William. Papers. Library of Congress
Townsend Family Papers. New York Public Library
Van Vechten, Abraham. Papers. New York State Archives
Washington, George. Papers. Library of Congress
Wirt, William. Papers. Maryland Historical Society

Cases

Brown v. Bd. of Educ. of Topeka, Kansas, 347 U.S. 483 (1954)

Carter v. Carter Coal Co., 298 U.S. 238 (1936)

Cohens v. Virginia, 19 U.S. (6 Wheat.) 264 (1821)

Cooley v. Bd. of Wardens of the Port of Philadelphia, 53 U.S. 299 (1852)

Donaldson v. Beckett, 4 Burr. 2408, 98 Eng. Rep. 257 (1774)

Elkison v. Deliesseline, 8 F. Cas. 493 (C.C.D.S.C. 1823) (No. 4,366)

Fairfax's Devisee v. Hunter's Lessee, 11 U.S. (7 Cranch) 603 (1813)

Fulton Steamboat Co. v. Livingston, L456 J0070 (1822)

Gibbons v. Livingston, 6 N.J. Law 236 (1822)

Gibbons v. Livingston, unreported case (C.C.S.D.N.Y. 1820)

Gibbons v. Ogden, 6 N.J. Law 585 (1822)

Gibbons v. Ogden, 17 Johns. 488 (1820)

Gibbons v. Ogden, 19 U.S. (6 Wheat.) 448 (1821)

Gibbons v. Ogden, 22 U.S. (9 Wheat.) 1 (1824)

Gibbons v. Ogden, New York Court of Chancery (1818)

Gibbons v. Trumbull, Court for the Treatment of Small Essex County Causes (1818)

Gonzales v. Raich, 545 U.S. 1 (2005)

Groves v. Slaughter, 40 U.S. 449 (1841)

Hammer v. Dagenhart, 247 U.S. 251 (1918)

Heart of Atlanta Motel v. United States, 379 U.S. 241 (1964)

Heirs of Fulton and Livingston v. Shreve, unreported case (C.C.D. La.1817)

In re Vanderbilt, 4 Johns. 57 (1819)

Katzenbach v. McClung, 379 U.S. 294 (1964)

Lawrence v. Fulton, New York Court of Chancery (1816)

License Cases, 46 U.S. 504 (1847)

Livingston v. Cutting, no. L126 J0087–82, New York Court of Chancery (1819)

Livingston v. Cutting, no. L126 J0071, New York Court of Chancery (1820)

Livingston v. Fulton Steam Boat Co., no. L597 J0070, New York Court of Chancery (1821)

Livingston v. Gibbons, 4 Johns. Ch. 571 (1820)

Livingston v. Gibbons, 5 Johns. Ch. 250 (1821)

Livingston v. Livingston, no. L596 J0070, New York Court of Chancery (1820)

Livingston v. Ogden and Gibbons, 4 Johns. Ch. 48 (1819)

Livingston v. Ogden and Gibbons, 4 Johns. Ch. 95 (1819)

Livingston v. Tompkins, 4 Johns. 415 (1820)

Livingston v. Van Ingen, 9 Johns. 507. (1811)

Livingston v. Van Ingen, 15 F. Cas 697 (C.C.D.N.Y. 1811) (No. 8,420)

Martin v. Hunter's Lessee, 14 U.S. (1 Wheat.) 304 (1816)

McCulloch v. Maryland, 17 U.S. (4 Wheat.) 316 (1819)

Millar v. Taylor, 4 Burr. 2303, 98 Eng. Rep. 201 (1796)

National Labor Relations Bd. v. Jones & Laughlin Steel Corp., 301 U.S. 1 (1937)

North River Steam Boat Co. v. Hoffman, 5 Johns Ch. 300 (1819)

North River Steam Boat Co. v. Livingston, 1 Hopk. Ch. 149 (1824)

North River Steam Boat Co. v. Livingston, 3 Cow. 713 (1825)

Ogden and Gibbons v. Rutherford, New Jersey Court of Chancery (1803)

Ogden v. Gibbons, 4 Johns Ch. 174 (1819)

Ogden v. Gibbons, 5 N.J.L. 612 (1819)

Passenger Cases, 48 U.S. 283 (1849)

Schechter Poultry Corp. v. United States, 295 U.S. 495 (1935)

State v. Dayton, 4 N.J.L. 64 (1818)

State v. Gibbons, 4 N.J.L. 45 (1818)

Sullivan v. Fulton Steam Boat Co., 19 U.S. (6 Wheat.) 450 (1821)
Swift v. United States, 196 U.S. 375 (1904)
The Wilson v. United States, 30 F. Cas. 239 (C.C.D. Va. 1820) (No. 17,846)
Trustees of Dartmouth College v. Woodward, 17 U.S. (4 Wheat.) 518 (1819)
United States v. Butler, 297 U.S. 1 (1936)
United States v. Carolene Prods. Co., 304 U.S. 144 (1938)
United States v. E. C. Knight Co., 156 U.S. 1 (1895)
United States v. Lopez, 514 U.S. 549 (1995)
United States v. Morrison, 529 U.S. 598 (2000)
Wabash, St. Louis, & Pacific Railway Co. v. Illinois, 118 U.S. 557 (1886)
Wickard v. Filburn, 317 U.S. 111 (1942)
Willson v. Blackbird Creek Marsh Co., 27 U.S. 245 (1829)

Newspapers and Periodicals

Albany Argus
American Citizen
Augusta Chronicle
Boston Commercial Gazette
Boston Daily Advertiser
Boston Daily Atlas
Charleston City Gazette
Charleston Courier
Charleston Mercury
Cincinnati Gazette
Cincinnati Western Spy
Columbian Magazine
Connecticut Courant
Connecticut Mirror
Connecticut Whig
Dedham Gazette
Elizabethtown Gazette
Georgia Patriot
Kentucky Gazette
Lehigh Herald
Lexington Reporter
Louisiana Gazette
Louisiana Gazette and Daily Advertiser
Louisiana Monitor
Louisville Public Advertiser
Maryland Gazette
Missouri Republican (St. Louis)
Mobile Commercial Register
National Advocate
National Gazette
National Intelligencer (Washington, DC)
New Brunswick Fredonian
New London Gazette
New Orleans Courier
New York Columbian
New York Commercial Advertiser
New York Daily Advertiser

New York Evening Bulletin
New York Evening Post
New York Gazette and General Advertiser
New York National Advertiser
New York National Union
New York Spectator
New York Statesman
New York Times
Niles' Register
Norwich Courier
Ohio Federalist
Pennsylvania Gazette
Pittsburgh Gazette
Pittsfield Sun
Rhode Island Republican
Richmond Enquirer
Savannah Daily Georgian
Southern Patriot
Trenton Federalist
Trenton State Gazette
United States Gazette
Washington Daily National Advertiser
Washington Daily National Intelligencer
Washington National Intelligencer
Washington (GA) Gazette
Washington (GA) News
Western Sun (Vincennes, IN)

Published Primary Sources

Anon. *An Examination of Cadwallader D. Colden's Book, Entitled, "A Life of Robert Fulton," by a Friend of John Fitch, Deceased.* London: n.p., 1818.

Barnard, Daniel D. *A Discourse on the Life, Character, and Public Services of Ambrose Spencer.* Albany, NY: J. Munsell, 1849.

Barnes, Joseph. *Remarks on Mr. John Fitch's Reply to Mr. James Rumsey's Pamphlet.* Philadelphia: Joseph James, 1788.

———. *Treatise on Justice, Policy, and Utility of Establishing an Effectual System of Promoting the Progress of Useful Arts . . .* Philadelphia: Francis Bailey, 1792.

Claiborne, Nathaniel Herbert. *Notes on the War in the South: With Biographical Sketches of the Lives of Montgomery Jackson, Sevier, the Late Gov. Claiborne and Others.* Richmond, VA: William Ramsay, 1819.

Colden, Cadwallader D. *Life of Robert Fulton.* New York: Kirk and Mercein, 1817.

———. *A Review of the Letter Addressed by William Alexander Duer, to Cadwallader Colden in Answer to Strictures Contained in His "Life of Robert Fulton" . . .* New York: Kirk and Mercein, 1818.

———. *A Vindication by Cadwallader D. Colden, of the Steam Boat Right Granted by the State of New-York (to Livingston and Fulton) in the Form of an Answer to the Letter of Mr. Duer, Addressed to Mr. Colden.* New York: W. A. Mercein, 1818.

Coxe, Tench. *An Address to an Assembly of the Friends of American Manufactures . . .* Philadelphia: R. Aitken, 1787.

De Pauw, Linda Grant, Charlene Bangs Bickford, and Helen E. Veit, eds. *Documentary History of the First Federal Congress of the United States of America, March 4 1789–March 3, 1791.* 17 vols. Washington, DC: Government Printing Office, 1972–2004.

Dircks, Henry, ed. *The Life, Times and Scientific Labors of (Edward Somerset) the Second Marquis of Worcester, to Which Is Added, a Reprint of His Century of Inventions*. London: Quaritch, 1865.

Dodd, William E., ed. *The John P. Branch Historical Papers of Randolph-Macon College*. Vols. 1 and 2. Richmond, VA: Taylor and Taylor Printing, 1901–2.

Duer, William A. *A Letter, Addressed to Cadwallader D. Colden, Esquire, in Answer to the Strictures, Contained in His "Life of Robert Fulton"*. . . . Albany, NY: E. and E. Hosford, 1817.

———. *New-York as It Was, during the Latter Part of the Last Century*. New York: Stanford and Swords, 1849.

———. *A Reply to Mr. Colden's Vindication of the Steam-Boat Monopoly*. Albany, NY: E. and E. Hosford, 1819.

Elliot, Jonathan. *The Debates in the Several State Conventions on the Adoption of the Federal Constitution, as Recommended by the General Convention at Philadelphia in 1787*. 2nd ed. Philadelphia: J. B. Lippincott, 1859.

Fairfax, Fernando. *Memorial of Fernando Fairfax against the Extension of the Patents Granted to Robert Fulton for Improvements in Propelling Vessels by Steam*. Washington, DC: Edward De Krafft, 1816.

Fitch, John. *The Autobiography of John Fitch*. Edited by Frank D. Prager. Philadelphia: American Philosophical Society, 1976.

———. *The Original Steam-Boat Supported* . . . Philadelphia: Zachariah Poulson, 1788.

"Fitch's Steamboat." *Scientific American* 2 (October 1846): 1.

Johnson, Allen, ed. *Readings in American Constitutional History, 1776–1876*. New York: Houghton Mifflin, 1912.

Kennedy, John Pendleton. *Memoirs of the Life of William Wirt, Attorney General of the United States*. 2 vols. Philadelphia: Lea and Blanchard, 1849.

Kent, James. *Commentaries on American Law*. 4 vols. New York: O. Halsted, 1826–30.

Latrobe, Henry Benjamin. *The Correspondence and Miscellaneous Papers of Benjamin Henry Latrobe*. Edited by John C. Van Horne and Lee W. Formwalt. 3 vols. New Haven, CT: Yale University Press, 1984–88.

"The Life of Robert Fulton." Pts. 1 and 2. *American Monthly Magazine and Critical Review* 1 (August 1817): 250–57; 2 (January 1818): 233.

Livingston, William. *The Papers of William Livingston*. Edited by Carl Prince, Dennis P. Ryan, Pamela B. Schafler, and Donald W. White. 5 vols. New Brunswick, NJ: Rutgers University Press, 1979–88.

Lowrie, Walter, and Walter S. Franklin, eds. *American State Papers: Miscellaneous*. Vol. 2. Washington, DC: Trales and Seaton, 1834.

Marcus, Maeva, and James R. Perry, eds. *The Documentary History of the Supreme Court of the United States, 1789–1800*. 8 vols. New York: Columbia University Press, 1985–2007.

Marshall, John. *An Autobiographical Sketch*. Ann Arbor: University of Michigan Press, 1937.

———. *The Papers of John Marshall*. 12 vols. Edited by Herbert A. Johnson et al. Chapel Hill: University of North Carolina Press, 1974–2006.

New York State Legislature. *Report of the Committee to Whom Was Referred the Memorial and Petition of Aaron Ogden*. Albany, NY: n.p., 1814.

Ogden, Aaron. *Autobiography of Col. Aaron Ogden of Elizabethtown*. Paterson, NJ: Printing Press and Publishing, 1893.

Purple, Edwin R. "Notes Biographical and Genealogical of the Colden Family." *New York Genealogical and Biographical Record* 4 (1873): 161–83.

Randolph, John. *The Life of John Randolph of Roanoke*. 2 vols. Edited by Hugh A. Garland. New York: D. Appleton, 1851.

Rumsey, James. *A Short Treatise on the Application of Steam* . . . Philadelphia: Joseph James, 1788.

Savery, Thomas. *The Miners Friend, or an Engine to Raise Water by Fire Described*. London: W. Clowes, 1702.

Stockton, Lucius Horatio. *A History of the Steamboat Case, Lately Discussed by Counsel before the Legislature of New Jersey, Comprised in a Letter to a Gentleman at Washington.* Trenton, NJ: Privately printed, 1815.

Story, Joseph. *Commentaries on the Constitution of the United States.* 3 vols. Boston: Hilliard, Gray, 1833.

———. *The Life and Letters of Joseph Story.* Edited by William Wetmore Story. 2 vols. Freeport, NY: Books for Libraries Press, 1971.

Sullivan, James Langdon. *A Demonstration of the Right to the Navigation of the Waters of New York.* Cambridge, MA: Hilliard and Metcalf, 1821.

Taylor, John. *New Views of the Constitution of the United States.* Washington, DC: Way and Gideon, 1823.

Thornton, William. *Papers of William Thornton.* Edited by C. M. Harris. Vol. 1. Charlottesville: University Press of Virginia, 1995.

———. *A Short Account of the Origins of Steamboats.* Washington, DC: Eliot's Patent Press, 1814.

Todd, Charles B., ed. *Life and Letters of Joel Barlow: Poet, Statesman, Philosopher.* New York: DaCapo, 1970.

United States, Congress, House. *Journal of the House of Representatives of the United States.* Washington, DC: Government Printing Office, 1789–.

———, Senate. *Journal of the Executive Proceedings of the Senate of the United States of America.* Washington, DC: Government Printing Office, 1789–.

United States, Continental Congress. *Journals of the Continental Congress, 1774–1789.* Edited by Worthington C. Ford et al. 34 vols. Washington, DC: Government Printing Office, 1904–37.

Ward, John, ed. "An Account of the Steamboat Controversy." *Proceedings of the New Jersey Historical Society.* Vol. 9, *1860–1864.* Newark: New Jersey Historical Society, 1864.

Washington, George. *The Diaries of George Washington.* Edited by Donald Jackson and Dorothy Twohig. 6 vols. Charlottesville: University Press of Virginia, 1976–79.

Wiltse, Charles M., and Harold Moser, eds. *The Papers of Daniel Webster: Correspondence,* vol. 1, *1798–1824.* Hanover, NH: University Press of New England, 1974.

Wright, Benjamin F., ed. *The Federalist Papers: The Famous Papers on the Principles of American Government.* New York: Metrobooks, 2002.

Secondary Sources

Articles

Abel, Albert S. "The Commerce Clause in the Constitutional Convention and Contemporary Comment." *Minnesota Law Review* 25, no. 4 (1941): 432–93.

———. "Commerce Regulation before *Gibbons v. Ogden:* Interstate Transportation Enterprise." *Mississippi Law Journal* 18 (May 1947): 335–81.

———. "Commerce Regulation before *Gibbons v. Ogden:* Interstate Transportation Facilities." *North Carolina Law Review* 25, no. 2 (1947): 121–71.

Birkner, Michael. "Samuel L. Southard and the Origins of *Gibbons v. Ogden.*" *Princeton University Library Chronicle* 40 (Winter 1979): 171–82.

Brandt, Clare. "Robert R. Livingston, Jr., the Reluctant Revolutionary." *Hudson Valley Regional Review* 4 (March 1987): 8–20.

Breckin, J., and Jennifer Tamm. "The International Diffusion of the Watt Engine, 1775–1825." *Economic History Review* 31 (November 1978): 541–64.

Burke, John G. "Bursting Boilers and the Federal Power." *Technology and Culture* 7 (Winter 1966): 1–23.

———. "The History of the Patent System under the Prerogative and at Common Law." *Law Quarterly Review* 46 (April 1896): 141–54.

Campbell, Thomas. "Chancellor Kent, Chief Justice Marshall, and the Steamboat Cases." *Syracuse Law Review* 25, no. 2 (1974): 497–513.

Chenault, William W., and Robert C. Reinders. "The Northern Born Community of New Orleans in the 1850s." *Journal of American History* 51 (September 1964): 232–47.

Church, William E. "A Forgotten Episode—*Gibbons v. Ogden.*" *Illinois Law Review* 4, no. 6 (1910): 420–24.

Cooke, Frederick H. "The *Gibbons v. Ogden* Fetish." *Michigan Law Review* 9 (1911): 324–33.

Couch, Randall R. "William Charles Cole Claiborne: An Historiographical Review." *Louisiana History* 36 (Fall 1995): 453–65.

Countryman, Edward. "Consolidating Power in Revolutionary America: The Case of New York, 1775–1783." *Journal of Interdisciplinary History* 6 (Spring 1976): 645–77.

Cummins, Light T. "Anglo Merchants and Capital Migration in Spanish Colonial New Orleans, 1763–1803." *Gulf Coast Historical Review* 4 (Fall 1988): 7–28.

Cushman, Robert Eugene. "The National Police Power under the Commerce Clause of the Constitution." *Minnesota Law Review* 3 (April 1919): 290–319, 380–483.

Donner, Irah. "The Copyright Clause of the U.S. Constitution: Why Did the Framers Include It with Unanimous Approval?" *American Journal of Legal History* 36 (October 1992): 361–90.

Ellis, David M. "Yankee-Dutch Confrontation in the Albany Area." *New England Quarterly* 45 (June 1972): 262–70.

Federico, P. J. "Early Interferences and the Case of *Robert Fulton v. John L. Sullivan.*" *Journal of the Patent Office Society* 19 (August 1937): 761–66.

Feller, Daniel. "The Market Revolution Ate My Homework." *Reviews in American History* 25 (September 1997): 408–15.

Greenberg, Dolores. "Reassessing the Power Patterns of the Industrial Revolution: An Anglo-American Comparison." *American Historical Review* 87 (December 1982): 1237–61.

Halsey, Harlan I. "The Choice between High-Pressure and Low-Pressure Steam Power in America in the Early Nineteenth Century." *Journal of Economic History* 41 (December 1981): 723–44.

Hart, W. O. "Mrs. Louise Livingston, Wife of Edward Livingston." *Louisiana Historical Quarterly* 5 (July 1922): 352–56.

Harvey, Peter. *Reminiscences and Anecdotes of Daniel Webster.* Boston: Little, Brown, 1877.

Hatcher, William B. "Edward Livingston's View of the Nature of the Union." *Louisiana Historical Quarterly* 24, no. 3 (1941): 698–728.

Henretta, James. "Families and Farms: *Mentalité* in Pre-industrial America." *William and Mary Quarterly*, 3rd ser., 35 (January 1978): 3–32.

Hindle, Brooke. "James Rumsey and the Rise of Steamboating in the United States." Special issue, *West Virginia History* 48 (1989): 33–42.

Hulme, E. Wyndham. "The History of the Patent System under the Prerogative and at Common Law." *Law Quarterly Review* 46 (April 1896): 141–54.

———. "On the Consideration of the Patent Grant, Past and Present." *Law Quarterly Review* 51 (July 1897): 313–18.

Hunter, Louis C. "The Invention of the Western Steamboat." *Journal of Economic History* 3 (November 1943): 201–20.

Kemp, Emory. "James Rumsey and His Role in the Improvements Movement." Special issue, *West Virginia History* 48 (1989): 1–6.

Kendall, D. "Mr. Gibbons and Colonel Ogden." *Michigan State Bar Journal* 26 (February 1947): 22–25.

Kim, Sung Bok. "Robert Livingston and Moral Judgment." *Hudson Valley Regional Review* 4 (March 1987): 1–7.

Kulikoff, Allan. "The Transition to Capitalism in Rural America." *William and Mary Quarterly*, 3rd ser., 46 (January 1989): 120–44.

Lamoreaux, Naomi R., Daniel M. G. Raff, and Peter Temin. "Beyond Markets and Hierarchies: Towards a New Synthesis of American Business History." *American Historical Review* 108 (April 2003): 404–33.

243

Lamplugh, George. "Up from the Depths: The Career of Thomas Gibbons, 1783–1789." *Atlanta Historical Journal* 25, no. 3 (1981): 38–43.

Layton, Edwin T., Jr. "James Rumsey: Pioneer Technologist." Special issue, *West Virginia History* 48 (1989): 15.

Maass, Alfred R. "Daniel French and the Western Steamboat Engine." *American Neptune* 56 (Winter 1996): 29–44.

———. "The Right of Unrestricted Navigation on the Mississippi, 1812–1818." *American Neptune* 60 (January 2000): 53–54.

Matson, Cathy, and Peter S. Onuf. "Toward a Republican Empire: Interest and Ideology in Revolutionary America." *American Quarterly* 37 (Fall 1985): 496–531.

McFarland, George F. "The Old Stone Mill at Morley." *St. Lawrence County Historical Association Quarterly* 36 (Fall 1991): 1–5.

Mendelson, Wallace. "New Light on *Fletcher v. Peck* and *Gibbons v. Ogden*." *Yale Law Journal* 58 (March 1949): 567–73.

Musson, A. E., and E. Robinson. "The Early Growth of Steam Power." *Economic History Review* 11 (April 1959): 418–39.

Pesser, Edward. "Who Has Power in the Democratic Capitalistic Community? Reflections on Antebellum New York City." *New York History* 58 (April 1977): 136–39.

Pfaff, Caroline. "Henry Miller Shreve: A Biography." *Louisiana Historical Quarterly* 10 (April 1927): 192–239.

Philip, Cynthia Owen. "Robert R. Livingston: Enthusiastic Inventor, Prudent Entrepreneur." *Hudson Valley Regional Review* 4 (March 1987): 74–80.

Popper, Deborah Epstein. "Poor Christopher Colles: An Innovator's Obstacles in Early America." *Journal of American Culture* 28 (June 2005): 178–90.

Prager, Frank D. "Brunelleschi's Patent." *Journal of the Patent Office Society* 28 (February 1946): 109–35.

———. "The Steamboat Pioneers before the Founding Fathers." *Journal of the Patent Office Society* 37 (July 1955): 486–522.

Preston, Daniel. "The Administration and Reform of the U.S. Patent Office, 1790–1836." *Journal of the Early Republic* 5 (Fall 1985): 331–53.

Proctor, L. B. "Abraham Van Vechten, the Founder of the Bar of the State of New York." *Albany Law Journal* 58 (July 30, 1898): 60–69.

———. "Chancellors Livingston, Lansing, and Kent." *Albany Law Journal* 45 (January–July 1892): 17–22.

Ringwald, Donald C. "First Steamboat to Albany." *American Neptune* 23 (July 1964): 157–71.

Robinson, Eric H. "The Early Diffusion of Steam Power." *Journal of Economic History* 34 (March 1974): 91–107.

Roper, Donald M. "The Elite of the New York Bar as Seen from the Bench: James Kent's Necrologies." *New York Historical Society Quarterly* 56 (July 1972): 199–237.

Rumsey, James. "Letters of James Rumsey, Inventor of the Steamboat." *William and Mary Quarterly*, 1st ser., 24 (January 1916): 154–74.

———. "Letters of James Rumsey, Inventor of the Steamboat (Concluded)," *William and Mary Quarterly*, 1st ser., 25 (July 1916): 21–34.

Sheehan, Donald. "The Manchester Literary and Philosophical Society." *Isis* 33 (December 1941): 519–23.

Skaaren, Lorna. "John R. Livingston and the American Revolution." *Hudson Valley Regional Review* 4 (March 1987): 311–20.

Skemer, Don C. "The Institutio Legalis and Legal Education in New Jersey: 1783–1817." *New Jersey History* 96 (Autumn–Winter 1978): 123–33.

Stecker, Dora. "Constructing a Navigation System in the West." *Ohio Archaeology and Historical Society Publications* 22 (January 1913): 18–21.

Stern, Robert L. "The Commerce Clause and the National Economy." *Harvard Law Review* 59 (May 1946): 645–93, 883–947.

Thomson, David Whittet. "The Great Steamboat Monopolies, Part 2: The Hudson." *American Neptune* 16 (October 1956: 270–280).

Treagle, Joseph G., Jr. "Early New Orleans Society: A Reappraisal." *Journal of Southern History* 18 (February 1952): 20–36.

Walterscheid, Edward C. "Inherent or Created Rights: Early Views on the Intellectual Property Clause." *Hamline Law Review* 19 (Fall 1995): 81–98.

———. "Patents and the Jeffersonian Mythology." *John Marshall Law Review* 29 (Fall 1995): 283–86.

———. "Thomas Jefferson and the Patent Act of 1793." *Essays in History* 40 (July 1998): 5.

———. "To Promote the Progress of Science and Useful Arts: The Background and Origin of the Intellectual Property Clause of the United States Constitution." *Journal of Intellectual Property Law* 2 (Fall 1994): 45–54.

Warren, Charles, ed. "The Story-Marshall Correspondence (1819–1831)." *William and Mary Quarterly*, 2nd ser., 21 (January 1941): 1–26.

"Whitehall Plantation." Pts. 1–3. *Georgia Historical Quarterly* 25 (December 1941): 341–62; 26 (March 1942): 40–64; 26 (June 1942): 129–155.

Winters, John D. "William C. C. Claiborne: Profile of a Democrat." *Louisiana History* 10 (Summer 1969): 189–210.

Books

Albion, Robert G. *Rise of New York Port.* New York: Charles Scribners' Sons, 1939.

Appleby, Joyce. *Inheriting the Revolution: The First Generation of Americans.* Cambridge, MA: Belknap, 2000.

Balleisen, Edward J. *Navigating Failure: Bankruptcy and Commercial Society in Antebellum America.* Chapel Hill: University of North Carolina Press, 2001.

Bartlett, Irving H. *Daniel Webster.* New York: W. W. Norton, 1978.

Bathe, Greville, and Dorothy Bathe. *Oliver Evans: A Chronicle of Early American Engineering.* Philadelphia: Historical Society of Pennsylvania, 1935.

Baxter, Maurice G. *One and Inseparable: Daniel Webster and the Union.* Cambridge, MA: Harvard University Press, 1984.

———. *The Steamboat Monopoly: Gibbons v. Ogden, 1824.* New York: Alfred A. Knopf, Inc., 1972.

Beltzhoover, George M., Jr. *James Rumsey, the Inventor of the Steamboat.* Wheeling: West Virginia Historical and Antiquarian Society's Publication, 1900.

Bender, Thomas. *New York Intellect: A History of Intellectual Life in New York City from 1750 to the Beginnings of Our Own Time.* New York: Alfred A. Knopf, 1987.

Beveridge, Albert J. *The Life of John Marshall.* 4 vols. Boston: Houghton Mifflin, 1916–19.

Billings, Warren M., and Mark F. Fernandez, eds. *In Search of Fundamental Law: Louisiana's Constitutions, 1812–1974.* Lafayette, LA: University of Southwestern Louisiana, 1993.

———. *A Law unto Itself? Essays in the New Louisiana Legal History.* Baton Rouge: Louisiana State University Press, 2001.

Bloomfield, Maxwell. *American Lawyers in a Changing Society.* Cambridge, MA: Harvard University Press, 1976.

Boyd, Thomas. *Poor John Fitch, Inventor of the Steamboat.* New York: G. P. Putnam's Sons, 1935.

Branch, Taylor. *Pillar of Fire: America in the King Years 1963-65.* New York: Simon and Schuster, 1999.

Brandt, Clare. *An American Aristocracy: The Livingstons.* Garden City, NY: Doubleday, 1986.

Breen, Timothy. *The Marketplace of Revolution: How Consumer Politics Shaped American Independence.* New York: Oxford University Press, 2004.

Broers, Michael. *Europe under Napoleon, 1799–1815.* London: Hodder Arnold, 1996.

Brown, Gordon S. *Incidental Architect: William Thornton and the Cultural Life of Early Washington, D.C., 1794–1828.* Athens: Ohio University Press, 2009.

Bruegel, Martin. *Farm, Shop, Landing: The Rise of a Market Society in the Hudson Valley, 1780–1860.* Durham, NC: Duke University Press, 2002.

245

Bruun, Geoffrey. *Europe and the French Imperium, 1799–1814.* New Haven, CT: Greenwood, 1983.

Burstein, Andrew. *America's Jubilee.* New York: Alfred A. Knopf, 2001.

Casto, William R. *The Supreme Court in the Early Republic: The Chief Justiceships of John Jay and Oliver Ellsworth.* Columbia: University of South Carolina Press, 1995.

Cayton, Andrew R. L. *The Frontier Republic: Ideology and Politics in the Ohio Country, 1780–1825.* Kent, OH: Kent State University Press, 1986.

Cayton, Andrew R. L., and Peter Onuf. *The Midwest and the Nation.* Bloomington: Indiana University Press, 1990.

Chester, Alden. *Legal and Judicial History of New York.* 3 vols. New York: National Americana Society, 1911.

Clark, Christopher. *Roots of Rural Capitalism.* Ithaca, NY: Cornell University Press, 1990.

Cooke, Jacob E. *Tench Coxe and the Early Republic.* Chapel Hill: University of North Carolina Press, 1978.

Cornog, Evan. *The Birth of Empire: DeWitt Clinton and the American Experience, 1769–1828.* New York: Oxford University Press, 1998.

Corwin, Edwin S. *John Marshall and the Constitution: A Chronicle of the Supreme Court.* New Haven, CT: Yale University Press, 1919.

Crosskey, William W. *Politics and the Constitution in the History of the United States.* 3 vols. Chicago: University of Chicago Press, 1953–80.

Cudahy, Brian J. *Over and Back: The History of Ferryboats in New York Harbor.* New York: Fordham University Press, 1990.

Cushman, Barry. *Rethinking the New Deal Court: The Structure of a Constitutional Revolution.* New York: Oxford University Press, 1998.

Dangerfield, George. *Chancellor Robert R. Livingston of New York, 1746–1813.* New York: Harcourt, Brace, 1960.

———. *The Era of Good Feelings.* New York: Harcourt, Brace, and Smith, 1952.

Dickinson, H. W. *Robert Fulton, Engineer and Artist: His Life and Works.* London: John Lane, 1913.

Dohan, Mary Helen. *Mr. Roosevelt's Steamboat: The First Steamboat to Travel the Mississippi.* New York: Dodd, Mead, 1981.

Dorsey, Florence L. *Master of the Mississippi: Henry Miller Shreve and the Conquest of the Mississippi.* New York: Literary Classics, 1941.

Douglass, Elisha P. *The Coming of Age of American Business: Three Centuries of Enterprise, 1600–1900.* Chapel Hill: University of North Carolina Press, 1971.

Douty, Esther Morris. *Hasty Pudding and Barbary Pirates: A Life of Joel Barlow.* Westminster, England: Westminster Press, 1975.

Dunbaugh, Edwin L. *Night Boat to New England, 1815–1900.* New York: Greenwood, 1992.

Dunne, Gerald T. *Justice Joseph Story and the Rise of the Supreme Court.* New York: Simon and Schuster, 1971.

Elkins, Stanley, and Eric McKitrick. *The Age of Federalism.* New York: Oxford University Press, 1993.

Ellis, David Maldwyn. *New York: City and State.* Ithaca, NY: Cornell University Press, 1979.

Ellis, Franklin. *History of Columbia County, New York.* Philadelphia: Everts and Ensign, 1878.

Ellis, Joseph J. *American Sphinx: The Character of Thomas Jefferson.* New York: Alfred A. Knopf, 1997.

Ellis, Richard E. *Aggressive Nationalism: McCulloch v. Maryland and the Foundation of Federal Authority in the Young Republic.* New York: Oxford University Press, 2007.

———. *Jeffersonian Crisis: Courts and Politics in the Young Republic.* New York: Oxford University Press, 1971.

———. *The Union at Risk: Jacksonian Democracy, States' Rights and the Nullification Crisis.* New York: Oxford University Press, 1987.

Elmer, Lucius Q. C. *Reminiscences of the Bench and Bar during More Than Half a Century.* Newark, NJ: Martin R. Dennis, 1872.

Farrand, Max. *The Records of the Federal Convention of 1787.* Vol. 3. New Haven, CT: Yale University Press, 1911.

Fehrenbacher, Donald. *The South and Three Sectional Crises*. Baton Rouge: Louisiana State University Press, 1995.

Feller, Daniel. *The Jacksonian Promise: America, 1815–1840*. Baltimore, MD: Johns Hopkins University Press, 1995.

Finkelman, Paul. *Slavery and the Founders: Race and Liberty in the Age of Jefferson*. Armonk, NY: M. E. Sharpe, 2001.

Fisher, David Hackett. *The Revolution of American Conservatism: The Federalist Party in the Era of Jeffersonian Democracy*. New York: Harper and Row, 1965.

Fitch, C. E. *Encyclopedia of Biography of New York*. 3 vols. New York: American Historical Society, 1916.

Fletcher, R. A. *Steam-Ships: The Story of Their Development to the Present Day*. London: Sidgwick and Jackson, 1910.

Flexner, James Thomas. *Steamboats Come True: American Inventors in Action*. New York: Fordham University Press, 1992.

Forbes, Robert Pierce. *The Missouri Compromise and Its Aftermath: Slavery and the Meaning of America*. Chapel Hill: University of North Carolina Press, 2007.

Fox, Dixon Ryan. *The Decline of Aristocracy in the Politics of New York*. New York: Columbia University Press, 1919.

Frankfurter, Felix. *The Commerce Clause under Marshall, Taney, and White*. Chapel Hill: University of North Carolina Press, 1937.

Freeman, Joanne B. *Affairs of Honor: National Politics in the Early Republic*. New Haven, CT: Yale University Press, 2001.

Frese, Joseph R., and Jacob Judd, eds. *An Emerging Independent American Economy, 1815–1875*. Tarrytown, NY: Sleepy Hollow Press, 1980.

Friedman, Lawrence M. *A History of American Law*. New York: Simon and Schuster, 1973, 1985.

Friedman, Leon, and Fred L. Israel, eds. *The Justices of the United States Supreme Court, 1789–1969: Their Lives and Major Opinions*. New York: Chelsea House, 1969.

———. *The Justices of the United States Supreme Court, 1789–1995: Their Lives and Major Opinions*. New York: Chelsea House Publishers, 1995.

Galie, Peter J. *Ordered Liberty: A Constitutional History of New York*. New York: Fordham University Press, 1996.

Gamble, Thomas. *Savannah Duels and Duelists, 1733–1877*. Savannah, GA: Review Publishing and Printing, 1923.

Garraty, John A., ed. *Quarrels That Have Shaped the Constitution*. Rev. ed. New York: Harper and Row, 1987.

Garraty, John A., and Mark C. Carnes, eds. *American National Biography*. New York: Oxford University Press, 1999.

Gerber, Scott Douglas. *Seriatim: The Supreme Court before John Marshall*. New York: New York University Press, 1998.

Gilje, Paul A., ed. *Wages of Independence: Capitalism in the Early American Republic*. Madison, WI: Madison House Publishers, 1997.

Goodnow, Frank J. *Social Reform and the Constitution*. New York: Macmillan, 1911.

Goodrich, Carter. *Government Promotion of American Canals and Railroads, 1800–1890*. New York: Columbia University Press, 1960.

Greene, Jack, and J. R. Pole, eds. *Colonial British America: Essays in the New History of the Early Modern Era*. Baltimore, MD: Johns Hopkins University Press, 1984.

Gunn, L. Ray. *The Decline of Authority: Public Economic Policy and Political Development in New York, 1800–1860*. Ithaca, NY: Cornell University Press, 1988.

Gunther, Gerald, comp. *John Marshall's Defense of McCulloch v. Maryland*. Palo Alto, CA: Stanford University Press, 1969.

Haines, Charles. *The Supreme Court in American Government and Politics, 1789–1835*. Berkeley: University of California Press, 1944.

Hamlin, Talbot. *Benjamin Henry Latrobe*. New York: Oxford University Press, 1955.

Hanger, Kimberly S. *A Medley of Cultures: Louisiana Culture at the Cabildo*. New Orleans: Louisiana Museum Foundation, 1996.

Hanyan, Craig, and Mary L. Hanyan. *De Witt Clinton and the Rise of the People's Men*. Ottawa: McGill-Queens University Press, 1996.

Harris, J. R. *Industrial Espionage and Technology Transfer: Britain and France in the Eighteenth Century*. Aldershot, England: Ashgate, 1998.

Harrison, Richard A. *Princetonians, 1769–1775: A Biographical Dictionary*. Princeton, NJ: Princeton University Press, 1980.

Hartz, Louis. *Economic Policy and Democratic Thought: Pennsylvania, 1776–1860*. Cambridge, MA: Harvard University Press, 1947.

Harvey, Peter. *Reminiscences and Anecdotes of Daniel Webster*. Boston: Little, Brown, 1879.

Hatcher, William B. *Edward Livingston: Jeffersonian Republican and Jacksonian Democrat*. Baton Rouge: Louisiana State University Press, 1940.

Hatfield, Edwin Francis. *History of Elizabeth, New Jersey: Including the Early History of Union County*. New York: Carlton and Lanahan, 1868.

Hatfield, Joseph T. *William Claiborne: Jeffersonian Centurion in the American Southwest*. Lafayette: University of Southwestern Louisiana, 1976.

Hendrick, Burton J. *Bulwark of the Republic: A Biography of the Constitution*. Boston: Little, Brown, 1937.

Hershkowitz, Leo, and Milton Klein, eds. *Courts and Law in Early New York: Selected Essays*. Port Washington, NY: Kennikat Press, 1978.

Hindle, Brooke. *Emulation and Invention*. New York: New York University Press, 1981.

Hobson, Charles F. *The Great Chief Justice: John Marshall and the Rule of Law*. Lawrence: University Press of Kansas, 1996.

Horton, John T. *James Kent: A Study in Conservatism, 1763–1847*. New York: D. Appleton-Century, 1939.

Horwitz, Morton. *The Transformation of American Law, 1780–1860*. Cambridge, MA: Harvard University Press, 1977.

———. *The Transformation of American Law, 1870–1960: The Crisis of Legal Orthodoxy*. New York: Oxford University Press, 1992.

Howe, Daniel Walker. *What Hath God Wrought: The Transformation of America, 1815–1848*. New York: Oxford University Press, 2007.

Hunt, Louise Livingston. *Memoir of Mrs. Edward Livingston*. New York: Harper and Brothers, 1886.

Hunter, Louis C. *Steamboats on the Western Rivers: An Economic and Technological History*. New York: Octagon Books, 1969.

Hurst, J. Willard. *Law and the Conditions of Freedom in the Nineteenth-Century United States*. Madison: University of Wisconsin Press, 1956.

Ifkovic, John W. *Connecticut's Nationalist Revolutionary*. Hartford: American Revolution Bicentennial Commission of Connecticut, 1977.

Ireland, Robert. *The Legal Career of William Pinkney, 1764–1822*. New York: Garland Press, 1986.

Irwin, Ray Watkins. *Daniel D. Tompkins: Governor of New York and Vice President of the United States*. New York: New-York Historical Society, 1968.

Jabour, Anya. *Marriage in the Early Republic: Elizabeth and William Wirt and the Companionate Ideal*. Baltimore, MD: Johns Hopkins University Press, 1998.

Johnson, Herbert A. *The Chief Justiceship of John Marshall, 1801–1835*. Columbia: University of South Carolina Press, 1997.

Johnston, William Preston, *The Johnstons of Salisbury: With a Brief Comment on the Hancock, Strother, and Preston Families*. New Orleans, LA: I. Graham and Son, 1897.

Jones, Eliot, and Homer B. Vanderblue. *Railroads: Cases and Selections*. New York: Macmillan, 1925.

Jordan, Francis, Jr. *The Life of William Henry of Lancaster, Pennsylvania, 1729–1786*. Lancaster, PA: New Era Printing, 1910.

July, Robert William. *The Essential New Yorker, Gulian C. Verplanck*. Durham, NC: Duke University Press, 1951.

Karsten, Peter. *Heart versus Head: Judge-Made Law in Nineteenth-Century America*. Chapel Hill: University of North Carolina Press, 1997.

Kasson, John. *Civilizing the Machine: Technology and Republican Values in America, 1776–1900*. New York: Viking Press, 1976.

Kennedy, John. *The History of Steam Navigation*. Liverpool, England: Charles, Birchall, 1903.

Kennedy, John Pendleton. *Memoirs of the Life of William Wirt, Attorney General of the United States*. 2 vols. Philadelphia: Lea and Blanchard, 1849.

Kierner, Cynthia A. *Traders and Gentlefolk: The Livingstons of New York, 1675–1790*. Ithaca, NY: Cornell University Press, 1992.

Klein, Maury. *The Power Makers: Steam, Electricity, and the Men Who Invented Modern America*. London: Bloomsbury Press, 2008.

Klein, Milton. *Empire State: A History of New York State*. Ithaca, NY: Cornell University Press, 2001.

Kline, Ronald R. *Consumers in the Country: Technology and Social Change in Rural America*. Baltimore, MD: Johns Hopkins University Press, 2000.

Konkle, Burton Alva. *Joseph Hopkinson, 1770–1842, Jurist-Scholar-Inspirer of the Arts: Author of Hail Columbia*. Philadelphia: University of Pennsylvania Press, 1931.

Kulikoff, Alan. *The Agrarian Origins of American Capitalism*. Charlottesville: University Press of Virginia, 1992.

Lamoreaux, Naomi R. *Insider Lending: Banks, Personal Connections, and Economic Development in Industrial New England*. New York: Cambridge University Press, 1994.

Lamplugh, George. *Politics on the Periphery: Factions and Politics in Georgia, 1783–1806*. Newark: University of Delaware Press, 1986.

Lane, Wheaton J. *Cornelius Vanderbilt: An Epic of the Steam Age*. New York: Alfred A. Knopf, 1942.

———. *From Indian Trail to Iron Horse: Travel and Transportation in New Jersey, 1620–1860*. Princeton, NJ: Princeton University Press, 1939.

Larson, John Lauritz. *Internal Improvement: National Public Works and the Promise of Popular Government in the Early United States*. Chapel Hill: University of North Carolina Press, 2001.

Latrobe, John H. B. *The First Steamboat Voyage on the Western Waters*. Baltimore: Maryland Historical Society, 1871.

———. *A Lost Chapter in the History of the Steamboat*. Baltimore: Maryland Historical Society, 1871.

Lawler, Thomas Bonaventure, and Thomas Hamilton Murray, eds. *The Journal of the American-Irish Historical Society*. Boston: American-Irish Historical Society, 1907.

Leuchtenburg, William E. *The Supreme Court Reborn: The Constitutional Revolution in the Age of Roosevelt*. New York: Oxford University Press, 1995.

Livingston, Edwin Brockholst. *The Livingstons of Livingston Manor*. New York: Knickerbocker Press, 1910.

Lloyd, James T. *Lloyd's Steamboat Directory and Disasters on Western Rivers*. Cincinnati, OH: James T. Lloyd, 1906.

MacAvoy, Paul W. *The Economic Effects of Regulation: The Trunk-Line Railroad Cartels and the Interstate Commerce Commission Picture 1900*. Cambridge, MA: MIT Press, 1965.

MacLeod, Christine. *Inventing the Industrial Revolution: The English Patent System, 1660–1800*. Cambridge: Cambridge University Press, 1988.

Malone, Dumas, ed. *Dictionary of American Biography*. 22 vols. New York: Charles Scribner's Sons, 1928–58.

Martin, Scott C. *Cultural Change and the Market Revolution in America, 1789–1860*. Lanham, MD: Rowman and Littlefield, 2005.

Marx, Leo. *The Machine in the Garden: Technology and the Pastoral Ideal in America*. New York: Oxford University Press, 1967.

McCall, Edith. *Conquering the Rivers: Henry Miller Shreve and the Navigation of America's Inland Waterways*. Baton Rouge: Louisiana State University Press, 1984.

McGraw, Judith A. *Early American Technology: Making and Doing Things from the Colonial Era to 1850*. Chapel Hill: University of North Carolina Press, 1994.

Meyer, David R. *Networked Machinists: High-Technology Industries in Antebellum America.* Baltimore, MD: Johns Hopkins University Press, 2006.

Minnigerode, Meade. *Certain Rich Men.* New York: G. P. Putnam's Sons, 1927.

Montgomery, M. R. *Jefferson and the Gunmen: How the West Was Almost Lost.* New York: Crown Publishers, 2000.

Morgan, Donald G. *Justice William Johnson: The First Dissenter.* Columbia: University of South Carolina Press, 1954.

Morison, Samuel Eliot. *The Oxford History of the United States, 1783–1917.* 2 vols. Oxford: Oxford University Press, 1927–28.

Nelson, William E. *The Americanization of the Common Law: The Impact of Legal Change on Massachusetts Society, 1760–1830.* Cambridge, MA: Harvard University Press, 1975.

Newmyer, R. Kent. *John Marshall and the Heroic Age of the Supreme Court.* Baton Rouge: Louisiana State University Press, 2001.

———. *Supreme Court Justice Joseph Story: Statesman of the Old Republic.* Chapel Hill: University of North Carolina Press, 1986.

North, Douglass C. *The Economic Growth of the United States, 1790–1860.* Englewood Cliffs, NJ: Prentice Hall, 1961.

Novak, William J. *The People's Welfare: Law and Regulation in Nineteenth-Century America.* Chapel Hill: University of North Carolina Press, 1996.

Patterson, C. Perry. *Presidential Government in the United States: The Unwritten Constitution.* Chapel Hill: University of North Carolina Press, 1947.

Perry, Lewis. *Boats against the Current: American Culture between Revolution and Modernity, 1820–1860.* New York: Oxford University Press, 1993.

Petersen, William J. *Steamboating on the Upper Mississippi.* Iowa City: State Historical Society of Iowa, 1937.

Peterson, Merrill D. *The Great Triumvirate: Webster, Clay, and Calhoun.* New York: Oxford University Press, 1988.

Philbrick, Francis S. *The Rise of the West, 1754–1830.* New York: HarperCollins, 1965.

Philip, Cynthia Owen. *Robert Fulton: A Biography.* New York: Franklin Watts, 1985.

Preble, G. H. *A Chronological History of the Origin and Development of Steam Navigation.* Philadelphia: L. R. Hamersly, 1895.

Prime, Nathaniel S. *Long Island, from Its First Settlement by Europeans to the Year 1845.* New York: Robert Carter, 1845.

Prince, Carl E. *New Jersey's Jeffersonian Republicans: The Genesis of an Early Party Machine, 1789–1817.* Chapel Hill: University of North Carolina Press, 1964.

Prude, Jonathan. *The Coming Industrial Order: Town and Factory Life in Massachusetts, 1810–1860.* New York: Cambridge University Press, 1983.

Randall, Willard Sterne. *Thomas Jefferson: A Life.* New York: Henry Holt, 1993.

Ranlet, Philip. *The New York Loyalists.* Knoxville: University of Tennessee Press, 1986.

Reigart, J. Frank. *The Life of Robert Fulton.* Philadelphia: G. C. Henderson, 1856.

Remini, Robert. *Daniel Webster: The Man and His Time.* New York: W. W. Norton, 1997.

Renehan, Edward J., Jr. *Commodore: The Life of Cornelius Vanderbilt.* New York: Basic Books, 2007.

Rigal, Laura. *The American Manufactory: Art, Labor and the World of Things in the Early Republic.* Princeton, NJ: Princeton University Press, 1998.

Robarge, David Scott. *A Chief Justice's Progress: John Marshall from Revolutionary Virginia to the Supreme Court.* Westport, CT: Greenwood, 2000.

Ronda, James P. *Jefferson's West: A Journey with Lewis and Clark.* Chapel Hill: University of North Carolina Press, 2002.

Roper, Donald M. *Mr. Justice Thompson and the Constitution.* New York: Garland Press, 1987.

Rosen, Deborah A. *Courts and Commerce: Gender, Law, and the Market Economy in Colonial New York.* Columbus: Ohio State University Press, 1997.

Roth, David M. *Connecticut's War Governor: Jonathan Trumbull.* Chester, CT: Pequot, 1974.

Rowley, Warren C., Alexander Seward, and Rees G. Williams, eds. *Transactions of the Oneida Historical Society, at Utica*. Utica, NY: Ellis H. Roberts, 1881.

Russell, Kirk. *Randolph of Roanoke: A Study in Conservative Thought*. Chicago: University of Chicago Press, 1951.

Sale, Kirkpatrick. *The Fire of His Genius: Robert Fulton and the American Dream*. New York: Free Press, 2001.

Sellers, Charles. *The Market Revolution: Jacksonian America, 1815–1846*. New York: Oxford University Press, 1991.

Semmes, John E. *John H. B. Latrobe and His Times*. Baltimore, MD: Norman, Remington, 1917.

Shaw, Ronald E. *Erie Water West: A History of the Erie Canal, 1792–1854*. Lexington: University of Kentucky Press, 1966.

Sheriff, Carol. *The Artificial River: The Erie Canal and the Paradox of Progress, 1817–1862*. New York: Hill and Wang, 1996.

Shewmaker, Kenneth E., ed. *Daniel Webster, "The Completest Man."* Hanover, NH: University Press of New England, 1990.

Simon, James F. *What Kind of a Nation: Thomas Jefferson, John Marshall, and the Epic Struggle to Create a United States*. New York: Simon and Schuster, 2002.

Smith, Henry Nash. *Virgin Land: The American West as Symbol and Myth*. Cambridge, MA: Harvard University Press, 1950.

Smith, Jean Edward. *John Marshall: Definer of a Nation*. New York: Henry Holt, 1996.

Smith, Merritt Roe, and Leo Marx, eds. *Does Technology Drive History? The Dilemma of Technological Determinism*. Cambridge, MA: MIT Press, 1994.

Sobel, Robert. *Panic on Wall Street: A History of America's Financial Disasters*. Frederick, MD: Beard Books, 1999.

Stellhorn, Paul A., and Michael J. Birkner, eds. *The Governors of New Jersey: Biographical Essays, 1664–1974*. Trenton: New Jersey Historical Commission, 1982.

Stokes, Melvyn, and Stephen Conway, eds. *The Market Revolution in America: Social, Political, and Religious Expressions, 1800–1880*. Charlottesville: University Press of Virginia, 1996.

Sutcliffe, Alice Crary. *Robert Fulton*. New York: Macmillan, 1915.

———. *Robert Fulton and the "Clermont."* New York: Century, 1909.

Sutcliffe, Andrea J. *Steam: The Untold Story of America's First Great Invention*. New York: Palgrave Macmillan, 2004.

Taylor, George Rogers. *The Transportation Revolution, 1815–1860*. New York: Rinehart, 1951.

Thayer, Theodore. *As We Were: The Story of Old Elizabethtown*. Elizabeth, NJ: Grassman, 1964.

Treese, Joel D., ed. *Biographical Directory of the United States Congress, 1774–1996*. Washington, DC: Congressional Quarterly Press, 1996.

Turnbull, Archibald Douglas. *John Stevens: An American Record*. New York: Century, 1928.

Turner, Ella May. *James Rumsey, Pioneer in Steam Navigation*. Scottdale, PA: Mennonite Publishing House, 1930.

Van Santvoord, George. *Sketches of the Lives and Judicial Services of the Chief-Justices of the Supreme Court of the United States*. New York: Charles Scribner, 1854.

Waldstreicher, David. *In the Midst of Perpetual Fetes: The Making of American Nationalism, 1776–1820*. Chapel Hill: University of North Carolina Press, 1997.

Walterscheid, Edward C. *The Nature of the Intellectual Property Clause: A Study in Historical Perspective*. Buffalo, NY: W. S. Hein, 2002.

———. *To Promote the Progress of Useful Arts: American Patent Law and Administration, 1798–1836*. Littleton, CO: F. B. Rothman, 1998.

Warren, Charles. *The Supreme Court in United States History*. Boston: Little, Brown, 1922.

Weinberg, Meyer. *A Short History of American Capitalism*. Amherst, MA: Meyer Weinberg, 2002.

Welke, Barbara Young. *Recasting American Liberty: Gender, Race, Law and the Railroad Revolution, 1865–1920*. Cambridge: Cambridge University Press, 2001.

Westcott, Thompson. *The Life of John Fitch: The Inventor of the Steamboat.* Philadelphia: J. B. Lippincott, 1857.

Wheeler, William Ogden. *The Ogden Family in America, Elizabethtown Branch, and Their English Ancestry.* Philadelphia: J. B. Lippincott, 1907.

White, G. Edward. *The Marshall Court and Cultural Change, 1815–1835.* New York: Oxford University Press, 1991.

White, Leonard D. *The Federalists: A Study in Administrative History, 1789–1801.* New York: Macmillan Books, 1954.

Wilentz, Sean. *Chants Democratic: New York City and the Rise of the American Working Class, 1788–1850.* New York: Oxford University Press, 1986.

Williams, William Appleman. *The Contours of American History.* Cleveland, OH: World Publishing, 1961.

Wilson, James Grant, ed. *The Memorial History of the City of New York: From Its First Settlement to the Year 1892.* 4 vols. New York: New-York History, 1892–93.

Wood, Gordon S. *Radicalism of the American Revolution.* New York: Alfred A. Knopf, 1991.

Woodress, James. *A Yankee's Odyssey: The Life of Joel Barlow.* Philadelphia: J. B. Lippincott, 1958.

Wyatt-Brown, Bertram. *Southern Honor: Ethics and Behavior in the Old South.* Oxford: Oxford University Press, 1983.

York, Neil Longley. *Mechanical Metamorphosis: Technological Change in Revolutionary America.* Westport, CT: Greenwood, 1985.

Dissertations

Annis, David L. "Mr. Bushrod Washington, Supreme Court Justice on the Marshall Court." PhD diss., University of Notre Dame, 1974.

Burke, Joseph Charles. "William Wirt: Attorney General and Constitutional Lawyer." PhD diss., Indiana University, 1965.

Dubois, Roy Louis. "John Stevens: Transportation Pioneer." PhD diss., New York University, 1973.

Gregg, Dorothy. "The Exploitation of the Steamboat: The Case of Colonel John Stevens." PhD diss., Columbia University, 1951.

Robinson, Thomas P. "The Life of Thomas Addis Emmet." PhD diss., New York University, 1955.

INDEX

A page number in italic refers to an illustration on that page. The letter *n* following a page number refers to a note on that page.

Index

259

www.ingramcontent.com/pod-product-compliance
Lightning Source LLC
Chambersburg PA
CBHW021855020426
42334CB00013B/345